THE WELSH SOCIETY
OF PHILADELPHIA
1798–1839

Swansea
South Wales Record Society
2021

Published by the South Wales Record Society
Kim Collis – Treasurer, c/o West Glamorgan Archive Service,
City and County of Swansea, Civic Centre, Swansea, SA1 3SN

First published 2021

ISBN 978-1-9998326-6-7

Introduction and editorial matter Richard C. Allen, 2021

THIS BOOK IS DEDICATED TO

THE MEMBERS OF THE WELSH SOCIETY OF PHILADELPHIA AND THE SPECIAL COLLECTIONS STAFF (PAST AND PRESENT) AT THE LUTNICK LIBRARY, HAVERFORD COLLEGE, PENNSYLVANIA

The image on the cover of the book is taken from the present Welsh Society of Philadelphia. With grateful thanks to the members of the Society for granting permission to use their emblem.

TABLE OF CONTENTS

Acknowledgements vii
Editing the Minutes.. ix
List of Illustrations and Tables xi

PART ONE

The Early History of the Welsh Society of Philadelphia,
1798–1839 1

PART TWO

Governance

The First Constitution and Rules Adopted by the Welch Society.... 57

The Second Constitution Adopted by the Welch Society
on the 1st day of March Anno Domini 1802 62

Bye-Laws of the Welch Society 68

Supplemental Rules and Regulations Adopted by the Welch Society ... 69

PART THREE

Minutes of Meetings, Volume 1: 1798–1839...................... 71

PART FOUR

Select Biographies of Early Members and Associates 443

Bibliography 503

Index 530

ACKNOWLEDGMENTS

This first volume of minutes of the Welsh Society of Philadelphia came about as a consequence of a Gest Fellowship at Haverford College in Pennsylvania. Diana Franzusoff Peterson and Ann Upton were responsible for drawing my attention to the records of the Society, while more recently Mary A. Crauderueff has been very helpful in answering all my queries. Equally, I am grateful to Charles Lentz, David Walker, Charles Wenzel and Jack Williams for taking a strong interest in my efforts to transcribe the records and to contextualise the philanthropic and cultural activity of the Society. Their support has been invaluable over many years, while their kind-heartedness and friendship to this regular visitor to Philadelphia certainly mirrors those of earlier generations of Society members. Indeed, the Society is still active and grants scholarships to students of Welsh descent for their undergraduate studies who live in the Greater Philadelphia area and it also promotes other Welsh cultural and artistic activities.

I am extremely grateful to the executive committee and members of the South Wales Record Society for providing a home for this work. As a charitable organisation their investment in a series of volumes from 1982 onwards has been instrumental in providing a rich source for a better understanding of Wales from the medieval period to the twentieth century. I am indebted to Dr Ben Curtis, the Series Editor, who has patiently and swiftly responded my various queries and to the anonymous reader whose very helpful report helped to shape some of the final observations made in the book.

Financial assistance from various sources must be acknowledged, including the aforementioned Haverford College Gest Fellowship and the British Academy. Alan Fear and Carol Phelps O'Connor at the former School of Education, University of Wales, Newport, not only provided additional financial support but also allowed me time to develop my deeper understanding of the early history of the Society and to employ Erica Canela as a research assistant for the project. I am grateful for Erica's expert assistance in helping me to transcribe the first draft of the minutes. My wife, Joan, has regularly listened to tales of Welsh Philadelphians, old and new, and has often provided timely historical correctives to my narrative.

Finally, the reasons why the Welsh Society of Philadelphia continues to flourish is in no small part due to their collective vision of lasting fellowship, philanthropic ideals and community spirit.

EDITING THE MINUTES

As with other volumes in this South Wales Record Society series, the overarching principle has been to be produce a comprehensive and yet accessible and readable study. Covering a period of just over forty years (1798–1839) this unabridged transcription of the unpaginated quarterly and annual meeting minutes of the Welsh Society of Philadelphia has been a lengthy undertaking but certainly worth the effort.

The records of the Welsh Society of Philadelphia are housed in the Quaker and Special Collections at Haverford College, Pennsylvania. The extant records document the long and on-going cultural and philanthropic associations of generations of Welsh-Americans in Philadelphia, Pennsylvania, and America more generally.[1] Following the completion of this volume, the intention is to transcribe and publish the later records of the Society from 1840 onwards and thereby bring a complete history of this important organisation to greater public attention.

For the current volume there are, however, some archival and methodological points that require a brief explanation. The minutes have separate italicised explanatory sub-headings such as *Annual Dinner, Membership, Finance, Organisation* etc. to help guide the reader through the extant records. Detailed footnotes have been provided to assist the reader where some points needed exemplification.

The preponderance of upper-case letters was common in the eighteenth and nineteenth centuries on both sides of the Atlantic, but

---

1 Lutnick Library, Quaker and Special Collections, Haverford College, Haverford, Pennsylvania (hereafter HC), MC-1186, Welsh Society of Philadelphia records.

for the sake of consistency these have largely been removed to allow the text to run more smoothly. The spelling has been left in the original format, but occasionally the syntax has been modernised. The names of those members attending the meetings have been faithfully reproduced although there have been insertions of full-stops and superscription of abbreviated phrases. For example, dec^d (deceased) and Honr^y (Honorary) etc. The interchangeability of Welsh/Welch, Welshmen/Welchmen has been left as in the original.

The dates are reflective of the American style of dating – January 1, 1800 rather than 1 January 1800, while the specific years have been inserted at the beginning of every set of minutes for that particular year.

Finally, in Part Four I have provided an insight into the varied and often influential lives of those individuals who comprised the Welsh Society of Philadelphia either as fully paid-up members or as honorary appointments. Obviously, it is not always possible to track down every member – there are just too many Joneses etc to trace! As such, some lengthier entries are offered and others are much shorter, but hopefully all of these will provide future researchers with some basic biographical details for these Welsh-Americans.

ILLUSTRATIONS

Plate 1.	'Arch Street Ferry, Philadelphia', c.1800	16
Plate 2.	Advertisement for the Annual Meeting of the Welch Society on 1 March 1799	18
Plate 3.	Reporting the Annual Meeting, 1 March 1799	19
Plate 4.	'South East Corner of Third and Market Streets, Philadelphia', c.1800	23
Plate 5.	The St David's Day Festivities, March 1798 (and transcript)	24
Plate 6.	'High Street, from Ninth Street, Philadelphia', c.1800	55
Plate 7.	'Bank of the United States, in Third Street, Philadelphia', c.1800	56
Plate 8.	The First Constitution and Rules adopted by the Welch Society, 1798	58
Plate 9.	'Second Street North from Market Street with Christ Church, Philadelphia', c.1800	70
Plate 10.	'Congress Hall and New Theatre, in Chestnut Street, Philadelphia', c.1800	442
Plate 11.	'The City & Port of Philadelphia, on the River Delaware from Kensington', c.1800	502

TABLES

Table 1. Welsh Society of Philadelphia Investments, 1820...... 23

Table 2. Assistance to Welsh Emigrants provided by the Welsh Society of Philadelphia, 1818........................... 44

Table 3. Assistance to Welsh Emigrants provided by the Welsh Society of Philadelphia, 6 September 1830.... 52

Table 4. Assistance to Welsh Emigrants provided by the Welsh Society of Philadelphia, 6 December 1830..... 53

PART ONE

THE EARLY HISTORY OF THE WELSH SOCIETY OF PHILADELPHIA, 1798–1839.[1]

At noon on 1 March 1798, sixty-four male citizens of Philadelphia gathered at the house of William Ogden, a tavern on Chestnut Street, to launch a Welsh Society. The Welsh Society of Philadelphia has had a continuous history to the present day and a long-lasting association with Welsh-Americana, particularly in its promotion of Welsh cultural activities and the annual St David's Day festival.[2] This was one of many similar Welsh societies which sprang up in the eighteenth and nineteenth

---

1   HC, MC-1186, Vol 1. Unpaginated Minute Book of the Records of the Welsh Society of Philadelphia (4 June 1798–2 December 1839) and Copy of the Original Association, 1 March 1798. The following study was first published in Richard C. Allen, 'The Origins and Development of Welsh Associational Life in Eighteenth-Century Philadelphia', *Transactions of the Honourable Society of Cymmrodorion: Trafodion Anrhydeddus Gymdeithas y Cymmrodorion* (hereafter THSC), New Series, 15, 2008 (2009), 105–26. This is, however, a greatly expanded assessment. I am grateful to the Honourable Society of Cymmrodorion for allowing me to republish this work.
2   For details of the Society and its activities see https://www.philadelphiawelsh.org/ [accessed 1 October 2021].

centuries in Britain, America and elsewhere.³ This introductory essay scrutinises the development of the Welsh Society of Philadelphia and its predecessor, the Society of the Sons of Ancient Britons c.1729, with particular attention paid to its early membership and the social and political influence of members in Philadelphia – the spiritual home of Welsh exiles in America.⁴ Part of its remit was a commitment to provide moral support, financial assistance and practical relief for Welsh exiles who might otherwise struggle in a foreign land without help.

---

3   For example, see Prys Morgan, *The Eighteenth Century Renaissance* (Llandybïe: Christopher Davies, 1981), pp. 54–62; R. T. Jenkins and Helen M. Rammage, *The History of the Honourable Society of Cymmrodorion, 1751–1951* (London: The Honourable Society of Cymmrodorion, 1951). For wider discussions of Welsh/British associational life from the late-sixteenth century onwards see Peter Clark, *British Clubs and Societies 1580–1800: The Origins of an Associational World* (Oxford: Clarendon Press, 2000), pp. 75, 252, 259, 297–9; Heather Hughes, '"How the Welsh became White in South Africa": Immigration, Identity and Economic Transformation from the 1860s to the 1930s', *THSC*, n.s. 7 (2001), 112–27; Bill Jones, 'Desiring and Maintaining a Welsh Australia: The Cambrian Society of Victoria in the 1830s and 1940s', *Australian Studies*, 19/1 (Summer 2004), 113–46; Robert Ll. Tyler, *The Welsh in an Australian Gold Town: Ballarat, Victoria, 1850–1900* (Cardiff: University of Wales Press, 2010); Joan Allen and Richard C. Allen, '"Competing identities": Irish and Welsh Migration and the North-East of England', in A. J. Pollard and A. G. Green (eds), *Regional Identities in North-East England 1300–2000* (Woodford: Boydell and Brewer, 2007), pp. 133–60.
4   For details of associational life in Philadelphia in the eighteenth century see Daniel R. Gilbert, 'Patterns of Organization and Membership in Colonial Philadelphia Club Life, 1725–1755', University of Pennsylvania, Ph.D. thesis, 1952, pp. 156–7; Aaron Sullivan, '"That Charity which begins at Home": Ethnic Societies and Benevolence in Eighteenth-Century Philadelphia', *Pennsylvania Magazine of History and Biography* (hereafter *PMHB*), 134/4 (October 2010), 305–37; Jessica Choppin Roney, *Governed by a Spirit of Opposition: The Origins of American Political Practice in Colonial Philadelphia* (Baltimore, MD: Johns Hopkins University Press, 2014), particularly pp. 69–79 (Welsh associational activity is mentioned on p. 71).

PART ONE

Welsh Migration and the Creation of the Welsh Tract

The migratory patterns of the Welsh as indentured servants on plantations in the Caribbean, as well as traders who settled on the east coast of America, can be traced back to the mid-seventeenth century,[5] but it was the emigration of hundreds of Welsh people, particularly members of the Religious Society of Friends (Quakers) escaping persecution from the 1680s onwards, that led to the establishment of identifiable Welsh settlements in Pennsylvania.[6] In May 1681 an agreement was signed in London between William Penn and the British Quakers which enabled them to purchase shares in his newly acquired holding of 600,000 square miles. Twelve influential Welsh Quakers took an interest in the project and consequently seven Welsh companies were established. They purchased 62½ square miles (40,000 acres) in Pennsylvania and persuaded others to invest, thus setting in train the first great wave of Welsh emigration.[7]

The 'Welsh Tract' was to be a 'Welsh barony' and 'a Holy Christian

---

5   Between 1654 and 1685 the Port Books of Bristol record that approximately 4,000 Welsh people, mainly from south Wales, set sail for the plantations in Barbados as indentured labourers and servants. Others left Wales in search of riches and adventure, notably Howell Powell of Brecon who emigrated to Virginia in 1642 and Lewis Morris of Tintern who initially settled in Barbados before settling in New York. See D. H. Sacks, *The Widening Gate: Bristol and the Atlantic Economy, 1540–1700* (Berkeley and Oxford: University of California Press, 1991); David Hussey, *Coastal and River Trade in pre-Industrial England: Bristol and its Region, 1680–1730* (Exeter: University of Exeter Press, 2000); Samuel S. Smith, *Lewis Morris. Anglo-American Statesman, ca.1613–1691* (Atlantic Highland, New Jersey: Humanities Press, 1983).

6   On 4 March 1681, in response to a £16,000 debt owed to his father by Parliament, Penn had been granted a Charter at Westminster to colonise the former Dutch Colonies. For details, see T. M. Rees, *A History of the Quakers in Wales and their Emigration to North America* (Carmarthen: W. Spurrell & Son, 1925), p. 179.

7   Further details of the Welsh land companies are provided in T. A. Glenn, *Merion in the Welsh Tract* (Norristown: Herald Press, 1896), p. 21; C. S. Browning, *The Welsh Settlement of Pennsylvania* (Philadelphia: W. J. Campbell, 1912), passim.

Community', with the right of self-government. This is not, however, the place to critique the explanation for Welsh Quaker emigration, or indeed the failure to realise the plan for a self-governing Welsh settlement.[8] It is sufficient to note that between 1682 and 1700 hundreds of Welsh emigrants 'braved the horrible Atlantic crossings to create their pioneer settlements in a new world'.[9] They settled along the Schuylkill River and throughout the colony to which they allocated Welsh place-names, most notably, Bryn Mawr, Radnor, Haverford, Upper and Lower Merion, Gwynedd, and Tredyffrin. The terms of their settlement on the Welsh Tract were ratified in 1687, but the dream of an independent colony that would preserve the cultural and linguistic distinctiveness of the

---

8   For details, see Richard C. Allen, '"In Search of a New Jerusalem". A Preliminary Investigation into Welsh Quaker Emigration to North America c.1660–1750', *Quaker Studies*, 9/1 (September 2004), 31–53; Richard C. Allen, *Quaker Communities in Early Modern Wales: From Resistance to Respectability* (Cardiff: University of Wales Press, 2007), chap. 7; Richard C. Allen, 'The Making of a Holy Christian Community: Welsh Quaker Emigrants to Pennsylvania, c.1680–1750', in Tim Kirk and Luda Klusáková (eds), *Cultural Conquests, 1500–2000* (Prague: Philosophica et Historica, Studia Historica, 2009), pp. 45–61. For wider studies see Jordan Landes, *London Quakers in the Trans-Atlantic World: The Creation of an Early Modern Community* (Basingstoke: Palgrave Macmillan, 2015), Naomi Pullin, F*emale Friends and the Making of Transatlantic Quakerism, 1650–1750* (Cambridge: Cambridge University Press, 2018); Esther Sahle, *Quakers in the British Atlantic World, c.1660–1800* (Woodbridge: Boydell Press, 2021).

9   G. A. Williams, *When Was Wales?* (pbk edn. London: Penguin, 1985), p. 136. This was out of an estimated total of 23,000 emigrants. See David Hacket Fischer, *Albion's Seed: Four British Folkways in America* (Oxford: Oxford University Press, 1989), p. 421. Further details of British emigration are also provided in David Armitage and Michael J. Braddick (eds), *British Atlantic World, 1500–1800* (Basingstoke: Palgrave Macmillan, 2002); Eric Richards, *Britannia's Children: Emigration from England, Scotland, Wales and Ireland since 1600* (London and New York: Hambledon, 2004); H. V. Bowen (ed.), *Wales and the British Overseas Empire: Interactions and Influences, 1650–1830* (Manchester: Manchester University Press, 2012); Donald MacRaild, Tanya Bueltmann and J. C. D. Clarke (eds), *British and Irish Diasporas: Societies, Cultures and Ideologies* (Manchester: Manchester University Press, 2019).

Welsh was not to last.¹⁰ Indeed, two years earlier the Welsh Tract had been politically and geographically subdivided into Philadelphia and Chester Counties, and by 1690 the rights that had been granted to the Welsh townships of Haverford, Merion and Radnor were transferred by the Provincial Government to more orthodox township authorities.¹¹

Further townships in the Welsh Tract were added in due course and populated by new settlers from England, Ireland, the Netherlands and Germany who quickly established their own township authorities. The Welsh bitterly resented this loss of power and status, especially as this ran counter to the agreements they had signed with Penn.¹² They wrote several letters of complaint and in 1697, after the collapse of the Susquehanna Land Company, Penn, the Governor of the Colony, was called 'diwyneb' ('faceless'/'two-faced') for breaking his promise to provide the Welsh with dedicated land in Philadelphia.¹³ There were nevertheless some positive developments. Between 1697 and 1698 a further 7,820 acres in Pennsylvania were purchased for £508 by two Welsh Quakers, William ap John and Thomas ap Evan. They subsequently sold the land on for £6.10s. per 100 acres which, in turn, prompted the settlement of thirty Welsh families in the Gwynedd township, Montgomery County.¹⁴ This area rapidly developed and by 1741 it had become a particularly affluent part of the colony. The Welsh also settled in other parts of Pennsylvania, notably in Berks and Bucks Counties, and to a lesser extent in Lancaster County. Thus, the

---

10   Allen, 'The Making of a Holy Christian Community', pp. 54–8.
11   Fischer, *Albion's Seed*, p. 591.
12   Details of the squabbles that developed between the leaders of Pennsylvania in the late-seventeenth century are recounted in Glenn, *Merion in the Welsh Tract*, pp. 47–52; R. C. Simmons, *The American Colonies: From Settlement to Independence* (New York: D. McKay Co., 1976), p. 143; E. T. Ashton, *The Welsh in the United States* (Hove: Caldra House, 1984), pp. 47–8, 51; Barry Levy, *Quakers and the American Family* (Cambridge: Cambridge University Press, 1988), chap. 5; Allen, 'In Search of a New Jerusalem', 39–40.
13   Rees, *History of the Quakers in Wales*, pp. 181–3.
14   Howard M. Jenkins, 'The Welsh Settlement at Gwynedd', *PMHB*, 8 (1884), 175–6.

Welsh were in evidence all along the Susquehanna River. As the colony expanded areas such as Merion that were once described as 'a wilderness' became 'a fruitful field'.[15] By the turn of the eighteenth century over two thousand houses had been erected in Philadelphia alone, and many Welsh emigrants occupied executive posts in the province.[16]

The Welsh Language in Colonial Pennsylvania

In the late-seventeenth century the Welsh language was the primary means of communication. Penn and leading Welsh Quakers had agreed in May 1681 that in these Welsh settlements 'all causes, quarrels, crimes and disputes might be tried and wholly determined by officers, magistrates and juries of our own language'.[17] As a result they established discernible Welsh Quaker and Welsh-speaking enclaves. The retention of the Welsh language and customs, and the lasting affection for Wales, demonstrates the resolve of some of the settlers to defend their Welsh heritage and retain their national identity in Pennsylvania. The letters of emigrants to relatives and former neighbours in Wales provide insights into these early experiences and induced others to join them in the new colony. The publication in 1721 of Ellis Pugh's *Annerch i'r Cymru* – the first Welsh language text published in America – would also suggest that the Welsh emigrant community were still clearly attached to their

---

15 Anon., 'John Roberts of Merion', *PMHB*, 19 (1895), 262–3.
16 For example, see Jenkins, 'Welsh Settlers at Gwynedd', 182–3; G. H. Jenkins, 'From Ysgeifiog to Pennsylvania: The Rise of Thomas Wynne, Quaker Barber-Surgeon', *Flintshire Historical Society Journal*, 28 (1977–8), 39–61.
17 Also, see W. F. Dunaway, 'Early Welsh Settlers of Pennsylvania', *Pennsylvania History: A Journal of Mid-Atlantic Studies* (hereafter *PH*), 12 (1945), 252–3.

language.[18] Although John Jones was born and raised in Pennsylvania, he viewed the colony as a 'distant and foreign land'. In 1725 he wrote a letter to Hugh Jones in Wales about Welsh place-names and exclaimed 'it affords me great delight even to think of them... I long to see them.'[19] Boyd Schlenther has reservations about whether the linguistic purity of the first settlers of the Welsh Tract was maintained, and whether Penn ever truly intended these parts of Pennsylvania to be exclusively Welsh. He notes that even in the early Welsh settlements there were some who had learned English as a second language, or wrote in English, and there were bilingual meetings in the Welsh Tract to accommodate those who did not speak the Welsh language.[20] Yet evidence suggests that the survival of language varied from one township to another. For example, in 1702 an English visitor to the Gwynedd township required the services of an interpreter.[21]

---

18 Ellis Pugh, *Annerch ir Cymru, iw galw oddiwrth y llawer o bethau at yr un peth angenrheidiol er mwyn cadwedigaeth eu heneidiau* (Philadelphia: Andrew Bradford, 1721). An English version was provided six years later. See Ellis Pugh, *A Salutation to the Britons: to call them from the many things, to the one thing needful for the saving of their souls: Especially, to the poor unlearned tradesmen, plowmen and shepherds, those that are of a low degree like myself... Translated from the British language by Rowland Ellis, revised and corrected by David Lloyd* (Philadelphia: S. Keimer, 1727).
19 The translated version is provided in Anon., 'John Jones to Hugh Jones, c.1725', in A. C. Myers (ed.), *Narratives of Pennsylvania, West New Jersey and Delaware, 1630–1707* (New York: Charles Scribner's Sons, 1912; rept. New York: Barnes & Noble, 1967), pp. 454–5. A Welsh copy was published in *PMHB*, 14 (1890), 227–31.
20 Boyd S. Schlenther, '"The English is Swallowing Up Their Language": Welsh Ethnic Ambivalence in Colonial Pennsylvania and the Experience of David Evans', *PMHB*, 114 (1990), 201–28 (202–4).
21 Rees, *History of the Quakers in Wales*, p. 181. The predominance of Welsh-speakers in Radnor township in c.1707 meant that Anglicans also had to preach to their congregations in Welsh. See A. H. Dodd, 'The Background of the Welsh Quaker Migration to Pennsylvania', *Journal of the Merioneth Historical and Record Society*, 3/2 (1958), 111–27 (124).

The Society of the Sons of Ancient Britons

During the early decades of the eighteenth century, emigration from Wales slowed, and virtually dried up in the second quarter of the century. From being an influential minority group in the late-seventeenth century, the Welsh became simply one of many ethnic communities in Pennsylvania. Indeed, by the end of the eighteenth century the Welsh population, which had constituted a considerable proportion of the colony in its early decades, now had to share the land with other migrants. Naturally with such a great influx of other settlers the identity of the Welsh community, their language and their culture was increasingly under threat.[22] Later migration streams made it difficult for the Welsh to sustain their language, and English became prioritised. Most Welsh settlers accepted that for practical reasons they should acquire new linguistic skills.[23] Language was, however, central to the survival of other cultural signifiers and some were determined to defend their Welsh heritage. On 25 February 1729, the *Pennsylvania Gazette* announced that 'several Gentlemen and other Persons of Reputation, of the honourable stock of ancient *Bretons*, design to erect themselves into a Society, to meet together annually on the first day of March, or St David's Day'.[24] Interested parties were invited to hear a

---

22   For a history of the colony see Randall M. Miller and William Pencak (eds), *Pennsylvania: A History of the Commonwealth* (University Park: Pennsylvania State University Press; Harrisburg, Pa.: Pennsylvania Historical and Museum Commission, 2002).

23   For the decline of the Welsh language, especially in nineteenth-century Pennsylvania, see W. D. Jones, 'The Welsh Language and Welsh Identity in a Pennsylvanian Community', in G. H. Jenkins (ed.), *Language and Community in the Nineteenth Century: A Social History of the Welsh Language* (Cardiff: University of Wales Press, 1998), pp. 261–86; Aled Jones and Bill Jones, *Welsh Reflections: Y Drych and America, 1851–2001* (Llandysul: Gomer Press, 2001), chap. 5.

24   *Pennsylvania Gazette*, 25 February 1729. See also Horatio Gates Jones, *Welsh Society Charter and Bye Laws* (Philadelphia: William Mann, 1880), p. 3. This is also available at the Historical Society of Pennsylvania, Philadelphia, MS. 1454. Series VIII. Cadwallader Collection. Box 22. Folder 4. Morris Family.

sermon preached 'in the antient *British* Language' and a Psalm played on the organ; members would then 'partake of a handsome Collation', at the *Queen's Head* owned by Robert Davis at King Street, Philadelphia, which would include a sermon, songs and ale. It was to be a 'ticket only' affair.[25]

On 1 March 1729 the Society of the Sons of Ancient Britons, one of the oldest benevolent societies in America, was duly inaugurated. As the *Pennsylvania Gazette* reported:

> many Gentlemen and others of the ancient Bretons met, and walk'd in a regular Order with Leeks in their Hats to the Church, where was preach'd in the old British language... an excellent Sermon... From thence they return'd... to the *Queen's Head*, where an handsome Dinner [was prepared], After which the following Healths were drank...
>
> The King and the Church; Queen Caroline; the Prince and Royal Family; prosperity to the ancient Bretons and this Province; the Proprietor's health, and his honour, Governor Gordon's, and many other healths.[26]

The Society aimed to promote 'Love and Friendship' and similar gatherings were held in various parts of England, in the American colonies, and in other Welsh settlements across the globe.[27] In 1730 members met at the *Sign of the Crown* in Market Street, Philadelphia, and the 1731 celebrations, for which tickets were sold at 5s. per head, were held at Owen Owen's *Indian King* in Market Street.[28] The

---

25 *Pennsylvania Gazette*, 25 February 1729.
26 *Pennsylvania Gazette*, 1 March 1729.
27 Very few records survive but some information can be found in Jones, *Welsh Society Charter*, pp. 5–6, and citing *Pennsylvania Gazette*, 1 March 1729.
28 *American Weekly Mercury*, 528 (Tuesday, 10 February–Thursday, 19 February 1730); 530 (3 March 1730); *Pennsylvania Gazette*, 16 February 1731; Jones, *Welsh Society Charter*, p. 6. For further details of the *Indian King* see Peter Thompson, *Rum Punch and Revolution: Taverngoing and Public Life in Eighteenth-Century Philadelphia* (Philadelphia: University of Pennsylvania Press, 1998), pp. 58–67, 130–1.

Pennsylvania Gazette observed that the event was a great success with drinking and cannonfire as the order of the day, and the proceedings were closed with a Ball at the home of Captain Hopkins. For much of the eighteenth century annual meetings were held and members enjoyed 'Musick, Mirth and Friendship'.[29] In 1741, however, their merrymaking had unfortunate consequences. The revellers inadvertently killed Thomas Scott, mate of the Liverpool registered *Phoenix*, when one of the cannons was 'overcharg'd with Powder, and besides imprudently ramm'd with rough Stones, which were to be shot at a Cask on the Ice, burst in Pieces'. Scott suffered a fractured skull and died a few hours later.[30]

Eighteenth Century London-Welsh Associational Life

The activities of this Society were consistent with the associational life of the London-Welsh and the founding, in 1715, of 'the most Honourable and Loyal Society of Ancient Britons' whereby Welsh exiles sought to recreate something of the cultural life of their homeland, albeit an imagined Welsh heritage.[31] In 1718 the London-Welsh Society established a charity school in Grays Inn which provided an education along with clothing and lodging for eighty boys and twenty-five girls of Welsh parentage.[32] As the *Pennsylvania Gazette* observed, the Society

---

29 *Pennsylvania Gazette*, 4 March 1731.
30 *Pennsylvania Gazette*, 5 March 1741.
31 For further details of this cultural shift see Prys Morgan, 'From a Death to a View: the Hunt for the Welsh Past in the Romantic Period', in Eric Hobsbawm and Terence Ranger (eds), *The Invention of Tradition* (Cambridge: Cambridge University Press, 1983), pp. 43–100; S. Smiles, *The Image of Antiquity: Ancient Britain and the Romantic Imagination* (New Haven and London: Yale University Press, 1994); Colin Kidd, *British Identities Before Nationalism: Ethnicity and Nationhood in the Atlantic World, 1600–1800* (Cambridge; New York: Cambridge University Press, 1999); Clark, *British Clubs and Societies*, pp. 75, 252, 259, 297–9.
32 For details, see *London Gazette*, 12 February 1715; Jenkins and Rammage, *History of the Honourable Society of Cymmrodorion*, p. 14.

of the Sons of Ancient Britons was

erected in Imitation of a useful Society in London, who annually meet on the same Day, and is encourag'd there by Persons of the first Rank; their late Royal Highnesses the Prince and Princess of Wales contributing largely to its Support and Reputation.[33]

The London-based Society of Ancient Britons, its successor the Honourable Society of Cymmrodorion (1751),[34] and other Welsh-American Societies, were part of a 'Celtic Revival' which extended across much of Europe.[35] Like its British counterpart, the Philadelphia-based society expressed its loyalty to Britain and to the monarchy, but why did they do this? Prys Morgan has suggested that the Welsh sought 'a proper recognition of their part in British history' rather than to 'separate themselves from Britain'. He contends that the Welsh cultural renaissance of the eighteenth and early-nineteenth centuries was predicated on a decline in Welsh traditionalism, but conversely an increasing 'interest in things Welsh'. Moreover, in the passing of 'Merrie Wales', the Welsh became self-conscious of themselves as a separate people and intent on preserving a distinctive Welshness. This, he argued, ushered in

a new generation... passionately devoted to rescue, restore and revive what they could of the old. As the new generation appeared, so many features of novelty, freshness and resourcefulness appeared in Wales which would in effect make the revival quite unlike any other episode in the Welsh past.[36]

---

33 *Pennsylvania Gazette*, 25 February 1729.
34 Emrys Jones, 'A Concise History of the Society', *THSC*, n.s. 9 (2003), 4–28 (5).
35 For example, the Cymmrodorion intended to promote 'friendship and good understanding among the people of Wales residing in the City of London'. See Jenkins and Rammage, *History of the Honourable Society of Cymmrodorion*, p. 74.
36 Morgan, *Eighteenth Century Renaissance*, p. 39.

Clearly, the Philadelphian Welsh were of the same mind. They wanted to understand their past, or at least to recover some of it. Others would suggest that this sort of associational activity often reflected 'a mechanism of conformity not dissent' in the host country, as well as 'a device by which separate identity might be articulated for whatever purpose, whenever necessary'.[37] This was expressed by James Jones Levick, a much later Philadelphian-Welshman, who stated in his 1890 address to the Welsh Society on behalf of 'The Ancient Britons': 'every one of us likes to be associated with the oldest families and I know no older... no better families than were the ancient Britons, your ancestors and mine'. He acknowledged the benefits of being Welsh:

> It is true that the Egyptians are an ancient people, but I am personally acquainted with no gentlemen of Egyptian ancestry who takes an active part in the civil government, or in the public charities of Philadelphia, whereas in both these particulars the descendants of the ancient Britons are most conspicuous. You need but look around this table to have the truth of this statement confirmed. And so it has been since the early days of this colony.

Pointing out the pre-eminent colonial positions held by Welshmen and their claims to be descended from ancient British stock, Levick asked 'who were those ancient Britons?':

> By this term we mean the different tribes, clans or nations inhabiting Britain before the time of the Roman invasion, and their descendants. Before the Roman invasion? Yes, for centuries before! Why, my Welsh brethren, we had a written history four centuries before Caesar was born... It was a right royal race that Brutus... brought with him and

---

37 P. Payton, *The Cornish Overseas* (Fowey: Cornwall Editions, 1999), p. 383, and cited in Jones, 'Desiring and Maintaining a Welsh Australia', 115. For a stimulating discussion of transnationalism and Wales see Paul O'Leary, 'Power and Modernity: Transnational Wales, c.1780–1939', *Llafur: Journal of Welsh People's History/Clychgrawn Hanes Pobl Cymru*, 12/4 (2019/20), 33–55.

landed, he and his sons, on the shores of that little island.[38]

Modern historians are more cautious in their comments about the Welsh, particularly exiles and the attachment to their cultural identity. Schlenther has argued that while the first Welsh-American society exhibited a 'modest burst of cultural self-consciousness' this 'pointed to the essential weakness of the Welsh language and culture in Pennsylvania, rather than to their increasing strength'.[39] By the middle of the eighteenth century, the ability to speak English enabled the Welsh to fraternise with a wider mixture of ethnic groups and became the preferred method of communication. Yet these early Welsh societies, both the London-based and Pennsylvanian examples, provided much more than simply a cultural identity for the Welsh exile. They were, as Bill Jones has observed for later Welsh societies, promoting 'their nationality's presence and its perceived contribution to their adoptive country's development'.[40] As will be shown, these Welsh societies offered practical and financial assistance to poor Welsh migrants and thereby they occupy a significant place in the history of emigration to the American colonies.

Philadelphia in the Eighteenth and Nineteenth Centuries – a wider historical context

It ought to be noted that the city of Philadelphia in which these Welshmen gathered on a regular basis underwent significant demographic, political, social and economic changes, from the emergence of the Society of the Sons of Ancient Britons in 1729 to the establishment of the Welsh Society of Philadelphia at the end of

---

38   National Library of Wales, MS. 2703F, 'Crynwyr Cymru ac UDA', particularly James Jones Levick, 'The Ancient Britons spoken at the Annual Dinner of the Welsh Society of Philadelphia ... March 1st 1890', 1–3.
39   Schlenther, 'The English is Swallowing Up Their Language', 225. Also, see Sally Schwartz, *'A Mixed Multitude': The Struggle for Toleration in Colonial Pennsylvania* (New York & London: New York University Press, 1987), p. 293.
40   Jones, 'Desiring and Maintaining a Welsh Australia', 116–17.

the eighteenth century. After its founding by William Penn in 1682, Philadelphia steadily grew from a population that could be counted in the hundreds, to well over 10,000 in 1731, 44,000 by the end of the eighteenth century and a population that exceeded 110,000 in the early decades of the nineteenth century.[41] Although initially comprising Protestant settlers, notably Quakers, Philadelphia (and Pennsylvania more widely) would increasingly become the home of other ethnic peoples, especially Irish and German settlers, throughout this period.[42] These different communities added to the cultural diversity of the city as can be illustrated in the Mummers Parade held on New Year's Day. This event had its origins in the late seventeenth century and despite attempts to supress it in the eighteenth century it has continued to the present day.[43] Moreover, the city became an important centre for commerce, especially along its waterfront as the mercantile economy expanded.[44] There was also a rapidly developing artisan community

---

41 See Mary Maples Dunn and Richard S. Dunn, 'The Founding, 1681–1701', Edwin B. Bronner, 'Village into Town, 1701–1746', and Harry M. Tinkcom, 'Town into City, 1746–1765', in Russell F. Weighley, Nicholas B. Wainwright, Edwin B. Wolf, Joseph E. Illick and Thomas Wendel (eds), *Philadelphia: A 300-Year History* (New York and London: W. W. Norton & Co., 1982), pp. 1–32, 33–67, 68–108. For the demographic shifts see B. Smith, 'Death and Life in a Colonial Immigrant City: A Demographic Analysis of Philadelphia', *Journal of Economic History*, 37/4 (1977), 863–88; S. E. Klepp, 'Demography in Early Philadelphia, 1690–1860', *Proceedings of the American Philosophical Society*, 133/2 (1989), 85–111, and her *'The Swift Progress of Population': A Documentary and Bibliographic Study of Philadelphia's Growth, 1600–1859* (Philadelphia: American Philosophical Society, 1989); Gary B. Nash, *First City: Philadelphia and the Forging of Historical Memory* (Philadelphia: University of Pennsylvania Press, 2002), p. 108.
42 For some details see Allen Davis and Mark Haller (eds), *The Peoples of Philadelphia: A History of Ethnic Groups and Lower-Class Life, 1790–1940* (Philadelphia: University of Pennsylvania Press, 1973).
43 For details of this and other cultural activities see Susan G. Davis, '"Making Night Hideous": Christmas Revelry and Public Order in Nineteenth-Century Philadelphia', *American Quarterly*, 34/2 (1982), 185–99.
44 Nash, *First City*, pp. 47–53.

whose skilled work created a 'dense urban space of brick houses and mansions, small dwellings in crowded alleys, warehouses, workshops, churches, and taverns'.[45]

The spread of Enlightenment ideas was instrumental in galvanising Philadelphians to establish centres of learning such as the Library Company, the American Philosophical Society, and a myriad of other organisations, as well as to question their allegiance to Britain. Indeed, between 1775 and 1783, Philadelphia took centre stage in the fight to attain American independence. Apart from its leading citizens providing finance and supplies for the war effort, Philadelphia was a meeting place for delegates who signed the Declaration of Independence in 1776 at the Second Continental Congress and the Constitution at the Philadelphia Convention of 1787. As such, 'the commercial city' became 'the city of revolution', while for ten years from December 1790 the national government resided in Philadelphia.[46]

Post-revolution, Philadelphia once again resumed its importance as a trading centre and manufacturing hub. It was a city full of opportunities and this led further waves of migrants to seek a new life there.[47] Unfortunately, as the Welsh Society's minutes reveal this was often unrealised. Indeed, as Gary Nash emphatically remarked, 'rapid industrial expansion and heavy immigration proved an explosive mix, so filling the city with political, religious, and economic strife that the

---

45 For these important developments see Nash, *First City*, pp. 53–63; Jean R. Soderlund, 'Colonial Era' in 'The Encyclopedia of Greater Philadelphia', https://philadelphiaencyclopedia.org/archive/colonial-philadelphia/ [accessed 4 October 2021].
46 For full details see Richard G. Miller, 'The Federal City, 1783–1800', in Weighley, Wainwright, Wolf, Illick and Wendel (eds), *Philadelphia: A 300-Year History*, pp. 155–207; Nash, *First City*, pp. 78–114, 122–33 (quote on p. 78).
47 For these developments see Edgar P. Richardson, 'The Athens of America, 1800–1825' and Nicholas B. Wainwright, 'The Age of Nicholas Biddle, 1825–1841', in Weighley, Wainwright, Wolf, Illick and Wendel (eds), *Philadelphia: A 300-Year History*, pp. 208–57, 258–306.

Plate 1. 'Arch Street Ferry, Philadelphia', c.1800.[48]

old concept of brotherly love seemed a lost and distant memory'.[49] In these days of urban strife and poverty, members of the Welsh Society of Philadelphia nevertheless offered some relief, and it is to their exertions that attention will now be drawn.

A New Beginning – the Welsh Society of Philadelphia

It is unclear when the Society of the Sons of Ancient Britons ceased to function as an effective cultural and benevolent body, but it may be that the War of Independence interrupted some of their activities. After all, the executive were close to the heart of government. Evidence

---

48   W. Birch and Son, *The City of Philadelphia, in the State of Pennsylvania North America; As it Appeared in the Year 1800: Consisting of Twenty-Eight Plates* (Philadelphia: W. Birch, 1800), plate 4.
49   Nash, *First City*, pp. 144–75 (quote on p. 144).

suggests that a St David's Society continued to meet before and during the revolution.[50] From 1798 onwards the Welsh in Philadelphia were once again eager to establish a society that would serve their cultural and philanthropic interests.[51] (Plate 2 and Plate 3) In 1802 the Welsh Society was legally endorsed by the Supreme Court of Pennsylvania, and had an elaborate organisation with a Constitution, Charter, Rules, and Bye-Laws.[52] Its committee structure was complex and included the usual officers, two counsellors, two physicians, and seven stewards to organise the quarterly meetings and the St David's Day dinner. It was agreed that twenty-one members ought to form the quorum for quarterly meetings and a two-thirds majority had the 'power to expel a member for disorderly behaviour'.[53] These formalities underline the Society's elitist ethos and indicate the extent to which they saw themselves as a respectable and influential sector of Philadelphian society. Those who sought membership had to secure nomination and election by ballot. In addition, some honorary members were admitted even if they were 'not citizens of this country' or could potentially offer invaluable services to the Society.[54] This was the case with Thomas Barton Zantzinger (1776–

---

50 See a testimony to Richard Price provided in HC, MC-1186, Vol. 1, 2 September 1822.
51 For statistical information relating to Philadelphia at this time see Susan E. Klepp, 'The Demographic Characteristics of Philadelphia, 1788–1801: Zachariah Poulson's Bills of Mortality', *PH*, 53/3 (July 1986), 201–21.
52 In 1838 it was agreed to produce in a pamphlet two hundred and fifty copies of the Charter and Bye-Laws for 'the use of the members of the Society'. HC, MC-1186, Vol. 1, 1 March 1838.
53 HC, MC-1186, Vol. 1, 4 February 1799. Rules and Regulations. The stipulation of having twenty-one members to ensure that the meeting was quorate was later regarded as 'extremely inconvenient'. HC, MC-1186, Vol. 1, 7 December 1801.
54 For discussions held at meetings concerning honorary members see HC, MC-1186, Vol. 1, 2 June 1800. The position of honorary members was confirmed in a minute from 1802: 'the members who are not residents of this State and those whose names have from the necessity of the case been excluded from the Charter of Incorporation shall be considered and established as honorary members of this Society'. HC, MC-1186, Vol. 1, 7 June 1802.

1847), a merchant, whose nomination and subsequent election in 1800 indicates the extent to which the Welsh had integrated with the Dutch-German communities, or Enos Bronson (1774–1823), the proprietor of the Federalist *Gazette of the United States*, who was a leading member between 1804 and 1820.[55] In March 1806 Bronson was the chairman of the Society (*pro-tem*) for the election of officers despite being from Connecticut and having no discernible Welsh connections.[56] His membership probably turned upon his close business ties with other members of the Society, particularly Thomas Biddle, and Elihu and Thomas Chauncey. Other members sought honorary status when they left the State for personal or professional reasons.[57]

WELCH SOCIETY.

THE members of the Welch Society are requested to attend the annual meeting on the first of March next, at one o'clock, at Ogden's Tavern, No. 86, Chesnut-street, to choose officers for the ensuing year—a dinner will be provided and on the table at 3 o'clock precisely.

OWEN FOULK, Secretary.

feb 25

Plate 2. Advertisement for the Annual Meeting of the Welch Society on 1 March 1799.[58]

---

55 Thomas B. Zantzinger was proposed in December 1800 by Richard Maris. Enos Bronson was proposed by Griffith Evans and resigned from the Society in 1820 due to ill-health. See HC, MC-1186, Vol. 1, 1 December 1800, 4 June 1804, 5 June 1820.
56 HC, MC-1186, Vol. 1, 1 March 1806.
57 For example, in December 1811 John S. Willett left Pennsylvania but requested 'to be placed on the list of honorary members'. HC, MC-1186, Vol. 1, 2 December 1811.
58 *Gazette of the United States & Philadelphia Daily Advertiser*, 27 February 1799, p. 2.

> At an annual meeting of the Welch S‑
> ciety, held at the houfe of William Ogden,
> No. 86, Chefnut-ftreet, on Friday laft, the
> firft of March, the following perfons were
> chofen officers for the enfuing year.
> —viz.—
>
> *President.*
> Samuel Meredith.
> *Vice-President.*
> Jacob Morgan,
> *Treasurer.*
> Thomas Cumpfton,
> *Secretary.*
> Owen Foulke,
> *Register.*
> Morgan I. Rhees,
> *Counsellors.*
> Benjamin R. Morgan,
> Edward Tilghman,
>
> *Physicians.*
> Dr. Thomas C. James,
> Dr. Jofeph Strong,
> *Stewards.*
> Robert Wharton,
> William Jones,
> John Evans,
> Jonathan Jones,
> John Davis,
> Michael Roberts,
> Richard Price.

Plate 3. Reporting the Annual Meeting, 1 March 1799.[59]

Financing the Society

The Society was financed by annual subscriptions while appeals were made urging members to provide further sums of money to help poor and indigent Welsh settlers. In June 1802 it was reported that the Treasurer and committee members had expended a considerable amount to assist these migrants and a minute recorded that 'it is probable that the Society may be called upon ere long for large sums of money to assist the emigrants that may be expected daily to arrive'. It called on members to contribute 'a sum sufficient to discharge the debt already contracted by them and also to raise a further sum to aid the usual funds of this Society'.[60] Such was the commitment to provide both financial as well as well as practical help. In addition, fines were imposed

---

59 *Gazette of the United States & Philadelphia Daily Advertiser*, 5 March 1799, p. 3.
60 HC, MC-1186, Vol. 1, 7 June 1802.

for non-attendance at annual, special and quarterly meetings.[61] As early as June 1799, however, the Treasurer reported that several members had refused to pay their contributions and fines to the Society. This was reiterated in March and June 1801 when it was recorded that there were several 'delinquents' in arrears. It was agreed that if they did not pay by the next meeting they would 'be reported as disorderly and a question of expulsion' would be considered.[62] Eighteen months later a bye-law firmed up this position. It stated that if members were in arrears for more than twelve months, they would be called on to pay their fines and contributions within a three-month period. After that the Secretary would forward their names to the next meeting and they would be expelled.[63] Moreover, in March 1805 James Rolph was censured by Robert Thomas for a numbered of unspecified misdemeanours, but his expulsion was deferred by the Society.[64]

Society minutes suggest that their efforts to recoup these arrears were often ineffectual.[65] Significantly, in 1814 it was discovered that upon his death John Jones, the Society's fees collector ('messenger'), had mismanaged some of their affairs. A committee reviewed the ledgers

---

61   HC, MC-1186, Vol. 1, 4 February 1799. Rules and Regulations, nos. 7–9.
62   HC, MC-1186, Vol. 1, 3 June 1799, 2 March 1801, 1 June 1801.
63   HC, MC-1186, Vol. 1, 6 December 1802. This was confirmed in a meeting on 1 March 1803.
64   HC, MC-1186, Vol. 1, 1 March 1805, 3 June 1805. He was, however, expelled in 1811 for not paying his fees. See HC, MC-1186, Vol. 1, 2 December 1811. The first expulsion was that of Thomas Jones in early 1799. It was recorded that his name was to be 'expunged' from the membership list and that he was 'no longer to be considered as a member of this Society'. Equally, William Preston was warned that the non-payment of fines and contributions would result in expulsion. He was expelled the following month. HC, MC-1186, Vol. 1, 4 February 1799, 2 September 1805, 2 December 1805.
65   For details, see HC, MC-1186, Vol. 1, 1 March 1820. William Meredith and William Read advised the Society that they had resigned years previously, several others were dead or could not be located, while Edmund Kinsey informed the Society that, although he was in debt to them, they 'must know he cannot afford to pay & intends sending in his resignation'. Also, see HC, MC-1186, Vol. 1, 5 June 1820 for further resignations.

that he kept but stated that it was with 'regret' there appeared a debt due from him for $347. Moreover, his personal finances would make it difficult for the Society to recoup the funds speedily from his estate while 'a material loss' was likely.[66] Several years later the Society appealed to new members to help recover some of the very heavy debts incurred by the Society,[67] but repeated resignations from the late-1810s onwards not only caused the Society to lose a valuable income stream but also questioned whether its usefulness as a philanthropic body would be seriously compromised. At this time (c.1823), defaulting members owed over $888, and a List of Outstanding Debts was made. It was comprised of twenty-three names. Six members were honorary, while a further member had died – all of these were taken off the register; an additional four had previously had their circumstances satisfactorily reviewed, and twelve were contacted to pay what they owed or 'of such part as they can conveniently pay'. In the case of the latter, the Society would then keep them on the current register but would be prepared to exonerate them from any unpaid fees and/or accept their resignation if that was their preferred choice. Of the twelve it was later noted that two of them had died.[68] By 1825 the situation demanded a further examination and the question of the legality of fining members was fully debated.[69]

Although various members persistently defaulted in paying their dues the Society nevertheless could accrue sizeable revenues. In 1808 the Society received a hundred Rupees from R. Williams of Calcutta for the express purpose of assisting Welsh emigrants. In response, the Society granted honorary membership as 'a benevolent Cambrian and worthy gentleman'. The Society also sought to benefit from the 'premium of exchange between Calcutta and Philadelphia'. The letter from Williams to William Jones and William Smith which accompanied the bequest reflected the benevolent attitude of the Society:

---

66   HC, MC-1186, Vol. 1, 6 June 1814.
67   HC, MC-1186, Vol. 1, 1 March 1821.
68   HC, MC-1186, Vol. 1, 1 March 1823.
69   HC, MC-1186, Vol. 1, 5 September 1825.

Dear Sirs,

I was much pleased with your description of the Welsh Society and as a Cambrian I feel interested in any thing that may tend to my countryman's good, particularly when the intention is to assist the unfortunate emigrant who, in the hope of bettering his prospects in life, visits a foreign clime finds himself on his arrival friendless. The Institution does honor to my countryman and tho' at a distance from it I beg you will present in my name the enclosed bank bill of one hundred Rupees. It is a mite, but with a large family my circumstances [does] not allow me to be a liberal as I wish.[70]

The coffers were further boosted the next year when John Snead who had settled in the city with his family left some property 'which was in danger of being lost, unless some suitable person was legally authorized to take charge of it'. The Society acted quickly and secured the legacy which they intended for the use of Snead's two orphaned children who were apprenticed to Thomas Wilkinson of Chester County.[71] In the same year members received a bequest from John Keble who donated just over $3,000,[72] and in 1837 the Society received part of the legacy of Dr Pierre Antione (Peter Anthony) Blénon of Hamilton Village, west Philadelphia.[73] The Society invested their funds judiciously, spreading their assets in a few banks and shares. In March 1820, the Society's funds were dispersed as illustrated below. (Table 1):

---

70 HC, MC-1186, Vol. 1, 6 June 1808.
71 HC, MC-1186, Vol. 1, 5 June 1809. For the administration of John Snead's Will, see Philadelphia (Pennsylvania), Register of Wills. Administration Files, no. 54 (1809).
72 HC, MC-1186, vol. 1, 4 September 1809. Again, in the same year and following, Robert Montgomery left money to various charitable institutions of which the Welsh Society was one. HC, MC-1186, Vol. 1, 4 December 1809, 4 June 1810.
73 HC, MC-1186, Vol. 1, 4 September 1837.

Table 1. Welsh Society of Philadelphia Investments, 1820.

	$
Stock of the Bank of North America 3 Shares	1800
Ditto of United States Six per cents	4129.72
Water Loan of the City	1500
And there is in his hands the sum of	20.34
	Total of 7450.06

This excluded the $900 owed to the Society in unpaid subscriptions,[74] which included, among others, the subscription of Enos Bronson. The following June, Bronson's long illness forced his resignation and members exonerated him from the debt.[75]

Plate 4. 'South East Corner of Third and Market Streets, Philadelphia', c.1800.[76]

---

74 HC, MC-1186, Vol. 1, 1, 1 March 1820.
75 HC, MC-1186, Vol. 1, 5 June 1820.
76 Birch and Son, *The City of Philadelphia*, plate 8.

An Elaborate Organisation

The Society's organisation was elaborate and careful. In some respects members drew upon a model with which they were already familiar, namely the Quaker business meetings.[77] Yet here the stewards had a key role in organising and coordinating social functions. In 1799, for example, they arranged 'a suitable dinner provided by William Ogden at his House on the first of March, and that a roast (a kid) be the first dish at the head of the Table'. They ensured that all wines were of a good quality and that liquor was provided only to those with the necessary ticket.[78] (See Plate 5 and the transcription which follows).

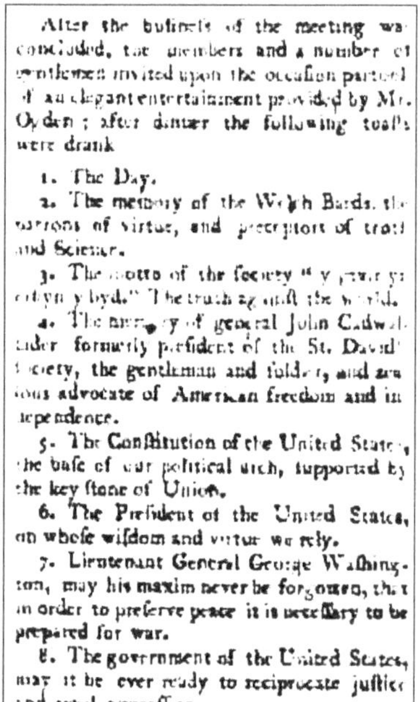

Plate 5. The St David's Day Festivities, 1 March 1799 (and transcript).[79]

---

77 For details of the Quaker impact on Pennsylvania and on associational life in Philadelphia see J. W. Frost, *A Perfect Freedom: Religious Liberty in Pennsylvania* (University Park, Pa.: Pennsylvania State University Press, 1993); Levy, *Quakers and the American Family*; Roney, *Governed by a Spirit of Opposition*, pp. 63–6.
78 HC, MC-1186, vol. 1, 4 February 1799.
79 *Gazette of the United States & Philadelphia Daily Advertiser*, 5 March 1799, p. 3.

PART ONE

[Transcription:]

After the business of the meeting was concluded, the members and a number of gentlemen invited upon the occasion partook of an elegant entertainment provided by Mr Ogden; after dinner the following toasts were drank:

1. The Day

2. The memory of the Welsh Bards, the patrons of virtue, and preceptors of truth and science.

3. The motto of the Society "y givir [sic] yr erbyn y byd" – The truth against the world.

4. The memory of General John Cadwallader formerly President of the St David's Society, the gentleman and soldier, and zealous advocate of American freedom and independence.

5. The Constitution of the United States, the base of our political arch, supported by the key stone of Union.

6. The President of the United States on whose wisdom and virtue we rely.

7. Lieutenant General George Washington, may his maxim never be forgotten, that in order to preserve peace it is necessary to be prepared for war.

8. The government of the United States, may it be ever ready to reciprocate justice and repel aggression.

9. The citizens of the United States, may unanimity, love of country and determination to support and defend its laws, liberties and independence, be their distinguishing characteristic.

10. The navy of the United States, may the venerable and expansive live oak of which it is formed, prove emblematical of its future strength, greatness and durability.

11. Our ministers abroad, may they guard the interest and support the dignity of our country in defiance of foreign influence.

12. The agriculture, manufactures and commerce of the United States.

13. Our adventurous ancestors who fought and found in the Western hemisphere the enjoyment of civil and religious liberty.

14. Our fair countrywomen.

15. The benevolent institutions throughout the United States.

16. The commonwealth of Pennsylvania.

Given the fourteenth toast to 'Our fair countrywomen', it is worth noting here that this was a male-only society. In this respect it was similar in its composition to many other organisations of the period with patriarchal attitudes governing membership, including several other contemporary London-Welsh societies such as the Cymmrodorion, Gwyneddigion, Caradogion, and Cymreigyddion, although the Abergavenny (Monmouthshire) based Cymdeithas Cymreigyddion y Fenni did have Augusta, Georgina Waddington (wife of Benjamin Hall, MP), and Lady Elizabeth Coffin-Greenly of Titley Court, Hereford, as members when it was established in 1833.[80] Among members of the Welsh Society of Philadelphia there was also an entrenched fear that female migrants were less capable of coping with the pressures of life in America and more likely to need financial or practical assistance. Equally, those women who were associated with the Society, particularly

---

80 Others include the Canorion, the Gomerians, the Ofyddion, St David's Society, Undeb Cymry, and Ymofynwyr Cymreigyddawl. For further details of Cymmrodorion, Gwyneddigion and versions of the Cymreigyddion Societies see W. D. Leathart, *The Origin and Progress of the Gwyneddigion Society of London, instituted MDCCLXX* (London; Hugh Pierce Hughes, 1831); Jenkins and Rammage, *History of the Honourable Society of Cymmrodorion*.

the wives of members, were politely thanked for their services but this did not alter their position on the fringe of the organisation.[81]

In contrast to its attitude to Philadelphian-Welsh women as members, up to thirty non-Welsh male 'guests' could be invited by the Society's stewards to the annual dinner, including officers of the St George,[82] St Andrew,[83] St Herman[84] and Hibernian Societies.[85] This was quickly scaled back in subsequent years with only eight guests being allowed.[86] In 1818 there was a determination to secure a regular host in Philadelphia in which they could hold the quarterly meetings and annual dinner. The Washington Hall was chosen and for $75 'a

---

81   See HC, MC-1186, Vol. 1, 1 March 1819 and later discussions in this introductory essay.
82   This group first met on 23 April 1772 at Patrick Byrne's tavern, Front Street; the first president was the Rev. Richard Peters. For details see Society of the Sons of St George, *List of the Members of the Society of the Sons of St George, Established at Philadelphia/ Revised and Corrected the 23rd of April, 1802* (Philadelphia: James Humphreys, 1802); Anon., *An Historical Sketch of the Origin and Progress of the Society of the Sons of St George* (Philadelphia: W. W. Bates & Co., 1872); Society of the Sons of St George, Philadelphia, *History of the Society of the Sons of St George, Philadelphia* (Philadelphia: T. C. Knauff, 1923); and the more rounded study of English migration and associational life in America by Tanya Bueltmann and Donald MacRaild, *The English Diaspora in North America: Migration, Ethnicity and Association, 1730s–1950s* (Manchester: Manchester University Press, 2017), particularly chap. 2.
83   See Scots Thistle Society of Philadelphia, *Constitution of the Scots Thistle Society of Philadelphia* (Philadelphia: John Bioren, 1799); Roney, *Governed by a Spirit of Opposition*, pp. 95–6 (St Andrew's Society). A wider study is provided in Tanja Bueltmann, *Clubbing Together: Ethnicity, Civility and Formal Sociability in the Scottish Diaspora to 1930* (Liverpool: Liverpool University Press, 2014), chap. 2.
84   See HC, MC-1186, Vol. 1, December 1807. Also, see B. Pfleger, *Ethnicity Matters: A History of the German Society of Pennsylvania* (Washington DC: German Historical Institute, 2006).
85   John H. Campbell, *History of the Friendly Sons of St Patrick and of the Hibernian Society for the Relief of Emigrants from Ireland: March 17, 1771– March 17, 1892* (Philadelphia: Hibernian Society, 1892).
86   HC, MC-1186, vol. 1, 2 December 1799.

capacious and comfortable apartment for their stated meetings to be lighted and warmed' was agreed.[87]

Despite the good relations between these various societies, the committee was highly selective about how their funds were spent. In 1811 members met to consider an appeal by the St David's Society to help fund a burial ground for the Welsh and their descendants in Philadelphia. After some discussion, the Society declined to help stating that 'the funds of this Society should not be placed at the disposal of any other institution. But are to be devoted, under the direction of our own members to the humane and charitable purposes for which we associated'.[88] Nevertheless, the St David's Society succeeded in establishing their burial ground when William Hamilton donated part of his estate for the purpose.[89] Ironically, when the last trustee died in 1834, the burial ground was conveyed to the Welsh Society.[90] There were a number of regulations about burial arrangements:

> Rule 1st. That no person be interred therein unless known to be of Welsh descent.
>
> 2nd. That no person be interred unless by a written order from at least one of those persons to be appointed by the acting committee, from time to time for that purpose.
>
> 3rd. That the burial ground shall be divided in the center by a walk, extending from the north to the south, in width not less than six feet and that the graves shall be dug east and west, commencing at the north corner and the first

---

87   HC, MC-1186, Vol. 1, 28 February 1818.
88   HC, MC-1186, Vol. 1, 1, 1 March 1811, 3 June 1811.
89   Jones, *Welsh Society Charter*, p. 13.
90   HC, MC-1186, Vol. 1, 2 June 1834; 1 September 1834; 28 February 1835 includes the rules governing the 'Welsh Burying ground'. In December 1834 the Welsh Society of Philadelphia spent $394 on repairs to the burial ground and continued to provide repairs thereafter. See HC, MC-1186, Vol. 1, 1 December 1834, 1 March 1839.

row, extend next [to] the wall, from north to south.[91]

More striking was the fact that the growth in the number of Welsh emigrants during the nineteenth century forced them to sell-off the old burial ground and purchase the much larger Mount Moriah cemetery in 1863.[92]

Significant Early Members[93]

The Welsh Society was composed of well-to-do merchants, religious leaders, attorneys, and other professionals. They invested enormous amounts of time and energy to the service of the Society. Richard C. Jones (c.1767–1809), an early secretary of the Society, had a lengthy testimonial written after his death. Clearly a very well-respected member, the Society certainly mourned his departure and were determined that his memory would not be forgotten:

> to the future members of the Society it may be useful that a portion of our records should be devoted to preserve the remembrance of one whose deportment presents so fair and favorable a model of capacity, fidelity and zeal as a member and an officer of this institution.

Jones had joined the Society in 1798 and initially acted as a steward. His philanthropy was well-known to Welsh emigrants. Indeed, Jones 'felt not the influence of coldness or insensibility, but a genial warmth

---

91 HC, MC-1186, Vol. 1, 28 February 1835.
92 On 29 December 1863 Henry P. Connell and his wife conveyed land to the Mount Moriah Cemetery Association of Philadelphia. This was ratified in an indenture on 2 April 1864, which also stated that a plot of land was to be provided for the use of the Welsh Society of Philadelphia for the sum of $1,500. I am grateful to Charles D. Wenzel for the details of this purchase. See his 'The Mount Moriah Cemetery of the Welsh Society of Philadelphia'; https://www.peoplescollection.wales/sites/default/files/Mt.%20Moriah.pdf [accessed 5 October 2021].
93 For additional details see Part 4: Select Biographies.

impelled his charities and a sound prudence directed them to the proper objects'. This was nowhere more apparent when yellow fever swept the city in the later 1790s and he risked his life assisting the infected citizens and sought to 'alleviate the miseries of a numerous body of emigrants from Wales'.[94] It was recorded that he embodied the spirit of the Welsh Society:

> Fearless of the danger, and regardless of fatigue, Mr Jones devoted himself to an unremitting service, for the relief of these afflicted strangers from the multiplied distress with which they were surrounded. Early and late, he attended the hospital administering to the wants of the necessitous, and imparting comfort and consolation to the distressed. The widow and the orphan were peculiar objects of his solicitude and attention, and this numerous family of sick and comfortless strangers experienced that fellowship and humanity which our association professes to promote.

His exposure to this disease undermined his health and he never fully recovered his former strength. Undeterred, he was appointed to serve on the Society's Orphan Committee, which he undertook with 'fatherly and friendly care, congenial with the benevolence of his own heart and in happy fulfillment of the charitable views of the institution'. Jones died after a short illness on 9 January 1809 and the Society observed that in his humanitarianism and dedication to their aims he 'left behind him no superior'.[95]

---

94 Although not specified this was probably the epidemic that occurred between 1797 and 1799. It followed on from the devastating 1793 epidemic. For details see Anita DeClue and Billy G. Smith, 'Wrestling the "Pale Faced Messenger": The Diary of Edward Garrigues during the 1798 Philadelphia Yellow Fever Epidemic', *PH*, 65, Special Supplemental Issue (1998), 243–68; Sean Taylor, '"We Live in the Midst of Death": Yellow Fever, Moral Economy, and Public Health in Philadelphia, 1793–1805', Northern Illinois University, Ph.D. thesis, 2001; Simon Finger, *The Contagious City: The Politics of Public Health in Early Philadelphia* (Ithaca: Cornell University Press, 2012), especially chap. 8.
95 HC, MC-1186, Vol. 1, 1 March 1809.

PART ONE

Equally, Richard Price (1736–1822), who had been a member of the St David's Society before and after the Revolution, was 'actively instrumental' in the organisation of the new Welsh Society in the late-1790s. He was one of the first stewards – an office he held until his death – and was 'distinguished by activity and fidelity in the discharge of his duties, and by ardent devotion to the objects and interests of the Institution'. Moreover,

> the kindness of his affection, the mildness and serenity of his temper, and the cheerfulness which marked his social hilarity to the last period of a protracted life, will long be in remembrance and the anniversary of the Society will not return without the recollection of its having been cheered, for so many revolutions, by the heartfelt joy which it always awakened in the breast of Mr Price.[96]

Collectively and individually, they anchored the Welsh community at the heart of respectable Pennsylvanian society and the influence of key members was felt at all levels of the political, religious and judicial system. Among them were George Clymer (1739–1813), a member of the Philadelphia Committee of Safety in 1773 who later signed the Declaration of Independence. He was elected to the Continental Congress and remained in Philadelphia during Sir Henry Clinton's occupation, but his prominent position in the Continental Congress made him the target of reprisals. After the Battle of Brandywine in 1777 the British troops destroyed his family residence in Chester County. Clymer was twice elected to the Pennsylvania Legislature (1780 and 1784) and in 1787 he represented the State at the Constitutional Convention before his election to the United States Congress two years later. He was later the President of Philadelphia Bank and Pennsylvania Academy of Fine Arts.[97] Morgan John Rhees (1760–1804), another prominent member, was a Baptist minister from Glamorgan who had

---

96 HC, MC-1186, Vol. 1, 2 September 1822.
97 For a useful study of Clymer, see Jerry Grundfest, 'George Clymer, Philadelphia Revolutionary, 1739–1813', unpublished University of Columbia, Ph.D. thesis, 1973.

been deeply influenced by French Revolutionary ideas to the extent that he established 'The Welsh Treasury', a body which attacked the immorality of the church and state. Like so many of his fellow dissenters he was forced to seek a more enlightened refuge in America. In 1798 he purchased a large tract of land for his followers in Pennsylvania which he called Cambria and named his capital 'Beulah'.[98] Robert Wharton (1757–1834) was a member of a merchant family who originally came from Westmoreland in England. He was elected mayor of Philadelphia fifteen times between 1798 and 1824, and elected Brigadier-General of the State militia. He was President of the renowned Fox-Hunting Club of Gloucester, New Jersey, a position he held until 1818; President of the Schuylkill Fishing Company between 1812 and 1828; and a founding member and Vice-President of the Washington Benevolent Society. In 1796, as a Philadelphia alderman, he helped to contain a riot among sailors in the city and two years later was effective in helping to disperse the Walnut Street prison rioters.[99]

Many early members of the Society were involved in the American Revolution at the highest levels, but curiously there is hardly any mention of their military rank or role during this momentous period in the Society's minutes. The first President of the Society was Samuel Meredith (1741–1817) who, at first glance, seems to have been a prosperous merchant and property speculator. Yet on further investigation this son of a Welsh Quaker from Radnorshire turns out to be a close confidant of George Washington and had, along with others, financially supported the war effort. Meredith became a General in the Continental Army during the War of Independence and fought at Trenton and Brandywine.

---

98 G. A. Williams, *The Search for Beulah Land: The Welsh and the Atlantic Revolution* (London: Croom Helm, 1979); H. M. Davies, '"Very Different Springs of Uneasiness": Emigration from Wales to the United States of America during the 1790s', *Welsh History Review*, 15/3 (1991), 368–98.

99 For details of Robert Wharton see Anne Hollingsworth Wharton, *Genealogy of the Wharton Family of Philadelphia, 1664 to 1880* (Philadelphia: privately published, 1880), pp. 18–28; E. D. Baltzell, *Philadelphia Gentlemen: The Making of a National Upper Class* (Philadelphia: University of Pennsylvania Press, 1979), pp. 87–8.

He was three times a member of the Pennsylvania Colonial Assembly as well as a Member of the Continental Congress between 1786 and 1788. More significantly, Meredith was the first United States Treasurer under the new Constitution, a position he held from 11 September 1789 until his resignation on 31 October 1801.[100] Another notable member was Clement Biddle (1740–1814), a Quaker merchant, who in 1776, along with his brother Owen (1737–1799),[101] abandoned pacifism and was actively involved in the war against the British.[102] He joined the 'Free Quakers', organised the 'Quaker Blues' – a company of volunteers in 1775 – and became known as the 'Quaker soldier'. As a Colonel in Washington's army he took part in various campaigns, most notably the battles at Princeton, Germantown, Trenton, Brandywine and Valley Forge. Politically adroit, he was instrumental in drafting the revolutionary State Constitution (1776) and framing the Federal Constitution (1787). President Washington also appointed him as Marshall of Pennsylvania.

The Society was to be a model for 'true patriotism' as these men accepted that they were 'Citizens of the World and the Nation',[103] but with a special tie to their Welsh ancestry. This was despite those events which had forced them to sever links with the British State. Although the Society formally honoured a Saint and the previous body

---

100 See Richard C. Allen, 'Samuel Meredith (1741–1817): American Patriot and Welsh Philanthropist', in Maurice Jackson and Susan Kozel (eds), *Quakers and their Allies in the Abolitionist Cause, 1754–1808* (London: Routledge, 2015), pp. 73–84, 167–75. His death was communicated to the Society in March 1817 along with a letter dated 8 December 1816 where he resigned his position as President. See HC, MC-1186, Vol. 1, 1 March 1816.

101 They were the son of John and Sarah (Owen) Biddle. For additional details see Library of the Society of Friends, London, unpublished Dictionary of Quaker Biography (Biddle, Clement; Biddle, Owen); Henry D. Biddle, *A Sketch of Owen Biddle... A List of His Descendants* (Philadelphia: privately published, 1892).

102 On 25 October 1765, in response to the Stamp Act, they signed up to the 'non-importation resolutions'.

103 HC, MC-1186, Vol. 1, The First Constitution and Rules adopted by the Welch Society.

had largely been a Protestant organisation,[104] the new Welsh Society insisted that 'the religious or political opinions of a candidate shall not influence his election'.[105] There were, on occasion, eminent industrialists, businessmen, judges, attorneys and publishers, whose Welsh origins were questionable but who were still admitted to the membership often as honorary members.[106] As Horatio Gates Jones acknowledged the mercantile, legal and clerical, and medical professions were all represented in the Society 'by names "familiar as household words"'.[107]

Motivation and Philanthropy

It is interesting to consider why men of this calibre involved themselves in Welsh associational life, but most obviously for the Welsh, Pennsylvania, and particularly Philadelphia, was their second home. The long history of emigration, along with positions of influence in the colony, had instilled a sense of comradeship and an acceptance that an association of the Welsh in Philadelphia could continue to promote 'love and friendship'. In a meeting in 1824 the committee called on members to 'duly appreciate the objects for which they associated… [and]… remember that social and continual intercourse is a strong tie to hold them together',[108] while a later President of the

---

104 The Ancient Britons largely derived much of its support from St David's Church in Radnor.
105 HC, MC-1186, Vol. 1, The First Constitution and Rules adopted by the Welch Society, Rule 3.
106 For an example of a member with no obvious Welsh roots, but who had married into a Welsh Philadelphian family see Burton Alva Konkle, 'Enos Bronson, 1774–1823', *PMHB*, 57 (1933), 355–8; Richard C. Allen, '"There Burst a Noble Heart": Enos Bronson (1774–1823), Federalist and Editor of the *United States Gazette*', (forthcoming).
107 Jones, *Welsh Society Charter*, p. 10.
108 HC, MC-1186, Vol. 1, 1 March 1824. This sentiment was repeated the following March when the clerk impressed upon members the necessity of increasing membership and thereby revenue. See HC, MC-1186, Vol. 1, 1 March 1825.

Society, the aforementioned Horatio Gates Jones, is said to have been 'an enthusiastic lover of Wales, the home of his fathers'. This patriotism was, to him at least, 'a religious sentiment'.[109] It would appear that the later Society was 'the direct, lineal, continuous successor of the Sons of the Ancient Britons'.[110] This new formulation of the Society embraced the aims of its precursor and evinced similar charitable objectives:

> To revive and increase social intercourse and mutual attachments are objects worthy the greatest characters, when combined with benevolent intentions, the attachment is still more desirable and the cement becomes more cohesive.[111]

High on the list of stated priorities was the belief that the Society ought to provide charitable assistance to the needy.[112] Charity, the Society recognised, began at home, but should also be dispensed to the 'remotest parts of the Earth'. This is fully articulated in the preamble to the Constitution of 4 February 1799 which stated:

> 'Ye know the heart of a stranger' it is as susceptible of impressions as the sensitive plant, on his first arrival in a new country it is of great importance to himself and the community that he form favourable ideas of its inhabitants, and be attached to his situation; that his love of country may center in that spot where his person and property are protected and where liberty and hospitality have made their residence. We shall therefore discharge one of the first duties enjoined on us as men, by taking our emigrant

---

109 He was President of the Society and a Pennsylvania State senator between 1875 and 1882.
110 Jones, *Welsh Society Charter and Bye Laws*, pp. 9–10.
111 HC, MC-1186, Vol. 1, The First Constitution and Rules adopted by the Welch Society.
112 HC, MC-1186, Vol. 1, Preamble to the Constitution; Jones, *Welsh Society Charter and Bye Laws*, p. 9. Also, see Priscilla Ferguson Clement, *Welfare and the Poor in the Nineteenth-Century City: Philadelphia, 1800–1854* (Fairleigh: Dickinson University Press, 1985).

brother by the hand instructing him in what he is ignorant of and providing for his immediate necessities.[113]

There have been many studies of Welsh migration to America, including those by Alan Conway,[114] Glanmor Williams,[115] Maldwyn A. Jones,[116] Anne Kelly Knowles,[117] and Ronald Lewis,[118] while Hywel Davies's work and Bill Jones's study of the Welsh in Scranton and elsewhere in America further outline the causes for migration[119] and

---

113 HC, MC-1186, Vol. 1. The First Constitution and Rules adopted by the Welch Society.
114 Alan Conway, 'Welsh Emigration to the United States', in Donald Fleming and Bernard Bailyn (eds), *Dislocation and Emigration: The Social Background of American Immigration, Perspectives in American History* 7 (Cambridge, MA: Harvard University Press, 1974), pp. 177–271, and his *The Welsh in America: Letters from the Immigrants* (Cardiff : University of Wales Press, 1961).
115 Glanmor Williams, 'A Prospect of Paradise? Wales and the United States, 1776–1914', in G. Williams, *Religion, Language and Nationality in Wales* (Cardiff: University of Wales Press, 1979), pp. 21–36.
116 Maldwyn A. Jones, 'From the Old Country to the New: The Welsh in Nineteenth Century America', *Flintshire Historical Society*, 27 (1975–6), 85–100.
117 Anne Kelly Knowles, *Calvinists Incorporated: Welsh Immigrants in Ohio's Industrial Frontier* (Chicago: Chicago University Press, 1997).
118 Ronald Lewis, *Welsh Americans: A History of Assimilation in the Coalfields* (Chapel Hill: University of North Carolina Press, 2009).
119 The 'push and pull' arguments and the more persuasive reasons for emigrating are provided in Davies, 'Very Different Springs of Uneasiness', and in Bill Jones, '"Raising the Wind": Emigrating from Wales to the USA in the Late Nineteenth and Early Twentieth Centuries', Canolfan Uwchefrydiau Cymry America, Prifysgol Caerdydd / The Cardiff Centre for Welsh American Studies, Cardiff University, Annual Public Lecture for 2003. Published on-line in 2004, see http://orca.cf.ac.uk/48163/1/RaisingTheWind.pdf [accessed 15 February 2021]. Here Jones observes that 'expulsive or magnetic forces' were at work. Agricultural workers were battling grinding poverty, land and food shortages, as well as social, religious and linguistic discrimination. Similarly, in the industrial centres working and living conditions were extremely poor and, as he points out, life was generally 'precarious and insecure'.

settlement patterns.[120] More recently Robert Tyler's examination of various Welsh settlements in Pennsylvania and throughout America, provide insights into cultural maintenance and the occupational profiling of the Welsh settlers.[121] These migrants invariably required financial and emotional assistance, to enable them to make a new home in America. In the case of John Jones, formerly of Montgomeryshire, he appealed to the Society in June 1828 to help him secure work as an assistant apothecary. In the following year George Williams, aged twenty-one, from Caernarfonshire sought work in conveyancing, but could not secure work in Philadelphia in that trade. The Society loaned him ten dollars for his bed and board and to travel to New York, where he immediately found work.[122]

Any poor Welsh person could draw upon the Society's benevolence, particularly those who were vulnerable such as the sick, elderly, widowed or orphaned. On arrival at Newcastle, Pennsylvania, or in Philadelphia itself, those who were sick or required some financial support were identified and helped. The first reference in the Society's minutes appears on 1 September 1800: 'The Ship *Thomas* at New castle with nearly two hundred persons, all of whom have paid their passage but in consequence of their arrival... additional expense was incurred to assist them on their way to the city, and towards their support until suitable situations were obtained'. Records show that almost all of the passengers were settled independently, apart from Elizabeth Owen, whose husband had died a few days after their arrival. Elizabeth, who had five children

---

120 For details of nineteenth century Welsh emigration in Pennsylvania see William D. Jones, *Wales in America: Scranton and the Welsh 1860–1920* (Cardiff: University of Wales Press; Scranton, Pa.: University of Scranton Press, 1993).

121 For a wider appreciation of Welsh settlement in the nineteenth century and the maintenance of the Welsh language and culture throughout America see Robert Ll. Tyler, *Wales and the American Dream* (Newcastle: Cambridge Scholars Publishing, 2015). He has also provided several microhistories which examine Welsh settlements in the late nineteenth and early twentieth centuries. See the Bibliography.

122 HC, MC-1186, Vol. 1, 2 June 1828, 7 September 1829.

and was heavily pregnant with her sixth child, remained in the care of the Society. At the same time the Society satisfied themselves that the thirty passengers on board the *Lavinia* which docked at Philadelphia did not require their assistance.[123] The following December it was noted that Elizabeth Owen had been housed and provided for, but the family of Lewis Miles were in dire straits. Lewis, his wife and seven children, had become so sick 'as to create great alarm in the neighbourhood'.[124] The family were subsequently housed by the Society at the Lazaretto in Delaware County. Built in 1799 this was the first quarantine station for the Port of Philadelphia.[125] The care of sick migrants was an ongoing concern, for, as the clerk observed, their ill-health was due 'in a great measure... to the length and severity of their passage'.[126] The initial costs were born by the Philadelphia Board of Health, but a request for payment for three Welsh families that had been housed at the Lazaretto from Edward Garrigues, the President of the Board between 1799 and 1800, was quickly dealt with by the Society.[127]

An indication of the dangers posed by the transatlantic journey at this time is provided in the correspondence of Welsh migrants. George Roberts of Edensburg, Cambria County, Pennsylvania, wrote to his parents in Wales in October 1801 that he had received communication from Richard Lewis in Baltimore of the terrible conditions faced by recent migrants. During the journey or while waiting to be processed

---

123 HC, MC-1186, Vol. 1, 1September 1800.
124 HC, MC-1186, Vol. 1, 1 December 1800.
125 The Lazaretto was in Tinicum Township, Delaware County, Pennsylvania. It was known as the 'Pest House' or the 'Old Lazaretto', and the building was subsequently sold in 1802 to make way for a new Lazaretto six miles away. For details of the efforts to quarantine passengers and a brief history of the Lazaretto see Wilson Jewell, *Historical Sketches of Quarantine: Address, Delivered before the Philadelphia County Medical Society, January 28, 1857* (Philadelphia: T. K. and P. G. Collins,1857), pp. 8–15; Henry Burnell Shafer, 'Medicine in Old Philadelphia', *PH*, 4/1 (January 1937), pp. 21–31 (especially 29–30).
126 HC, MC-1186, Vol. 1, 1 December 1800.
127 HC, MC-1186, Vol. 1, 1 June 1801.

in Baltimore harbour, forty adults and eight children had died. This tragedy was coupled with the previously ill-fated journey undertaken by Roberts's sisters who had witnessed over half of the passengers die at sea (53 out of 102). The two sisters were now recovering at his home, but he was acutely aware of the causes of their ailments – the length of the journey, a contaminated water supply and excessive heat. Roberts's letter also noted the fate of other Welsh passengers who were travelling to Morgan John Rhys [Rhees]'s Beulah territory, but died before reaching their destination. Those who were responsible for the orphaned children thereafter sought assistance from the Welsh Society.[128] In a much later minute there is a clear reference to the assistance provided. A sub-committee (the Orphan Committee) reported that they had succeeded in providing three children, Thomas Harris, Richard Jones and John Jones, with 'proper situations' of employment as apprentices. In the case of Richard Jones this apprenticeship was subject to arbitration by the 'Rule of Court', which decided the terms on which the young emigrant was bonded to Richard Lloyd of Lower Darby, Delaware. Thomas Harris was later apprenticed as a house carpenter under the guidance of Benjamin Gardner.[129]

There was also recognition of those benevolent individuals who had been responsible for safeguarding the wellbeing of emigrants. In December 1801, the Society elected Jacob Broome of Wilmington, Delaware, as an honorary member. They presented him with a certificate 'for his humane attention to the Welsh emigrants who arrived at Wilmington in the ship *Liberty*'. Equally, the Society gave Dr Thomas

---

128 National Library of Wales, Aberystwyth. MS. 14094D. The Rev. George Roberts of Ebensburg (1769–1853) to Evan, his father, and mother, Llanbrynmair, Montgomeryshire, 13 October, 1801 (in Welsh). This letter is partially translated in A. H. Dodd (ed.), 'Letters from Cambria County, 1800–1823', *PH*, 22/2 (April 1955), 134–45 (particularly pp. 136–9). For Beulah and Rhys see Williams, *The Search for Beulah Land*; E. W. James, 'Morgan John Rhys a Chaethwasiaeth Americanaidd', in D. G. Williams (ed.), *Canu Caeth: Y Cymry a'r Affro-Americaniaid* (Llandysul: Gwasg Gomer, 2010), pp. 2–25.

129 HC, MC-1186, Vol. 1, 1 March 1806, 1 September 1806, 1 December 1806, 4 December 1809.

C. James a silver plate and $150 for his services 'to the unfortunate sick emigrants at the City Hospital on the banks of the Schuylkill'.[130] Beyond the perils of trans-Atlantic crossings, migrants were ill-equipped to deal with the Pennsylvanian climate. In December 1803 Joshua Sylvanus was 'afflicted with lunacy in consequence of a stroke from the sun' and was taken to hospital. Although he died two days later his hospital fees of $5.50 were paid by the Society.[131]

In the early decades of the nineteenth century emigration continued unabated and so did the demands on the Society.[132] Assistance with travel, accommodation, and medical expenses, which included hospitalisation and amputations, was provided. In 1802, the Society gave help to 'a man affected with a lame arm', while in 1810 they paid for the amputation of John Jones's leg and his rehabilitation afterwards at a cost of $84.09. In 1813 the Society noted that they had under their care John Roberts, his wife and four young children. They provided medical treatment and twenty-six dollars to assist Roberts's family, but members accepted the fact that additional costs were likely to be incurred. The following December, Jonathan Smith, the Register of the Society, provided further details concerning Roberts and his family.

---

130 HC, MC-1186, Vol. 1, 7 December 1801. For details of the establishment of hospitals in Philadelphia c.1751 onwards see Thomas G. Morton and Frank Woodbury, *The History of the Pennsylvania Hospital 1751–1895* (Philadelphia: Times Printing House, 1895); Francis R. Packard and Florence M. Greim, *Some Account of the Pennsylvania Hospital from 1751 to 1938* (2nd edn. Philadelphia: Pennsylvania Hospital, 1957); William H. Williams, *America's First Hospital: The Pennsylvania Hospital, 1751–1841* (Wayne, Pa: Haverford House, 1976); Gary B. Nash, 'Poverty and Poor Relief in Pre-Revolutionary Philadelphia', *William and Mary Quarterly*, Third Series, 33/1 (January 1976), 3–30 (7–8).

131 HC, MC-1186, Vol. 1, 5 December 1803.

132 For examples, see Monique Bourque, 'Populating the Poorhouse: A Reassessment of Poor Relief in the Antebellum Delaware Valley', *PH*, 70/3 (Summer 2003), 235–67. For a wider study of emigration and realities of settlement in the nineteenth century see Charlotte Erikson, *Leaving England: Essays on British Emigration in the Nineteenth Century* (Ithaca and London: Cornell University Press, 1994).

After emigrating from Wales (no specific details are provided), Roberts had secured employment and conducted himself so well 'as to obtain the approbation and esteem of those by whom he was employed'. And yet his wages as a day labourer were meagre and he was barely able to maintain his family. During the summer he had contracted 'a very severe disease which would in all probability have terminated in death had it not been for the great care and attention of Doctor [Thomas] James, one of the physicians of the Society'. James and Dr Thomas Parke, another physician in the Society, were able to successfully treat Roberts and he fully recovered from his illness. The financial assistance he was provided with amounted to forty-six dollars which clearly shows the generosity of the Society as well as the potential risks of seeking a new life in America.[133] A later example from the early 1830s again demonstrates the generosity of the Society, even when the person they were helping had left the city. John Price, a painter from north Wales, had arrived in Philadelphia in November 1829 but failed to secure sufficient employment in the city and thereafter worked as a labourer on a small fishing vessel near Smith Island, Maryland. An accident to his hand however left him temporarily incapacitated and unable to work. The Society loaned him $10 on the understanding that he would pay this back when he was able.[134]

Employment was also provided as was helping any Welsh emigrant who was disabled, while the education for 'poor children of Welch parents',[135] and funeral costs were all met under the Society's benevolent remit. Earlier in the century (c.1804) Edward Price, who members found 'destitute in every respect', was given $20 to secure his passage to the West Indies.[136] Society disbursements

---

133 See HC, MC-1186, Vol. 1, 1 March 1802, 3 September 1810, 6 September 1813, 6 December 1813, 1 March 1814.
134 HC, MC-1186, Vol. 1, 1 March 1830.
135 This involved a change in the Charter of the Society and was first proposed in December 1811 but was not pursued. HC, MC-1186, Vol. 1, 2 December 1811, 2 March 1812.
136 HC, MC-1186, Vol. 1, 3 December 1804.

could be substantial, especially in 1817 when a hundred dollars was provided for seven Welsh emigrants to 'enable them to go into the Western Country'.[137] In a lengthy statement in February 1818 the Society set out its rationale for assisting forty-four migrants. They stated that among those who had made their way to Pennsylvania and Philadelphia in particular, Welsh emigrants had 'landed among strangers, friendless, pennyless, and many of them under the pressure of disease'. Many sought to make a new life in the western reaches of the State or further west, and the Society felt duty bound to support their additional travel requirements.[138] The committee appointed by the Society to facilitate these demands noted the 'temperate, frugal and industrious' nature of these people. Although tempered by a sense of their own heritage and somewhat patronising in its tone, the committee observed that as these emigrants were used to hard work and privations in Wales, they would be 'admirably qualified for the task they have undertaken' and would be successful. Moreover, those who were skilled had received the plaudits of employers in Philadelphia as they had conducted themselves with sobriety and orderliness. As such, the committee felt they had thereby 'justified the good opinion we have always entertained of our Welch countrymen... to be useful members of society'. The report testified that these emigrants had received financial support, medical treatment where needed, while women and children were provided with transportation

---

137 HC, MC-1186, Vol. 1, 1 September 1817. This was alongside assistance provided for a further five emigrants and Thomas Prichard and his family, they being 'distressed emigrants' who required accommodation for two weeks at a cost of fifteen dollars.

138 For details of the expansion of Welsh settlement from the eighteenth century onwards see Anne Kelly Knowles, 'Immigrant Trajectories through the Rural-Industrial Transition in Wales and the United States 1759–1850', *Annals of the Association of American Geographers*, 85/2 (1995), 246–66; William E. Van Vugt, 'Welsh Emigration to the United States during the Mid-Nineteenth Century', *WHR*, 15/4 (December 1991), 545–61. For examples of Welsh settlement in Ohio, see HC, MC-1186, Vol. 1, 1 March 1824, 7 September 1824 when Richard Jenkins was loaned ten dollars to assist him to proceed to Steubenville, Ohio, and Evan Evans who was loaned $20 to enable him and his family to settle in the State.

and their limited baggage on the journey to Pittsburgh. The cost to the Society in this year alone over $342.[139]

Occasionally the Society heard from those they had helped. Not only were loans repaid, but there were expressions of gratitude 'for the timely relief'.[140] In 1818 many others were assisted at a total cost of $234.50 (See Table 2 overleaf).[141] At the next meeting in March 1819 the committee continued to report on its successes and outlined the dangers faced by many of these newcomers and the necessary commitment of members to provide for those who were socially and economically disadvantaged. For example, excessive drinking in many of the taverns in Philadelphia and elsewhere in the United States was 'the baleful curse that seems to await all emigrants to this otherwise favor'd land'. And yet the Welsh were largely sober citizens which the committee alleged was 'a national trait'.[142] There were further calls for members to pay their general and annual subscriptions, and to remember that during their annual festivities in March 'the coldness and the asperities of life are forgotten, and the hand of the fellowship extended with kindness is received with

---

139 HC, MC-1186, Vol. 1, 28 February 1818. Also, see 1819 for another account of the Society's philanthropy. HC, MC-1186, Vol. 1, 1 March 1819.

140 This was the case in June 1818 when John Morgan sent a letter thanking the Society for the assistance they had provided. HC, MC-1186, Vol. 1, 1 June 1818. Also, see HC, MC-1186, Vol. 1, 1 March 1821, another emigrant who had gone 'westwards' repaid five dollars to the Society. During this year Joseph S. Lewis, the Vice-President of the Society, twice visited these settlers in Pittsburgh and noted that they had employment and had 'a grateful sense of the benefit conferred on them by the Society, by whose assistance a great number of them had been enabled to find their way to Pittsburgh and were evidently solicitous to repay the Society the sums advanced to them for that purpose'. HC, MC-1186, Vol. 1, 4 June 1821, 3 December 1821. Also, see HC, MC-1186, Vol. 1, 1 March 1825 when Evan Rees repaid $10 of a $15 loan that helped him travel westwards from Philadelphia.

141 HC, MC-1186, Vol. 1, 7 December 1818.

142 This can be compared to evidence from Wales in the nineteenth century which would challenge this assessment. See William Rees Lambert, *Drink and Sobriety in Victorian Wales, c.1820–c.1895* (Cardiff: University of Wales, 1980).

cordiality'. They focused on cultivating 'this bond of friendship' and not to lose sight of the honourable intentions of their predecessors. Significantly, the committee also praised the largely unsung work of two women, Mary Linn and Mrs Joseph Simons, and acknowledged that they had administered to the needs of the emigrant families during the harsh winter months and formally recognised their contribution in the Society's minutes.[143]

Table 2. Assistance to Welsh Emigrants provided by the Welsh Society of Philadelphia, 1818.

	$
William Lewis Senior had advances made him	10
Reese Jenkins and wife [had advances made him]	15
Thos Morgan, wife & 3 children [had advances made him]	20
Edward Wilkins [had advances made him]	10
Edward Hughes had advances made him	2
Thomas Jones [had advances made him]	2
Reese Jenkins [had advances made him]	15
David Davis [had advances made him]	10
The widow Brien and family have had advanced on them at sundry times in cash and for various articles of furniture	86.56
Evan Evans had advanced him	30
William Lewis Jr and Evan Evans had two weeks board allowed them	4
Jacob Watkins had advanced him	15
George Watkins [had advances made him]	15

In 1820, $538.58 was spent in helping more than seventy Welsh emigrants. William P. Williams was singled out for praise for giving

---

143 HC, MC-1186, Vol. 1, 1 March 1819.

a home to 'forty-one, aged and youth' at various times.[144] Recipients included David Jeffreys who was given financial support to travel to Pittsburgh. He secured suitable employment, repaid the Society the costs of his relocation expenses and, subsequently, in March 1822 the committee assisted the passage of his family from Philadelphia to Pittsburgh into 'the arms of an anxious husband and father'. That same month the committee gave Thomas Watkins and his four daughters $20 to help them travel to Ebensburg in Cambria County to join their family.[145] It was this level of support that in 1823 paid for a physician and medicines for the Jennings family, and the hospital costs of both Joseph Jenkins and his pregnant wife.[146] The Rogers of Montgomeryshire were typical of those whose ill-health placed them in a vulnerable position. When members visited their home in 1828, they found the family in 'great distress', suffering from sickness, without any medical treatment and 'scarcely strength in either to assist the others to a glass of water'. It was largely thanks to the Society's financial support that they recovered from their illnesses.[147]

Equally, the elderly couple, Thomas Morris and his wife were provided with $20 in 1827 because they were a 'respectable pair' and 'too old for labour', while in the same year an additional $4 was spent on helping the sixty-year-old Robert Owen and his teenage son, John, to travel to Birmingham Mills, New Jersey.[148] The Society was frequently called upon to defray the costs of funerals, including the purchase of a

---

144   HC, MC-1186, Vol. 1, 1 March 1820.
145   HC, MC-1186, Vol. 1, 1 March 1822.
146   HC, MC-1186, Vol. 1, 1 September 1823. The family lived two miles outside of Philadelphia on the Ridge Road. Also, see HC, MC-1186, Vol. 1, 1 March 1824 where it was reported that Jenkins had recovered and was seeking work 'in the country'. The costs of his treatment had exceeded $95. The next month it was further agreed that $40 could be expended to help them settle in Pike Township, Bradford County, north-eastern Pennsylvania, while the board and lodging of Mrs Jenkins and her two children were also paid ($30). HC, MC-1186, Vol. 1, 7 June 1824.
147   HC, MC-1186, Vol. 1, 1 December 1828.
148   HC, MC-1186, Vol. 1, 1 March 1827, 4 June 1827.

coffin, funeral clothes and burial. Earlier (c.1821), the committee who had taken responsibility for the well-being of the elderly David Davies made further provision to cover the cost of his funeral.[149]

Assistance to Female Migrants

Women were often the primary beneficiaries of the Society's relief, particularly when they were sick, widowed or bereaved. The first woman to be assisted and referred to in the minutes was Elizabeth Robinson in March 1799,[150] while Mary Pritchet [Prichard?] was provided for when she was dying of consumption in 1808. The committee who looked after her noted that they were at least consoled by the knowledge that 'her last days were rendered in some measure comfortable'.[151] In September 1826 the Society gave $10 to Elizabeth Lewis, a widow with four children whose husband had died on the journey west from Philadelphia, and helped her secure employment as a nurse. Until she established herself the committee continued to provide financial support.[152] The sum of $10 was advanced to another widow, Ann Comey, formerly of Llanfihangel Genau'r-glyn. Her husband had left home in a small open boat to travel a regular journey of fifteen miles but was presumed drowned. Although her cousin in Pittsburgh was willing to provide for her and her family, Mrs Comey had no other funds. After some deliberation, the Stewards agreed to cover these costs.[153] Women migrants not only applied to the Society for food, shelter and medical treatment but also for protection, especially in legal matters about which they had limited knowledge. In June 1803, a committee was appointed to investigate Mary Phillips's complaint that money she was owed after

---

149 HC, MC-1186, Vol. 1, 3 December 1821. In 1824 John Thomas, 'a poor distressed young Welchman' was treated in the Pennsylvania Hospital but subsequently died of his ailments. The Society paid for his treatment and funeral expenses. HC, MC-1186, Vol. 1, 7 June 1824.
150 HC, MC-1186, Vol. 1, 1 March 1799.
151 HC, MC-1186, Vol. 1, 1 March 1808.
152 HC, MC-1186, Vol. 1, 4 September 1826; 1 March 1827.
153 HC, MC-1186, Vol. 1, 1 September 1828.

providing the services of two of her servants was 'unjustly detained'.[154] The Society also had the necessary authority to secure the release of Bridget Williams from imprisonment in 1820 and recover her wages and clothing. By expending $10.05 they 'saved her from further molestation' by her employer, who had her jailed by falsely claiming an indenture.[155]

The Society recognised that their own members could face severe hardship and were prepared to help where they could. This was the case in 1827 when they assisted Hannah, the widow of John Roberts, their former Secretary. They acknowledged the care he had taken to aid Welsh emigrants, but his death after a 'lingering disease' left his wife and large family in a precarious financial situation. Subsequently, the Society provided $200 as a donation to his wife 'in consideration of his faithful services'.[156]

Anxieties Over Relief Payments

Emigration to Philadelphia was, however, not always the best solution. The Society stressed that they were able to help, but only as a last resort to those in need. In March 1821 the committee tasked with assisting emigrants stated that, even if they had the financial means, they could not justify giving

> money to those who are in good health and able to earn their subsistence. On the contrary they would recommend a more strict adherence to the course formerly pursued & to appropriate the pecuniary means of the Society to the relief of those only who are unable to provide for themselves.[157]

---

154 HC, MC-1186, Vol. 1, 6 June 1803. Frustratingly there are no further references in the minutes relating to this concern or its outcome.
155 HC, MC-1186, Vol. 1, 5 June 1820, 1 March 1821.
156 HC, MC-1186, Vol. 1, 3 September 1827, 3 December 1827.
157 HC, MC-1186, Vol. 1, 1 March 1821.

In the cases of John Francis, Samuel Reynolds and David Davis assistance was provided as they had become separated from friends 'on whom they entirely relied for future success'. Moreover, they had young families who were unaccustomed to the climate and thereby susceptible to disease. In this period, fourteen Welsh emigrants were assisted at a cost of sixty dollars.[158] In the autumn of the same year, however, William Prosser received $20 to help him to return to Wales.[159] Equally those who had secured passage to New York were assisted on their way to Pittsburgh to avoid them becoming a burden by remaining in either New York or Philadelphia where linguistic difficulties would have made it difficult to secure employment. In all $145 was expended and this included food and medicines.[160]

All claims for assistance were carefully assessed. If the claimant was infirm or employment was not available, he/she would be assisted in kind to minimize the burden on the Society. Recipients had to satisfy the conditions outlined under the Society's Constitution, notably that assistance was normally restricted to those residing within the boundaries of Philadelphia. In December 1822 John Evans, 'a distressed Welshman' from Baltimore whose wife had died of yellow fever, appealed to the Society after travelling to Philadelphia. A bout of illness forced him to return to his family of seven children, but the Society was unable to cover the costs.[161] The Society also became increasingly concerned that there was a misapprehension in Wales that they would provide financial assistance to emigrants 'free from any expense to themselves' for onward travel to Pittsburgh or elsewhere in the United States. They wrote to various clergymen and dignitaries in Wales explaining the conditions

---

158 HC, MC-1186, Vol. 1, 1 March 1821.
159 HC, MC-1186, Vol. 1, 3 September 1821.
160 HC, MC-1186, Vol. 1, 1 September 1823; 1 December 1823 where John Thomas from Llanfyllin in Montgomeryshire, his wife and seven children were assisted. They had arrived in New York before moving on to Philadelphia. Here they were provided with two weeks accommodation and a loan of forty-five dollars to help them purchase a wagon for their journey westwards.
161 HC, MC-1186, Vol. 1, 2 December 1822.

of relief in order to 'prevent persons emigrating to this country from coming here under the false impression that they can rely totally on the Society'.[162]

In March 1824 it was noted that the letter had been widely circulated to various newspapers,[163] and members agreed that they could do no more than show the emigrants 'the best and cheapest methods of proceeding to their destinations'.[164] The misrepresentation of the Society's charitable remit, however, continued. In June 1829 Hannah Lewis and her daughter arrived from Swansea with a letter from her sister who had settled in Lawrenceburg, Indiana, providing the following advice:

> If possible enter a vessel to Philadelphia, if you are scarce of money and as there is provision made at Philad[elphia] to help the Welsh people to any part of the United States, you must enquire for some Welsh family and they will tell you what to do, as there is money there to help the Welsh people on their way.

Clearly the committee were anxious to dispel these rumours. They sent a strongly worded letter to Lewis's sister counselling that she was ill-advised to 'give such information to her connections in Wales, observing that such misrepresentations would have a tendency to mislead a number of persons to come over, only to be disappointed'.[165]

Increasing Emigration and Continued Support

From this period onwards the Society faced similar demands for assistance. And yet they provided as much support as they could both in practical terms as well as via loans. The meeting of December 1829 recorded in some detail the large numbers of Welsh emigrants entering

---

162 HC, MC-1186, Vol. 1, 1 December 1823.
163 HC, MC-1186, Vol. 1, 1 March 1824.
164 HC, MC-1186, Vol. 1, 7 September 1824.
165 HC, MC-1186, Vol. 1, 1 June 1829.

America,[166] the difficulties they faced, and the level of assistance provided. These ranged from Elizabeth Jones, 'a distressed widow', and Elizabeth Garrett, a poor widow with an ailing teenage son, and their relocation to the new settlements that were being developed, such as Mount Carbon;[167] to negotiating with those who were detaining the meagre but essential luggage of emigrants on account of unpaid medical expenses ('hospital money'); to treatment by well-known surgeons such as Dr Philip Syng Physick. The committee procured his assistance to treat the twelve-year-old daughter of Ann Jones of a diseased hip. She was taken to the Pennsylvania hospital and the committee recorded that they had 'frequently called to see her, and are happy to say, that she is doing well'.[168]

During the 1830s members were equally busy dispensing aid. The annual meeting in 1830 noted the assistance given to the family of Robert Humphreys of Denbighshire who had lost 'everything' on board the *Mary*. They had encountered a hurricane during their passage to New York and were forced to eventually disembark in Boston in October 1829 in a 'wretched state'. The heavily pregnant Mrs Humphreys and her family were provided with clothing, accommodation, and further assistance to relocate to Philadelphia. Unfortunately, Mrs Humphreys's baby died ten days after arriving in the city. The Society, however, continued to provide the family with support, including lodging,

---

166 For example, over sixty had travelled from Liverpool in the *Washington* the previous September. John Morris and his family, Baptists from Montgomeryshire, had sailed on the *Minerva* from Liverpool and had disembarked at New York before making their way to Philadelphia en route to Pittsburgh. They were given a loan of $25, but the committee took his promissory note, payable on demand. HC, MC-1186, Vol. 1, 7 December 1829.

167 Mount Carbon is in Schuylkill County, Pennsylvania. In 1828 the small settlement comprised six houses, a store, a warehouse, and the collector's office. For further details see Anon., *History of Schuylkill County, Pa.: with Illustrations and Biographical Sketches of Some of Its Prominent Men and Pioneers* (New York: W. W. Munsell & Co., 1881), pp. 250–1.

168 HC, MC-1186, Vol. 1, 7 December 1829.

medical treatment, and employment for the daughter, aged eleven, while her two boys went to school. In the meantime Robert, the father, sought work in Pottsville in Schuylkill County where there was an anthracite coalworks.[169]

The level of assistance provided during 1830 was nearly $375 (Tables 3 and 4) and in March 1831 the Society recorded spending over $475. Indeed, the outlay was outstripping the income of the Society and the Treasurer was forced to sell off $150 worth of shares that members had invested in the Schuylkill Navigation Company.[170] The situation was exacerbated by having to expend a further $45 returning one migrant family to Wales. The committee tasked with providing relief offered the following detailed account of this particular case:

> It becomes the duty of the acting committee to lay before the Society a particular statement of the case of Elizabeth Vaughan and her three children who arrived here from Liverpool in the month of September last in the Barque *Huskinson* with every reasonable expectation of meeting her husband, either in this city or at Pottsville. He had written for her and stated that he was settled at Pottsville and that she and her children must join him at that place, so soon as she could raise a sufficient sum to defray the expense of their passages – this was accomplished with great difficulty, and on her arrival she had the mortification and disappointment to learn that he had return'd to Wales, without leaving for her either the means for her support or return. The committee advised her to remain with her friends until her husband could be heard from and advanced her money for her board and the passage of herself and children to Pottsville where her friends resided. After remaining there a few weeks she received a letter from her husband, expressing his determination

---

169   HC, MC-1186, Vol. 1, 1 March 1830.
170   HC, MC-1186, Vol. 1, 1 March 1831.

to remain in Wales, and directing her to return as soon as possible without however having provided funds for the payment of necessary expenses. She returned to this city forthwith and applied to your committee for the means of returning to Wales; after due deliberation the committee determined that it would be advisable to send her home, in preference to being at the expense of the maintenance of herself and her children during the winter. Accordingly, a contract was enter'd into with Capt Dixey for the passage of herself and children to Liverpool for the sum of $45 – he to find every necessary for their comfort and support during the passage. In so doing the committee believe they have somewhat exceeded their legitimate authority, but believe that they have acted in conformity with the true interests of the Society. And therefore hope their act will meet their approbation.[171]

Table 3. Assistance to Welsh Emigrants provided by the Welsh Society of Philadelphia, 6 September 1830.[172]

March 1	To William Tegan	20	David Davis	20
30	Wm Meredith	10	Thos Williams family	12
April 6	Wm Williams	5	Wm Davis & family	10
June 10	Richd Evans	15	Thos Davis & family	26.32
25	Thos Llewellyn & family	50	Mary Williams	28
26	T. Rees, J. Anthony & J. Phelps	20	Wm Jones (deaf & dumb)	7
July 3	J. Reese & Fanny Griffith	40		
6	Reese Evans & family	20		
6	J^{no} Reese & family	15		

---

171 HC, MC-1186, Vol. 1, 1 March 1831.
172 HC, MC-1186, Vol. 1, 6 September 1830.

PART ONE

Table 4. Assistance to Welsh Emigrants provided by the Welsh Society of Philadelphia, 6 December 1830.[173]

	$
Ann Richards and Elizabeth Vaughan	22.00
James Ewing, E. Hitchens & R. Hawkins	23.00
C. O'Donnell, board of A. Richards & E. Vaughan	6.25
Henry James $8. & Robert Popkins $10. E Vaughan $6.	24.00
Decr 6. 1830	$75.25

The expenditure, although slightly less in early 1832 at $174.50, was still draining the Society of its funds. Nevertheless, the commitment to assist emigrants was accepted as 'the means of doing much good', but a few months later it was clear that many of the incoming Welsh immigrants were 'penniless' and in desperate need of help. The Society willingly provided loans amounting to $274 to assist thirty-one adults and fifty-two children and a further $297 to thirty-eight adults and forty-seven children in March 1833. There was, however, a cautious approach as members were warned to be on their guard against those who might 'represent themselves as Welsh'.[174] By the end of the 1830s members were assisting fewer emigrants, with thirteen adults and twenty-two children being provided for. The sums varied from $5 to $30, and collectively amounting to $104, while the Society had a healthy balance of $1023 and over $9400 in investments.[175]

Conclusion

This analysis of Welsh associational life has advanced some insights into the long history of emigration to Pennsylvania, and how the Welsh strove to retain their cultural identity. These efforts brought together a dynamic group of the wealthiest and most influential sections of Philadelphia society. Cultural networking was crucial to the successful

---

173 HC, MC-1186, Vol. 1, 6 December 1830.
174 HC, MC-1186, Vol. 1, 1 March 1832, 3 September 1832, 1 March 1833.
175 HC, MC-1186, Vol. 1, 1 March 1839.

establishment of businesses and professional careers in this fast-growing commercial city. At first sight the declining use of the Welsh language would seem to suggest that the settlers were prepared to relinquish their heritage and culture, and thereby assimilate into Pennsylvania life. And yet, it could be argued, that this actually spurred Welsh migrants into proactive mode and led to the creation of a cluster of Welsh associations.[176] As Philadelphians they were under some pressure to demonstrate an unequivocal loyalty to their city, defending it as well as contributing to its growth and prosperity.

The benevolent objectives that lay at the heart of both the Society of the Sons of Ancient Britons and the Welsh Society of Philadelphia served to unify otherwise scattered individuals and bring the Welsh community together. They also offered a refuge and cultural home to those who travelled to Philadelphia thereafter. The Society managed its affairs judiciously and soon accrued a healthy surplus revenue. In dispensing charity, members were able to assist their fellow Welsh migrants and it is clear from the Society's records that this endeavour sprang from generous impulses. Nonetheless, this level of conspicuous philanthropy also served to profile the Society's status and respectability. After all, the presence of too many indigent Welsh migrants in what was perceived to be the cradle of government was undesirable, and any suggestion that the Welsh were disreputable citizens had to be avoided at all costs. Restrictions were put in place to ensure that demand did not exceed resources, but in the main those genuinely in need were rarely refused assistance. Influenced by higher ideals to serve others, the members readily believed in 'the golden chain of Fellowship' and sought to provide advice and relief to their compatriots whenever and wherever they needed it.[177]

---

176 Welsh migration in the nineteenth century offered new opportunities to privilege Welsh culture and heritage. These are recounted in Jones, 'The Welsh Language and Welsh Identity in a Pennsylvanian Community', pp. 261–86.
177 HC, MC-1186, Box 1, Preamble to the First Constitution. The first rule was to have 'a seal emblematic of its charitable designs'.

Plate 6. 'High Street, from Ninth Street, Philadelphia', c.1800.[178]

---

178 Birch and Son, *The City of Philadelphi*a, plate 12.

Plate 7. 'Bank of the United States, in Third Street, Philadelphia', c.1800.[179]

---

179 Birch and Son, *The City of Philadelphia*, plate 17.

PART TWO

GOVERNANCE

The First Constitution and Rules Adopted by the Welch Society

To Welchmen and their Descendants within the United States of America

The spirit of migration from Wales, till of late years having partly subsided the friendship and fraternization which usually existed between the ancient Britons and this country became thereby less fervent than at former periods.

To revive and increase social intercourse and mutual attachments are objects worthy the greatest characters; when combined with benevolent intentions, the attainment is still more desirable and the cement becomes more cohesive.

To be good citizens of the World and the nation we live in, yet to have special fellowship with the descendants of our ancestors, is perfectly consistent with true patriotism and universal philanthropy. That charity which begins at home defuses its influence to the remotest parts of the earth.

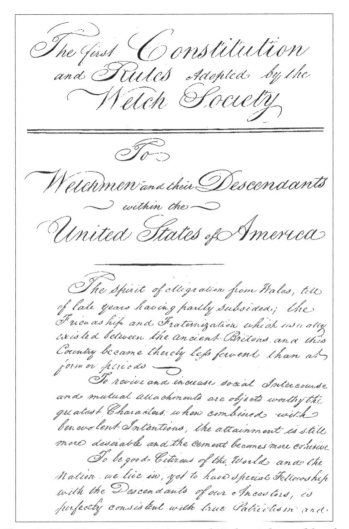

Plate 8. The First Constitution and Rules Adopted by the Welch Society, 1798.[1]

---

1 HC, MC-1186, Vol 1. Unpaginated Minute Book of the Records of the Welsh Society of Philadelphia (4 June 1798–2 December 1839) and Copy of the Original Association, 1 March 1798, End of Volume. The image is reproduced with the permission of the Welsh Society of Philadelphia and Lutnick Library, Quaker and Special Collections, Haverford College, Haverford, Pennsylvania.

'Ye know the heart of the stranger' it is as susceptible of impressions as the sensitive plant, on his first arrival in a new country it is of great importance to himself and the community that he form favourable ideas of its inhabitants, and be attached to his situation; that his love of country may center in that spot where his person and property are protected and where Liberty and hospitality have made their residence. We shall therefore discharge one of the first duties enjoined on us as men by taking our emigrant brother by the hand instructing him in what he is ignorant of and providing for his immediate necessities.

Influenced by such motives – that golden chain of fellowship may be brightned & that their compatriots may receive advice & relief the subscribers have adopted the following

Constitution

1st. The Institution shall be called 'the Welch Society for the advice and assistance of emigrants from Wales' and shall have a seal emblematic of its charitable designs.

2. Every member of the society shall pay an annual subscription of one dollar and upon signing the constitution and paying four dollars shall receive his certificate of membership. Any person known to be of Welch descent and proposed as a candidate by a member shall be balloted for at the next meeting and if the votes of two thirds of the members present shall appear in the affirmative such candidate shall be declared duly elected. Previous to the next meeting after the election of any member he shall sign the constitution and pay into the hands of the Treasurer four dollars when he shall receive a certificate of his admission and the seal of the Society signed by the President and attested by the Secretary. Honorary members shall be admitted by the same rules.

3. The religious or political opinions of a candidate shall not influence his election; nor shall controversies on those subjects be introduced whilst the President is in the chair, under the penalty of five dollars for the use of the Society.

4. The Society shall meet on the first Monday in June, September and December at a place appointed, to enact the necessary laws. Twenty-one members shall form a quorum two thirds of whom shall have the power to expel a member for disorderly behaviour. And on the first day of March annually convene to elect by ballot a President, Vice President, Treasurer, Secretary, Register, two Counsellors, two Physicians, and seven Stewards, the whole to form an acting committee to transact and execute all the affairs of the establishment.

5. The President (or in his absence the Vice President) shall take the chair and preserve order at all the meetings, put all questions to vote which shall be decided by the majority, sign the laws and see them executed, and on particular occasions shall call extra conventions.

The Treasurer shall take charge of all the property and give such security as the Society requires, render a just statement of his accounts at the annual meetings, pay all orders signed by the chairman of the committee or (in the case of imminent distress) by any two of its members provided the sum do not exceed five dollars.

The Secretary shall keep their records of all the transactions of the Society and committee give notices &c.

The Register shall record all applications for advice or employment and advertise in certain cases for suitable situations.

In all difficult cases opinions of the Counsellors shall be taken, but no suit shall be commenced unless agreed to by a majority of the committee present.

The Physicians shall at the request of the committee visit the sick, and administer to their relief; or if the case be urgent on application to them by any two of its members.

The Stewards also shall pay particular attention to the sick and distressed and cooperate with other officers in their respective duties.

The committee shall meet once every month to receive applications and deliberate on the report of its officers and subcommittees, seven members shall form a quorum.

In case of the absence of any of the officers temporary ones may be elected; and every absentee whether officer or member residing in the city or suburbs shall forfeit the sum of twenty five cents for every omission except at the annual meeting he shall [pay] one dollar.

No alteration or amendment shall be made on the above constitution without the consent of two thirds of the members which improvement shall be proposed three months prior to its discussion.

The Second Constitution and Rules adopted by the Welch Society on the 1ˢᵗ Day of March Anno Domini 1802

The Charter and Bye Laws of the Welch Society

Introduction

It is an opinion hardly to be controverted, that the inhabitants of this country are, in a special manner, bound to respect the virtue of hospitality to the stranger and the unfortunate; whilst familiar circumstances seem to indicate this important truth, it must strike the intelligent mind, as no less worthy of observation of gratitude that, when divine goodness imposed upon man a duty so essential to his nature and happiness, it was to be accompanied with a pleasure and satisfaction in the exercise thereof, which loses not its reward even in this life. On the contrary, 'I was a stranger and ye took me not in,' is an address that few minds can contemplate without emotions of horror, and which even the misanthrope will rather depricate than envy.

Although the wretched of no clime nor condition should be excluded from our aid and commiseration, yet we hold the maxim to be both just and natural, that those of the country and people of our ancestors have claims of greater sensibility and of stronger obligation than others.

Under the influence of those sentiments and impressions, the Sons of St David in the City of Philadelphia and its vicinity have long since instituted a Society for the humane and benevolent purposes of dispensing advice and assistance to Welchmen in distress.

This ancient institution, so much the pride and honor of its founders and supporters, and so much the object of grateful remembrance by the many who have shared in its bounty and assistance, having been accommodated to existing circumstances from time to time, with respect to form, is now established by an Act of Incorporation and presented to the Society in the plan of the following constitution.

PART TWO

Charter incorporating the Welch Society

Article 1.

For the purpose of more effectually affording advice and assistance to emigrants from Wales, the following named persons, vizt. Samuel Meredith, Clement Biddle, Morgan J. Rhees, Benjamin R. Morgan, Robert Wharton, Jacob Morgan, Benjamin Morgan, William Jones, Richard Price, Jonathan Jones, Thomas Cumpston, Samuel Clarke, Samuel Price, George Thompson, Michael Roberts, Robert Jones, John Davis, Richard Maris, Cadwallader Evans Junr, Owen Foulke, Caleb Foulke Junr, John M. Price, Joseph Price, Lewis Walker, Peter Evans, Joseph Roberts, John Evans, Edward Thompson, Richard C. Jones, William Lewis, Joseph Simons, Joshua Humphreys, John Morgan, John Thomas, Samuel Miles Junr, John Wharton, James Read, John Cadwallader, Josiah Roberts, Griffith Evans, Franklin Wharton, David Ellis, James Ralph, William Ogden, William Nichols, Samuel Jones, Samuel Miles, Edward Jones, Israel Jones, Robert Morris, Enoch Thompson, Cadwallader Evans, Joseph Cadwallader, Edward Tilghman, Richard Peters, Peregrine Wharton, Edward Roberts, David Evans Junr, Joseph Strong, Samuel Wheeler, John J. Parry, Elijah Griffith, John Bowen, Matthew Randall, James Smith, Samuel Whetherill, Joseph North, Chandler Price, Joseph Snowden, George Clymer, John Haines, William L. Maddock, Isaac H. Jackson, William Smith, Thomas Wharton Jr, Jonathan Walker, Thomas C. James, Richard H. Morris, Paschal Hollingsworth, Richard Edwards, John Palmer, Owen Jones, Isaac Jones, John Owen, William Jones, Charlton Yeatman, William Preston, John Read Junr, John Jones, John Lewis, John Philips, Benjamin Jones, James Crukshank, Benjamin Price, William Read, William Meredith, Joseph S. Lewis, Clement Humphreys, Samuel Parish, Thomas B. Zantzinger, Thomas Jones, Samuel Humphreys, Edward Edwards, Joseph Ball, Thomas Humphreys, Jonathan Smith, Pearson Hunt, Thomas Cadwallader, Joseph Higbee, Wilson Hunt, James Hamilton, William Hamilton, David Edwards, Ezekiel E. Maddock,

Joshua Edwards, Joseph P. Norris, Thomas Parke, Gideon H. Wells, Thomas Gibson, Thomas Chew Junr, Robert Thomas, Richard Peters Junr, Abiah Brown, John Clifton, Daniel Smith, Thomas Allibone, Isaac Wayne, Charles Cadwallader, Henry Jenkins, Isaac Jones, Thomas Biddle, being Citizens of the Commonwealth of Pennsylvania, and such others as they shall hereafter associate with themselves being Citizens of the said Commonwealth are hereby erected into a body politic and corporate by the name, style, and title of The Welch Society, and by the same name, style, and title, shall have perpetual succession, and may purchase, take, and hold, by gift, grant, demise, bargain, and sale, devise and bequest, or by any other mode of lawful conveyance, any lands, tenements, goods or chattels, real, personal or mixed estate, and the same or any part thereof, from time to time, may sell, alien [align], convey and dispose of, and shall and may have a common seal, which they may alter and renew at their pleasure.

Provided always nevertheless, that the clear yearly value or income of the messuages, houses, lands, and tenements, rents, annuities, or other hereditaments and real estate of the said corporation, and the interest of money by them lent, shall not exceed the sum of five hundred pounds.

Article 2nd

Any person known to be of Welch descent, and proposed as a candidate by a member, shall be balloted for at the next meeting, and provided the votes of two thirds of the members present appear in the affirmative, shall be declared duly elected. Previous to the next meeting after the election of any member, he shall sign the Constitution, and pay into the hands of the Treasurer eight dollars, when he shall be entitled to receive a certificate of his admission under the seal of the Society, signed by the President and Treasurer, and attested by the Secretary.

Honorary members, however may be admitted without being subject to the aforesaid conditions.

Article 3rd

Religion and politics shall not be introduced whilst the President is in the chair, under a penalty of five dollars, for the use of the Society.

Article 4th

The Society shall meet on the first Monday in June, September and December, at a place appointed; thirteen members shall form a quorum to transact the usual business of the Society, but for the admitting and expelling of a member, for the enacting or repealing any bye-law, it shall require twenty one members present, two thirds of whom shall agree in such cases, and no member shall be expelled, or bye-law enacted or repealed, without three months notice. If at any meeting the quorum shall not be formed, the members present shall have power to adjourn. And on the first of March annually, convened to elect, by ballot a President, Vice President, Treasurer, Secretary, Register, two Counsellors, two Physicians, and seven Stewards, the whole to form an acting committee to transact and execute all the affairs of the establishment; but in the absence of the other officers, a majority of the Stewards shall be competent to transact business.

Article 5th

The President, Vice President or, in the absence, a Chairman to be chosen pro tem, shall take the chair half an hour after the time appointed for meeting. He shall be the absolute judge of order, allowing an appeal, however, if demanded by six members, in which case the Society shall decide as on other questions, but without debate; and, at the request of two thirds of the acting committee present, have power to call extra meetings.

The Treasurer shall take charge of all the property, and give such security as the Society may require; pay all orders signed by the chairman of the acting committee, or, in the case of extreme distress, by any two of its members; submit a just statement of his accounts to a committee for the purpose appointed, who shall report at the annual meetings.

The Secretary shall keep fair records of all the transactions of the Society, and give notice of the time and place of meeting.

The Register shall record all applications for advice or employment, and advertise in certain cases for suitable situations.

In all difficult cases, opinions of the Counsellors shall be taken; but no suit at law shall be commenced unless agreed to by a majority of the committee.

The Physicians shall, at the request of the committee, visit the sick, and administer to their relief; or, if the case be urgent, on application to them by any two of its members.

The Stewards also shall pay particular attention to the sick and distressed, and cooperate with other officers in their respective duties.

Article 6th

The acting committee shall meet once every month to receive applications, and deliberate on the report of its officers and sub committee; three members shall form a quorum.

In the case of absence of any of the officers, temporary ones may be elected, and every absent member residing in the city or suburbs, shall forfeit the sum of fifty cents for each omission except at the annual meeting, when he shall pay one dollar. And the President, Vice President, Treasurer, Secretary, and Register shall respectively pay one dollar for non-attendance at special and quarterly meetings.

Article 7th

If any officer of the Society shall die, remove out of the state, or resign, another shall be chosen to serve the remainder of the year; and if any member chosen officer refuse to serve he shall pay a fine five dollars.

Article 8th

The acting committee shall report their proceedings to the Society quarterly.

Article 9th

No alteration or amendment shall be made in the above Constitution without the consent of twenty five members, which alteration shall be proposed three months prior to its discussion.

Article 10th

The Society at any of the stated meetings shall, on the notice herein before mentioned, have power from time to time, to make, alter, and repeal such bye-laws, rules and regulations, prescribing the duties of the officers and for conducting the affairs of the institution, as to them shall appear expedient. Provided always, that the said bye-laws, rules and regulations, or any of them be not repugnant, to the constitution and laws of this Commonwealth, or to the foregoing instrument.

Officers for the present year

Samuel Meredith	President
Robert Wharton	Vice President
Thomas Cumpston	Treasurer
Richard C. Jones	Secretary
Joseph S. Lewis	Register

Bye-Laws of the Welch Society

1st. On the President assuming the chair, the Secretary shall call over the names of the members; and as soon as convenient, furnish the Treasurer with a certified copy of the names and fines of the absentees; the business next in order shall be to read the minutes of the last meeting.

2nd. No business to be acted upon but by motion, seconded and committed to writing if requested; nor shall any member depart from the Society while the President is in the chair, without his leave, under the penalty of fifty cents.

3rd. When a motion is before the Society, no other shall be received by the chair, unless immediately relative to the original motion, except a motion for adjournment, the question upon which shall be taken without debate.

4th. The Chairman of the meeting shall nominate one of the members to superintend and adjust the expence incurred during the time of business which he shall ascertain before the meeting adjourns and receive the same from the members present.

5th. The Stewards shall have the direction, superintendence and arrangement of the annual entertainment, towards the expence thereof, thirty dollars shall be appropriated out of the funds of the Society, the remaining expence to be equally paid by the members present at such entertainment.

6th. The fines for non attendance at special meetings shall be the same as for quarterly meetings, and all fines shall be paid into the general fund of the institution.

7th. The acting committee shall appoint a messenger and pay him such compensation as they may think adequate for his services; it shall be the duty of the messenger to carry the notices of meetings to the members; and, under the direction of the Treasurer, collect the fines and contributions, and attend the meetings of the Society.

PART TWO

Supplemental Rules and Regulations adopted by the Welch Society vizt

1803 December 5th

Whereas provision has not been made in the Act of Incorporation for the collection of the annual contribution. Therefore, resolved that the contribution to be paid annually by each member for the use of the Society shall be two dollars to be collected and paid into the hands of the Treasurer.

1807 December 7th

The Stewards shall have the direction, superintendence and arrangement of the annual dinner, and the expence of the guests invited by order of the Society, shall be paid out of the general fund, the remaining expence to be equally paid by the members present at such entertainment.

Plate 9. 'Second Street North from Market Street with Christ Church, Philadelphia', c.1800.[2]

---

2   Birch and Son, *The City of Philadelphia*, plate 15.

PART THREE

MINUTE BOOK, 1798–1839[1]
WELCH SOCIETY[2]
[INDEX OF MEMBERS][3]

A
~~Allibon, Thomas~~

B
Biddle, Clement
dec[d]
Ball, Joseph
dec[d]
~~Brown, Abiah~~[4]
dead
Biddle, Thomas

C
Cumpston, Thomas
dec[d]

~~Clarke, Samuel~~
Clymer, George
~~Cruckshanks, James~~
dead
Cadwallader, Thomas
Clifton, John
dec[d]
Chauncey, Charles
Chauncey, Elihu
Craig, William
Clay, Curtis Jr
dec[d]
Chew, Benjamin Jr

---

1 HC, MC-1186, vol. 1.
2 A red volume with Welch Society rather than Welsh Society written in gold leaf on the cover. The volume was given to the Society by James Crukshank – there are various spellings of his last name in the volume of minutes.
3 This is for the years 1802–3 and noted the attendance of members.
4 Unless indicated the crossing out of the name would signify the death, resignation or expulsion of the member.

D

~~Davis, John~~
expelled
~~Dowers, John~~ Jr
Davis, Edward
Dewees, William R[5]

E

Evans, Peter
Evans, John
~~Evans, Griffith~~
resigned
~~Ellis, David~~
declined[6]
~~Edwards, Richard~~
dead
~~Edwards, Edward~~
dead
Edwards, Joshua
~~Evans, Issachar~~
decd
Ellis, William Coxe
Honr^{y7}
Evans, Samuel
Ellis, Rowland
dec^d

Eddy, Lewis
dec^d
Evans, Thomas
Evans, Thomas (of Peters)[8]

F

Foulke, Owen
Honr^y dec^d
Foulke, Caleb Jr
Honr^y
Fraser, Robert
Fisher, James C.
Fisher, Joshua
dead
Freeman, Tristram B.
Fisher, Redwood
dec^d
Fisher, Miers
dec^d
Fisher, William W.
dec^d
Foulke, Charles
dec^d

G

~~Griffith, Robert C.~~
declined

---

5   Resigned.
6   Occasionally a nominated member would decline membership.
7   Some members were granted honorary membership of the Society, especially if they provided assistance to the emigrants.
8   St Peter's, Philadelphia.

Gibson, James
~~Gillaspy, George~~
Doctor resigned
Gilpin, Joshua
Garrigues, Benjamin F.
dec^d
Gray, Edward
dec^d

H

Humphreys, Joshua
dec^d
~~Harris, John~~
expelled
Hollingsworth, Paschal
~~Humphreys, Clement~~
dead
Humphreys, Samuel
Humphreys, Thomas
Hunt, Pearson
Hon^{ry}
Higbee, Joseph
Hon^{ry}
~~Hunt, Wilson~~
resigned
Huddle, Joseph Jr
Hamilton, James
dec^d
~~Hopkinson, Joseph~~
resigned
Hale, Thomas
resigned
Harrison, John

dec^d
Hughes, John
dec^d
Howell, Joseph E.
dec^d
Hemphill, Joseph
Howell, George
Howell, Benjamin B.
Howell, William E.
dec^d
Hendy, William Capt
Hallowell, John
dec^d
Howell, William W.
dec^d

J

Jones, William Capt
dec^d
Jones, Jonathan
Hon^{ry}
~~Jones, Richard S.~~
dead
~~Jones, Israel~~
resigned
Jackson, Isaac H.
Hon^{ry}
James, Thomas C. Doctor
dec^d
~~Jones, Isaac~~
dead
Jones, William
~~Hon^{ry}~~

Jones, Benjamin
~~Jones, Thomas~~
deceased
Jenkins, Henry
Hon^{ry}
Jones, Isaac Tob^9
Jones, Lloyd Capt
~~Jones, John C.~~
resigned
~~Jones, Isaac H.~~
resigned
Jones, Saml U.
declined
Jones, John
Jones, Rich^d B.
dec^d
Jacobs, Samuel Havard

[Added out of sequence]

Jones, William J.
Jones, Joseph
dec^d

K

Kinsey, Edmund

L

Lewis, William
dec^d

~~Lewis, John~~
dead
Lewis, Joseph S.
dec^d
Lewis, David
dec^d
Lewis, Reece
dec^d
Lewis, Saml Neave
Lewis, John D.
Lewis, Lawrence

M

Meredith, Samuel
dec^d
Morgan, Benjamin R.
Maurice, Richard
Morgan, John
~~Maddock, William L.~~
Morris, Richard H.
~~Hon^{ry}~~
Meredith, William
Maddock, Ezekiel C.
~~Michael, Joseph~~
deceased
Marshall, Charles Jr
dec^d
Mifflin, John F.
Morgan, Geo W.
dec^d
Murdock, Robert

---

9   This abbreviation (Tob/Tob^a) is presumably 'Tobias' and is used to differentiate from the other Isaac Jones specified in the list.

Milnor, James
Morris, Thomas
Mayberry, Thomas
Morgan, William H.
Miles, Lewis
Meredith, David
dec^d
Morgan, Thomas

N

~~North, Joseph~~
dead
Norris, Joseph S.
Nichols, Samuel
Nicholas, Charles J.

O

~~Ogden, William~~
expelled
~~Owen, John~~
dead
Otto, Jacob S.
dec^d

P

Price, Richard
dec^d
Price, Samuel
resigned
Price, Joseph
Price, John M.
dec^d

Price, Chandler
dec^d
~~Palmer, John~~
dead
~~Preston, William~~
expelled
~~Phillips, John~~
deceased
Price, Benjamin
Hon^{ry}
Parrish, Samuel
dec^d
Parke, Thomas Doct^r
dec^d
Peters, Richard Jr
dec^d
Poulson, Zachariah
Prosser, James
Parker, William

R

~~Roberts, Michael~~
dead
Roberts, Joseph
absent
~~Read, James~~
dec^d
Roberts, Josiah
absent
~~Rolph, James~~
expelled
Randall, Matthew
dec^d

Read, John Jr
resigned
Read, William
Hon^{ry}
Read, Collinson
Hon^{ry} dec^d
Reinholt, George
dec^d
Relf, Samuel
dec^d
Roberts, Algernon
Hon^{ry} dec^d
Rogers, William
expelled
Read, James Junr
Roberts[10]
Roberts, Thomas P.

S

Simons, Joseph
dec^d
Strong, Joseph Doct^r
deceased
Smith, James
dec^d
Smith, William W.
dec^d
Smith, Jonathan
dec^d
Smith, Joseph
Sharpless, Jesse

resigned
Shaw, Joseph
dec^d
Strawbridge, John
Hon^{ry}
Shaw, William A.
dec^d

T

Thompson, George
resigned
Thomas, John
resigned
Thompson, Enock
resigned
Tilghman, Edward
resigned
Tilghman, William
dec^d
Thomas, Robert
dead 1805
Tatim,[11] James
Tilghman, Edwd Jr
dec^d
Thompson, Jonah
Thomas, Benjamin

V

Vaux, George
dec^d

---

10 No further entry details.
11 Elsewhere as Tatem.

W

Wharton, Robert
dec^d
Walker, Lewis
Wharton, John
dec^d
Wharton, Franklin
dec^d
Wharton, Peregrine H.
dec^d
Wetherill, Samuel Jr
dec^d
Wharton, Thomas C.
dec^d
Wells, Gideon H.
Hon^{ry} dec^d
Waln, Robert
dec^d
Wistar, John
Williams, Joseph
dec^d
Wistar, Charles
Worrell, Joseph[12]
Wildes, Joseph
dec^d
Waln, Jesse
Wharton, Fishbourn
Watson, John
dec^d
Wheeler, John J.
W̶i̶l̶l̶e̶t̶t̶,̶ ̶J̶o̶h̶n̶ ̶S̶.̶
Hon^{ry}

Ware, Richard
dec^d
Williams, James
dec^d

Out of sequence

Williams, Thomas Capt

Z

Zantzinger, Thomas B.

Honorary Members

B

Bloomfield, Joseph
Trenton
Broome, Jacob
Wilmington

C

Cadwallader, John
dead
Cadwallader, Joseph
dead
Cadwallader, Lambert
C̶h̶e̶w̶,̶ ̶B̶e̶n̶j̶a̶m̶i̶n̶ ̶J̶r̶
Cadwallader, Charles
Craig, William

---

12 Elsewhere as Worrall.

D

Dickinson, Philemon
Dickinson, Samuel

E

Evans, Cadwallader
Edwards, Revd David
Ellis, William Cox[13]

H

Howell, Joshua L.
dec^d New Jersey
Hamilton, William
dec^d
Hastings, John

J

Jones, Samuel Penypack
Jones, Edward Washington
Jones, John Merion
Jones, Thomas W.
~~Jones, Richard B.~~
Jones, David C. New York

L

Lewis, Josiah
dec^d

M

Morgan, Benjamin
Miles, Samuel Senr
dec^d
Miles, Samuel Jr
dec^d
Morris, Robert
dec^d

N

Nichols, William
dec^d

P

Picton, Thomas[14]
Peters, Richard Senr
dec^d
Paulin, Levy
dec^d

R

Read, George Newcastle dec^d
Rhees, Morgan J.
Read, James Capt
Roberts, Richard

---

13   Elsewhere as Coxe.
14   Elsewhere as Pickton.

Roberts, Algernon
Roberts, John
Roberts, [Thomas][15]

S

Snowden, Joseph
dec[d]
Strawbridge, John

T

Thomas, Evan
New Castle

V

Vaux, George
dec[d]

W

Wheeler, Samuel
dec[d]
Wayne, Isaac
dec[d]
White, John Moore
Woodruff, A[a]ron D.
Walker, Jonathan
Woodruff, Abner
~~Williams, Joseph~~
Willett, John S.
dec[d]

Y

Yeatman, Charleton

---

15 Name faint or rubbed out.

Organization: Beginnings of the Association

Welsh Society

Copy of the Original Association

We the Subscribers Welchmen and descendants of Welchmen do agree to meet at the house of William Ogden[16] on the first day of March 1798 at 12 o'clock for the purpose of forming ourselves into a Society for the relief of such emigrants as may arrive in this country from Wales.

Samuel Meredith
Clement Biddle
Morgan J. Rhees
William Griffiths
Benjamin R. Morgan
Robert Wharton
Jacob Morgan
Isaac Price
Thomas Morgan
Benjamin Morgan
William Jones
Richard Price
Jonathan Jones
Thomas Cumpston
Samuel Clarke
Samuel Price
George Thompson
Michael Roberts
Robert Jones
John Davis
James Read

Richard Maris
Cadwallader Evans Junr
Owen Foulke
Caleb Foulke Junr
John M. Price
Joseph Price
Lewis Walker
Peter Evans
Joseph Roberts
John Evans
Edward Thompson
Richard E. Jones
William Lewis
Joseph Simons
Joshua Humphreys
Mordecai Lewis
John Morgan
John Thomas
Samuel Miles Junr
John Wharton

---

16 This was William Ogden's Tavern, 86 Chestnut Street, Philadelphia. See Pennsylvania Historical and Museum Commission, Harrisburg, Pa. Records of the House of Representatives; Records of the General Assembly, Record Group 7. Septennial Census Returns, 1779–1863. Box 1026, p. 136 (no. 262).

PART THREE

John Cadwallader
Josiah Roberts
Griffith Evans
Franklin Wharton
David Ellis
James Rolph
Robert E. Griffith
William Ogden
William Nichols   Hon^ry
Samuel Jones   Pennypack[17]
Samuel Miles
Edward Jones
Israel Jones
Robert Morris   Frankfort[18]
Enoch Thompson
Cadwallader Evans
Joseph Cadwallader
Edward Tilghman
Richard Peters   Honorary
Perrigrine Wharton
Edward Roberts
John Jones   M
David Evans Junr

---

17   This is in north-east Philadelphia.
18   This is in north-east Philadelphia, about ten miles from the city.

Organization: Proposal to Establish a Welsh Society

At a meeting of Welchman and descendants of Welchman at the house of William Ogden March 1st 1798 for the purpose of forming a Society for the advice and assistance of emigrants from Wales.

Mr Samuel Meredith in the Chair

Resolved that the persons who have signed the association for the above purpose be associated under the name of THE WELCH SOCIETY

Organization: Appointment of a Committee to draft the Constitution

Resolved that a committee of three be appointed for the purpose of drafting a Constitution to report to a meeting to be held on the 24th Instant.

Messrs Rhees, Biddle & Thomas were appointed.

Organization: Election of Officers

Resolved that the company present proceed to the election of a President, Vice President, Treasurer and two Secretaries on counting the votes it appeared that

Samuel Meredith	was chosen President
Jacob Morgan	[was chosen] Vice President
Thomas Cumpston	[was chosen] Treasurer
Owen Foulke	
William Griffith	[were chosen] Secretaries

Adjourned to meet on 24th Instant

(signed) Owen Foulke Sec^y

PART THREE

1798

At an Adjourned Meeting of the Welch Society held March 24th 1798.

Present

Jacob Morgan   Vice President
Morgan J. Rhees
Thomas Cumpston
John Cadwallader
Richard Price
William Griffith
Richard Jones
Joseph Price
John Morgan
Jacob Morgan
Caleb Foulke
John M. Price
Samuel Miles Jun[r]

Organization: Constitution and Book of Minutes

Mr Rhees of the committee to prepare a Constitution made report which with certain amendments was adopted and ordered to be transcribed into the Book of Minutes.

Organization: Seal and Certificate of Membership

On notion agreed that Mess[rs] Rhees, Cumpston & J. Jones be appointed a committee to provide the Society with a Seal and form of certificate of membership with suitable embellishments.

Adjourned

signed Owen Foulke Sec[y]

At a Special Meeting of the Welch Society held April 24th 1798.

Present

Samuel Meredith	President
Jacob Morgan	Vice President

Richard Maris	Joseph Price
John M. Price	Michael Roberts
Samuel Miles Junr	Benjamin Morgan
Caleb Foulke Junr	Thomas Cumpston
Joseph Thomas	Peter Evans
John Evans	Joshua Humphreys
[unspecified]¹⁹ Roberts	Lewis Walker
Richard Price	William Jones
Samuel Clarke	Franklin Wharton
Owen Foulke	

Organization: Election of Officers

The Society proceeded to the election of two Councellors, two Physicians, a Register and seven Stewards. The following persons were duly elected

Joseph Thomas	Counsellors
Benjn R. Morgan	
Samuel P. Griffiths	Physicians
Thomas C. James	
William Griffith	Register
Robert Wharton	Stewards
Morgan J. Rhees	
Richard Price	
William Jones	
John Evans	
Jonathan Jones	
Michael Roberts	

---

19   Edward?

PART THREE

Organization: Certificate of Association

The committee appointed to provide the Society with a form of certificate &c., produced a drawing by Mr Barolet which was approved of. The committee are directed to have the same executed as soon as possible.

Membership: New Members

The following persons following at a former Meeting were balloted for and duly elected members of the Society vizt

Col. William Nichols Honorary	
Samuel Jones of Pennypack a member	proposed by Thomas Cumpston
Samuel Miles	proposed by S. Miles Jun[r]
Edward Jones	[proposed by] Jonathan Jones
Israel Jones	
Enoch Thompson	[proposed by] Richard Price
Rob[t] Morris Frankfort	
Cadwallader Evans	[proposed by] Caleb Foulke Jun[r]
Joseph Cadwalleder	[proposed by] Morgan J. Rhees
Edward Tilghman	[proposed by] Joseph Thomas
Richard Peters Hon[ry]	
Perrigrine Wharton	[proposed by] Richard Price
Edward Roberts	
David Evans Jun[r]	

Organization: Bye-Laws

On a motion agreed, that Thomas Cumpston, William Jones and Owen Foulke be appointed a committee to prepare a set of Bye-Laws for the regulation of the Society to report to the next meeting.

Finance: Amendments to the Constitution

Moved and seconded, that the words four dollars in the second Article of the Constitution be struck out for the purpose of inserting a larger sum to be determined on at a future meeting.

Finance: Fees

On motion agreed, that each member pay four dollars to the Treasurer before the next meeting.

Sixty-four dollars was paid to the Treasurer by the members present agreeably to the foregoing motion.

Adjourned

signed Owen Foulke Sec^y

At a Meeting of the Welch Society, June 4th 1798.

Present

Samuel Meredith	President
William Griffith	
Robert Wharton	
Benjamin Morgan	
William Jones	
Thomas Cumpston	
Samuel Clarke	
Michael Roberts	
Owen Foulke	
Perigrine Wharton	
Joseph Price	
John Evans	
Joshua Humphreys	
Josiah Roberts	
Franklin Wharton	
David Ellis	
William Ogden	
Israel Jones	

Organization: Bye-Laws

The committee appointed to prepare Bye-Laws are requested to report them to the next meeting.

Finance: Amendments to the Constitution

The consideration of the motions to strike out four dollars from the second article of the Constitution is postponed until next meeting.

Membership: New Members

The following persons proposed at a former meeting were duly elected vizt

Thomas Pickton	proposed by Morgan J. Rhees
Lloyd Jones	
Joseph Strong	
John J. Parry	
Elisha Griffith	
John Bowen	
Matthew Randall	[proposed] by Richard Price
James Smith	
Griffith Edwards	[proposed by] Joseph Price
Samuel Wetherill Jun[r]	[proposed by] J. M. Price
Joseph Snowden	
Honorary	[proposed by] Benjamin R. Morgan
Joseph North	
Chandler Price	
Henry Hill	[proposed by] Samuel Meredith]
George Clymer	

Finance: Sundry Payments

The Treasurer reported that he had received seventy-two dollars since last meeting and paid the following orders drawn by the Chairman of the acting committee.

Four dollars to E. Jones

Ten dollars to ditto on loan
Fifty dollars to Mr Barolet on acco^t of the plate
Five dollars to Elias Jones

Adjourned to meet on the first Monday in September next

signed Owen Foulke Secretary

At a Meeting of the Welch Society, December 3rd 1798.

Present

Samuel Miles
Thomas Cumpston
Richard Price
Michael Roberts
Samuel Miles Junr
Jonathan Jones
Richard Smith
Richard Jones
Joseph Price
John M. Price
Caleb Foulke Junr
Owen Foulke

Organization: Chairing the Meeting

Neither the President or Vice President attending Col. Samuel Miles was called to the chair.

Organization: Bye-Laws

The committee appointed to prepare a set of Bye-Laws not being ready to report are continued and requested to report to next meeting.

Organization: Seal of the Society

The committee appointed to obtain a seal for the Society produced one which they are directed to deposit in the hands of the Treasurer.

An order drawn on the Treasurer in favor of James Smither[20] for twenty-five dollars being his charge for engraving the seal.

Finance: Accounts

The Treasurer reports that he has received twelve dollars since last meeting.

Organization: Constitution

On motion agreed, that Samuel Miles, William Jones, Thomas Cumpston and Owen Foulke be appointed a committee to revise the Constitution and report to a special meeting, who are authorized to call such meeting when ready to report.

Membership: New Members

The following persons were proposed at former meeting were duly elected:

John Haines	proposed by Robt Wharton
Aaron D. Woodruff	[proposed by] Michael Roberts
Govr Richd Howells	
William E. Maddock	[proposed by] Joseph Price
Isaac H. Jackson	[proposed by] Wm Jones
William Smith	[proposed by] Joseph Price
Thomas Wharton Junr	[proposed by] Jos^a Humphreys
Jonathan Walker of North[21]	[proposed by] Owen Foulke

Adjourned

signed Owen Foulke Secretary

---

20 An engraver in Philadelphia.
21 Northumberland was founded in 1772 and is now a borough in Northumberland County, Pennsylvania. Joseph Priestley (1733–1804), the British theologian, dissenter and political theorist lived there from 1794 until his death.

1799

At a Special Meeting of the Welch Society held February 4th 1799.

Present

Samuel Meredith	Morgan J. Rhees
James King	Richard C. Jones
Matthew Randall	Isaac H. Jackson
Lewis Walker	Owen Foulke
Thomas Cumpston	Joseph Price
Benjam^n R. Morgan	Samuel Clarke
Richard Price	Chandler Price
Edward Jones	Benjamin Morgan
David Ellis	John Haines
Israel Jones	William Ogden
Joseph Simons	Caleb Foulke Junr
Robert Wharton	

Organization: Rules and Regulations

The committee appointed at a former meeting to prepare Rules and Regulations for the further government of the Society reported which with certain amendments and additions was adopted as follows.

RULES AND REGULATIONS for the further government of the Society.

1st The President, Vice President or in their absence, the Chairman appointed (pro-tem) shall take the chair half an hour after the time appointed for meeting.

2nd As soon as the members come to order the Secretary shall call over the names of the members, the business next in order shall be, to read over the minutes of the last proceeding meeting.

3rd The decisions of the President, Vice President or Chairman of the meeting on questions of order shall be immediately submitted to unless appeal be regularly made to the meeting by three members in which case the meeting shall decide as upon other questions.

4th No business to be acted upon but by motion seconded and committed to writing if required.

5th When a question is before the Society no other motion shall be received by the Chair, unless immediately relating to the business before the Society except a motion for adjournment which shall be decided without debate.

6th The President, Vice President, or Chairman of the Meeting shall nominate one of the Stewards or in their absence some other member to superintend and adjust the expence incurred during the time of business, which he shall ascertain before the meeting adjourns and apportion the same amongst the members present and receive and pay for the same to the landlord immediately.

7th The Stewards shall have the direction superintendence and arrangement of the annual entertainment towards the expence thereof, each member shall pay one dollar and fifty cents exclusive of the fine for non-attendance at the annual meeting. The remaining expence to be equally paid by the members present at such entertainment.

8th The fines for non-attendance at special meetings shall be the same as for quarterly meetings.

9th The President, Vice President, Treasurer Secretary, Register and Stewards shall respectively pay fifty cents for non-attendance at special or quarterly meeting.

10th The Treasurer and Secretary shall appoint a messenger and pay him such compensation as they shall think adequate to his services. It shall be the duty of the messenger to carry the notices of meeting to the members and to collect the fines and contributions, he shall attend the Society upon public occasions.

11th If any officer of the Society should die, remove out of the State or resign another shall be chosen to serve the remainder of the year, and if any member be chosen an officer and refuse to serve he shall pay to the Society Stock five dollars.

12th The acting committee shall report their proceedings to the Society quarterly.

Annual Dinner

The acting committee submitted to the consideration of the Society the following management for the annual dinner on the first of March which was agreed to.

That all Stewards shall have a suitable dinner provided by William Ogden at his house on the first of March that a kid be the first dish at the head of the table. The Stewards shall also attend to the quality of the wines and other liquors necessary for the occasion and that no liquor be called for on that day except by the Stewards who shall issue cards or tickets specifying expressly their orders which cards shall be produced by the landlord as necessary vouchers for the settling of his charge. And that the Stewards or a committee of them shall prepare a set of sentiments or toasts suitable for the occasion, and in compliance with the custom usual by other societies upon those occasions and to return civilities shewn to the officers of this Society. The Stewards may send cards of invitation to such characters as they may think proper not exceeding thirty in number.

Organization: Constitutional Amendments – Stewards

On motion made and seconded, the following alteration in the Constitution was agreed to vizt

That the fourth of the Constitution be altered, so that the acting committee shall consist of the Stewards only four of whom shall be a quorum sufficient to do business.

PART THREE

Discipline: Expulsion of a Member

On motion made and seconded, Joseph Thomas's name was expunged from the list of members and no longer to be considered as a member of this Society.

Membership: New Members

The following persons proposed at a former meeting were duly elected

Richard H. Morris   proposed by Jon^a Jones
Paschal Hollingsworth
Richard Edwards
John Palmer
Joshua L. Howell   [proposed] by Thos Cumpston

At the Annual Meeting of the Welch Society, March 1st 1799.

Present

Samuel Meredith   Israel Jones
Samuel Miles   Isaac H. Jackson
Thomas Cumpston   David Ellis
Michael Roberts   Richard Price
Morgan J. Rhees   John Evans
Joshua Humphreys   Joseph Roberts
John Davies   John Haines
Benjamin Morgan   Richd C. Jones
Lewis Walker   James King
Joseph Price   Chandler Price
William Ogden   Robert Wharton
Richard Maris   Caleb Foulke Junr
John M. Price   Owen Foulke
George Clymer   Jonathan Jones

Membership: New Members

The following persons proposed at a former meeting were duly elected members of the Society, vizt

Spafford Drury	proposed by R. Wharton
John Owen	[proposed by] David Ellis
William Jones	[proposed by] Richard Price

Assistance to Welsh Emigrants

The petition of Elizabeth Robinson praying for relief from the Society was read and referred to the acting committee to report or act upon as they shall think proper.

Organization: Constitution and Bye-Laws

On motion, agreed that a committee of three members be appointed to superintend and direct the printing of the Constitution and Bye-Laws of the Society with the power to revise retaining the original principles. Messrs George Clymer, Morgan J. Rhees and Jonathan Jones were accordingly appointed.

Organization: Election of Officers

The following persons were elected officers of the Society for the present year

Samuel Meredith	President
Jacob Morgan	Vice President
Thomas Cumpston	Treasurer
Morgan J. Rhees	Register
Owen Foulke	Secretary
Benjamin R. Morgan	Counsellors
Edward Tilghman	
Thomas C. James	Physicians
Joseph Strong	

Robert Wharton   Stewards
William Jones
John Evans
John Davis
Richard Price
Michael Roberts

adjourned to first Monday in June

signed Owen Foulke Sec^y

At a Meeting of the Welch Society held June 3rd 1799.

Present

Samuel Meredith	Richard C. Jones
James King	Caleb Foulke
Richard Price	John Wharton
John Davis	John Owen
Thos Cumpston	William Ogden
Michael Roberts	Owen Foulke
Benjn Morgan	Joseph Price
Isaac H. Jackson	Chandler Price
William Jones	Franklin Wharton

Membership: New Members

The following persons proposed at a former Meeting were duly elected members of the Society.

Philemon Dickinson   proposed by Robert Wharton
Owen Jones
William Cliffton Junr
Isaac Jones
William Gray

Jonathan Robeson
Joseph Bloomfield [proposed by] Morgan J. Rhees
Dr Charleton Yeatman [proposed by] Richard Price
William Preston
Samuel Dickinson [proposed by] Jonathan Jones

Finance: *Refusal to Pay Arrears and Fines*

The Treasurer reported that several members had refused to pay their contribution & fines due to the Society.

On motion, agreed that the Treasurer furnish the Stewards with a list of the delinquents who are directed to call upon them in order to ascertain their reasons for refusal and to report to the next meeting the names of those who remain delinquent.

Adjourned

signed Owen Foulke Sec[y]

At a Meeting of the Welch Society, December 2nd 1799.

Present

Samuel Meredith
George Thompson
William Smith
Jonathan Jones
William Jones
Isaac H. Jackson
Isaac Jones
Morgan J. Rhees
Michael Roberts
Joseph Strong

Thomas Cumpston
Richard Price
John Davis
Caleb Foulke Jun[r]
Joseph M. Price
Charleton Yeatman
James Rolph
John Owen
Joseph Price
Owen Foulke

PART THREE

Financial Matters: Amendments to the Constitution

The motion made at a meeting held April 24th 1798 for striking out the words four dollars in the second article of the Constitution for the purpose of inserting a larger sum was taken into consideration and determined in the affirmative and five dollars inserted in the place thereof.

On motion, agreed that the words, one dollar be stricken out from the second article of the Constitution and the words two dollars be inserted.

Annual Dinner: Invitations to St George's, St Andrew's and Hibernian Societies

Resolved that the stewards be directed to provide a dinner for the Society on the first day of March next, and that they are directed to invite the officers of the St George's, St Andrew's and Hibernian Societies and such other persons as they may think proper not exceeding eight in number.

Membership: New Members

The following persons were duly elected Members:

John Reed	proposed by Samuel Meredith
John Jones (of Merion)	by Jonathan Jones
John Lewis	by Thomas Cumpston

1800

At a Meeting of the Welch Society held 1ˢᵗ March 1800.

Present

Samuel Meredith	President
Isaac Jones	
Michael Roberts	
Morgan J. Rhees	
Richard Price	
James Rolph	
Jonathan Jones	
Caleb Foulke Junʳ	
R. Edwards	
William Jones	
John Wharton	
Isaac H. Jackson	
Richard C. Jones	
Joseph Price	
Owen Foulke	

Membership: New Members

The following persons proposed at a former meeting were duly elected members

John Phillips	proposed by Morgan J. Rhees
Benjamin Jones	[proposed] by William Jones
James Cruckshank	[proposed] by William Smith
Benjamin Price	[proposed] by Richard Price
Lambert Cadwallader	[proposed] by Jonathan Jones
George Read of Newcastle	[proposed] by P. Dickinson
William Read of Philᵃ	
William Meredith	[proposed] by Caleb Foulke

PART THREE

Organization: Election of Officers

The following persons were duly elected officers of the Society for the present year

Samuel Meredith	President
Jacob Morgan	Vice President
Thomas Cumpston	Treasurer
Owen Foulke	Secretary
Morgan J. Rhees	Register
Benjamin R. Morgan	Counsellors
Edward Tilghman	
Thomas C. James	Physicians
Joseph Strong	
Robert Wharton	Stewards
William Jones	
John Evans	
Jonathan Jones	
John Davis	
Richard Price	
Michael Roberts	

At a Quarterly Meeting of the Welch Society held June 2nd 1800.

Present

Samuel Meredith	Isaac H. Jackson
Thomas Cumpston	Richard Price
C. Yeatman	Caleb Foulke
William Jones	Peregrine Wharton
John Phillips	John Davis
Benjamin Price	Owen Foulke
John Lewis	Robert Wharton

Membership: Honorary Members

The motion made by Morgan J. Rhees at last meeting for presenting honorary members not citizens of the country with certificates of membership at the expence of the Society be postponed for further consideration.

Membership: New Members

The following persons proposed at a former meeting were duly elected members

Abia[h] Brown	proposed by Wm Jones (Market St)
John Cliffton	[proposed] by Isaac Jones
Daniel Smith	
Thomas Alibone	
Isaac Wayne	[proposed] by Wm Nichols
Chas Cadwallader	[proposed] by J. Cadwallader

Adjourned

signed Owen Foulke Sec^y

At a Quarterly Meeting of the Welch Society held September 1st 1800.

Present

Robert Wharton	Joseph Strong
William Jones	Isaac Jones
Thomas Cumpston	Richard Price
William Jones	Benjamin Price
William Smith	David Ellis
Richard Maris	John Evans
Richard C. Jones	John Lewis
John Phillips	John Owen
Michael Roberts	

PART THREE

Membership: New Members

Robert Wharton being chosen Chairman the Society proceeded to the election of those persons recollected by the members present to have been nominated at a former meeting, the Secretary being out of town on business & the book not being before the Society.

The following persons were duly elected

Joseph S. Lewis
Josiah Lewis
Clement Humphreys
Samuel Parish

The acting committee made the following report

Emigrants from Wales

The Stewards of the Society report

That since the last quarterly meeting the following vessels have arrived from Liverpool with emigrants from Wales –

The Ship *Thomas* at New castle with nearly two hundred persons all of whom have paid their passage but in consequence of their arrival at New Castle additional expence was incurred to assist them on their way to the city, and towards their support until suitable situations were obtained, nearly the whole of the above number are now provided for except Elizabeth Owen widow of John Owen who died a few days after their arrival and has left five small children, and his widow now pregnant. This family remains under the care of the Stewards subject to the future orders of the Society.

The *Lavinia* from Liverpool with thirty persons who have all paid their passage, and it is not apprehended that the Society will incur any expence on their account.

Philadelphia September 1st 1800

Signed on behalf of the Committee

John Evans

Adjourned

signed R. C. Jones, Sec^y protem

**At a Quarterly Meeting of the Welch Society
held December 1st 1800.**

Present

Robert Wharton
Caleb Foulke
Perigrine Wharton
Isaac H. Jackson
Joseph Price
R. Maris
Franklin Wharton
John Phillips
David Ellis
Morgan J. Rhees
C. Yeatman

William Jones
Richard Price
John Davis
Isaac Jones
William Meredith
John Evans
Joseph S. Lewis
Owen Foulke
John Owen
Richard Edwards
James Read

Organization: Acting President

Neither the President or Vice President being present Robert Wharton Esqr President

Membership: New Members

The following persons proposed at a former meeting were duly elected vizt

PART THREE

Thomas B. Zantzinger   proposed by Richd Maris
Thomas Jones   [proposed by] Isaac Jones

Assistance to Welsh Emigrants: Liaising with the Board of Health

A letter from Edward Garrigues, late President of the Board of Health,[22] respecting a charge for the accommodation of three Welch families at the Lazaretto was read.[23]

On motion, agreed that Robert Wharton, Jonathan Jones & Owen Foulke be a committee to confer with the Board of Health respecting their charge.

Annual Dinner

Resolved that the Stewards be directed to provide a dinner for the Society on the second day of March next at 3 o'clock and that they are directed to invite the officers of St George, St Andrew and Hibernian Societies, and such other persons as they may think proper not exceeding eight in number.

---

22 Edward Garrigues (1756–1845), a Quaker, of Cherry Street, Philadelphia, was a carpenter and master builder by trade, and elected to the Carpenters' Company in Philadelphia in 1793. Towards the end of the eighteenth century (c.1798) he was among the wealthiest citizens residing in the city. His wealth did not affect his humanitarian concern for the citizens of Philadelphia. He was known for his humanitarianism, especially during the yellow fever epidemic in 1798 and he was the President of the Philadelphia Board of Health between 1799 and 1800. See Historical Society of Pennsylvania, MS. Am.0895. Copy of a diary by Edward Garrigues, and transcribed by Anita DeClue and Billy G. Smith, 'Wrestling the "Pale Faced Messenger": The Diary of Edward Garrigues during the 1798 Philadelphia Yellow Fever Epidemic', *Pennsylvania History: A Journal of Mid-Atlantic Studies* (hereafter *PH*), 65, Special Supplemental Issue (1998), pp. 243–68.
23 The Lazaretto was the first quarantine station for the Port of Philadelphia.

Assistance to Welsh Emigrants

The acting committee report that the following cases have come under their notice since their last report vizt

The relief of Elizabeth Owen and family. That they found her in a very distressed situation with five small children and in a state of pregnancy. That they have taken a house for her accommodation for six months and furnished her with such other aid as appeared to be immediately necessary.

And they likewise found the family of Lewis Miles consisting of himself, wife and seven children in a very sickly state so as to create great alarm in the neighbourhood of their residence that they caused them to be removed to the Lazaretto where they will remain at the expence of the Society.

Also, the widow of Evan Richards and four small children.

And that the distresses of the above-mentioned families may in a great measure be attributed to the length and severity of their passage.

Adjourned to meet the second day of March next at 12 o'clock.

PART THREE

1801

At an Annual Meeting of the Welch Society held March 2nd 1801.

Present

Jonathan Jones
Michael Roberts
John M. Price
Joseph Price
James Crukshank
Thomas B. Zantzinger
Richard Edwards
William L. Maddock
P. H. Wharton
John Owen
William Read
William Smith
Richard Price
Isaac Jones

Joseph S. Lewis
James Read
Spafford Drury
Lewis Walker
Samuel Parish
Joshua L. Howell
Thomas Pickton
Thomas Cumpston
Saml Wetherill
Robert Wharton
Owen Foulke
Richard C. Jones
Caleb Foulke
James Rolph

Assistance to Welsh Emigrants: Liaising with Board of Health

The committee appointed to confer with the Board of Health respecting their charge, report that the Board of Health will not relinquish their demand.

On motion, agreed that the further consideration of the demand of the Board of Health be referred to the next quarterly meeting.

THE WELSH SOCIETY OF PHILADELPHIA, 1798–1839

Membership: New Members

The following persons were duly elected members of the Society

Samuel Humphreys	proposed by R. Edwards
Thomas Johns Honorary	[proposed by] M. J. Rhees
Edward Edwards	proposed by John Davis
Joseph Ball	[proposed by] Owen Foulke
Thomas Humphreys	
Jonathan Smith	[proposed by] Jon^a Jones
Pearson Hunt[24]	
Thomas Cadwallader	[proposed by] Owen Foulke
Lewis Jones Jardine	[proposed by] M. J. Rhees
Joseph Higbee	[proposed by] Jon^a Jones
Wilson Hunt	[proposed by] Genl Dickinson
James Hamilton	
William Hamilton	

Finance: Accounts

The Treasurer exhibited an account by which it appears that the sum of six hundred and ten dollars 68/^{100} has been disbursed since the first of March 1800, and a balance of sixty-four dollars 38/^{100} in favor of the Treasurer.

Discipline: Arrears in Contributions

On motion agreed that the Treasurer furnish the Stewards with the list of delinquents and that the Stewards notify each delinquent that unless the arrears respectively due from them, are discharged by the next quarterly meeting, their names be presented to the Society.

Adjourned

signed Owen Foulke Secretary

---

24   Pearson Hunt of Trenton, New Jersey (1766–4 November 1828)?

PART THREE

At a Quarterly Meeting of the Welch Society held June 1ˢᵗ 1801.

Present

Robert Wharton
Joseph S. Lewis
Lewis Walker
Isaac Jones
James Read
Joseph Price
John Owen
Samuel Parish
Owen Foulke
Thomas Cumpston
T. B. Zantzinger
David Evans Junʳ

Richard C. Jones
William Jones
William Ogden
Richard Price
Michael Roberts
Wᵐ Meredith
Joseph Simons
William Smith
Caleb Foulke
John Phillips

Assistance to Welsh Emigrants: Liaison with Board of Health

The Treasurer reported that he had paid the Board of Health their demand.

Membership: New Members

The following persons proposed at a former meeting were duly elected members of the Society

Joseph Huddle Junʳ   proposed by Robᵗ Wharton
The Revᵈ David Edwards   [proposed by] Thoˢ Pickton
Ezekiel C. Maddock   [proposed by] P. H. Wharton
Joshua Edwards   [proposed by] Owen Foulke
Joseph Petorris   [proposed by] James Read
Doctʳ Thoˢ Parke
Gideon H. Wells
James Gibson
Benjⁿ Chew Junʳ   [proposed by] P. Dickinson
Robert Thomas   [proposed by] John Davis

Discipline: Arrears in Contributions

On motion agreed that the acting committee inform the delinquents that if they do not pay their arrearages by the next quarterly meeting their conduct will be reported as disorderly and a question of expulsion taken thereon.

Adjourned

signed Owen Foulke Secretary

At a Meeting of the Welch Society held September 7th 1801.

Present

Robert Wharton
James Read
John Phillips
Richard C. Jones
William Jones
Owen Foulke
Henry Jenkins
John Evans
John Davis

Joshua L. Howell
Thomas Pickton
Peter Evans
Michael Roberts
Benjamin Price
Caleb Foulke
William Ogden
James Gibson

Organization: Meeting Not Quorate

Adjourned for want of a quorum to proceed to business.

signed Owen Foulke Secretary

At a Meeting of the Welch Society held December 7th 1801.

Present

Richard Price	Griffith Evans
William W. Smith	Jonathan Smith
Thos Cumpston	John Evans
Richard C. Jones	Isaac Jones
Thomas Humphreys	Joseph Price
Joseph Huddle Junr	J. Crukshank
Owen Foulke	Thomas Jones
Henry Jenkins	Joseph S. Lewis
William Ogden	John Owen
John Phillips	Caleb Foulke
Michael Roberts	Lewis Walker

Membership: New Members

The following persons proposed at a former meeting were duly elected

Richard Peters Junr	proposed by Thos Cumpston
Thomas W. Jones	[proposed by] Joseph Simons
Henry Jenkins	[proposed by] Thos Cumpston
William Tilghman	
Evan Thomas of New Castle	[proposed by] Richard C. Jones
Jacob Broome of Wilmington an Honorary Member	

Membership: Honorary Membership – Jacob Broome of Wilmington for Assistance to Welsh Emigrants

Resolved that Jacob Broome of Wilmington who being elected an Honorary Member of the Society be presented with a framed certificate for his humane attention to the Welch emigrants who arrived at Wilmington in the Ship *Liberty*.

Assistance to Welsh Emigrants: Work of Dr Thomas C. James

Resolved that the thanks of the Society be publickly given to Doctor Thomas C. James for his humane attention to the unfortunate sick emigrants at the City Hospital on the banks of Schuylkill and that the acting committee on behalf of the Society present him with a piece of silver plate with one hundred fifty dollars.

Organization: Amendments to the Constitution

Whereas it has been found extremely inconvenient in transacting the business of the Society on account of the 4th Section of the Constitution requiring that 21 members be a quorum. Therefore, resolved that John Evans, Richard C. Jones, Joseph S. Lewis, Griffith Evans and Jonathan Smith be a committee to consider and report any alterations in the Constitution of the Society for the purpose of having the same incorporated.

Organization: Acting Committee Report

The acting committee reported their proceedings since the first of June last which was approved by the Society.

Annual Dinner

Resolved that the Stewards be directed have a dinner provided on the 1st March for the Society and that they are directed to invite the officers of St George's, St Andrew's and Hibernican Societies and such other persons as they think proper not exceeding eight in number.

Adjourned

signed Owen Foulke Secretary

PART THREE

1802

At an Annual Meeting of the Welch Society held at Francis Hotel[25] March 1ˢᵗ 1802.

Present

Samˡ Meredith
Robert Wharton
Richard Price
Joseph Price
Morgan J. Rhees
John Evans
Griffith Evans
Franklin Wharton
Doct Jos. Strong
Joshua L. Howell
Isaac Jones

John Owen
William Jones
John Lewis
William Meredith
Joseph S. Lewis
Samuel Parrish
Thomas B. Zantzinger
Thomas Jones
Jonathan Smith
Thoˢ Cadwallader
Henry Jenkins
Richard C. Jones

The acting committee reported that since their last report to which they begged leave to refer the Society little business had occurred worthy of attention. That they have relieved a distressed widow of the house of Thomas Philips and also a man affected with a lame arm.

The Treasurer reported his accounts. Balance in his favor $2.16.

---

25 Presumably, this was John Francis's Union Hotel on Market Street. It was originally built in 1767 by Mary Lawrence Masters. Five years later it was used by Richard Penn as the Governor's Mansion for the colony of Pennsylvania. It was later the British headquarters of General Sir William Howe (1777–8), while after c.1780 it was briefly owned by Robert Morris. Morris conducted his work in the building as the Superintendent of Finance before it was rented for the use of Presidents George Washington (1790–7) and John Adams (1797–1800).

The committee appointed to revise the Constitution reported the form as printed which was unanimously adopted.

On motion of Mr Jonathan Smith resolved that a committee be appointed to apply to the proper authorities for the purpose of having the Society Incorporated.

Whereupon the acting committee were directed to attend to this business.

Membership: New Members

The following gentlemen were unanimously elected

Isaac Jones   proposed by Thomas Cumpston
Thomas Biddle   [proposed by] Richd C. Jones

Organization: Election of Officers

The election of officers being entered into & closed the following gentlemen were returned duly elected

President   Samuel Meredith
Vice President Robert Wharton
Treasurer   Thomas Cumpston
Secretary   Richard C. Jones
Register   Joseph S. Lewis
Stewards   Michael Roberts
                John Evans
                Isaac Jones
                Richard Price
                William Jones
                Jonathan Smith
                James Cruckshanks

Adjourned

signed Richard C. Jones Secr^y

PART THREE

At a Quarterly Meeting of the Welch Society held at William Ogdens June 7th 1802.

Present

Samuel Meredith
William Jones
John Evans
James Rolph
Jon^a Smith
Joseph S. Lewis
John Philips
James Cruckshank

Franklin Wharton
Lewis Walker
Joshua L. Howell
Joseph Price
Dr Parke
Henry Jenkins
William Ogden
Richard C. Jones

Organization: Act of Incorporation / Assistance to Welsh Emigrants

The acting committee reported that agreeably to the directions of the Society they have procured the Act of Incorporation which is now laid before them with a copy of the Bye-Laws thereto annexed and having relieved several persons whose necessities required assistance.

Finance: Limited Funds

They further report that from the Treasurers accounts the finances of the Society are in very low state and that he and several other individuals are in advance.

June 7th 1802

John Evans Chairman

Organization: Honorary Members

On motion resolved that the members who are not residents of this State and those whose names have from the necessity of the case been excluded from the Charter of Incorporation shall be considered and established as honorary members of this Society.

113

Membership: New Members

The following gentlemen were proposed as members

Zacha[h] Poulson	[proposed] by Richard C. Jones
Robert Frazer	[proposed by] Jonathan Smith
George Biddle	[proposed by] Richard C. Jones
Capt. Jos. Meredith	[proposed by] William Ogden
John Moore White	[proposed by] Joshua L. Howell

Assistance to Welsh Emigrants

On motion of Mr Jonathan Smith seconded by Mr Joseph S. Lewis

As the acting committee have reported that the Society is largely indebted to the Treasurer and other members of that committee and as it is probable that the Society may be called upon ere long for large sums of money to assist the emigrants that may be expected daily to arrive. Therefore, resolved that it be recommended to the individual members of this Society to contribute a sum sufficient to discharge the debt already contracted by them and also to raise a further sum to aid the usual funds of this Society.

On motion, resolved that Mess[rs] Ja[s] Cruckshanks, Jonathan Smith, John Evans, Robert Wharton, Col. Joshua L. Howel, Aaron D. Woodruff, Ja[s] S. Lewis and Richard C. Jones be a committee to call upon the members respectively for the purpose mentioned in the foregoing resolution.

Adjourned

signed Rich[d] C. Jones Sec[y]

PART THREE

At a Meeting of the Welch Society held at John Dunwoodys[26] Septr 6th 1802.

Present

Doct^r Thomas Parke Richard Price
James Cruckshank Robert Wharton
Thomas Humphreys Richard C. Jones

Organization: Election of Temporary President

Richard Price was elected President pro tem.

Organization: Not Quorate

There not being a quorum to transact business it was moved to adjourn. The members therefore adjourned

signed Richard C. Jones Secretary

At a Quarterly Meeting of the Welch Society held at Wm Ogdens on Monday the 6th of December 1802.

Present

Robert Wharton J. Clifften
John Evans Richd C. Jones
Isaac Jones J. Cruckshank
Joseph S. Lewis Dr Parke
Clem^t Humphreys H. Jenkins
Capt. J. Wharton Richard Price
T. B. Zantzinger Jonathan Smith
Joseph Huddle Saml Humphreys
Thomas Wharton Thomas Cumpston
Thos Cadwallader William Ogden
Capt. Michael

---

26 This would have been Dunwoody's Tavern on Market Street.

Finance: Collections and Accounts

The collecting committee reported progress and were continuing.

The acting committee reported that since their last report to the Society, noting material had occurred. That the Treasurer had reported to them his accounts as follows

Balance in his favour $217.25

Besides which there is due to individuals for advances made by them as follows

	$
To Robert Wharton	50
Isaac Jones	25
John Evans	25
Michael Roberts	25
	125
	342.25

signed by Joseph S. Lewis

Register

Finance: Arrears in Contributions and Expulsion

On motion, resolved that the following be recommended to the next meeting to be passed into a Bye-Law of this Society. vizt

That it shall be the duty of the Secretary to give notice to such members who are in arrears to the Society for more than twelve months, that unless they pay up their fines and contributions &c. within three months after the notice shall be given that their names will be reported to the Society for expulsion as provided for by the Constitution.

Organization: Purchasing of a Minute Book

Resolved that the Secretary be authorized to procure a book for the fair entry of the minutes of this Society.

Annual Dinner

On motion made and seconded resolved that the acting committee be directed to provide a dinner on the first of March for the Society and that they are directed to invite the officers of St George's, St Andrew's and Hibernian Societies and such other persons as they think proper not exceeding eight in number.

Membership: New Members

The following gentlemen were proposed as members

Robert Waln	[proposed] by Thomas Cumpston
Collinson Read	
James C. Fisher	
David Lewis	
Samuel Nicholas	[proposed] by Richard C. Jones
Reece Lewis	
Chas Marshall Junr	
Joseph Smith	
Joshua Fisher	
George Reinholdt	[proposed] by Jonathan Jones

The following gentlemen were elected as members of this Society

Zachariah Poulson
Robert Frazer
George Biddle
Capt Joseph Michael
John Moore White Honorary

Adjourned

signed Richd C. Jones

1803

At an Annual Meeting of the Welch Society held at John Hain[e]s's the first of March 1803.

Members Present

Joseph Bell
Thos Cumpston
Ja^s Cruckshanks
Griffith Evans
Robert Frazer
John Haines
Thos Humphreys
Capt Wm Jones
Jonathan Jones
Richard C. Jones
Richard Price
Joseph Price
Dr Thos Parke
Zach^a Poulson
James Rolph
Jonathan Smith
Joshua L. Howell

Robt Wharton Vice Pres'dt
Isaac Jones
William Jones
Thomas Jones
Henry Jenkins
Isaac Jones Tob^a
John Lewis
Joseph S. Lewis
Richard Maris
Richd H. Morris
Jos. P. Norris
John M. Price
John J. Parry
Richd Peters Junr
James Read
William Smith
Robert Thomas

Organization: No Formal Business

The acting committee reported that agreeably to the Constitution they had met from time to time and attended to such business as had occurred; but had nothing to mention particularly deserving the notice of the Society.

Treasurer's Accounts

The Treasurer reported his accounts which were examined. Balance in favour of the Society $8.75.

PART THREE

Organization: Bye-Law – Fines and Expulsion for Non-Payment of Fees

The following resolution was enacted into a Bye-Law and is recorded accordingly vizt

BYE LAW That it shall be the duty of the Secretary to give notice to such members who are in arrears to the Society for more than twelve months. That unless they pay up their fines and contributions & within three months after the notice shall be given. Their names shall be reported to the Society for expulsion as provided for by the Constitution.

Membership: New Members

The following gentlemen nominated at the last meeting were elected members of this Society.

Robert Waln
Collinson Read
James C. Fisher
David Lewis
Samuel Nichols

Reece Lewis
Chas Marshall Jun[r]
Joseph Smith
Joshua Fisher
George Reinholdt

The following gentlemen were proposed as members to be balloted for at next meeting

John C. Jones
John Wistar
John F. Mifflin
Joseph Hopkinson
Thomas Flynson
John Dowers Jun[r]
Abner Woodruff
Jesse Sharpless
Edmund Kinzey

proposed by Isaac Jones
[proposed by] Robert Wharton
[proposed by] Thomas Cumpston

not [proposed by] James Rolph hon[ry]
[proposed by] George Thompson
[proposed by] Mich[l] Roberts Honry
[proposed by] Robert Wharton
[proposed by] William Jones

Organization: Election of Officers

The election being entered into and closed the following gentlemen were returned duly elected

President	Samuel Meredith
Vice President	Robert Wharton
Treasurer	Thomas Cumpston
Secretary	Richard C. Jones
Register	Joseph S. Lewis
Stewards	John Evans
	Michael Roberts
	Isaac Jones
	Jonathan Smith
	Richard Price
	William Jones
	James Cruckshanks
Counsellors	Benjamin R. Morgan
Physicians	Edward Tilghman
	Doct[r] Thomas C James
	Doct[r] Joseph Strong

Adjourned

signed Richard C. Jones Sec[y]

PART THREE

Welch Society[27]

At a Quarterly Meeting of the Welch Society held at William Ogdens June 6th 1803.

Members Present

Thomas Cumpston
James Cruckshank
John Evans
Doct^r Thomas C. James
Isaac Jones
William Jones
Henry Jenkins
Joseph S. Lewis
Reece Lewis

William Maddock
William Ogden
Richard Price
Benjamin Price
Dr Thomas Parke
Zachariah Poulson Junr
James Read
Collinson Read
Jonathan Smith

Acting Committee Report and Assistance to Welsh Emigrants

The acting committee reported that since the last meeting they have relieved a family in extreme distress in North Second Street and that they are still under the care of the Society.

John Evans has received eight pounds sterling on account of the children of Richard Jones who died at the Lazaretto 25th August 1801. He has been requested by the committee to hold the same in his hands for the use of the heirs of the said Jones.

The committee being informed that certain wages due to Mary Philips from the services of her two servants are unjustly detained from her and conceiving that as she was under the care of the Society it would be proper to interfere in her behalf have appointed a committee for that purpose who now have the business under their care.

---

27 The minutes now specify 'Welch [*sic*] Society' before the meeting is recorded.

Finance: A Call for Supplementary Funds

The committee appointed on the 7th June 1802 to solicit contributions from the members in aid of the funds of the Society report that they have called on nearly all the members and have received the following sums – there are a few yet to be called in on whom they expect to see before the next meeting

	$
James Cruckshank John Evans and Isaac Jones	121
Robert Wharton	62
Joseph S. Lewis	35
	218

the committee was continued.

Organization: Bye-Law – Fines for Non-Payment of Fees

On motion resolved that the following be recommended to the next meeting to be passed into a Bye-Law of this Society.

Whereas provision has not been made in the Act of Incorporation for the collection of fines from the members absenting themselves from the meetings of the Society – Therefore resolved that every member who shall be absent at any quarterly or special meeting shall forfeit and pay fifty cents and for every such absence at an annual meeting one dollar for the use of the Society.

Membership: New Members

The following gentlemen were elected members of this Society

John C. Jones
John Wistar
John F. Mifflin

Joseph Hopkinson
John Dowers Jun[r]
Abner Woodruff

PART THREE

George W. Morgan was proposed as a member to be balloted for at the next meeting by Wm Ogden

Adjourned

signed Rich. C. Jones Secretary

Welch Society

At a Meeting of the Welch Society held at William Ogdens September 5th 1803.

Members Present

Richard Rice
Isaac Jones
Dr Joseph Strong
Thomas Cumpston
Zach^a Poulson
John C. Jones
William Jones
Edmund Kinsey
Richard C. Jones

Ezekiel C. Maddock
Henry Jenkins
Robert Wharton
Rich. Hill Morris
John Parry
Thomas Morris
Dr Thomas Parke
Franklin Wharton

Finance

The committee appointed to receive contributions were continued.

Finance: Treasurer's Accounts

The Treasurer reported his accounts balance in favour of the Society $248.63.

Organization: Bye-Law – Annual Membership Fee

On motion resolved that the following be recommended to the Society to be passed as a Bye-Law

Whereas provision has not been made in the Act of Incorporation for the collection of the Annual Contribution – Therefore resolved that the contribution to be paid annually by each member for the use of the Society shall be $2 to be collected and paid into the hands of the Treasurer.

Membership: New Member

George W. Morgan was elected a member

Adjourned

signed Rich[d] C. Jones Sec[y]

Welch Society

At a Meeting of the Welch Society held at William Ogdens December 5th 1803.

Members Present

Robert Wharton
Richard Price
Jon[a] Smith
Joseph S. Lewis
Joseph Price
Richard C. Jones
Benjamin Price
Michael Roberts
Zach[a] Poulson
W[m] L. Maddock
Robert Frazer
James Cruckshank
James Wistar
John C. Jones
Griffith Evans

Sam[l] Meredith
Capt F. Wharton
John Cliffton
Joseph Smith
Dr Thomas Parke
Dr Thomas C. James
Collinson Read
Samuel Parrish
Reece Lewis
Perigrine H. Wharton
Henry Jenkins
Richard Maris
Joseph Hopkinson
Jesse Sharpless

PART THREE

Finance

On motion resolved that the committee for receiving contributions be discontinued.

The acting committee reported that they had met once since the last meeting but that nothing material requiring the attention of the committee had occurred.

Assistance to Welsh Emigrants

Thomas Cumpston informed the committee that in the month of August last a Welch man of the name of Joshua Sylvanus was afflicted with lunacy in consequence of a stroke from the sun and that he was taken to the hospital where he died in two days. The committee desired T. Cumpston to pay the expences attending the business amounting to $5.50.

Organization: Bye-Law – Annual Membership Fee

The following resolution was passed as a

BYE LAW

Whereas provision has not been made in the Act of Incorporation for the collection of the Annual Contribution. Therefore, resolved that the contribution to be paid annually by each member for the use of the Society shall be two dollars to be collected and paid into the hands of the Treasurer.

Annual Dinner

On motion of Collinson Read Esq[r] resolved that the acting committee be directed to provide a dinner on the first of March for the Society and that they be directed to invite the officers of St George's, St Andrew's and Hibernian Societies, and such other persons as they think proper not exceeding eight in number.

Membership: New Members

The following gentlemen were proposed as members

Joseph Shaw [proposed] by Joseph Smith
James Prosser [proposed by] Joseph Price
Charles Chauncey [proposed by] Thomas Jones
Elihu Chauncey
Thomas Hale [proposed by] Thomas Biddle

Adjourned

signed Rich[d] C. Jones Secretary

PART THREE

1804
Welch Society

At an Annual Meeting of the Welch Society held at Francis Hotel March 1st 1804.

Members Present

Samuel Meredith
Robert Wharton
Richard Price
Jonathan Smith
Thomas Biddle
Thomas Cumpston
James Cruckshank
Griffith Evans
Robert Frazer
Thomas Humphreys
Joseph Price
Dr Thomas Parke
James Rolph
Dr Joseph Strong
William W. Smith
Dr Thos C. James
Isaac Jones
Thomas Jones
Thomas Cadwallader

Henry Jenkins
Isaac Jones Tob.
Joseph S. Lewis
Reece Lewis
Richard Maris
Richard H. Morris
John J. Parry
Zachariah Poulson
James Read
Joseph Smith
Jesse Sharpless
Lewis Walker
Lloyd Jones
Chandler Price
Franklin Wharton
John Cliffton
William Meredith
William Jones

Assistance to Welsh Emigrants

The acting committee reported that they had met from time to time as the affairs of the Society required but had but one call on their charity since their last report when relief was afforded to the amount of D[rs28] 5.

---

28   Dollars.

Finance: Accounts

The Treasurer reported his account for the last year balance due to the Society $319.31

Membership: New Members

The following gentlemen nominated at the last meeting were elected members vizt

James Prosser
Charles Chauncey
Elihu Chauncey

Joseph Shaw
Thomas Hale

Organization: Election of Officers

The election being entered into and closed the following gentlemen were returned duly elected

President	Samuel Meredith
Vice President	Robert Wharton
Treasurer	Thomas Cumpston
Secretary	Richard C. Jones
Register	Joseph S. Lewis
Stewards	Richard Price
	John Evans
	Michael Roberts
	Isaac Jones
	Jonathan Smith
	James Cruckshank
	John M. Price
Physicians	Doct^r Thomas C. James
	Joseph Strong
Counsellors	Benjamin R. Morgan
	Robert Frazer

Adjourned

signed Richard C. Jones Secretary

By Jos. S. Lewis

PART THREE

Welch Society

At a Quarterly Meeting of the Welch Society held at Hardy's Hotel[29] June 4th 1804.

Members Present

Thomas Cumpston
Richard Price
Joseph S. Lewis
Dr Thos Parke
James Cruckshank
Elihu Chauncey
Edmund Kinsey
Joseph Price
Henry Jenkins

Joseph Smith
John C. Jones
William Jones
Griffith Evans
William L. Maddock
Reece Lewis
James Prosser
Richard Maris

Organization: No Formal Business

The acting committee reported that since the last meeting they had attended to the duties of the Society but that nothing particular had occurred to communicate to the Society.

Organization: Bye-Laws and Fines

On motion of Joseph S. Lewis, seconded by James Cruckshank the following resolution was submitted for the consideration of the Society to be passed as a Bye- Law.

Whereas there appears an obscurity in the Sixth Article of the Constitution with respect to the fines. Therefore, resolved that in future the fine for non-attendance at roll call shall be twenty-five cents and for total absence fifty cents except at the Annual Meeting when the fines shall be doubled.

Finance: Accounts

The Treasurer reported his accounts balance in favor of the Society $347.4/[100]

---

29 This was 98 Market Street, Philadelphia.

Membership: New Members

Joseph Williams was proposed by Mich[l] Roberts
Enos Bronson [proposed] by Griffith Evans
Adjourned

signed Richard C. Jones Secretary

Welch Society

At a Quarterly Meeting of the Welch Society held at Hardys Hotel September 3rd 1804.

Members Present

John Evans	John C. Jones
Richard Price	Charles Chauncey
Robert Frazer	Richard Maris
Isaac Jones	Henry Jenkins
Dr Thomas C. James	Thomas Cumpston
Dr Thomas Parke	Elihu Chauncey
Zacha[h] Poulson	William Jones
John Phillips	Joseph Smith
Thomas Jones	Richard C. Jones

Organization: Meeting not Quorate

There not being a constitutional quorum to enact Bye-Laws the resolution proposed at the last meeting was defer[r]ed for further consideration.

Assistance to Welsh Emigrants

Richard C. Jones represented to the Society the situation of a certain Thomas Thomas who requested a loan might be granted him. Whereupon it was resolved that the Secretary be directed to draw upon the Treasurer for $20 as a loan to the said Thomas Thomas.

PART THREE

Membership: New Members
Joseph Williams and Enos Bronson were elected members.
Adjourned
signed Richd C. Jones Sec^y

Welch Society
At a Meeting of the Welch Society held at Hardy's Hotel
December 3rd 1804.

Members Present

Robert Wharton	Isaac Jones
Thos Cumpston	Jonathan Smith
Richard Price	Joseph Smith
W. W. Smith	Griffith Evans
John M. Price	Joseph S. Lewis
Doct^r Strong	Reece Lewis
Zach^a Poulson	John Morgan
Jesse Sharpless	Ja^s Cruckshank
Henry Jenkins	John C. Jones
Thomas Jones	John Prosser
Doct^r Parke	Richard C. Jones
Robert Frazer	

Organization: Amendment to Bye-Laws
The resolution brought forward as a Bye-Law was rejected.

Assistance to Welsh Emigrants
The acting committee reported that since the last meeting of the Society there had been but one case of distress under their notice vizt Edward Price a Welchman whom they found destitute in every respect, they accordingly took him under their protection and advanced him $20 and appointed a committee to procure him a passage to the West Indies.

Finance: Accounts

The Treasurer reported his accounts. Balance in favour of the Society $341.4/^{100}

Annual Dinner

On motion resolved that the acting committee be directed to provide a dinner on the first of March for the Society and that they are directed to invite the officers of St George's, St Andrew's and Hibernian Societies and such other persons as they think proper not exceeding eight in number.

Membership: New Members

Joshua Gilpin proposed [by] David Lewis
Charles Wistar [proposed by] John M. Price

Adjourned

signed Rich[d] C. Jones Secretary

PART THREE

1805
Welch Society

At an Annual Meeting of the Welch Society held at Francis's Hotel March 1st 1805.

Members Present

Samuel Meredith
Robert Wharton
Thomas Cumpston
Joseph S. Lewis
Isaac Jones
James Read
Richard Maris
Isaac Jones (Tob^a)
Dr Thos C. James
William Meredith
Zach^a Poulson
Thomas Biddle
Thos Cadwallader
Reece Lewis
Joseph Price
Richd C. Jones

John Philips
Enos Bronson
Benjn R. Morgan
Elihu Chauncey
James Cruckshank
David Lewis
Thos B. Zantzinger
John C. Jones
Henry Jenkins
Robert Thomas
Doct^r Strong
Thos Humphreys
Richard Price
Jesse Sharpless
John M. Price

Membership: New Members

The following gentlemen were balloted for and duly elected vizt

Joshua Gilpin
Charles Wistar

Assistance to Welsh Emigrants

The acting committee reported that since the last meeting of the Society they have met from time to time, have relieved such cases of distress as came under their notice and have transacted generally such business as they found requisite without however having anything requiring to be particularized to the Society.

Treasurer's accounts

The Treasurer reported his accounts. Balance in favour of the Society $317.94

Finance: Accounts

On motion of Robert Wharton Esqr seconded by Thomas Cumpston Esqr the following resolution was adopted

Whereas by the Treasurers account there appears a balance in favour of the Society. Therefore, resolved that the acting committee be directed to dispose of it and such future sums as may be received in such way as shall appear to them most conducive to the interest of the Society.

Discipline: Expulsion of a Member

The following note being handed to the chair and duly seconded was directed to be entered on the minutes.

To the President of the Welch Society

Sir

I move that James Rolph a member be expelled from said Society for various reasons

yours with respect

Robt Thomas

March 1st 1805

Organization: Election of Officers

The President having left the chair in order that the members might enter upon the election. Benjn R. Morgan Esqr was chosen chairman and

PART THREE

Doct. Thomas C. James and Reece Lewis appointed Tellers. After the election was gone through the certificate was handed to the Secretary for record

We whose names are hereunto subscribed certify that the foregoing and annexed lists contain the names of the members of the Welch Society who voted at an election of officers for the same held March 1st 1805 at Francis's Hotel that the following gentlemen were duly elected to the several offices over their respective names mentioned

Benjn R. Morgan   Chairman

Thomas C. James   Tellers
Reese Lewis

President   Samuel Meredith
Vice President   Robert Wharton
Treasurer   Thomas Cumpston
Secretary   Rich. C. Jones
Register   Joseph S. Lewis
Stewards   John Evans
                          Richard Price
                          Isaac Jones
                          Jonathan Smith
                          James Cruckshank
                          John M. Price
                          Thomas Parke
Physicians   Doct. Thomas C. James
                          Doct[or] Joseph Strong
Counsellors   Benjamin R. Morgan
                          Edward Tilghman

Adjourned

signed Richd C. Jones Sec^y

Welch Society

At a Quarterly Meeting of the Welch Society held at Hardys Hotel June 3rd 1805.

Members Present

Samuel Meredith
Thomas Cumpston
Jonathan Smith
Isaac Jones
James Cruckshank
Thomas Cadwalader
Thomas Biddle
Doctor Strong
Robert Thomas
Perigrine H. Wharton
Edmund Kinsey
John Evans
Doctor Parke
Joseph Price
John Morgan
Samuel Humphreys

Robert Wharton
Joseph Hopkinson
Lewis Walker
John Philips
Elihu Chauncey
Samuel Parrish
Enos Bronson
Griffith Evans
John C. Jones
Richard Price
George Thompson
Richard C. Jones
Joseph Smith
James Rolph
Zach[a] Poulson
William Meredith

Assistance to Welsh Emigrants

The acting committee reported that they have since the last meeting of the Society attended to their duty and have relieved such cases of distress as came under their notice, but at present have nothing to communicate that requires the attention of the Society.

Finance: Accounts

The Treasurer reported his accounts. Balance in favor of the Society $293.94

PART THREE

Discipline: Expulsion of a Member

On motion of Jonathan Smith seconded by Isaac Jones resolved that the consideration of the charge against James Rolph be postponed.

Adjourned

signed Richd C. Jones Sec^y

Welch Society

At a Quarterly Meeting of the Welch Society held at Hardys Hotel September 2nd 1805.

Members Present

Robert Wharton
James Cruckshanks
Richard Maris
Doctor Strong
Edmund Kinsey
Joseph S. Lewis
Richard C. Jones
John Philips
Joseph Price
Jonathan Smith

Joseph Smith
John C. Jones
Henry Jenkins
Zach^a Poulson
Jesse Sharpless
James Prosser
Samuel Parrish
Thomas B. Zantzinger
Richard Price
John Wharton

Organization: Acting Committee Report

The acting committee reported that they have since the last meeting of the Society attended to such business as had occurred but had nothing interesting to communicate.

Sept 2nd 1805

(signed) Jos. S. Lewis Reg^r

Discipline: Expulsion of a Member

The Secretary reported that agreeably to the duty enjoined on him by the Bye-Law passed the first of March 1803 he had given notice to William Preston that unless his fines and contributions were paid his name would be reported to the Society for expulsion.

Whereupon a motion of Joseph S. Lewis seconded by Jonathan Smith it was resolved that the Secretary shall give notice to William Preston that unless he complies with the regulations of the Society with which he was furnished in May last he will be expelled at the next meeting.

Membership: New Members

Members proposed

Matthew L. Beaven	[proposed] by Joseph Smith
Levi Paulin	[proposed] by Jona[than] Jones

Adjourned

signed Rich. C. Jones Sec^y

Welch Society

At a Quarterly Meeting of the Welch Society held at Hardys Hotel December 2nd 1805.

Members Present

Jonathan Smith	Edmund Kinsey
Richard Price	Geo. W. Morgan
Dr Thos Parke	Joseph Smith
James Cruckshank	Griffith Evans
John C. Jones	Samuel Nicholas
Zach^a Poulson	Henry Jenkins
Richard Maris	William W. Smith
Thomas Jones	Peter Evans
Joseph Price	Richard C. Jones

Thomas Wharton Samuel Parrish
Joseph Huddle James Prosser
Collinson Read

Discipline: Expulsion of a Member

The acting committee reported that they and their sub-committee had attended their different duties, but nothing requiring the attention of the Society has come within their notices. Except that William Preston having neglected to pay his fines and contributions agreeably to a resolution of the Society at their last meeting, they beg leave to recommend the following resolution

Resolved that William Preston be expelled from the Society.

Whereupon it was resolved that William Preston be expelled and hereafter no longer be considered a member of this Society.

Annual Dinner

On motion made and seconded. Resolved that the acting committee be directed to provide a dinner on the first of March for the Society and that they are directed to invite the officers of St George's, St Andrew's & Hibernian Societies, and such other persons as they think proper not exceeding eight in number.

Membership: New Members

The following gentlemen were proposed as members

William Craig [proposed] by Thomas Jones
William Tatem [proposed by] Thos Cumpston
Samuel Relf [proposed by] Jonathan Smith
John Harrison
George Gillaspy [proposed by] Enos Bronson
Tristram B. Freeman [proposed by] Chandler Price

Adjourned

signed Rich. C. Jones Sec^y

1806
Welch Society

At an Annual Meeting of the Welch Society held at Vogdes Hotel, March 1st 1806.

Members Present

Samuel Meredith
Robert Wharton
Thomas Cumpston
Jon.ᵃ Jones
Joseph S. Lewis
James Read
W.ᵐ W. Smith
Doct.ʳ Parke
Thomas Hale
Zach.ᵃ Poulson
Jos. P. Norris
Doctor Strong
Samuel Clarke
Reece Lewis
T. B. Zantzinger
Enos Bronson
Jesse Sharpless
Samuel Parrish
Thomas Biddle
Robert Frazer

Joseph Huddle Jr
Edmund Kinsey
Elihu Chauncey
Charles Chauncey
John M. Price
Richard Price
Chandler Price
George W. Morgan
John C. Jones
Joseph Smith
Doctor James
Thomas Humphreys
Capt. Michael
John Phillips
Charles Wistar
S. Wetherill Jr
Joseph Price
Lewis Walker
Henry Jenkins
Rich. C. Jones

Assistance to Welsh Emigrants: Orphans

The acting committee reported that since the last meeting they have attended to the general business of the Society. That their Orphan Committee have had the following children bound in proper situations vizt

Thomas Harris
Richard Jones
John Jones

Annual Dinner

And that agreeably to the directions of the Society they have caused a dinner to be provided at this place which will be on table at 3 o'clock

Finance: Accounts

The Treasurer reported his accounts. Balance in favour of the Society $409.62

Organization: Election of Officers

The President having left the chair in order that the members might enter upon the election of officers. Mr Enos Bronson was chosen Chairman and Messrs Thomas Barton Zantzinger and Reece Lewis were appointed Tellers. After the election was gone through the following certificate was handed to the Secretary for record.

Philad^a March 1st 1806

We whose names are hereunto subscribed certify that the foregoing and annexed lists contain the names of the members of the Welch Society who voted at an election of officers for the same held 1st March 1806 at the Shakspeare Hotel,[30] and that the following gentlemen were duly elected to the several offices mentioned over their respective names

signed

Enos Bronson	Chairman
Thos B. Zantzinger	Tellers
Reece Lewis	

---

30   Located at the north-west corner of Sixth and Chestnut Streets.

President   Samuel Meredith
Vice President   Robert Wharton
Treasurer   Thomas Cumpston
Secretary   Richard C. Jones
Register   Joseph S. Lewis
Physicians   Doctor James
    Doctor Strong
Counsellors   Edward Tilghman
    Benjamin R. Morgan
Stewards   John Evans
    Richard Price
    Isaac Jones
    Jonathan Smith
    Dr Thomas Parke
    James Cruckshank
    Chandler Price

Membership: New Members

The chair being resumed by the President the following gentlemen propose at a former meeting were elected members of this Society vizt

William Craig
William Tatem
Samuel Relf
John Harrison
George Gillasspy
Tristram B. Freeman

Adjourned

signed Rich[d] C. Jones Sec[y]

PART THREE

Welch Society

At a Quarterly Meeting of the Welch Society held at Hardys Hotel, June 2nd 1806.

Members Present

Robert Wharton
Jon^a Smith
Doct^r Parke
Isaac Jones
Richard Price
Ja^s Cruckshank
Doctor Strong
Enos Bronson
Elihu Chauncey
John Clifton
Griffith Evans

Lewis Walker
Joseph Price
Charles Chauncey
Thomas Jones
Richard Maris
Joseph Smith
T. B. Zantzinger
Henry Jenkins
John Philips
Richard C. Jones

Organization: Meeting Adjournment

The Treasurer and Register being absent no report was received either from the acting committee or the Treasurer therefore the Society adjourned.

Membership: New Member

Isachar Evans was proposed as a member of the Society by T. Cumpston

signed Rich C. Jones Sec^y

Welch Society

At a Quarterly Meeting of the Welch Society held at Kenedys Hotel, September 1st 1806.

Members Present

Robert Wharton
Jonathan Smith
Isaac Jones
Doctor Parke
Richard Price
Thos Cumpston
Chandler Price
Ja^s Cruckshank
Elihu Chauncey
Robert Frazer
Thomas Biddle
Joseph Price

Joseph Smith
Richard Maris
Jesse Sharpless
John Jones C.
Isaac Jones Tob.
Z. Poulson
Lewis Walker
Edmund Kinzey
Matthew L. Beavan
John Philips
Henry Jenkins
Richard C. Jones

Finance: Accounts

The Treasurer reported his accounts stating four shares of Water Loan to the credit of the Society and a balance of $147.54 cash.

Assistance to Welsh Emigrants: Dispute Concerning an Orphaned Apprentice

The Orphan Committee reported that the difference between Richard Lloyd & the Society respecting his apprentice lad Richard Jones is referred by Rule of Court to Thomas Norton and John Palmer.

Membership: New Members

Iscahar Evans   proposed by Thos Cumpston was elected as a member.
Isaac H. Jones proposed by Isaac Jones (Tob^a)
Adjourned

(signed) Richd C. Jones, Sec^y

PART THREE

Welch Society

At a Meeting of the Welch Society held at the City Hotel late Hardys, December 1ˢᵗ 1806.

Members Present

Robert Wharton
Jaˢ Cruckshank
Richard Maris
Thomas Wharton
Doctor Parke
Zachaʰ Poulson
John Davies
Robert Frazer
Henry Jenkins
Edmund Kinzey
Joseph Price

Richard Price
Jonathan Smith
John Clifton
Isaac Jones
Matthew L. Beavan
Captain Michael
Geo. W. Morgan
John Harrison
William Craig
Richard C. Jones

Finance: Accounts

The Treasurer reported his accounts. Balance in cash in favour of the Society $147.04

Assistance to Welsh Emigrants: Dispute Concerning an Orphaned Apprentice

The Orphan Committee reported that the difference between the Society and Richard Lloyd of Darby had been settled against them.

Annual Dinner

On motion resolved that the acting committee be directed to provide a dinner on the first of March and that they are directed to invite the officers of the St George's, St Andrew's and Hibernian Societies and such other persons as they might think proper not exceeding eight in number.

Membership: New Members

Isaac H. Jones proposed at a former meeting was duly elected a member.

The following gentlemen were proposed as members of this Society

Samuel W. Jones [proposed] by William Craig
Samuel N. Lewis [proposed] by Richard C. Jones
Jesse Johns Hon^y [proposed] by Robert Frazer

Adjourned

Signed Rich. C. Jones Sec^y

PART THREE

1807
Welch Society

At an Annual Meeting of the Welch Society held at the Mansion House, February 28th 1807.

Members Present

Samuel Meredith
Robert Wharton
Joseph S. Lewis
Jonathan Smith
Thomas Wharton
Thomas Jones
William Craig
Isaac H. Jones
John Jones (Tob[a])
Joseph Huddle Jr
Thomas Cumpston
Richard Price
Matthew L. Beavan
Jesse Sharpless
John Philips
Joseph Smith
Benjamin Jones
Isaac Jones
Geo. W. Morgan
Elihu Chauncey
Griffith Evans
Enos Bronson
Richard C. Jones

Joseph Price
John Davis
Richard Maris
John Harrison
Samuel Relf
Doctor Parke
Edmund Kinzey
Zach[a] Poulson
Joseph P. Norris
John Morgan
Charles Wistar
James Read
Thomas Humphreys
Reece Lewis
Robert Frazer
David Lewis
John Clifton
Joseph Strong
James Cruckshank
Richard Peters Jun[r]
John M. Price
Samuel Wetherill Jun[r]

Assistance to Welsh Emigrants

The acting committee reported that the duties of the office had been attended to whenever it was found requisite and that they had distributed relief to all such cases as required it.

Finance: Accounts and Investments

That agreeably to the directions of the Society at a former meeting the Treasurer had under the sanction of the committee invested $400 in Water Loan of the City of Philadelphia and had still a balance of cash as would appear by the report of his accounts. That the committee would direct such further investment as the funds of the Society would allow.

The Treasurer reported his accounts. Balance in favour of the Society $84.04

Membership: New Members

The following gentlemen proposed at a former meeting were duly elected members

Samuel Neave Lewis
Samuel W. Jones
and Jesse Johns Honorary

Organization: Election of Officers

The President having nominated the Judges and Tellers of the election left the chair when the election for officers was entered upon. After the poll had closed the following certificate was handed to the Secretary for record

Philadelphia Feb[y] 28th 1807

We whose names are hereunto subscribed certify that the foregoing and annexed lists contain the names of the members of the Welch Society, who voted at an election of officers for the same, held the 28th day of February 1807 at the Mansion House Hotel, and that the following gentlemen were duly elected to the several offices mentioned after their respective names

signed

Jo^s Parker Norris
John Davis
Richard Maris
E. Bronson

President	Samuel Meredith
Vice President	Robert Wharton
Treasurer	Thomas Cumpston
Secretary	Rich. C. Jones
Register	Joseph S. Lewis
Counsellors	Edward Tilghman
	Benjn R. Morgan
Physicians	Doctor Thomas C. James
	Doctor Joseph Strong
Stewards	John Evans
	Jonathan Smith
	Richard Price
	Doctor Parke
	Chandler Price
	Isaac Jones
	James Cruckshands [sic]

Membership: New Member

Reese Brooks   proposed by Jonathan Jones.

Adjourned

signed Rich. C. Jones Sec^y

Welch Society

At a Meeting of the Welch Society held at the Mansion House, June 1st 1807.

Members Present

Samuel Meredith	Matthew L. Beavan
Robert Wharton	John Morgan
Thomas Cumpston	Zach^a Poulson
Joseph S. Lewis	Samuel Parrish
James Cruckshank	William Craig
Dr Thomas Parke	Joseph Price
Jonathan Smith	Edmund Kinzey
Isaac Jones	Lewis Walker
Richard Price	Jesse Sharples
Doct^r Strong	John Philips
Joseph Smith	Richard C. Jones

Finance: Accounts

The Treasurer reported his accounts. Balance in favour of the Society $431.94

Assistance to Welsh Emigrants

The acting committee reported that since the last meeting of the Society they have met as occasion required, but have had no claim on the funds of the Society.

Organization: Amendments to the Bye-Laws – 5th Article concerning the Annual Dinner

The committee having thought it necessary that some alterations should be made in the Bye-Laws of the Society appointed a sub-committee to revise them, who have prepared the following article as a substitute for Article the 5th which is accordingly recommended to the Society for consideration and if they think proper for adoption vizt

The Stewards shall have the direction, superintendance and management of the annual entertainment, and the expence of the guests invited by order of the Society shall be paid out of the general fund, the remaining expence to be equally paid by the members present at such entertainment.

June 1st 1807

signed Jos. S. Lewis Register

Membership: New Members

The following gentlemen were proposed as members

Reese Brooks	[proposed] by Jonathan Jones
Job Bacon	[proposed by] William Craig
Redwood Fisher	[proposed by] Rich. C. Jones

Adjourned

signed Rich. C. Jones Sec^y

Welch Society

At a Meeting held at the Mansion House, September 7th 1807.

Members Present

Jonathan Smith	Richard Price
Joseph Strong	Samuel N. Lewis
Joseph S. Lewis	Joseph Price
Joseph Huddle Junr	Samuel Parrish
Joseph Michael	Lewis Walker
Joseph Williams	Thomas Parke
Elihu Chauncey	Zach^a Poulson
John Davis	Chandler Price

Organization: Absence of President and Vice-President

The President and Vice President being absent Richard Price Esqr was chosen chairman pro-tem.

Finance: Accounts

The Treasurer reported his accounts. Balance in favour of the Society $483.19.

Acting Committee Report: No Business

The acting committee reported that they had nothing new to present to the notice of the Society.

Membership: Resignation

The resignation of Mr John Read Junr was read and accepted.[31]

Membership: New Members

Miers Fisher Jr   proposed by Jos[eph] S. Lewis
John Jones

Adjourned

signed Jos. S. Lewis

for Rich. C. Jones Sec^y

---

31   John Read Jr, a lawyer and senator, does not appear in the minutes, but was the Son-in-law of the President, Samuel Meredith.

PART THREE

Welch Society

At a Quarterly Meeting held at the Mansion House, December 7th 1807.

Members Present

Richard Price
Jonathan Smith
D. Geo. Gillaspy
Matt^w L. Beavan
James Prosser
Zach^a Poulson
Rich. C. Jones
Thomas Cumpston
Edmund Kinzey
Robert Frazer
Doct^r Strong
John J. Parry
Samuel N. Lewis

Robert Wharton
William Craig
Joseph S. Lewis
Joseph Price
Joseph Smith
Samuel Parrish
Samuel Williams
Jesse Sharpless
Reece Lewis
Dr Thomas C. James
Chandler Price
Elihu Chauncey

Financial: Investments

The acting committee reported that they had attended to their duty, and now have the pleasure to advise the purchase of an additional sum of $500 of the stock of the City of Philadelphia which makes the whole sum invested $800.

Discipline: Payment of Fines

The committee trust that the punctual payment of arrears of fines &c. due to the Society will enable them ere long to make an addition to the capital stock so necessary for the prosperity of the Society.

signed Jos. S. Lewis Register

Decr 7th 1807

Finance: Accounts

The Treasurer reported his accounts. Balance in favour of the Society $51.25.

Organization: Amendments to the Bye-Laws – 5th Article concerning the Annual Dinner

The following substituted for Article the 5th of the Bye-Laws was accepted and the Secretary directed to record it as a Bye-Law

BYE LAW

The Stewards shall have the direction, superintendence & arrangement of the annual dinner and the expence of the guests invited by order of the Society shall be paid out of the general fund. The remaining expence to be equally paid by the members present at such entertainment.

Annual Dinner

On motion resolved that the acting committee be directed to provide a dinner on the first of March and that they are directed to invite the officers of the St George's, St Andrew's, Hibernian and St Herman Societies and such other persons as they think proper not exceeding eight in number.

Membership: New Members

The following gentlemen were duly elected members of this Society

Reese Brooks
Job Bacon
Redwood Fisher
Miers Fisher Jun[r]
John Jones

PART THREE

The following gentlemen were proposed as members of this Society

George Vaux	[proposed] by Elihu Chauncey
John Bacon	[proposed by] William Craig
Joseph E. Howell	[proposed by] Joseph Smith
John Hughes	[proposed by] R. C. Jones
Richd B. Jones Hon^{ry}	[proposed by] John M. Price
David Davis	
Horace Binney	[proposed by] Jonathan Smith
Capt James Read	[proposed by] J. M. Price
Robert Murdock	[proposed by] David Lewis

Adjourned

signed Rich. C. Jones, Sec^y

1808
Welch Society

At an Annual Meeting of the Welch Society held at the Mansion House Hotel, March 1st 1808.

Members Present

Samuel Meredith
Thomas Cumpston
Joseph S. Lewis
Richard Price
Jonathan Smith
Chandler Price
Doct. Jos. Strong
Reece Lewis
Sam. N. Lewis
Geo. W. Morgan
Matt^W L. Beavan
Zach^a Poulson
David Lewis
John Jones
Redwood Fisher
Charles Wistar
Joseph P. Norris
James Read
John Harrison
Enos Bronson
Joseph Smith
Job Bacon
John Philips
Thomas Humphreys
Samuel Parrish
Samuel Relf
Richard Maris
Griffith Evans
Isacher Evans
Charles Chauncey
Jesse Sharpless
John Clifton
Lloyd Jones
Benjamin R. Morgan
Robert Wharton
Elihu Chauncey
Thos Cadwallader
Joseph Shaw
Rich. C. Jones

Finance: Accounts

The Treasurer reported his accounts. Balance in favour of the Society $103.42

PART THREE

Assistance to Welsh Emigrants

The acting committee reported that since their last communication the calls on the benevolence of the Society have been few, amongst them the most distressing was that of Mary Pritchet wife of Thomas Prichet whom the physicians of the Society found labouring under a consumption which afforded no hope of recovery, but as she was in extreme want of every necessary, the committee extended such relief as afforded them the consolation of knowing that her last moments were rendered in some measure comfortable. The committee have also furnished some cloathing to an orphan under their care.

Annual Dinner

Agreeably to the orders of the Society the committee have engaged a dinner for the Society at Mr Renshaws this day.

March 1st 1808

Signed Jos. S. Lewis Register

Membership: New Members

The following gentlemen proposed at the last meeting of the Society were duly elected as members

George Vaux [proposed by] Capt Ja^s Read; Joseph E. Howell; Robt Murdock

John Bacon
John Hughes
Richd B. Jones Hon^{ry}
Horace Binney

Organization: Election of Officers

The President having nominated the Judges & Tellers of the election left the chair when the Election for officers was entered upon. After the poll was closed the following certificate was handed to the Secretary for record.

157

We whose names are hereunto subscribed certify that the foregoing and annexed list contain the names of the members of the Welch Society who voted at an election of officers for the same held the 1st day of March 1808 at the Mansion House Hotel, and that the following gentlemen were duly elected to the several offices mentioned after their respective names

President   Samuel Meredith
Vice President   Robert Wharton
Treasurer   Thomas Cumpston
Secretary   Richard C. Jones
Register   Joseph S. Lewis
Counsellors   Benjn R. Morgan
                                  Edward Tilghman
Stewards   John Evans
                                  Richard Price
                                  Jonathan Smith
                                  Thomas Parke
                                  Chandler Price
                                  Reece Lewis
                                  Elihu Chauncey
Physicians   Doctor Thomas C. James
                                  Doctor Joseph Strong

Signed Ch. Chauncey
Jos. Parker Norris
Redwood Fisher

Membership: New Member

Thos Meredith proposed by Thos Cadwallader Esqr

Adjourned

signed Richard C. Jones Sec^y.

PART THREE

Welch Society

At a Quarterly Meeting of the Welch Society held at the Mansion House Hotel, June 6th 1808.

Members Present

Robert Wharton
Jonathan Smith
Joseph S. Smith
Doctor Parke
Charles Chauncey
Redwood Fisher
Robert Murdock
Reese Brooks
Joseph Michael
Edmund Kinsey

Joseph Price
Samuel N. Norris
Joseph Huddle Jr
Samuel Parrish
Reece Lewis
Samuel Relf
James Prosser
Zach^a Poulson
John Jones
Richard C. Jones

Finance: Gift to the Society

The acting committee reported that as usual they had attended to the ordinary business of the Society. And that they have the pleasure herewith to offer a letter they have received from Capt William Jones and Mr William W. Smith, members of this Society lately returned from Calcutta, enclosing a letter from Mr R. Williams of that place accompanying a present from that gentleman of one hundred Rupees to forward the benevolent views of our association. The committee under a full sense of this mark of national feeling beg leave to offer the following resolution for the adoption of the Society

Resolved that Mr R. Williams of Calcutta be admitted an Honorary Member of the Welch Society and that the President and Secretary be directed to transmit him a framed certificate thereof with our thanks for his donation.

By order

Signed Jos. S. Lewis Register

On motion the resolution was unanimously accepted

Philad^a 31st May 1808

Gentlemen

Enclosed is a letter from R. Williams Esquire of Calcutta, the sentiments and <u>contents</u> of which will speak the eulogy, of a benevolent Cambrian and worthy gentleman with more effect than the pathos of eloquence or the tear of pity. We need not suggest to you that which your own feelings will indicate of an appropriate and acceptable expression of the respect of the Society for the generous donor.

The Society will receive in addition to the 100 Rupees from Mr Williams the premium of exchange between Calcutta and Philadelphia.

We are very respectfully & truly yours

The acting committee of the Welch Society

signed Wm Jones for self
& Wm W. Smith

Dear Sirs,

I was much pleased with your description of the Welsh Society and as a Cambrian I feel interested in any thing that may tend to my countryman's good, particularly when the intention is to assist the unfortunate emigrant who, in the hope of bettering his prospects in life, visits a foreign clime finds himself on his arrival friendless. The Institution does honor to my countryman and tho' at a distance from it I beg you will present in my name the enclosed bank bill of one hundred Rupees. It is a mite, but with a large family my circumstances [does] not allow me to be a liberal as I wish.

Sincerely wishing you a pleasant voyage,

I am my dear Sirs

yours very truly

signed R. Williams

Wm Jones & Wm Smith Esqrs

Membership: New Members

Mr Thomas Meredith was duly elected an Honorary Member of the Society.

The following gentlemen were proposed as members

Edward Davis	[proposed] by Robert Wharton
Joseph Worrel	
John D. Lewis	[proposed] by Joseph S. Lewis
Edwd Tilghman Jr	
James Milnor	[proposed] by Richd C. Jones

Adjourned

signed Richd C. Jones Sec^y.

Welch Society

At a Quarterly Meeting of the Society held at the Mansion House Hotel, September 5th 1808.

Members Present

Robert Wharton
Richard Price
Reese Brooks
Zach^a Poulson
John Jones
Joseph Price
Jonathan Smith
Elihu Chauncey
Joseph S. Lewis
Dr Thos Parke

John C. Jones
Thomas Cumpston
Isaac H. Jones
Edmund Kinsey
Griffith Evans
Joseph Huddle Junr
Joseph Smith
Samuel Relf
Matthew L. Beaven
Charles Chauncey

Assistance to Welsh Emigrants

The acting committee reported that as usual they had extended relief to such cases as required it, but have nothing of particular notice to offer the Society.

Finance: Accounts

The Treasurer reported his accounts. Balance in favour of the Society $171.82.

Membership: New Members

The following gentlemen were duly elected

Edward Davis
Joseph Worrell
John D. Lewis
Edward Tilghman Jr
James Milnor

The following gentlemen were proposed as members

Algernon Roberts	[proposed] by Thos Cumpston
Curtis Clay Junr	[proposed] by Joseph Smith
Wm Coxe Ellis of Muncey[32]	[proposed] by Rich. C. Jones
Joseph Wilds	[proposed] by Reese Brooks
Jesse Waln	[proposed] by Rich. C. Jones
Captn Saml Evans	

Adjourned

signed Richd C. Jones Secy

---

32   Muncy is a borough in Lycoming County, Pennsylvania, and was derived from the Munsee people who inhabited this area before the European settlers.

PART THREE

Welch Society

At a Quarterly Meeting of the Society held at the Mansion House Hotel, December 5th 1808.

Members Present

Thomas Cumpston
Jonathan Smith
Richard Price
Reece Lewis
Thomas Parke
Joseph Smith
Reese Brooks
Zach^a Poulson
Griffith Evans
Samuel Parrish
William Craig
Robert Murdock
Miers Fisher Jr
Lewis Walker
Capt Jos. Michaels

Samuel N. Lewis
Job Bacon
Dr Joseph Strong
John Jones
Thomas Prosser
Edmund Kinsey
Wm W. Smith
William Jones
John C. Jones
Isaac H. Jones
Richard C. Jones
Thomas Biddle
Dr Geo. Gillaspy
John Clifton
Joseph Williams

Organization: Absence of President and Vice-President

The President and Vice President being absent Thomas Cumpston was called to the Chair.

Finance: Accounts

The Treasurer reported his accounts. Balance in favor of the Society $382.87.

Organization: Absence of Registrar

In consequence of the Register's indisposition no report was made by the acting committee.

Membership: New Members

The following gentlemen were duly elected members

Algernon Roberts
Curtis Clay Junr
Coxe Ellis
Joseph Wildes
Jesse Waln
Captn Saml Evans

The following gentlemen were proposed as members

Rowland Ellis	[proposed] by John C. Jones
Richard Roberts Hon^y	[proposed by] Reese Brooks
Fishbourn Wharton	[proposed by] Richard Price
William Rogers	[proposed by] James Prosser
Jacob S. Otto	[proposed by] Samuel Relf
Caleb Birchall	[proposed by] Joseph Smith
Jos. Ellis Bloomfield	[proposed by] Joseph S. Lewis
John Watson	[proposed by] Joseph Smith
John J. Wheeler	[proposed by] Robert Wharton
James Read Jr	[proposed by] James Read
William J. Jones	[proposed by] Joseph S. Lewis
Joseph Hemphill	[proposed by] Thos B. Zantzinger
Isaac Jones	[proposed by] Samuel Relf
William P. Dewees	[proposed by] Jonathan Smith

Annual Dinner

On motion resolved that the acting committee be directed to provide a dinner on the first of March next for the Society and that they be directed to invite the officers of the St George's, St Andrew's, Hibernian and St Herman Societies and such other persons as they may think proper not exceeding eight in number.

PART THREE

Adjourned

signed Jos. S. Lewis Register

for Richd C. Jones Secretary.

1809
Welch Society

At an Annual Meeting of the Society held at the Mansion House Hotel, March 1st 1809.

Members Present

Robert Wharton
Thomas Cumpston
Thomas Parke
Enos Bronson
Elihu Chauncey
Charles Chauncey
George Vaux
Joseph P. Norris
Griffith Evans
John Philips
Joseph Michaels
Joseph Worrell
Jesse Sharpless
Joseph Huddle Jr
John Wistar
Charles Wistar
Joseph Wildes
Zach^a Poulson
Chandler Price
Thos B. Zantzinger
John J. Parry
Matthew L. Beaven
Dr Thos C. James
Samuel Wetherill Jr
John M. Price
Robert Frazer

Reese Brooks
Redwood Fisher
Isaac H. Jones
Joseph S. Lewis
Samuel N. Lewis
Samuel Parrish
Job Bacon
Robert Murdock
John Jones
William Craig
Joseph Smith
Jonathan Smith
C. C. Maddock
Isachar Evans
Samuel Relf
David Lewis
Joseph Price
Thomas Humphreys
John Bacon
James Read
Curtis Clay Jr
Lewis Walker
Jesse Waln
Doct^r Jos. Strong
Peter Evans
William W. Smith

Richard Price
Reece Lewis
Dr Geo. Gillaspy
Benjn Chew Jr
James C. Fisher
Joshua Humphreys

Annual Dinner

The acting committee made the following report vizt

The acting committee agreeably to direction have engaged with Mr Renshaw to provide a dinner for the Society this day.

Finance: Accounts and Fines

The committee have the satisfaction to state to the Society that in consequence of a resolve adopted on the first March 1805 directing the acting committee to dispose of the monies of the Society in stock the Treasurer has from time to time invested the surplus funds in City Stock & that the Society now hold ten shares thereof.

The committee hope that a continued attention of the members to the punctual payment of fines and contributions will enable the Society to increase its stock so as to extend the benefits proposed by the institution of the Welsh Society.

March 1st 1809

signed Jos. S. Lewis Register

Finance: Accounts

The Treasurer reported his accounts. Balance due the Society $189.87.

Membership: New Members

The following named gentlemen were duly elected members vizt.

Rowland Ellis
Richd Roberts Hon^{ry}
Fishbourn Wharton
Joseph Hemphill
John Watson
John J. Wheeler

William Rogers
Jacob S. Otto
Caleb Birchall
Jos. Ellis Bloomfield

James Read Junr
William J. Jones
Joseph Jones
William P. Dewees

Organization: Indisposition of President

A letter was read from Mr Meredith our President stating that he was prevented from attending today on account of indisposition.

Membership: Death and Testimonial to Former Secretary – Richard C. Jones

Doctor Parke announced to the Society the death of our late valued Secretary Mr Richard C. Jones whereupon Doct^r Parke, Charles Chauncey and Doct^r James were appointed a committee to prepare a testimonial of our respect to his memory, who reported the following which was unanimously adopted, vizt

The committee appointed for the purpose of preparing a testimonial of the sence [*sic*] entertained by the Society of the merits of their lately deceased Secretary and of the regret excited by his death beg leave to report the following remarks and submit that they be preserved on the records as an expression of the sentiments and feelings of the Society on this mournful occasion.

Since the last meeting of the Welch Society its members have been called to mourn the departure of their beloved brother and highly valued Secretary Richard C. Jones. To the present members of this association, it would be necessary to present a view of the character and worth of their deceased friend. They have witnessed his excellence, and they justly feel and lament his loss. But, to the future members of the Society it may be useful that a portion of our records should be devoted to preserve the remembrance of one whose deportment presents so fair and favorable a model of capacity, fidelity and zeal as a member and an officer of this institution.

PART THREE

At the revival of the Society under its present arrangements in the year 1798 Richard C. Jones became a member and was one of the Stewards first appointed by the Society. The uniform conduct of Mr Jones from the day of his admission as a member to his death indicates with certainty that his motives in joining the Society were benevolent and his principle of action a desire to relieve from suffering and distress. In accordance with this primary impulse, his career was run with undeviating tenor and an unfaltering course. He felt not the influence of coldness or insensibility, but a genial warmth impelled his charities and a sound prudence directed them to the proper objects.

As a member of the acting committee, he was called on various occasions to a zealous service in the cause of the distressed. One memorable instance is within the recollection of many survivors, and cannot but be remembered with feeling and interest as long as the great objects of this association are dear to its members. On the occasion referred to, Mr Jones bore a conspicuous part and his indefatigable exertions, in concert with his associates of the committee, to alleviate the miseries of a numerous body of emigrants from Wales, were followed by effects upon his health, which he never entirely surmounted. The prevalence of a violent and infectious fever among these emigrants, caused them to be placed at the Hospital on Schuylkill and rendered extremely perilous the discharge of the offices of humanity towards them. Fearless of the danger, and regardless of fatigue, Mr Jones devoted himself to an unremitting service, for the relief of these afflicted strangers from the multiplied distress with which they were surrounded. Early and late, he attended the hospital administering to the wants of the necessitous, and imparting comfort and consolation to the distressed. The widow and the orphan were peculiar objects of his solicitude and attention, and this numerous family of sick and comfortless strangers experienced that fellowship and humanity which our association professes to promote. The exertions of Mr Jones amid this scene of sickness and distress were followed by an attack of the fever, from which after a painful illness, he recovered, but, as it is apprehended, with as constitution so impaired by its ravages, as never to regain its pristine vigour.

In consequence of the mortality, which prevailed among the Welch Emigrants before mentioned, the appointment of an Orphan Committee became necessary to accomplish the purposes of the Society. Mr Jones was appointed on this committee and discharged the duty with a fatherly and friendly care, congenial with the benevolence of his own heart and in happy fulfillment of the charitable views of the institution. For upwards of six years Mr Jones filled with perfect acceptation to all, the office of Secretary to the Society. His accuracy and fidelity as an officer coupled with a lively interest in the concerns of the Institution, cause his loss to be felt and sincerely deplored.

In the social and joyous scenes of the Society as well as in the severest path of duty our friend was accustomed to display qualities, which endeared him to all, and which will ever be remembered by those who have witnessed his generosity of feeling and complacency of manners. The last illness of Mr Jones was short, and his career of usefulness closed on the ninth of January one thousand eight hundred and nine.

It is no detraction from living worth to say, that as an active and faithful officer and as a zealous and useful member of the Welch Society, Richard C. Jones has left behind him no superior.

Membership: Resignation

A letter was received from Samuel Clarke resigning his membership, which was accepted.

Membership: New Members

The following named gentlemen were proposed as members, vizt.

Francis R. Wharton   [proposed] by William Craig
George Howell   [proposed] by Joseph Smith

Organization: Election of Officers

We whose names are hereunto subscribed certify that the annexed list contains the names of officers elected by the Welch Society for the ensuing year

March 1st 1809

(signed) James Read
Joseph P. Norris
E. Bronson

The list is as follows vizt

President	Samuel Meredith
Vice President	Robert Wharton
Treasurer	Thomas Cumpston
Secretary	Joseph S. Lewis
Register	Jonathan Smith
Counsellors	Benjamin R. Morgan
Treasurer	Edward Tilghman
Stewards	John Evans
	Richard Price
	Thomas Parke
	Chandler Price
	Reece Lewis
	Elihu Chauncey
	Matthew L. Beaven
Physicians	Doctor Thomas C. James
	[Doctor] Joseph Strong

Adjourned

Joseph S. Lewis Secretary

Welch Society

At a Quarterly Meeting held at the Mansion House Hotel on Monday June 5th 1809.

Members Present

Robert Wharton
Thomas Cumpston
Joseph S. Lewis
Jonathan Smith
Elihu Chauncey
Matthew L. Bevan
Joseph E. Howell
Zachariah Poulson
Horace Binney
John Jones
Joseph Smith

Curtis Clay Junr
Reese Brooks
Caleb Birchall
Edmund Kinsey
Joseph Price
Lewis Walker
Samuel Parrish
Edward Davies
John J. Parry
Richard Price
Thomas Parke

Finance: Accounts

The Treasurer reported his accounts. Balance due the Society $149.87.

Assistance to Welsh Emigrants

The acting committee made the following report vizt

The acting committee of the Welch Society report that they had received information that a certain John Snead who with his wife & children arrived some years since at Wilmington in the Ship *Liberty* from Wales had died in the neighbourhood of this city, and had left some property, which was in danger of being lost, unless some suitable person was legally authorized to take charge of it, in consequence of which the committee procured letters of administration on the deceased's estate, that the administrators had received some of the property, and expected to receive more which will probably amount to about one hundred dollars.

It is proposed to place the amount which may be received out at interest in the name of the Society for the benefit of two orphan children of the deceased (who are the only survivors of the family) and who were bound shortly after their arrival in the country to Thomas Wilkinson, a respectable inhabitant of Chester County, until they severally became of age.

The committee further report that they have bound Owen Howell an apprentice to a shoemaker and that they intend binding Thomas Harris an apprentice as soon as a suitable place can be procured for him, both those boys are Welch, & orphans and have been for some time under the care of the committee.

June 3 1809

signed Jon^a Smith Reg^r

Finance: Payment to Joseph S. Lewis for Copying minutes

On motion of Mr Bevan resolved that an order be drawn on the Treasurer in favour of Joseph S. Lewis for twenty-five dollars being so much paid by him for copying the former minutes and the Constitution of the Society.

Membership: New Members

William Craig who proposed Francis R. Wharton not being present his election was postponed to a future meeting.

George Howell who was proposed as a member at the last meeting was duly elected.

Membership: Resignation

The Secretary handed a letter from Isaac H. Lewis resigning his membership which was accepted.

Membership: New Members

The following mentioned gentlemen were proposed as members, vizt.

John Roberts Hon^ry	[proposed] by Thomas Cumpston
John Bevan	[proposed] by Matthew L. Bevan
John Strawbridge	[proposed] by Joseph Smith
Benjn B. Howell	[proposed] by Joseph S. Lewis

Adjourned[33]

Welch Society

At a Quarterly Meeting held at the Mansion House Hotel on Monday September 4th 1809.

Members Present

Robert Wharton	Samuel Parrish
John Jones	Jonathan Smith
Reese Brooks	John J. Wheeler
Joseph Wildes	Charles Chauncey
Thomas Parke	Joseph Smith
Richard Price	Thomas Cumpston
Joseph Price	Edward Davies
Joseph E. Howell	Samuel Relf
Joseph S. Lewis	Joseph Williams
Richard H. Morris	Edmund Kinsey
Zachariah Poulson	Matthew L. Bevan

Acting Committee Report and Assistance to Welsh Emigrants

The acting committee made the following report vizt

That they had as usual attended to the concerns of the Society and afforded such relief as was thought proper to such persons as stood in need and had claims on the Society.

---

33   The minutes were not signed off on this occasion.

PART THREE

Finance and Investments: Legacy of John Keble

The committee further report that having understood that the late Mr John Keble had by his Will bequeathed the residuary part of his estate for the benefit of charitable institutions to be appointed at the discretion of certain persons in his Will named for the purpose. They appointed a sub-committee to solicit on behalf of the Society a portion of the estate so bequeathed; application was accordingly made, and the committee have now the satisfaction to state that they have received from the executors of Mr Keble for the use of the Society the following property vizt

A mortgage with bond and warrant of attorney given by John Britton on 58 acres of land in Blockley Township for	$1333.33
On which the interest from 17th March 1807 to the 1st Sept 1809 – 2 years & 5½ months is due	$196.67 $1,530
A certificate of deferred 6 pct Stock nominal 946.75^{/100}$ equal to	$752.67
And in Cash	$781.45
	$3064.12

Amounting to three thousand and sixty-four dollars and twelve cents, the mortgage and bond and six p'cent Stock are assigned and transferred in the corporate name of the Society. By the Will of Mr Keble it appears that the principal of the mortgage cannot be demanded until three years after the death of the testator.

The committee beg leave to suggest to the Society the propriety of selling the deferred six p'cent Stock and of investing the proceeds in stock more permanent, a portion of this stock is redeemable annually but the sum so redeemed is so small that it would be difficult to reinvest it. In order therefore that the principal of the stock shall remain entire until the objects for which the Society was formed demand its expenditure the committee beg leave to recommend to the consideration of the Society the following resolution vizt

Resolved that the acting committee be authorised to sell the deferred six percent stock the property of this Society and invest the proceeds together with the balance of cash in the hands of the Treasurer including the sum in cash received from the executors of John Keble deceased in such stock as they may deem most for the interest of the Society.

signed Jon^a Smith Reg^r

The resolution accompanying the report being moved and seconded was unanimously adopted.

Finance: Accounts

The Treasurer reported his account. Balance due the Society $285.37.

Membership: New Members

Mr William E. Howell was proposed as a member by Samuel Parrish.

The election for members being gone into the following named gentlemen were duly elected vizt

John Roberts   Honorary
John Bevan
John Strawbridge
Benjamin B. Howell

Adjourned

PART THREE

Welch Society

At a Quarterly Meeting held at the Mansion House Hotel on Monday December 4th 1809.

Members Present

Robert Wharton
Thomas Cumpston
Richard Price
Reece Lewis
Jonathan Smith
Thomas Parke
Joseph S. Lewis
Edward Tilghman Jr
Caleb Birchall
Edmund Kinsey
Lewis Walker
Reese Brooks
Joseph Huddell Jr
John M. Price

George Howell
Joseph Smith
John Cliffton
Richard Hill Morris
Zachariah Poulson
James C. Fisher
Edward Davies
Joseph Jones
Chandler Price
John J. Wheeler
John Jones
Joseph Price
Matthew L. Bevan
Samuel Parrish

Finance: Investments

The acting committee made the following report vizt

That they have by virtue of a resolution of the Society passed at their last meeting relative to the investment of its funds sold the six p'cent Stock belonging to the Society and have invested the proceeds together with the balance of cash in the hands of the Treasurer in three shares of the Stock of the Bank of North America.

Finance: Legacy of Robert Montgomery

The committee having been informed that Mr Robert Montgomery lately deceased had bequeathed part of his property to charitable institutions appointed Mess[rs] Robert Wharton and Joseph S. Lewis a committee to apply to the executors of Mr Montgomery on behalf of this Society and request a portion of the estate so bequeathed.

Assistance to Welsh Emigrants – Thomas Harris

The committee further report the Orphan Committee have bound Thomas Harris, a minor from Wales (who has been under the care of the Society for a considerable period), to Benjamin Gardner a house carpenter.

December 4th 1809

signed Jona Smith, Reg^r

Membership: Resignation

The Secretary handed a letter which he had received from Edward Tilghman Esquire resigning his membership which was accepted.

Membership: New Member

The election being gone into Mr William E. Howell was duly elected a member.

Annual Dinner

On motion resolved that the acting committee be directed to provide a dinner on the first of March next for the Society and that they be directed to invite the officers of the St George's, St Andrew's, St Herman's & Hibernian & such other persons as they think proper not exceeding eight in number.

Membership: New Members

David C. Jones Honorary	[proposed by] Jonathan Jones
John Hastings [Honorary]	[proposed] by John M. Price
Benjamin Thomas	[proposed] by Richard Price
Capt Wm Hendy	[proposed] by Richard Price

William W. Fisher   [proposed] by Robert Wharton
Thomas Morris   [proposed] by Joseph S. Lewis
Jonah Thompson   [proposed] by Samuel Parrish
John Hallowell   [proposed] by George Vaux
Thomas Mayburry   [proposed] by Reese Brooks
Adjourned

1810
Welch Society

At the Annual Meeting of the Welch Society held at the Mansion House Hotel on March 1ˢᵗ 1810.

Members Present

Thomas Cumpston
Chandler Price
Elihu Chauncey
Richard Price
Samuel Parrish
Reese Brooks
Richard Hill Morris
George Vaux
John Wistar
William W. Smith
Caleb Birchall
Joseph Price
Robert Wharton
Curtis Clay
Joseph S. Lewis
John J. Wheeler
Richard Maris
Edward Tilghman Jr
Evan Thomas
James Tatem
Doctʳ Thomas C. James
John Bacon
Edmund Kinsey
John Phillips
David Lewis
James Read

Samuel N. Lewis
Reece Lewis
John M. Price
Doctʳ Joseph Strong
Samuel Meredith
John Bevan
Thomas Humphreys
William Craig
Isachar Evans
Joseph Huddell Jr
Griffith Evans
Zachariah Poulson
Enos Bronson
Thomas Parke
Joseph P. Norris
Joseph Worrell
John Jones
Charles J. Wistar
Charles Marshall Jr
George Vaux
Benjamin B. Howell
Samuel Wetherill
Joshua L. Howell
Joseph Williams
Thomas Cadwallader

PART THREE

Assistance to Welsh Emigrants and the Annual Dinner

The acting committee made the following report vizt

That since the last meeting of the Society they have attended to its interests [in] general and granted relief in such cases as presented & came within the view of the benevolent intentions of the institution, nothing however occuring which in the opinion of the committee requires the particular attention of the Society except that the annual dinner has been provided agreeably to its direction at this house and will be on table at 3 o'clock this afternoon.

March 1st 1810

Signed Jon^a Smith Reg^r

Finance: Accounts

The Treasurer reported his account. Balance due the Society $409.4/^{100}.

Membership: New Members

The following mentioned gentlemen proposed at the last meeting were duly elected members vizt

David C. Jones	Honorary New York
John Hastings	ditto
Benjamin Thomas	
Capt William Hendy	
William W. Fisher	
Thomas Morris	
Jonah Thompson	
John Hallowell	
Thomas Mayberry	

Organization: Election of Officers

The election being gone into, Griffith Evans & Enos Bronson were appointed Judges who reported the following gentlemen to be duly elected officers for the ensuing year vizt

President	Samuel Meredith
Vice President	Robert Wharton
Treasurer	Thomas Cumpston
Secretary	Joseph S. Lewis
Register	Jonathan Smith
Counsellers	Benjamin R. Morgan
	Charles Chauncey
Physicians	Doct. Thomas C. James
	[Doctor] Joseph Strong
Stewards	John Evans
	Richard Price
	Thomas Parke
	Chandler Price
	Reece Lewis
	Elihu Chauncey
	Matthew L. Beaven

Adjourned

Welch Society

At a Quarterly Meeting of the Society held at the Mansion House Hotel on Monday June 4th 1810.

Members Present

Robert Wharton	Joseph Price
Thomas Parke	Lewis Walker
Zachariah Poulson	Matthew L. Bevan
Ja^s E. Bloomfield	Edmund Kinsey
John Jones	Richard Price
John Philips	Reece Lewis
John Clifton	William W. Fisher
Jonathan Smith	Chandler Price

Membership: Resignation

A letter was read from Thomas Hale resigning his membership in this Society which was accepted.

Finance: Printing Costs

The account for printing notices to the members and cards for visitors amounting to $16.87 was produced whereupon it was ordered that a draft be drawn upon the Treasurer for that amount in favour of Joseph S. Lewis.

Assistance to Welsh Emigrants

The acting committee made the following report which was read and with the resolution annexed thereto adopted.

The acting committee of the Welch Society report

That they have attended to the duties of their appointment and afforded relief to such objects as the committee conceived had claims on the Society and came within its benevolent intentions.

Finance: Bequest and Investment of Funds

The committee also report to the Society they have (in addition to what had been received and mentioned in a former report from the estate of John Keble deceased) received from the executors a transfer of £202.63/^{100} of nominal deferred 6 p'cent stock equal on the first January last to $160.49/^{100}. That they have also received from the executors $16.21/^{100} being the amount of one years divided on the above mentioned stock.

The committee beg leave to recommend the adoption of the following Resolution vizt

Resolved that the acting committee of the Welch Society be and they are hereby directed to sell the $202.63/^{100} of six p'cent stock the property of this Society and invest the proceeds thereof together with any other monies in the hands of the Treasurer in such stock as they may think proper and that Thomas Cumpston, the Treasurer, be and is hereby authorised to make the necessary transfer.

June 1st 1810

signed Jon^a Smith Reg^r

which resolution was accordingly adopted.

Membership: New Member

John Sergeant was proposed as a member by Chandler Price.

signed Jon^a Smith

Sec^y pro:tem

Welch Society

At a Quarterly Meeting of the Society held at the Mansion House Hotel on Monday 3rd Sept[ember] 1810.

Members Present

Robert Wharton
Thomas Cumpston
Joseph S. Lewis
Richard Price
Thomas Parke
Jonathan Smith
Benjn R. Morgan
Thomas C. James
John J. Wheeler
Doct^r George Gillespy
Joseph Price
Joseph Huddell Jr

Joseph Worrell
Benjamin Thomas
Thos B. Zantzinger
Samuel Relf
Matthew L. Bevan
John Jones
John J. Parry
Edward Davies
Caleb Birchall
John Hallowell
Edmund Kinsey
John Philips

PART THREE

Assistance to Welsh Emigrants

The acting committee made the following report vizt

That since the last meeting of the Society the committee have attended to the business of the Society and have nothing of importance to report except in the case of a certain John Jones, an emigrant Welchman, whose situation made it necessary to place him in the Pennsylvania Hospital[34] where an amputation of his leg took place – after his recovery he has been sent home at the expense of the Society; in attending to the business the committee have expended $184.9/^{100}.

Sept. 3rd 1810

signed Jon^a Smith Reg^r

Finance: Accounts

The Treasurer reported his accounts. Balance due the Society $338.29/^{100}.

Membership: New Members

C. Price being absent the election of John Sergeant as a member was not gone into.

The following named gentlemen were proposed as members

James M. Broom of Wilmington
Honorary [proposed] by Thos Cumpston
William H. Morgan Resident [proposed by] Richard Price
John S. Willett [Resident] [proposed by] Reece Lewis

Adjourned

---

34 For details see William H. Williams, *America's First Hospital: The Pennsylvania Hospital, 1751–1841* (Wayne, Pa: Haverford House, 1976).

Welch Society

At a Quarterly Meeting of the Society held at the Mansion House Hotel on Monday 3rd December 1810.

Members Present

Richard Price
Thomas Parke
Joseph S. Lewis
Reece Lewis
Joseph Huddell
Robert Wharton
Jonathan Smith
Thomas Biddle

Jonah Thompson
Chandler Price
John Bevan
John Jones
Caleb Birchall
Capt. Wm Jones

Organization: Acting Committee Report

The acting committee made the following report vizt

That they have attended to the duties of their appointment, but have nothing that requires the particular attention of the Society to report at this time.

Philad^a Decr 3rd 1810

signed Jon^a Smith Reg^r

Discipline: Expulsion

The following motion made by Joseph S. Lewis and seconded by Reece Lewis was ordered to be placed on the minutes for the consideration of the Society at their next meeting vizt

Resolved that William Rogers not having paid the sum required by the Constitution for his admission be expelled [from] the Society.

Membership: Refusal to Join

George Thompson having thro' John Jones our messenger declined being a member it was resolved on motion that the Secretary erase his name from the list of members.

Annual Dinner

On motion resolved that the acting committee be directed to provide a dinner on the first day of March next for the Society and that they be directed to invite the officers of the St George's, St Andrew's, Hibernian and German Societies and such other persons as they may think proper not exceeding eight in number.

Membership: New Members

The following gentlemen were proposed as members vizt

Lawrence Lewis	[proposed] by David Lewis
Lewis Eddy	[proposed] by David Lewis
Edward Gray	[proposed] by Jonathan Smith
Benjn F. Garrigues	[proposed] by Matthew L. Bevan
Roberts Vaux	[proposed] by Elihu Chauncey
William Parker	[proposed] by David Lewis

Adjourned

1811
Welch Society

At the Annual Meeting of the Welch Society held at the Mansion House Hotel on March 1st 1811.

Members Present

Richard Price
Thomas Humphreys
Elihu Chauncey
Thomas Parke
Richd H. Morris
Zachariah Poulson
Reece Lewis
Joseph S. Lewis
Curtis Clay
Samuel Parrish
Dr Geo. Gillespy
Enos Bronson
Samuel Relf
George Vaux
Joseph Price
Joseph E. Howell
John Wister
John Jones
David Lewis
John Hallowell

Robert Murdock
James Read
Samuel Wetherill Jr
Thomas Cadwallader
John Clifton
Doct^r Joseph Strong
Samuel N. Lewis
Matthew L. Bevan
Reese Brooks
Benjamin B. Howell
Joseph Wildes
John Hughes
Caleb Birchall
James Milnor
Jonah Thompson
Joseph P. Norris
Benjamin Chew
Joseph Worrell
Thomas Cumpston
John Philips

Organization: Absence of President and Vice President

The President and Vice President being absent Doctor Thomas Parke was called to the chair.

PART THREE

Discipline: Expulsion

The resolution proposed at the last meeting for the expulsion of William Rogers was considered and unanimously adopted.

Membership: Resignation

A letter was read from John Dowers Junr resigning his membership which was accepted.

Finance: Investments

The following report was read from the acting committee vizt

That they have sold the six percent stock the property of the Society and invested the proceeds together with the balance in the hands of the Treasurer in the purchase of five shares of the City Loan, which shares are placed in the corporate name of the Society on the books of the City Treasurer.

Community Interaction: Request for Assistance from St David's Society to Purchase a Burial Ground

The committee beg leave to lay before the Society an application from the St David's Society soliciting a contribution to enable them, to purchase a burying ground.[35]

---

35 Although the above dates from c.1811, according to Charles R. Baker, the Welsh Burying Ground 'dates back to 1809 when the St David's Society purchased land to create a burial ground for its members. The ground extended from Market Street to Oak (now Ludlow Street) between 40th and 41st Streets. In 1834 the surviving members of the Society conveyed ownership to the Welsh Society. Owing to the rapid growth of the City of Philadelphia in the mid-1860s, the bodies were removed (c.1864) to Section 203, Mount Moriah Cemetery, and the property sold. Note that Mount Moriah Cemetery is the resting place of many people from the earliest of cemeteries and churches in Philadelphia'. See Charles R. Baker, *Publications of The Genealogical Society of Pennsylvania*, XI/1 (1931), 36 'Fragments from Old Philadelphia Graveyards'; XI/2 (1931), 144. For further developments see the minutes of the Welsh Society of Philadelphia from 1834.

Annual Dinner

In pursuance of the directions to the acting committee at the last meeting of the Society, the annual dinner has been prepared at the Mansion House Hotel by Mr Renshaw to be on table at 3 o'clock this day.

Philad^a March 1st 1811

Community Interaction: Request for Assistance from St David's Society to Purchase a Burial Ground

The letter from the St David's Society mentioned by the acting committee was referred to Thomas Cadwallader, Benjamin Chew and Joseph S. Lewis to consider and report on the subject at the next meeting.

Assistance to Welsh Emigrants

An account was presented by the executor of Richard C. Jones deceased for so much paid by him for clothes for Howell Jones an orphan under our care, and an order was drawn for the same six dollars and thirty cents in favour of Joseph S. Lewis.

Membership: New Members

The following gentlemen were elected members vizt

William H. Morgan
John S. Willett
Lawrence Lewis
Lewis Eddy
Edward Gray
Benjamin F. Garrigues
Roberts Vaux
William Parker

PART THREE

The following gentlemen were proposed as members vizt

Richard Ware	[proposed] by Joseph Worrell
Charles J. Nicholas	[proposed] by Thomas Cadwallader
James Williams	proposed] by Thomas Cumpston

Finance: Accounts and Investments

The Treasurer reported his accounts. Balance due the Society $60.23/^{100} and that the Society now possess three shares of the stock of the Bank of North America and fifteen shares City Stock.

Organization: Election of Officers

The election being gone into James Milnor and Enos Bronson the Tellers reported the following gentlemen as being duly elected officers for the ensuing year vizt

President	Samuel Meredith
Vice President	Robert Wharton
Treasurer	Thomas Cumpston
Secretary	Joseph S. Lewis
Register	Jonathan Smith
Counsellors	Benjamin R. Morgan
	Charles Chauncey
Physicians	Doct^r Thomas C. James
	Doct^r Joseph Strong
Stewards	John Evans
	Richard Price
	Thomas Parke
	Chandler Price
	Reece Lewis
	Elihu Chauncey
	Matthew L. Beaven

Adjourned

Welch Society

At a Quarterly Meeting of the Welch Society held at the House of David Kennedy[36] on Monday 3rd June 1811.

Members Present

Robert Wharton
Richard Price
Doct[r] Thomas Parke
Chandler Price
Samuel Parrish
Joseph S. Lewis
Jonathan Smith
William H. Morgan
Joseph Huddell Jr
William E. Howell
John Jones
James Prosser

Joseph Price
Zachariah Poulson
Caleb Birchall
Reese Brooks
Joseph Worrell
Reece Lewis
John Hallowell
William Parker
Benjamin Thomas
Joseph Jones
George W. Morgan
Edmund Kinsey

Community Interaction: Request for Assistance from St David's Society to Purchase a Burial Ground

The committee appointed to report upon the petition of the St David's Society, made the following report which was adopted and the Secretary desired to inform them thereof vizt

The committee to whom was referred a petition addressed to this Society by certain persons styling themselves the President, Treasurer and Secretary of the St David's Society, soliciting the aid of this Society in the purchase of a burial ground for the Welch and Welch descendants do report

---

36   A year earlier in 1810 David Kennedy was recorded as a tavernkeeper on 9 Laetitia Court, Philadelphia. See James Robinson (ed.), *The Philadelphia Directory... 1810* (Philadelphia: William Woodhouse, 1810), p. 157.

That in the opinion of your committee the petition ought not to be granted inasmuch as the funds of this Society should not be placed at the disposal of any other institution. But are to be devoted, under the discretion of <u>our own members</u> to the humane and charitable purposes for which we associated.

signed Thos Cadwallader
Benjamin Chew
Joseph S. Lewis

Philad^a Mar[ch] 4th 1811

Assistance to Welsh Emigrants

The acting committee made the following report vizt

That they have attended to the business of the Society and have afforded relief in such cases as occurred which appeared to them to come within the objects of the institution.

Organization: Stewardship of the Society

Since the last meeting of the Society the committee have to regret the resignation of Doct^r Thomas Parke one of the Stewards. The committee having considered it necessary that the vacancy should be filled they have therefore chosen Mr Samuel Parrish as a Steward of the Society until its next annual meeting.

Philad^a June 3rd 1811

signed Jon Smith Reg^r

Discipline: Concerns Relating to a New Member – Roberts Vaux

The Secretary stated that he had received a letter from Roberts Vaux expressing some hesitation in accepting the membership to which he was elected on 1st March last. Jonathan Smith & Joseph S. Lewis were appointed a committee to wait upon Mr Chauncey who proposed him and report at the next meeting upon the subject.

Organization: Rules Regarding the Distribution of Relief

The acting committee were directed to consult the Counsellors of the Society as to our powers in granting relief and the objects to which under the Charter we can apply our funds.

Membership: New Members

The following gentlemen proposed at the last meeting were duly elected members vizt

Richard Ware
Charles J. Nicholas
James Williams

Organization: Printing of the Charter and Bye Laws

Resolved that the Secretary be directed to have 500 copies of the Charter and Bye Laws printed for the use of the members.

Membership: New Member – Captain Thomas Williams

Capt Thomas Williams was proposed for membership by John Jones.

Adjourned.

Welch Society

At a Quarterly Meeting of the Society held at the House of David Kennedy on Monday 2nd Septr 1811.

Members Present

Robert Wharton
Richard Price
Samuel Relf
Chandler Price
Joseph S. Lewis

Thomas Cumpston
James Tatem
John Jones
William H. Morgan
Joseph Huddell Jr

John S. Willett
Edward Tilghman Jr
Reece Lewis
Caleb Birchal
Joseph Price

John Bevan
Elihu Chauncey
George Vaux
Doct^r Thomas Parke
Samuel Parrish

Community Interaction: Request for Assistance from St David's Society to Purchase a Burial Ground

The Secretary reported that he had communicated to the St David's Society the resolve of this Society on their petition.

Membership: New Member

The committee on the case of Roberts Vaux report that he accepted the membership in this Society.

Organization: Rules Regarding the Distribution of Relief

The acting committee made the following report vizt

That they have attended to the interests of the Society generally, and in particular to a resolution of the Society at their last meeting which directs them to consult the Counsellers as to its powers in granting relief and the objects to which under the Charter the Funds can be applied. The committee beg leave to submit to the Society a written opinion of the Counsellers on that subject.

September 2nd 1811

signed Jon^a Smith Reg^r

The opinion of the Counsellers was read as follows

The subscribers having considered the resolution of the Welch Society, upon which their opinion is requested by the acting committee of that Society by a reference to the Counsellers, under date of August 17th 1811 do report

That they are of opinion that the powers of the Society in granting relief are confined by the Charter to advice and assistance to emigrants from Wales, and that the funds of the association cannot with propriety be applied to any other objects. By emigrants they understand persons recently arrived and not persons who have gained a settlement in the country.

If it shall be considered desirable to attend the powers of the Society in the application of its funds, the subscribers respectfully suggest, that an application to the Legislature would be the proper mode of attaining the object.

August 31st 1811

Signed Benjn R. Morgan
Charles Chauncey

Organization: Printing of the Charter and Bye Laws

The Secretary reported that he had complied with the directions of the Society on having 500 copies of the Constitution printed and presented a bill for that and other printing amounting to $82.87/^{100} for which an order was drawn on the Treasurer in favour of Joseph Cruckshank.

Membership: Resignation

A letter was received from Robert Frazer resigning his membership which was accepted.

Adjourned.

PART THREE

Welch Society

At a Quarterly Meeting of the Society held at David Kennedy's Inn on Monday 2nd December 1811.

Members Present

Matthew L. Bevan
Reese Brooke
Caleb Birchall
Thomas Cumpston
James C. Fisher
Benjⁿ F. Garrigues
Benjⁿ B. Howell
William E. Howell
John Jones
Edmund Kinsey
John Morgan
Samuel Relf
William Parker

Reece Lewis
Samuel N. Lewis
Thomas Morris
Richard Price
Chandler Price
John Strawbridge
Robert Wharton
Richard Ware
James Williams
Joseph Price
William H. Morgan
Edward Davies

Membership: Honorary Membership

A letter was read from John S. Willett stating his intention to remove from the State and requesting to be placed on the list of honorary members which was agreed to.

Annual Dinner

On motion it was resolved that the acting committee be directed to provide a dinner on the first day of March next for the Society and that they be directed to invite the officers of the St George's, St Andrew's, Hibernian and German Societies and such other persons as they may think proper not exceeding eight in number.

Discipline: Fines for Non-Attendance / Expulsion

The Secretary having reported that notice had been given agreeably to the Bye-law of March 1ˢᵗ 1803 to John Davis and James Rolph and they not having since paid their dues, on motion, they were expelled [from] the Society.

Membership: New Member

Captⁿ Thomas Williams proposed as a member on 3ʳᵈ June last was duly elected.

Organization: Amending the Charter for Educational Provision

Mr Chandler Price offered the following resolution which was unanimously adopted vizt

Resolved that the acting committee be authorized to apply to the Legislature so to amend the Charter of the Society as to enable them to apply the funds of the Society to more general purposes and particularly to the educating poor children of Welch parents.

Membership: New Member

William A. Shaw was proposed as a member of this Society by Joseph S. Lewis.

Adjourned.

PART THREE

1812

Welch Society

At the Annual Meeting of the Society held at the Masonic Hall[37] on Monday 2nd March 1812.

Members Present

Matthew L. Bevan
Reese Brooks
Caleb Birchall
Thomas Cumpston
Thomas Cadwallader
John Clifton
Elihu Chauncey
Curtis Clay
Benjamin Chew
Edward Davies
William E. Howell
John Hallowell
Benjamin Jones
Richard Jones
David Lewis
Samuel Meredith
Richard Maris
William Meredith
George W. Morgan
Thomas Morris
Joseph P. Norris
Richard Price
Joseph Price

Peter Evans
Issacher Evans
Samuel Evans
Lewis Eddy
James C. Fisher
Benjn F. Garrigues
Thomas Humphreys
Joseph Huddell Jr
John Hughes
George Howell
Richard Peters Jr
Zachariah Poulson
William Parker
James Read
Samuel Relf
James Read Jr
Jonathan Smith
Joseph Smith
Edward Tilghman Jr
Robert Wharton
Samuel Wetherill Jr
John Wister
Charles Wister

---

37   The two-storey Masonic Hall, Chestnut Street, Philadelphia, was built between 1808 and 1811 on the designs of William Strickland. It burnt down in 1818 and was rebuilt two years later.

John M. Price John J. Wheeler
John J. Parry Richard Ware
Chandler Price James Williams
Dr Thomas Parke Jonathan Smith

Membership: Resignation

A letter was received from Jesse Sharpless resigning his membership in the Society which was accepted.

Organization: Amending the Charter for Educational Provision

The acting committee made the following report vizt.

That in pursuance of a resolution adopted at the last meeting of the Society they have prepared a memorial to the Legislature of this State; the object contemplated by the resolution being in the opinion of the committee of great importance they have thought it most prudent to lay the memorial before the Society at its annual meeting for consideration previous to taking any further steps in the business.

Annual Dinner

The committee have as usual attended to the concerns of the institution generally & have nothing further to report that requires the attention of the Society at present except that they have ordered a dinner to be prepared this day at this house at three o'clock PM.

Philad^a March 2nd 1812

(signed) Jon Smith Reg^r

Organization: Amending the Charter for Educational Provision

The above report with the memorial alluded to having been read, it was resolved that the subject to which the memorial refers be postponed indefinitely.

Organization: Salary of the Messenger

The annual salary of the messenger was fixed at one hundred dollars to commence the 1st Instant.

PART THREE

Finance: Accounts

The Treasurer presented his account. Balance due from him $261.56/[100].

Assistance to Welsh Emigrants

An application on behalf of a Mrs Pearce for relief was read and with sundry documents accompanying the same referred to the acting committee.

Membership: New Member

William A. Shaw proposed at the last meeting of the Society was duly elected a member.

Organization: Election of Officers

The Society then proceeded to elect officers for the ensuing year. John Hallowell & William Parker, the Tellers, reported the following gentlemen as being duly elected

President	Samuel Meredith
Vice President	Robert Wharton
Treasurer	Thomas Cumpston
Secretary	Joseph S. Lewis
Register	Jonathan Smith
Counsellors	Benjamin R. Morgan
	Charles Chauncey
Physicians	Doct[r] Thomas C. James
	Doct[r] Joseph Strong
Stewards	John Evans
	Richard Price
	Chandler Price
	Reece Lewis
	Elihu Chauncey
	Matthew L. Beaven
	Samuel Relf
Adjourned	

201

signed Jon Smith Reg^r
for Joseph S. Lewis Secretary

Welch Society

At a Quarterly Meeting of the Society held at the House of Peter Evans[38] on Monday 1st June 1812.

Members Present

David Lewis
Reece Lewis
Joseph S. Lewis
John J. Parry
Joseph Jones
Benjn R. Morgan
John Jones

Reese Brooke
Edmund Kinsey
Joseph Price
Robert Wharton
Caleb Birchal
Peter Evans

Absence of President and Temporary Absence of Vice-President

The President and Vice President being absent Benjamin R. Morgan was appointed Chairman after which the Vice President attended and took the Chair.

Assistance to Welsh Emigrants

The acting committee were directed to make report at the next meeting of the Society upon the case of Mrs Pearce.

---

38 Peter Evans was the proprietor of several taverns in Philadelphia. In 1808 he was located at the corner of Schuylkill High and Front Streets, which he continued to occupy in 1810. In 1817 he was recorded as occupying the City Hotel on the north-west corner of Chestnut and Seventh Streets, Philadelphia. See James Robinson (ed.), *The Philadelphia Directory... 1808* (Philadelphia: William Woodhouse, 1808), unpaginated (see under Evans, Peter); Robinson (ed.), *The Philadelphia Directory... 1810*, p. 95; James Robinson (ed.), *Robinson's Original Annual Directory... 1817* (Philadelphia: James Robinson, 1817), p. 162.

PART THREE

Death of Society's Physician

The secretary reported the decease of our respected member Doct^r Joseph Strong for many years a physician of the Society whereupon agreeably to the seventh article of the Charter the Society proceeded to elect a physician in his place when Doct^r Thomas Parke was duly elected of which Secretary is to inform him.

Membership: Resignation

A letter was read from Richard Peters Junr resigning his membership which was accepted.

Finance: Bequest and Investment of Funds

Mr Wharton reported that he had called several times at the request of the Treasurer upon John Britton for the interest due on his bond part of the legacy of John Keble and that he could not collect the interest, of which upwards of two years were due. Upon which the bond was directed to be delivered to Mr Morgan one of our Counsellors to enter up judgment to proceed to recover as soon as possible the principal and interest. The bond was accordingly delivered to Mr Morgan.

Adjourned

Welch Society

At a Quarterly Meeting of the Society held at the House of Peter Evans on Monday 7th September 1812.

Members Present

Caleb Birchall
Richard Ware
Reese Brooke
Job Bacon
Joseph S. Lewis

Jonah Thompson
Thomas Cumpston
Benjamin Thomas
Doct^r Thomas Parke
Peter Evans

Edmund Kinsey
John Jones
John Morgan
Joseph Price

Dr George Gillaspy
Robert Wharton
Edward Davies
John Bacon

Organization: Absence of President and Temporary Absence of Vice-President

The President and Vice President being absent Thomas Cumpston was appointed Chairman after which the Vice President appeared and took his seat.

Finance: Bequest and Investment of Funds

The Treasurer reported he had received the principal and interest of John Britton's bond whereupon the acting committee were directed to have the unappropriated monies in the hands of the Treasurer invested in such manner as they may deem most proper.

Assistance to Welsh Emigrants

The acting committee not having made report in the case of Mrs Pearce owing to the absence of the Register are required to do so at the next meeting.

An application was received from Rachel Michael, widow of our deceased member Capt[n] Joseph Michael stating her distress and requesting assistance which was referred to the acting committee for their early attention.

Adjourned

PART THREE

Welch Society

At a Quarterly Meeting of the Society held at the House of Peter Evans on Monday 7th December 1812.

Members Present

Thomas Cumpston
Chandler Price
Griffith Evans
Thomas Morris
William H. Morgan
Joseph Price
James Williams
Job Bacon
Edmund Kinsey
John Jones
John Bacon
Doct' Thomas Parke
Edward Gray

Jonathan Smith
Reese Brooke
Joseph Huddell Jr
Richard Ware
Edward Davies
Caleb Birchall
Peter Evans
Benjamin Thomas
Richard Price
John Hallowell
Dr George Gillaspy
William Parker
Samuel Relf

Organization: Absence of President, Vice-President and Secretary

The President and Vice President being absent, the Treasurer was appointed chairman and in the absence of the Secretary the Register acted in his place.

Assistance to Welsh Emigrants

The acting committee made the following report which was read, adopted and ordered to be entered on the minutes vizt

That they have attended to the business of the Society generally, but particularly to the objects referred to them at the last meeting on the application of Mrs Michael & Mrs Pearce the committee have to state that on recurring to the Act of Incorporation as also to the opinion of the Counsellors lately reported to the Society, they find the Society is not authorized to afford relief out of its funds.

Finance: Investment of Funds

The acting committee further reports that in pursuance of the directions of the Society they have purchased the sum of two thousand one hundred dollars of the Six Per Cent Stock of the United States of 1812 with interest from the first day of October last which stands in the name of "The Welch Society of Philadelphia" the certificates of which are deposited with the Treasurer.

December 7th 1812

Signed Jon^a Smith, Reg^r

Annual Dinner

On motion it was resolved that the acting committee be directed to provide a dinner on the first day of March next for the Society and that they be directed to invite the officers of the St George's, St Andrew's, Hibernian and German Societies and such other persons as they may think proper not exceeding eight in number.

Membership: New Members

The following were proposed as member of the Society vizt

Lewis Miles	[proposed] by Benjamin Thomas
Thomas Evans	[proposed] by Edmund Kinsey

Adjourned.

signed Jonathan Smith Register

PART THREE

1813
Welch Society

At the Annual Meeting of the Society held at the House of Peter Evans on Monday 1ˢᵗ March 1813.

Members Present

Robert Wharton
Benjⁿ R. Morgan
Richard Price
James Read Jr
Joseph Wildes
George Gillaspy
Zachariah Poulson
Joseph S. Lewis
Reese Brooke
Caleb Birchall
John Jones
John Hughes
Wᵐ H. Morgan
George W. Morgan
Lewis Walker
William Parker
Samuel Relf
Joseph Huddell Jr
Edmund Kinsey
Samuel N. Lewis
Jonah Thompson
John Wister
William Meredith
John J. Parry
Dr Thomas Parke
Joseph Simons

Joseph Williams
Edward Davies
Richard Ware
William W. Fisher
Griffith Evans
Dr Thomas C. James
Matthew L. Bevan
Joseph E. Howell
Enos Bronson
Thomas Cumpston
Joseph Price
Thomas Morris
Richard H. Morris
Joseph P. Norris
Ezekiel C. Maddock
Benjamin Chew
David Lewis
James Williams
James Read
Samˡ Wetherill Jr
Elihu Chauncey
Peter Evans
Tristram B. Freeman
Chandler Price
John J. Wheeler
John Bevan

Finance: Accounts

The Treasurer reported his Accounts, balance due the Society $372.86/^{100}.

Assistance to Welsh Emigrants

The acting committee made the following report vizt

that they have attended to the duties of their appointment; nothing on the subject of application for charity has occurred since the last meeting.

Annual Dinner

They have agreeably to the resolution of the Society engaged a dinner to be prepared by Mr Renshaw at the Mansion House Hotel this day at 3 o'clock.

Membership: Resignation and New Members

Samuel Humphreys offered his resignation of membership which was accepted.

Lewis Miles and Thomas Evans proposed as members at the last meeting were duly elected.

The following gentlemen were proposed as members vizt

Samuel Havard Jacobs	[proposed] by John J. Parry
David Meredith	[proposed] by Chandler Price
Thomas W. Morgan	[proposed] by Jonah Thompson

Organization: Election of Officers

The Society then proceeded to elect its officers for the ensuing year. William Meredith and Matthew L. Bevan being appointed Tellers reported the following gentlemen as being duly elected vizt

President	Samuel Meredith
Vice President	Robert Wharton
Treasurer	Thomas Cumpston

Secretary   Joseph S. Lewis
Register   Jonathan Smith
Counsellors   Benjamin R. Morgan
                 Charles Chauncey
Physicians   Thomas C. James
                 Thomas Parke
Stewards   John Evans
                 Richard Price
                 Chandler Price
                 Reece Lewis
                 Elihu Chauncey
                 Matthew L. Bevan
                 Samuel Relf

Adjourned

Welch Society

At a Quarterly Meeting of the Society held at the House of Peter Evans on Monday 7th June 1813.

Members Present

Thomas Cumpston
Jonathan Smith
Peter Evans
Lewis Walker
Reece Lewis
Thomas Evans
John Jones
Thomas Morris
Dr Thomas Parke

James Williams
Griffith Evans
Job Bacon
Elihu Chauncey
John Hughes
Caleb Birchall
Joseph Price
Richard Price
Robert Wharton

Organization: No Business

The acting committee reported that they had nothing to lay before the Society at present requiring its consideration.

Membership: Resignations

John C. Jones offered his resignation which was agreed to be accepted upon his paying the fines and contributions due.

The resignation of William Hunt was read and accepted.

Membership: Honorary Status

John Strawbridge informed the Society that he had removed to the country & requesting he might be exempted from payment of fines being willing to pay his annual contribution which was agreed to and his name ordered to be placed on the list of honorary members.

Membership: New Member

William W. Howell was proposed as a member by John M. Price.

Adjourned

for Joseph S. Smith Secretary

signed Reece Lewis

Welch Society

At a Quarterly Meeting of the Society held at the House of Peter Evans on Monday 6th Septr 1813.

Members Present

Thomas Parke
Lewis Walker
Wm H. Morgan
Joseph S. Lewis
Reece Lewis

Jonathan Smith
Thomas Cumpston
Matthew L. Bevan
Edmund Kinsey
Joseph Price

Peter Evans Thomas Evans
Richard Price Caleb Birchall
John Jones Thomas Morris

Organization: Absence of President, Vice-President and Secretary

The President and Vice President being absent Thomas Cumpston was appointed chairman.

Organization: General Business

The acting committee made the following report vizt

That they have attended to the business of the Society generally since its last meeting.

Assistance to Welsh Emigrants

That they have now under their care John Roberts, a Welch emigrant, and his family which consists of a wife and four small children. He has been sick for a considerable time past and has been attended by Doct^r James one of the Physicians of the Society, he is now nearly recovered. The committee have advanced for the relief of himself and family twenty-six dollars and are of opinion a further sum will be necessary.

September 6th 1813

signed Jon Smith, Reg^r

Membership: Resignations

The resignation of Joseph Hopkinson was read and accepted as was also that of Griffith Evans.

Discipline: Waiving of Fines and Contributions

In consequence of the indisposition of James Tatem it is resolved that the fines and contributions now due by him be remitted, and that he should not be charged for any in future until the further order of the Society on the subject.

Adjourned

Welch Society

At a Quarterly Meeting of the Society held at the House of Peter Evans on Monday 6th Dec[embe]r 1813.

Members Present

Reese Brooke
Caleb Birchall
Thomas Cumpston
Edward Davies
Peter Evans
Thomas Evans
John Jones
Reece Lewis
Richard Price
Joseph Price
John J. Parry
Dr Thos Parke

Jonathan Smith
Lewis Walker
Richard Ware
Matthew L. Bevan
Robert Wharton
Thomas Morris
John Bevan
John Griffith
William Parker
Edmund Kinsey
William H. Morgan
Robert Wharton[39]

Assistance to Welsh Emigrants

The acting committee made the following report vizt

That since the last meeting of the Society they have advanced a further sum for the relief of John Roberts and family and that he had recovered from a severe indisposition & that a comfortable situation for himself and family had been provided where they were now settled. The committee beg leave to state that Mr Roberts & family have recently arrived from Wales that during the short period that he had resided in this country, he had conducted himself so as to obtain the approbation and esteem of those by whom he was employed, that his wages as a day labourer was not more than barely sufficient to maintain his family which consists of himself a wife and four small children, that during the last summer he was attacked with a very severe disease which would in all probability have terminated in death had it not been for the great

---
39 Second citation in this list.

care and attention of Doctor James, one of the physicians of the Society, and the pecuniary aid afforded him from its funds. The whole amount advanced by the Treasurer for his relief is forty-six dollars.

December 6th 1813

signed Jon Smith Reg^r

Membership: Resignation

Charles Marshall Jr offered his resignation of membership and stated some difference in the amount due to the Society. The matter was referred to the acting committee.

Annual Dinner

The acting committee were directed to provide a dinner on the anniversary of the Society the first day of March next for the Society and to invite the officers of the St George's, St Andrew's, Hibernian and German Societies and such other persons as they may think proper not exceeding eight in number.

Membership: New Members

The following gentlemen were elected members vizt

Samuel Havard Jacobs	Thomas W. Morgan
David Meredith	William W. Howell

The following gentlemen were proposed as members of the Society vizt

Thomas Allibone	[proposed] by Richard Price
Daniel Thomas	[proposed] by John Jones
William Rawle Jr	[proposed] by Charles Chauncey
Ward Griffin	[proposed] by John Jones

Adjourned

signed Reece Lewis for

Joseph S. Lewis Secretary

1814
Welch Society

At the Annual Meeting of the Society held at the House of Peter Evans March 1st 1814.

Members Present

Samuel Meredith
Matthew L. Bevan
Reese Brook
Job Bacon
Caleb Birchall
Elihu Chauncey
William Craig
Peter Evans
Thomas Evans
Benjn F. Garrigues
John Hughes
Joseph E. Howell
William E. Howell
William H. Howell
Benjamin Jones
John Jones
John Bevan
Edward Davies
Edmund Kinsey
Joseph S. Lewis
Reece Lewis
Richard H. Morris
E. C. Maddock
George W. Morgan
William Parker

Robert Murdock
Thomas Morris
Wm H. Morgan
David Meredith
Richard Price
Joseph Price
John M. Price
Chandler Price
Dr Thomas Parke
Zachariah Poulson
Samuel Relf
James Read Jr
William A. Shaw
George Vaux
Robert Wharton
Samuel Wetherill Jr
John Wister
John J. Wheeler
Richard Ware
James Williams
Enos Bronson
Joseph Huddell
Joseph Simons
Edward Davies
Thomas Cadwallader

Finance: Accounts

The Treasurers report was read shewing a balance due to Society of $809.78/^{100}.

Assistance to Welsh Emigrants

The following report of the acting committee was read and adopted vizt.

That they have attended carefully to the interests of the Society since its last meeting particularly to the subjects referred to them at that time.

The committee in their last report to the Society on the case of John Roberts omitted to state that Doctor Parke attended him during his late illness as well as Doctor James whose name alone was mentioned, they therefore think it but justice to mention the inadvertent omission in this report.

Membership: Resignation

The committee on an examination of the subject of Mr Charles Marshall Jr's letter referred to them find he had paid what was required from him some time ago, at which time he had desired to resign his membership in the Society. Under these circumstances the committee beg leave to recommend an acceptance of his resignation.

Annual Dinner

The committee have in pursuance of the directions of the Society made the necessary arrangements with Mr Renshaw at the Mansion House for the annual dinner this day at 3 o'clock where the members are respectfully invited to attend.

March 1st 1814

signed Jon Smith Reg^r

Membership: Resignations

On motion Charles Marshall Jr resignation was accepted in pursuance of the recommendation of the acting committee.

A letter was read from George Gillaspy resigning his membership which was accepted.

Organization: Changes to Bye-Laws- Fines for Non-Attendance

On motion of Mr Bronson seconded by Mr Wharton resolved that a committee be appointed to consider and report the propriety of repealing or altering the Bye-Laws imposing an annual contribution and fines for non-attendance at the quarterly and annual meeting. Mr Bronson, Mr Jonathan Smith and Mr Joseph S. Lewis were appointed

Membership: New Members

Thomas Allibone   were elected members of the Society
Daniel Thomas
Wm Racole Jr
Ward Griffin

Organization: Election of Officers

Mr George Vaux and Mr Job Bacon were appointed judges of the election who reported the following gentleman as being chosen officers for the ensuing year vizt

President	Samuel Meredith
Vice President	Robert Wharton
Treasurer	Thomas Cumpston
Secretary	Joseph S. Lewis
Register	Jonathan Smith
Counsellors	Benjamin R. Morgan
	Charles Chauncey
Physicians	Doct^r Thomas C. James
	Doct^r Thomas Parke
Stewards	John Evans
	Richard Price

PART THREE

>Chandler Price
>Matthew L. Bevan
>Samuel Relf
>Thomas Morris
>Benjn B. Howell

Membership: New Member

Mr Charles Foulke was proposed as a member by John M. Price

Adjourned

Welch Society

At the Quarterly Meeting of the Society held at the House of Peter Evans June 6th 1814.

Members Present

Enos Bronson	Edmund Kinsey
Caleb Birchall	Joseph S. Lewis
Thomas Cumpston	Richard Price
Edward Davies	John M. Price
Peter Evans	Joseph Price
Samuel Evans	Samuel Relf
Thomas Evans	Jonathan Smith
William W. Howell	Robert Wharton
Richard Ware	Benjamin B. Howell
William H. Morgan	William W. Fisher
Dr Thos Parke	John Hallowell

Organization: Changes to Bye-Laws- Fines for Non-Attendance

The committee appointed at the last meeting 'to report on the propriety of repealing or altering the Bye-Laws imposing an annual contribution and fines for non attendance at the quarterly an[d] annual meetings' made the following report vizt

That your committee have diligently considered the subject and have found that the amount of fines has been prescribed by the Charter of Incorporation and cannot therefore be regulated by the Bye-Laws.

It is the opinion of your committee that under the present circumstances of the Society and the political condition of the country, the annual contribution might, without injury, be dispensed with, but as that for the present year has in part been paid and the money invested and as demands upon the Society may again be increased in consequence of events which may take place previous to the next annual meeting, your committee beg leave to lay upon the table the following resolution, and at the same time to recommend that the further consideration of it be postponed until the first of March next.

Resolved. That the eighth and last article of the Bye-Laws be and the same hereby is repealed.

signed E. Bronson
Jon Smith
Joseph S. Lewis

Whereupon the report was ordered to lay on the table.

Membership: Death of a Member and Significant Arrears

The acting committee made the following report vizt

That since the last meeting of the Society their messenger John Jones has died, that in consequence thereof they appointed a committee to examine the state of his account with the Society and to receive the effects that were in his possession. The committee has reported that the books and other property of the Society were immediately delivered up and are in the hands of the Secretary, but they regret to add that there appears a balance due from John Jones of $347 which from an examination of his effects it appears will not be speedily paid if even a material loss is not sustained. The committee on the subject are continued who will attend to the interest of the Society.

PART THREE

Membership: Death of a Steward

The committee have to announce with sincere regret the decease of their fellow officer John Evans. So many years distinguished by his attention to the duties of Steward and whose attachment to the interest of the Society and his universal benevolence will long be deplored by every member.

Philad^a June 6th 1814

signed Jon Smith Reg^r

New Member: Charles Foulke

Charles Foulke proposed at last meeting was duly elected a member.

Membership: New Members

The following gentlemen were proposed as members vizt

John B. Bowen	by Enos Bronson
Thomas Evans	by his father Peter Evans

Adjourned

Welch Society

At the Quarterly Meeting of the Society held at the House of Peter Evans September 5th 1814.

Members Present

Richard Price	William W. Howell
Thomas Cumpston	Thomas Evans
Richard Ware	Thomas Parke
Thos C. Wharton	Benjn Thomas
Lewis Miles	Caleb Birchall
Joseph S. Lewis	Edmund Kinsey
William H. Morgan	John J. Parry

Benjⁿ F. Garrigues
Elihu Chauncey
George Vaux

Joseph P. Norris
Peter Evans
Daniel Thomas

Organization: Absence of President and Vice-President

The President and Vice President being absent Mr Cumpston was appointed Chairman.

Organization: Appointment of Society Collector

The Secretary on behalf of the Register (who was absent on indispensable business) reported that the acting committee had appointed Mr Benjamin F. Garrigues collector in the place of Mr John Jones, deceased, who had accepted the office and given bond with surety, which bond was now delivered to the Treasurer.

Membership: Resignation of Member

A letter was read from James Milnor resigning his membership which was accepted.

Benevolence: Legacy of Robert Montgomery for Charitable Objects; Liaison with Other Ethnic Societies

On motion Robert Wharton, George Vaux and Joseph S. Lewis were appointed a committee to join any committee that may be appointed by the other benevolent Societies of this city for the purpose of obtaining a distribution of the money bequeathed by Mr Robert Montgomery dec^d for charitable objects. And that the Secretary give notice thereof to the German, St George's, Hibernian and St Andrew's Societies.

Adjourned

PART THREE

Welch Society

At the Quarterly Meeting of the Society held at the House of Peter Evans Monday evening 5th December 1814.

Members Present

Robert Wharton
Richard Price
Thomas Evans
Samuel Evans
Joseph S. Lewis
Jonathan Smith
Edmund Kinsey
John J. Parry
Caleb Birchall
Joseph P. Norris
Joseph Price
Lewis Miles
William H. Morgan

Thomas Cumpston
Ezekiel C. Maddock
Benjn F. Garrigues
Chandler Price
James C. Fisher
Edward Davies
Richard Ware
Thomas Allibone
Peter Evans
William E. Howell
Benjamin Thomas
Thomas Morris

Benevolence: Legacy of Robert Montgomery for Charitable Objects; Liaison with Other Ethnic Societies

The committee appointed at the last meeting to call upon the executors of Robert Montgomery are continued.

Membership: Resignation

A letter was read from Fishbourne Wharton tendering his resignation which was referred to Richard Price and Benjn F. Garrigues.

Organization: Bye-Law, 1803 – Fines and Expulsion

The Secretary reported that agreably [*sic*] to the Bye-Law of 1st March 1803 he had given notice to the following members who had not in consequence paid their fines vizt

John Haines
William Ogden

Whereupon on motion they were expelled from the Society.

Membership: New Member – Deferred

The election of John B. Bowen was postponed in consequence of the absence of Mr E. Bronson who proposed him.

Membership: New Member

Thomas Evans, son of Peter was duly elected a member.

Annual Diner Preparations

The acting committee are directed to provide a dinner on the anniversary of the Society on the first March next and to invite the Officers of the St George's, St Andrew's, Hibernian and German Societies and such other persons as they may think proper not exceeding eight in number.

No Further Business

The acting committee made the following report vizt

That they have attended to the concerns of the Society since its last meeting there has nothing however occurred which requires the attention of the Society at present.

signed Jon Smith Reg[r]

PART THREE

1815

Welch Society

At the Annual Meeting of the Society held at the Washington Hall Hotel[40] March 1st 1815.

Present

Richard Price
James C. Fisher
E. E. Maddock
Edward Davies
Joseph Price
James Read
William E. Howell
George W. Morgan
Daniel Thomas
Samuel Relf
Willm H. Morgan
George Vaux
Samuel Evans
Caleb Hughes
Thomas Evans
James Williams
William Parker
Thomas Parke
William Craig
Joseph S. Lewis
Thomas Cumpston
Matthew L. Bevan

Thomas Cadwallader
Elisha Chauncey
John Hallowell
James Read Junr
Edmund Kinsey
Joseph Williams
Jonathan Smith
William W. Fisher
Peter Evans
Zachariah Poulson
Job Bacon
John Bacon
Caleb Birchall
Benjn F. Garrigues
Richard Ward
Enos Bronson
David Lewis
Lawrence Lewis
Samuel Wetherell Jr
John Bevan
Robert Wharton
James Read

---

40 This was located at 122 South Third Street, Philadelphia, and owned by William Renshaw.

Organization: Absence of President and Vice-President

The President and Vice President being absent Mr Cumpston was appointed Chairman.

Organization: Bye-Laws

The resolution proposed for the consideration of the Society on the 6th June last year was this day taken up as follows vizt

Resolved that the eighth and last article of the Bye-Laws, be and the same are hereby repealed and on motion the same was disagreed to.

Benevolence: Legacy of Robert Montgomery for Charitable Objects; Liaison with Other Ethnic Societies

The committee appointed to call on the executor of Robert Montgomery reported they had done so and were answered there were several claims against the estate which are contested and unsettled, and that the distribution of the residue of the funds in their hands cannot be made until the year 1817, whereupon the committee are continued.

Membership: Resignation and Arrears of Fines

The committee on the case of Fishbourne Wharton reported that he had received his certificate of membership and had paid some of his fines, upon which it was resolved that his resignation cannot be accepted unless he pays the fines and contributions now due from him.

Global News: Peace with Britain

The acting committee reported, that since their last communication to the Society they have duly attended to its interests. The acting committee with great pleasure embrace this opportunity to congratulate the Society on the restoration of peace between our beloved country & that of our ancestors and that we have the pleasing prospect of shortly using our endeavours on applying our funds to the benevolent purpose for which the Society was formed.

PART THREE

Finance: Accounts and Investments

By the Treasurers account which accompanies this report, it appears that there is a balance due the Society, unappropriated of $1313.27/[100].

The committee take the liberty of requesting the direction of the Society as to the disposition of that sum.

Philadelphia, March 1st, 1815

(signed) Jon^a Smith Reg.

upon which it was resolved that the acting committee be directed to invest the balance in the hands of the Treasurer in such stock as they may deem proper.

Membership: New Members

John R. Mifflin
Charles Dixey
Thomas A. Morgan

were duly elected members

Organization: Election of Officers

Edmund Kinsey and Joseph Williams were appointed judges of the election for officers. After the close of the election they reported the following gentlemen as chosen for the ensuing year vizt

President	Samuel Meredith
Vice President	Robert Wharton
Treasurer	Thomas Cumpston
Secretary	Joseph S. Lewis
Register	Jonathan Smith
Stewards	Richard Price
	Chandler Price
	Matthew L. Bevan
	Samuel Relf
	Thomas Morris

	Benjamin S. Howell
Physicians	Doct^r Thomas C. James
	Doct^r Thomas Parke
Counsellors	Charles Chauncey
	Benjn R. Morgan

Membership: New Member

Wharton Lewis was proposed as a member by Robert Wharton.

Adjourned.

Welch Society

At the Quarterly Meeting held at the House of Peter Evans, June 5th 1815.

Present

Richard Price
Joseph P. Norris
Chandler Price
Thomas Evans
Joseph Simons
Joseph S. Lewis
Peter Evans
Samuel H. Jacobs
and Robert Wharton

Joseph Worrell
Thomas Allibone Junr
Caleb Birchall
Lewis Miles
Joseph Price
Job Bacon
Thomas Morris
Willm H. Morgan

Organization: Absence of President and Vice-President

The President and Vice President being absent Richard Price was appointed Chairman.

Organization: Meeting Not Quorate

No quorum being present for the election of members and no business offering the meeting adjourned.

PART THREE

Welch Society

At the Quarterly Meeting held at the House of Peter Evans Monday, 4 September 1815.

Present

Robert Wharton
Richard Price
George W. Morgan
John Bacon
Elihu Chauncey
Peter Evans
John J. Parry
Wm H. Morgan
Benjⁿ F. Garrigues
Thomas Allibone
Enos Bronson
Edward Davies

William E. Howell
Joseph Price
Reese Brookes
Thomas Evans of Peter[41]
Thomas Evans
Richard Ware
Benjamin Thomas
Edmund Kinsey
Lewis Miles
Jonathan Smith
Thomas Parker
Samuel H. Jacobs

Organization: No Business

The Register reported verbally that nothing had occurred since the last meeting that required the attention of the acting committee.

Membership: New Member

John O. Evans was nominated as a member by Samuel H. Jacobs.

Adjourned

---

41   St Peter's, Philadelphia.

Welch Society

At the Quarterly Meeting held at the House of Peter Evans Monday Evening, December 4th 1815

Present

Joseph P. Norris
Richard Price
Joseph Worrell
John Clifton
Thomas Evans of Peter
Edmund Kinsey
Willm H. Morgan
Caleb Birchall
John Bevan
Samuel Evans
Joseph Shaw
Lewis Miles

George W. Morgan
Thomas Evans
Jonathan Smith
Thomas Parke
Joseph S. Lewis
Peter Evans
John J. Parry
Samuel Relf
Benjamin Thomas
Joseph Simons
Joseph Huddell Junr

Organization: Absence of President and Vice-President

The President and Vice President being absent Jonathan Smith was appointed Chairman.

Membership: Resignations

A letter was received from Robert Vaux resigning his membership and also one from John J. Wheeler, both of which were accepted.

Finance: Accounts

The acting committee made a partial report. They are desired to make a full report of the funds at the next meeting.

Membership: New Members

Wharton Lewis and Joseph O. Evans were duly elected members.

Annual Dinner

The acting committee are directed to provide a dinner on the anniversary of the Society, the 1st March next and to invite the officer of the St George's, St Andrew's, Hibernian & German Society, and such other persons as they may think proper not exceeding eight in number.

Membership: New Members

Thomas Roberts was proposed as a member by Peter Evans.

adjourned.

1816
Welch Society

At the Annual Meeting of the Society, held at the House of Peter Evans March 1st 1816.

Present

Richard Price
James Read
Enos Bronson
Zach^h Poulson
John B. Bowen
Joseph P. Norris
Thomas Evans
Caleb Birchall
Jon^a Thompson
Joseph Price
Job Bacon
John Bevan
Edward Davies
Thomas Morris
John Bevan
Thomas Cumpston
William Craig
Joseph Ogden Evans
Thomas Evans of Peter
John Hughes
William E. Howell

Edmund Kinsey
Wharton Lewis
John Morgan
E. E. Maddock
Gale Morgan
Robert Murdock
Joseph Jones
Thomas Morris
Matthew L. Bevan
William H. Morgan
Thomas Parke
James Read Junr
Samuel Relf
Jonathan Smith
Jonah Thompson
Joseph Williams
Joseph Worrell
Richard Ware
James Williams
William Parker
Joseph S. Lewis

Organization: Absence of President and Vice-President

The President and Vice President being absent Mr Cumpston was called to the Chair.

PART THREE

Finance: Accounts and Investments

The acting committee reported that they have in pursuance of the directions of the Society purchased seventeen hundred and twenty dollars and seventy four cents of funded six per cent stock of the United States, which now stands in the name of the Society and that the whole amount of stock now belonging to the Society consists of three shares of the Bank of North America, fifteen shares of Water Loan and six per cent stock of the United States, amounting to three thousand six hundred & ninety four dollars 75/^{100} and making in the whole seven thousand and thirty nine dollars, seventy five cents in value.

Organization: General Business

The committee have attended to the interest of the Society generally, since the last meeting, but have nothing further to communicate at present that requires attention.

(signed) Jon^a Smith Reg^r

The Treasurer reported his accounts, balance due the Society 346.36/^{100} dollars.

Membership: New Member

Thomas Roberts was duly elected a member.

Organization: Election of Officers

This being the day of the annual election Thomas Parke and Enos Bronson were appointed Judges who reported the following result, vizt

President	Samuel Meredith
Vice President	Robert Wharton
Treasurer	Thomas Cumpston
Secretary	Joseph S. Lewis
Register	Jonathan Smith

Stewards	Richard Price
	Chandler Price
	Matthew L. Bevan
	Samuel Relf
	Thos Morris
	Benjn B. Howell
	Wm C. Howell
Physicians	Doct^r Thomas C. James
	Thomas Parke
Counsellors	Benjamin R. Morgan
	Charles Chauncey

Adjourned.

Welch Society

At the Quarterly Meeting of the Society, held at the House of Peter Evans June 3rd 1816.

Present

Samuel Relf	Peter Evans
Joseph S. Lewis	Thomas Evans
William H. Morgan	Joseph P. Norris
Richard Price	Thomas Evans of Peter
Thomas Morris	Reese Brooke
Richard Ware	Thomas Roberts

Organization: Meeting Not Quorate

The President and Vice President being absent Richard Price was appointed Chairman when the roll being called and a quorum not being present, the company

Adjourned.

PART THREE

Welch Society

At the Quarterly Meeting of the Society held at the House of Peter Evans September 2nd 1816.

Present

Richard Price
Thomas Parker
Joseph P. Norris
Joseph S. Lewis
Joseph O. Evans
Joseph Simons
and

Thomas Evans
Thomas Evans of Peter
Job Bacon
Richard Ware
William H. Morgan
Peter Evans
Lewis Miles

Organization: Absence of President and Vice-President

The President and Vice President being absent Richard Price was appointed Chairman.

Membership: Resignations

A letter was received from James Read resigning his membership on account of bodily infirmities which was accepted; also from Captn W. Hendry, which was accepted.

Adjourned.

Welch Society

At the Quarterly Meeting of the Society, held at the House of Peter Evans, December 2nd 1816.

Present

Doct^r James Parke
Thomas Cumpston
John Cliffton

William W. Fisher
Job Bacon
Joseph P. Norris

Benjamin Thomas
George W. Morgan
Samuel Relf
Joseph O. Evans
William H. Morgan
and

Joseph S. Lewis
Thomas Evans
Richard Ware
Peter Evans
Joseph Huddell
Edmund Kinsey

Organization: Absence of President and Vice-President

The President and Vice President being absent Thomas Cumpston was appointed Chairman.

Organization: New Collector

The acting committee have as usual paid attention to the current affairs of the Society and have to report further that Edward Garrigues having found his engagements would not permit his further attention as Collector, they had appointed Mr Thomas Evans in his place who has given bond accordingly.

Organization: New Registrer

Mr Smith, our late Register, having also declined from the same cause, Mr William W. Fisher has been named in his place.

Discipline: Letter to Samuel Meredith – Attendance

The committee have addressed a letter to our worthy President enquiring whether he will again be able to attend our meetings his presence being indispensable to sign certificates and if not to ascertain whether he is desirous of retaining his situation.

Finance: Accounts

There is in the hands of the Treasurer the sum of three hundred and seventeen dollars & thirty cents and the stocks remain as reported in March last.

(signed) W. W. Fisher Reg[r]

Annual Dinner

On motion the acting committee were directed to provide a dinner on the anniversary of the Society the 1st March next and to invite the officers of the St George's, St Andrew's, Hibernian and German Societies, and such other persons as they may deem proper not exceeding eight in number.

Membership: New Members

The following gentleman were proposed members

Robert Waln Junr	by Joseph S. Lewis
Clement C. Biddle	by W^m W Fisher
Richard L. Howell	by John M. Price
Willm T. Stockton	
Willm Chancellor	

1817
Welch Society

At an Annual Meeting of the Society, held at the House of William Renshaw, March 1st 1817.

Present

Thomas Allibone
Enos Bronson
Matthew L. Bevan
Job Bacon
John Bevan
William Craig
Charles Dixey
Peter Evans
Samuel Evans
Thomas Evans
Thomas Evans of Peter
Joseph O. Evans
William W. Fisher
Joseph Huddell Jr
William E. Howell
Edmund Kinsey
Joseph S. Lewis
David Lewis
Elisha Chauncey
John J. Parry
Benjn Thomas

Samuel N. Lewis
Ezekiel C. Maddock
Robert Murdock
Willm H. Morgan
Thomas W. Morgan
Richard Price
John M. Price
Doct^r Thomas Parke
Zachariah Poulson
William Parker
Samuel Relf
William Rawley
Thomas L. Roberts
William W. Smith
Samuel Wetherill
Joseph Williams
Joseph Worrell
Richard Ware
and Joseph J. Norris

Organization: Absence of President and Vice-President

The Vice President being absent, Richard Price was chosen Chairman.

Assistance to Welsh Emigrants

The acting committee made the following report viz.

The acting committee report that they have attended to the current concerns of the Welch Society and that they have granted the sum of ten dollars to a distressed emigrant from Wales.

Membership: Death of Samuel Meredith (Society President) and letter prior to his death

Since the committee made their last report they have received with much regret the account of the death of our late worthy President Samuel Meredith Esq from whom they had previously received a letter in answer to the one addressed by the committee to him resigning his office as President of the Society.

The letter the committee now submit.

Belmont December 8th 1816

> Gentlemen
>
> I received your favour of 22 November by the last post and take the first opportunity of acknowledging it. I lament that an omission on my part to tender a resignation which ought to have been made immediately on my leaving Trenton, should have exposed the Society, on whose behalf you address me, to any inconvenience.
>
> A variety of circumstances – highly important to myself and family had at first driven the subject from my thoughts and for the last six months continued indisposition.
>
> Present gentlemen to the very respectable Society of which you form a part my resignation with my best wishes for the welfare of each its members individually and for the success of their united exertions and my regrets that it is not in my power to participate in them. Accept for yourselves my

thanks for the friendly and respectful manner in which you have recalled to my attention to a subject, which have too long escaped it.

with much respect

I am Gentlemen

your most obed sev^t

Samuel Meredith

Messrs Samuel Relf & Thos Parke Esq^{rs} members of the acting committee of the Welch Society.

Annual Dinner

The committee also report that they have prepared a dinner for the Society.

(signed) William W. Fisher Reg^r

Testimonial to the former President of the Society

Whereupon it was resolved that Enos Bronson and Samuel Relf be appointed a committee to prepare a suitable testimonial to the memory of our late valuable and worthy deceased President Samuel Meredith Esquire.

Organization: Resignation of the Treasurer

A letter was received from our late Treasurer Thomas Cumpston Esquire, resigning his office and declining a reelection and at the same time handing his accounts. Balance in his hands five hundred and sixty-nine dollars and fifty cents, and also, stating there was due to the Society sixty dollars for dividends on stock of the Bank of North America.

Membership: Resignations

The following resignations of membership were received and accepted viz Joseph Smith, Joshua Gilpin and Curtis Clay.

PART THREE

Membership: New Members

The following gentlemen who were proposed as members at the former meeting were duly elected vizt

Robert Waln Junr [proposed by] Clement C. Biddle
Richard L. Howell [proposed by] William P. Stockton
and Willm Chancellor

Organization: Stewardship

A letter was read from Chandler Price declining a reelection as Steward.

Organization: Elections

Enos Bronson and T. W. Morgan were appointed Judges of the election of officers which being gone into, they reported the following mentioned gentlemen as elected for the ensuing year vizt

President	Robert Wharton
Vice President	Joseph S. Lewis
Treasurer	Thomas Morris
Secretary	Matthew L. Bevan
Register	William W. Fisher
Stewards	Richard Price
	Samuel Relf
	William E. Howell
	Samuel N. Lewis
	Jonah Thomson
	Job Bacon
	and Enos Bronson
Physicians	Doct^r Thomas C. James
	& Thomas Parke
Counsellors	Benjamin R. Morgan &
	Charles Chauncey

Adjourned

239

Welsh Society

At the Quarterly Meeting of the Welch Society, held at Rubicam's Hotel,[42] June 2nd 1817.

Present

Wm Craig
E. Kinsey
E. E. Maddock
Wm E. Howell
Jonah Thompson
Dr Thos Parke
Saml Relf
Thos Allibone
R. Ware
Job Bacon

B. R. Morgan
Wm W. Fisher
Jos^h Shaw
J. P. Norris
R^d Price
Jos^h Worrell
H. Morgan
Thos Evans of Peter
Thomas Morris
and M. L. Bevan

Organization: Absence of President and Vice-President

The President and Vice President being absent – Richard Price was appointed Chairman.

Organization: Legislation and Emigration

The acting committee reported that they have attended to the current business, under their notice and hand the following abstract of their proceedings.

It appears to the committee a bill has been before the Legislature of our State, which in their opinion is well calculated to prevent impositions on emigrants from Wales.

---

42   Daniel Rubicam (1763–1832) was the proprietor of the Washington Hotel, 20 South Sixth Street, Philadelphia. See Robinson (ed.), *Robinson's Original Annual Directory... 1817*, p. 377.

Finance: Investments

The Treasurer was requested to invest three hundred dollars in United States six per cent stock.

Discipline: Fines for Non-Attendance and Expulsion

They recommend the fines of Richard W. Norris & Jesse Waln Jr to be remitted and that they be informed they will in future be enforced. Also, that the following names be stricken from the list of members as they for some time have not considered themselves as such

Wm Reed	F. Wharton
Matthew Randall	John Strawbridge &
Rowland Ellis	

They also recommend that John B. Bowen be released for the payment of his original subscription and fines from his inability to pay the same.

Organization: Certificates of Membership and Assistance to Emigrants

Eight dollars was ordered to be paid by the Treasurer for printing fifty copies of certificates of membership and three dollars to be refunded Mr Richard Price – he having paid the same to Owen Davis, a distressed emigrant from Wales.

Finance and Discipline: Accounts, Arrears and Suspension of Members

Messrs S. Relf and Wm E. Howell were appointed a committee to examine and report on the Treasurers accounts.

(signed) W. W. Fisher Register

On motion of Mr Joseph Worrell the report of the acting committee so far as respects Matthew Randall was suspended he engaging to pay the arrearages of fines &c. against that gentleman should he not pay the same himself.

And on motion of Mr Samuel Relf, the name of Jesse Waln Junr was suspended and that the Treasurer be requested to settle on the best possible terms with him. The report thereon was confirmed and adopted.

Membership: Resignations

Letters were received from Horace Binn[e]y and R. H. Morris resigning membership which was accepted on condition of their arrearages being previously settled.

Membership: New Member

The following gentleman was proposed as a member

Caleb Griffith   by Richd Price

(signed) M. L. Bevan Sect^y

Welch Society

At the Quarterly Meeting of the Welch Society, held at Daniel Rubicam's Tavern, Sept[embe]^r 1st 1817.

Present

Richard Price
Matthew L. Bevan
John Bacon
Wm W. Fisher
Jonah Thompson
Wm E. Howell
Job Bacon
E. E. Maddock
Joseph Shaw
Benjn Thomas

Richd Ware
Samuel Evans
John Clifton
Thomas Evans of Peter
Dr Thos Parke
John Bevan
Edmund Kinsey
Jos^h Worrell
Thomas Evans
and Thomas Allibone

242

PART THREE

Acting Committee Report and Assistance to Welsh Emigrants

The acting committee made the following report which was adopted by the Society vizt

The acting committee of the Welch Society beg leave to report that they have attended to the current concerns of the Society and that since the last quarterly meeting they have granted the sum of one hundred dollars to the following named distress'd emigrants from Wales vizt

John Bowen, Samuel Lewis, Wm Williams, John Williams, Henry Bowen, David Haines, Wm Williams Junr (to enable them to go into the Western Country) and that they had given a receipt promising to refund the money to the Society whenever they are in a situation so to do.

The committee have also granted the sum of twelve dollars to Evan Jones, a distressed emigrant, and have taken the like receipt from him. They also granted five dollars to each of the following names distress'd emigrants vizt Daniel Edwards, Thomas Jones, Edward Davis and Thomas Thomas, and they gave a receipt to the same effect as the former ones.

The committee have drawn on the Treasurer for money advanced by Mr Thomas Evans to Thomas Prichard and family (they being distressed emigrants from Wales), for boarding said family two weeks amounting to fifteen dollars.

signed W. W. Fisher Register

Phil^a Sept 1 1817

Finance: Accounts

The committee appointed to examine the Treasurers account made the following report

The undersigned being a committee appointed to examine the books and papers of the Treasurers of the Welch Society beg leave to report that they have carefully attended to that duty and have the satisfaction to find all his books and papers in correct and neat order.

The balance of cash on hand is two hundred and thirty-nine dollars and fifty-nine cents and the amount of stock, bearing interest, held by the Treasurer in trust for the Society is seven thousand six hundred & sixty-nine dollars and twenty-one cents, making a total of seven thousand, six hundred and sixty-nine dollars & twenty-one cents.

all which is respectfully submitted

signed Samuel Relf, Wm E. Howell committee

Membership: Fines for Non-Attendance and a Previous Resignation (c.1799)

The following preamble was proposed and adopted.

Whereas it appears from information communicated to the Society that Matthew Randall resigned his right of membership in the year 1799.

Therefore resolved, that all arrearages of fines and other claims appearing against Matthew Randall as a member of the Society, since 1799, be and the same are hereby remitted.

Adjourned.

Welch Society

At the Quarterly Meeting of the Welch Society held at Washington Hall, Dec[embe]^r 1 1817.

Present

Enos Bronson
E. E. Maddock
W. W. Fisher
Job Bacon

T. B. Freeman
Matthew L. Bevan
Thos Morris
Jos^h Huddle Jr

Richd Price
Jos^h E. Howell
John Clifton
Jos^h Simmons
Jos^h S. Lewis
Thomas Evans
Benjn Thomas
S. N. Lewis
Richd Ware

John Bacon
Dr T. Parke
Wm E. Howell
Thomas Evans of Peter
Jos^h Shaw
Reece Lewis
Joseph O. Evans
Robt Wharton
and Jos^h P. Norris

Membership: New Member

Caleb Griffiths proposed by Richard Price was duly elected a member.

Membership: Resignations

Letters offering their resignation of membership were read from William Jones, James C. Fisher & Joseph Price, which were severally accepted.

Annual Dinner

On motion the acting committee were directed to provide a dinner on the anniversary of the Society on the first of March next and to invite officers of George's, St Andrew's, Hibernian & German Societies, and such other persons as they may think proper not exceeding eight in number.

Membership: New Members

John Smith	proposed by Enos Bronson
John R. Griffith	proposed by Jos^h S. Lewis
Josiah Evans	
George Worrell	[proposed by] Thomas Morris
Captn Thos Morgan	[proposed by] Jos^h S. Lewis

Adjourned

1818
Welch Society

At the Annual Meeting of the Society held at the Washington Hall February 28th 1818.

Present

Robert Wharton
Thomas Allibone
Enos Bronson
M. L. Bevan
Job Bacon
C. Chauncey
W. Craig
Thos Evans
Thos Evans of Peter
Wm W. Fisher
Joseph Huddle Jr
George Howell
Wm E. Howell
S. H. Jacobs
J. S. Lewis
Lawrence Lewis
E. E. Maddock

Thomas Morris
W. H. Morgan
Jacob S. Otto
Richard Price
Geo. W. Morgan
Doctor Thos Parke
Z. Poulson
Saml Relf
Jas Read Jr
Jonah Thompson
Benjamin Thomas
Joseph Simons
Saml Wetherill
Joseph Worrell
Richard Ware
Jas O. Evans
Jos. P. Norris

Acting Committee Report and Assistance to Welsh Emigrants

The acting committee made the following report of their proceedings during the past year.

The acting committee respectfully submit to the Society a concise view of their proceedings since the last annual meeting which will be found embraced in the following

Report.

PART THREE

Amongst the crowd of strangers who have been landed on our shores in the course of the past year, it was to be expected that many would be found who had emigrated from the country of our forefathers, towards whom the fostering care of the Society should be especially directed. These, it has been the business of your committee to seek out, to welcome, and to relieve; Landed among strangers, friendless, pennyless, and many of them under the pressure of disease, they had a twofold claim upon us as fellow men and fellow countrymen and your committee feel grateful for the opportunity afforded of administering that relief which as the organs of your country, it was their pleasing duty to impart.

The views of the newcomers having in general been directed to a settlement in the western States, it was deemed prudent to encourage that disposition, and measures were accordingly taken to facilitate their removal thither. Temperate, frugal and industrious, inured to labour and accustomed to privations, these people are admirably qualified for the task they have undertaken, and favoured with the blessings of Heaven, will doubtless meet with the success they merit. From some of them intelligence have been received, and the committee have the satisfaction of saying, that no disappointment in the expectations they might have indulged in, appears to have been experienced; whilst a due sense of the favors conferred by the Society, is reciprocally, manifested.

A few who were mechanics or artizans have been, advantageously placed in the city, where by their sober and orderly conduct they have thus justified the good opinion we have always entertained of our Welch countrymen, and bid fair to be useful members of society.

The whole number under the care of the committee since last report has been forty-four of whom one is since dead, his name was William Thomas. The sums expended for their relief, inclusive of medicine, subsistence here, the transportation of women and children, and some little baggage as far as Pittsburg[h], with some minor disbursements, amounts in the whole to dollars $342.25/^{100}$ for which orders have been drawn on the Treasurer, and paid out of the current funds of the Society not only without encroaching on the capital stock but affording room for a further investment as will appear from the Treasurers accounts.

Organization: Future Meetings of the Society

As part of the duty assigned them, your committee have been attentive to the future accommodation of the Society, as well for their quarterly meetings of business as in the celebration of their annual festival and they flatter themselves that the arrangements made will be met with approbation.

The expenses attendant on our quarterly meetings have hitherto been borne by the individual members – an inconvenience which was justly complained of and was without doubt, a great obstacle in the way of a more general and punctual attendance. This expense being now assumed by the Society it is to be hoped that we shall hereafter find the greater part if not all our members, assembled at the stated times, thereby enacting an increased interest in and zeal for promoting the praise worthy objects of our association.

By a contract entered into with the managing committee of the Washington Hall, the Society is to be furnished with a capacious and comfortable apartment for their stated meetings to be lighted and warmed at the cost of the aforesaid committee for the sum of seventy-five dollars P^r annum. In this room the customary annual entertainment provided agreeably to the resolution of the last quarterly meeting, will for the first time be prepared and the committee have the satisfaction of saying that the expense to each individual will on this and on all future occasions, be but little more than one half of what it ordinarily has been.

Finance: Accounts and Investments

The committee have attended to their duty in the examination of the Treasurer's accounts by which they have ascertained that the Society has invested in Public Securities bearing interest the sum of $7429.72 and a cash balance in the hands of the Treasurer $410.79. Making a total of $7840.51

For a more detailed account of which the committee ask leave to refer to the Treasurers annual report.

All which is Respectfully submitted.

signed Wm W. Fisher Register

Philadelphia Febr^y 28th 1818

Membership: Resignations

Letters were read from Mess$^{[rs]}$ David Lewis, Joseph Shaw & John Hughes offering their resignation which were severally accepted.

Membership: New Members

The following gentlemen proposed as members at a former meeting were duly elected viz.

John R. Griffiths	George Worrall
Josiah Evans	Capt. Thos. Morgan &
John R. Smith	

Organization: Election of Officers

The Society proceeded to the election of officers for the ensuing year. Enos Bronson and Zachariah Poulson were appointed Tellers who reported the following mentioned gentlemen as elected viz

President	Robert Wharton
Vice President	Joseph S. Lewis
Treasurer	Thomas Morris
Secretary	Matthew L. Bevan
Register	Wm W. Fisher
Physicians	Doc. T. C. James
	Doc. T. Parke
Counsellors	Benj R. Morgan
	Charles Chauncey

Stewards   Richard Price
                Samuel Relf
                Wm E. Howell
                Jonah Thompson
                Job Bacon
                Enos Bronson
                Jos. Simons

Adjourned

signed Matthew L Bevan Secr^ty

Welch Society

At a Quarterly Meeting of the Welch Society held at the Washington Hall June 1st 1818.

Present

Robert Wharton   Richard Price
Job Bacon   John M. Price
Thomas Evans   John G. Parry
Thomas Evans [of Peter]   Doct. T. Parke
Jos. E. Howell   James Read Jr
Wm E. Howell   Joseph Simons
S. H. Jacobs   Jonah Thompson
Reece Lewis   Richard Ware
S. N. Lewis   Joseph Huddle
E. E. Maddock   John R. Griffiths
W. H. Morgan   John Bevan
Lewis Mills   Josiah Evans
Capt. T. Morgan   M. L. Bevan

Welsh Emigration: Letter of Gratitude

A letter was received from John Morgan an emigrant expressing his gratitude for the timely relief of this Society.

PART THREE

Membership: Resignation

A letter from John Wister offering his resignation as a member which was accepted.

Adjourned

sign'd Matthew L. Bevan Secret^y

Welch Society

At a Quarterly Meeting of the Welch Society held in September 1818 at the Washington Hall.

Present

Doct. Thos Parke
William W. Fisher
Joseph Worrall
Charles Dixey
Richard Price
Matthew L. Bevan
Thomas Evans [of Peter]
Thomas Evans
Josiah Evans

Richard Ware
Joseph Huddle Jr
Job Bacon
John R Griffiths
Lewis Miles
Joseph Simons
Wm H. Morgan
E. E. Maddock

Acting Committee Report and Assistance to Welsh Emigrants

The President and Vice President being absent Richard Price was called to the chair. The acting committee reported verbally that since the last quarterly meeting they have attended to the current concerns of the Society and have awarded relief to the undermentioned emigrants – viz. Thomas Morgan, James Jones, Elias Reese, Susan his wife, and two children, William Jones, wife and three children, Wm Lewis Jr., Evan Roberts, Reese Jenkins and wife, Thomas Morgan, wife and three children, Thomas Jones, William Lewis and Evan Evans.

By such pecuniary aid as their situations seemed to require the several amounts advanced will be detailed at a future meeting.

Membership: Resignation and New Member

A letter from C. C. Biddle, offering his resignation as a member was read and accepted. Proposed as a member Isaac R. Jones by Joseph Simons.

Adjourned.

Sign'd Matthew L. Bevan Secretary

Welch Society

At a Quarterly Meeting of the Welch Society held December 7th 1818 at the Washington Hall.

Present

Job Bacon
John Clifton
Thomas Evans
Thomas Evans of Peter
Jos. O Evans
Josiah Evans
W[m] H. Morgan
Lewis Miles
Capt. T. Morgan
Jos. P. Norris
Joseph Simons
Benj Thomas
Robert Wharton
W[m] W. Fisher

Caleb Griffith
John R Griffith
Joseph S. Lewis
E. E. Maddock
Thomas Morris
Richard Ware
George Worrall
John Hallowell
Doct. Thos. Parke
William Parker
Richard L. Howell
John Bevan
and Matthew L. Bevan

Acting Committee Report and Assistance to Welsh Emigrants

The acting committee reported viz.

PART THREE

The acting committee of the Welch Society beg leave to report that they have attended to the current concerns of the Society, and since the last report they have relieved the following persons viz

	$
William Lewis Senior had advances made him	10
Reese Jenkins and wife [had advances made him]	15
Thos Morgan, wife & 3 children [had advances made him]	20
Edward Wilkins [had advances made him]	10
Edward Hughes had advances made him	2
Thomas Jones [had advances made him]	2
Reese Jenkins [had advances made him]	15
David Davis [had advances made him]	10
The widow Brien and family have had advanced on them at sundry times in cash and for various articles of furniture	86.56
Evan Evans had advanced him	30
William Lewis Jr and Evan Evans had two weeks board allowed them	4
Jacob Watkins had advanced him	15
George Watkins [had advances made him]	15
	$234.50

All of which is respectfully submitted

Philadelphia Dec[embe]r 7th 1818

sign'd Wm W. Fisher Register

Membership: Resignation and New Member

A letter from George W. Morgan offering his resignation was read and accepted.

Issac R. Jones proposed at the last meeting was duly elected a member of the Society.

Organization: General Business and the Annual Dinner

An account from J. Cruikshanks for printing amounting to $11.50 was presented & ordered to be paid; on motion the acting committee are directed to prepare a dinner on the anniversary of the Society on the first of March next and to invite the Officers of the St George's, St Andrew's, Hibernian & German Societies, and such other persons as they may think proper not exceeding eight in number.

Adjourned

Sign'd Matthew L. Bevan Secretary

PART THREE

1819
Welch Society

At the Annual Meeting of the Welch Society held March 1st 1819 at the Washington Hall Hotel.

Present

John Bacon	Reece Lewis
Job Bacon	Lawrence Lewis
E. Chauncey	E. E. Maddock
Benjamin Chew	Thomas Morris
Wm Chancellor	W. H. Morgan
Charles Dixey	Capt. T. Morgan
Peter Evans	R. Price
Samuel Evans	John M. Price
Thomas Evans	Doct. T. Parke
Thomas Evans (of Peter)	Z. Poulson
Jos. O. Evans	Samuel Relf
Josiah Evans	Jos. Simons
W. W. Fisher	John R. Smith
Caleb Griffith	W. Parker
John R. Griffith	Robert Wharton and
George Howell	Matthew L. Bevan
George Worrall	Joseph S. Lewis

Membership: Resignations and New Member

Letters from Jos. Williams, Samuel H. Jacobs, and Wharton Lewis offering their resignation which was accepted. William P. Williams proposed by Joseph S. Lewis at last meeting was duly elected a member.

Assistance to Welsh Emigrants Acknowledged

It was stated to the Society that Mr William P. Williams has seconded the benevolent views of the Society by giving a home to a number of distressed Welch emigrants at great expense and inconvenience to himself and family where they remained until otherwise provided for by the acting committee.

It was therefore resolved unanimously that he be presented with a certificate of membership handsomely framed at the expense of the Society.

Acting Committee Report

The acting committee reported their proceedings during the past year which was accepted and ordered to be placed on the minutes viz

Agreeably to the settled custom of the Society the acting committee have prepared a report of their proceedings since the last annual meeting which is now respectfully submitted.

Integrity of the Society and its Philanthropy

The character of the Welch Society for philanthropy and benevolence has been too well established from its earliest infancy to render it necessary at this time to investigate its claims to such honorable distinction. The proofs of it are to be found on its records where they remain a well-earned testimonial of the disinterested beneficence of its founders.

Your committee therefore confine themselves principally to a recital of the transactions during the period alluded to in which there have been abundant opportunities for the exercise of the trust committed to them. They cannot however deny themselves the gratification of felicitating the Society on its continued usefulness so eminently confirmed by the experience of the past year. They believe that under providence this association has been the means of rescuing from death or perhaps from a fate worse than death many of our unfortunate countrymen who driven from their native land by poverty or distress had sought an asylum amongst us; had it not been for the active benevolence of this Society, some of these wretched sufferers must have perished thro sickness and famine, the dying moments uncheered by the presence of sympathising friends, and embittered with all the pangs of disappointment.

We rejoice that it was our lot to avert this dismal catastrophe; we congratulate ourselves on having been the instrument of restoring to health and usefulness many whom we trust will hereafter fill their stations worthily as members of our community.

The efforts of your committee have also been directed to the advancement of those of our emigrant bretheren [*sic*] who stood in need of their counsel rather than pecuniary assistance; of these a pleasing number have been found whose correct and respectable deportment whilst it reflects credit on the Society has enabled them to settle themselves in comfort and to lay a foundation for future prosperity. From some of these letters have been received, extracts from which it has been thought proper to exhibit with this report.

Intoxication, the baleful curse that seems to await all emigrants to this otherwise favor'd land, has yet left our countrymen uncontaminated. Whatever may be their failings, temperance has been found uniformly to reside amongst them. In all their experience your committee have not met with one solitary instance in which there was an absence of this cardinal virtue. The committee feel a pride in holding up to view this national trait, the adherence to which in this country particularly marks a principle of moral rectitude that redounds highly to the credit of our Welch bretheren.

It is not to be supposed that the numerous calls upon the charity of the Society could have been answered without a corresponding expense. Accordingly, it will be found that notwithstanding our respectable resources (which some of our members have been willing to consider as even more than sufficient), there is still a balance against the Society for money disbursed beyond our income. This balance might be liquidated without difficulty if the annual contributions were punctually paid. The committee are sorry to say this is far from being the case; on the contrary, whilst a few individuals perform all the laborious duty necessary to carry into effect the benevolent designs of the association – they are also frequently compelled to advance considerable sums which of right should always be found in the Treasury. Such a state of things should never exist, and your committee are confident that the remedy will be applied as soon as the fact is made known. The committee again earnestly recommend to the meeting the adoption of efficient measures to induce a more general attendance of the members.

Few are aware of the importance of our Society in its salutary influence on the fortunes of our emigrant Countrymen, and still fewer are acquainted with the extent of the benefits annually conferred on them.

The committee are anxious that every individual of the Society should be familiar with its proceedings; they desire them to judge for themselves to hear and to see how their charity is dispersed; to banish that lukewarmness & indifference which threatens the very existence of our institution at a time when its usefulness has been most completely tested, and its continuance most ardently to be desired among the means to be resorted to for the accomplishment of this wished for object. Your committee are concerned that none will be found more efficacious than the encouragement of those social feelings which prevail in our annual entertainments on the first of March. It has been found in all similar associations that the free and unrestrained intercourse subsisting in such meetings has the strongest influence in binding together the individuals who compose them. There the heart is softened, and the most generous propensities of our nature have full play. The coldness and the asperities of life are forgotten, and the hand of the fellowship extended with kindness is received with cordiality.

Those who have hitherto been strangers are now brought to an acquaintance and are unconsciously led to emulate each other in deeds of philanthropy. Let us then cultivate this bond of friendship and draw still closer the bonds which knit us to each other. Remember the design of our association, do not loose [sic] sight of the example of our predecessors; but let us this day join in celebrating the feast of St David with the zest and animation which formerly was its proper characteristics. From an inspection of the minutes of the acting committee and the Treasurers' accounts it will appear that the whole number of persons relieved in the course of the year ending this day is sixty-one, and that the amount expended for that purpose is $781.46/$^{100.}$

The greater part of these individuals have emigrated westwards where judging from former experience we have just grounds for believing they will do well. Two families yet remain in the city under the supervision of the committee. For these suitable situations can be provided in the country in the course of the Spring.

The committee on the Treasurers' accounts report that, the sum belonging to the Society invested in public stock is	$7429.72
Cash bal^e in the hands of the Treasurer	$21.32
	$7451.04

Against the balance in the Treasurers hands are to come sundry orders drawn by the committee and yet unpaid, amounting to $195, leaving due from the Society to individual members $173.68 which your committee think it incumbent on the Society to immediately to discharge. The committee cannot close their report without expressing their high sense of the obligations of the Society is under to Mrs Mary Linn and Mrs Joseph Simons for their charitable exertions in behalf of more than one suffering family of emigrants who have been under our care with the most exalted benevolence; these ladies have administered to the wants & soothed the distress of the suffering strangers exposing their persons to the inclemencies of the weather & with liberal hands bestowing on them those comforts which feminine delicacy alone knows how to make most acceptable. The committee therefore deem it their duty thus publicly to express the gratitude of the Society to these honorable ladies and with this they close their report.

Philad^a, March 1st 1819.

The Society proceeded to the election of officers for the ensuing year. Z. Poulson and Wm Parker were appointed Tellers who made the following report viz.

Philadelphia March 1st 1819.

At the annual meeting of the Welch Society this day an election was held for officers to act for the present year when the following gentlemen were duly elected.

President	Robert Wharton
Vice President	Joseph S. Lewis
Secretary	Thomas Morris
Treasurer	Matthew L. Bevan
Register	Wm W. Fisher
Physicians	Doct. T. C. James
	Doct. T. Parke
Counsellors	B. R. Morgan
	Charles Chauncey
Stewards	Richard Price
	Samuel Relf
	William E. Howell
	Job Bacon
	Joseph Simons
	George Worrall
	Captn T. Morgan

Sign'd William Parker

Sign'd Z. Poulson

Judges of Election

Adjourned

Sign'd Matthew L. Bevan Secretary

PART THREE

Welch Society

At a Quarterly Meeting of the Welch Society held at Peter Evans's, Monday Evening, June 7 1819.

Present

M. L. Bevan
Charles Dixey
Peter Evans
Thomas Evans
Josiah Evans
Wm W. Fisher
George Howell
B. B. Howell
Joseph S. Lewis
Reece Lewis
Thos Morris
W. H. Morgan

Richard Price
Doct^r T. Parke
George Worrall
Thos Evans (of Peter)
John Bacon
E. E. Maddock
Robert Wharton
John R. Griffith
Benjn Thomas
Joseph Simmons
Joseph O. Evans
Captn T. Morgan

Membership: Resignations

Letters were received from J. S. Otto, S. N. Lewis, W. Craig, and Edward Tilghman resigning membership which were severally accepted on their paying their dues.

A verbal report from the acting committee that Mr W. W. Fisher, former Register, had resigned and that Mr Job Bacon was appointed Register to supply the vacancy untill the election.

Adjourned

Signed M. L. Bevan Secret^y

Welch Society

At a Quarterly Meeting of the Welch Society held at Peter Evans's Tavern, Sept[embe]^r 6th 1819.

Present

Joseph S. Lewis
Joseph Simmons
Joseph Worrall
Reece Lewis
Dr Thos Parke
Wm W. Fisher
E. E. Maddock
Thomas Morris

Peter Evans
M. L. Bevan
Thomas Evans
Josiah Evans
Wm H. Morgan
Lewis Miles
Joseph O. Evans

Membership: Resignations

A letter of resignation from Mr C. J. Wistar was read and accepted.

The Secretary stated that Mr William Meredith instructed him to offer his resignation as a member which was refused by the Society on the ground that it should be offered in writing and all arrearages paid before it could be accepted.

Assistance to Welsh Emigrants

The acting committee reported verbally that the benevolent objects of the Society continued to claim their attention, and that their proceedings will be particularly detailed at their annual meeting.

Adjourned

Signed M. L. Bevan Secret^y

PART THREE

Welch Society

At a Quarterly Meeting of the Welch Society held at Peter Evans's Tavern Decem[be]^r 6, 1819.

Present

Joseph S. Lewis
John J. Parry
Doct^r T. Parke
Joseph Simmons
Captn Charles Dixey
Thos Allibone
Benjamin Thomas
William P. Williams
John R. Griffiths
Thos Evans (of Peter)
& Matthew L. Bevan

Thomas Evans
Josiah Evans
E. E. Maddock
Lewis Miles
Isaac R. Jones
William Rawle Jr
Robert Wharton
Joseph O. Evans
Peter Evans
Jos. P. Norris

Acting Committee Report and Assistance to Welsh Emigrants

The acting committee made the following report:

The acting committee since the last meeting of the Welsh Society have had numerous applications for assistance and have extended relief as far as they were enabled to do by the state of the funds, and are happy to say they have relieved many deserving objects, all which will be detailed with their proceedings for the year at the March meeting.

Finance: Arrears of Members and Non-Payment of Fees

The committee regret to say that the means of usefulness have been much cramped by the delinquency of many of the members in the payment of their dues, some of them for the dinners of which they have partaken.

The committee addressed letters to several members who were in arrears, stating the distress of the Society for want of means, but they regret to say with little effect as little more than 30 dollars has been collected within the last two months.

They recommend the appointment of a committee of the Society, to assist in the collection of the dues.

Signed, Joseph S. Lewis

For the Register

Which was adopted and a committee of five as recommended in the report were appointed to aid in the collection of the arrearages due the Society which committee consists of:

Mess[rs] Charles Dixey Joseph Simmons
Thomas Morris W. W. Howell
Thomas C. Wharton

The following resolution was offered and adopted.

Resolved, that the report of the acting committee of 1 March last be printed and sent to each member of the Society, with such further observation on the state of the Society as they may deem proper, to invite the members to a more active attendance and attention to its interests.

Annual Dinner

On motion, the acting committee directed to prepare a dinner on the anniversary of the Society the first day of March next, and to invite the officers of St George's, St Andrew's, Hibernian, and German Society's and other persons as they may deem proper, not exceeding eight in.

Adjourned.

Signed M. L. Bevan Secret[y]

PART THREE

1820

Welch Society

At an Annual Meeting of the Welch Society held at the Washington Hall Hotel (Renshaw's) March, first 1820.

Present

M. L. Bevan
John Bevan
John Cliffton
Charles Dixey
Peter Evans
Thomas Evans
Thomas Evans (of Peter)
Joseph O. Evans
Josiah Evans
William W. Fisher
Caleb Griffith
John R. Griffith
Joseph Huddell
George Howell
J. R. Jones
Joseph S. Lewis
Reece Lewis
Lawrence Lewis

Benjamin R. Morgan
John Morgan
E. E. Maddock
Thomas Morris
William H. Morgan
Joseph P. Norris
Richard Price
John M. Price
Dr Thomas Parke
Zachariah Poulson
William Parker
James Read
Joseph Simons
Benjamin Thomas
Lewis Walker
Joseph Worrell
George Worrall
William L. Williams

Acting Committee Report and Assistance to Welsh Emigrants

The acting committee made the following report which was read and adopted.

Since the last annual report, the acting committee have had many call on the benevolence of the Society, & have had the satisfaction of affording relief to many deserving objects; they have also with pain, been obliged to refuse assistance to several who were in distress, from the narrowness of the means at their disposal which has occasionally subjected some of the members to pecuniary advances, which would not be required if a more particular attention was paid to the punctual discharge of the dues of the members.

The number of persons relieved amounts to more than seventy, of whom forty-one aged and youth, were at one time under our care at the house of William P. Williams, whose more than brotherly kindness & the inconvenience he & his family subjected themselves to deserve the thanks of the Society.

Finance: Accounts and Investments

The sum expended during the past year in relieving the distressed amounts to $538.58/^{100} and it appears by the Treasurers report that the following is the present state of our funds – to wit

	$
Stock of the Bank of North America 3 Shares	1800
Ditto of United States Six percents	4129.72
Water Loan of the City	1500
And there is in his hands the sum of	20.34
Total of	7450.06

exclusive of about $900 due from members much of which it is feared will be lost.

Philadelphia March 1st 1820

(for the Register)

(signed) Joseph S. Lewis

Discipline: Membership and Arrears

The committee appointed at the last quarterly meeting to aid in the collection of arrearages due the Society

PART THREE

Reported

The committee, appointed at the last meeting of the Society, to forward the collection of the dues have attended to that duty and beg leave to make the following report in part:

They have collected $32.50/^{100} & have seen and enquired respecting the following persons who do not pay, for the reasons mentioned opposite their respective names to wit

William Meredith	says he has resigned long since
James Prosser	deceased & has left nothing
William Read	considers himself as having resigned many years ago
Daniel Thomas	not to be found
Fishbourn Wharton	does not consider himself a member
Thomas Williams	not to be found
R. B. Jones	not to be found
Edmund Kinsey	says the Society must know he cannot afford to pay & intends sending in his resignation

They have also found on the list of dues a number of honorary members not liable to pay dues or fines, which dues they propose the Secretary should strike therefrom.

All which is respectfully submitted.

Philad^a March 1 1820

(signed) Charles Dixey
Thomas Morris
Joseph Simons

It was moved and seconded that the names of delinquents mentioned in the report of the committee be considered separately when it was carried, that the verbal resignation thro[ugh] the Secretary, of Mr William Meredith, at the September quarterly meeting, be now accepted.

It was also stated that Mr Fishbourn Wharton and Mr William Read had considered themselves as having resigned their membership some years back, when it was agreed by the Society that their respective fines &c. be remitted and their names stricken from the list of members.

The other names reported by the committee were ordered to be stricken off fines &c. remitted as was also Mr Isaac Jones.

Membership: Resignations

Letters of resignation were received from Mess[rs] Jonah Thompson, Elihu Chauncey, Benj. B. Howell, John Wharton & Thomas C. Wharton, which were severally accepted.

Membership: New Members

The following gentlemen proposed as candidates for membership viz

John Roberts	by Thomas Morris
Thomas Elliott	also by Thomas Morris and Timothy B. Mount

Benjamin Stephens by George Worrall & Thomas Tunis by Reece Lewis were duly elected.

The undermentioned were proposed as members.

Jacob Thomas	by W. P. Williams
Samuel Jenkins	by same

The Society proceeded into the election of officers for the ensuing year. Z. Poulson and Benjamin Thomas were appointed Tellers who reported the following gentlemen to be duly elected

President	Robert Wharton
Vice President	Joseph S. Lewis
Treasurer	Thomas Morris
Secretary	George Worrall
Register	Job Bacon

Physicians   Dr Thomas C. James
                Dr Thomas Parke
Counsellors   Benjamin R. Morgan
Stewards   Charles Chauncey
                Richard Price
                William E. Howell
                Joseph Simons
                Charles Dixey
                Thomas Morgan
                Reece Lewis
                John R. Griffith.

Adjourned.

M. L. Bevan Secr[y]

Welch Society

At a Quarterly Meeting of the Welch Society held at Peter Evans, June 5 1820.

Present

Joseph S. Lewis. VP   Job Bacon
Dr Thomas Parke   Peter Evans
Edward Davies   Josiah Evans
Charles Dixey   Reece Lewis
John B. Griffith   Timothy Mount
Lewis Miles   Joseph Worrell
Joseph P. Norris   William P. Williams
George Worrall   Joseph O. Evans
E. E. Maddock

Organization: Minutes of Previous Meeting

The roll being called according to order, the minutes of the last quarterly meeting were read, considered, & approved.

Membership: Resignations

A letter from Chancellor Price, addressed to the President of the Society was read, in which he resigned his right of membership and on motion the said resignation was accepted, on condition that all arrears to the Society be first paid & discharged.

A letter from John Cliffton was also received & read, resigning his right of membership, and, on motion the said resignation was accepted on payment of all debts due from him to the Society.

A letter from John J. Parry was also received & read, in which for the reasons therein stated he requested the Society to accept of his resignation & to exonerate him from the payment of the debts he owed, & which he was unable at this time to discharge. Whereupon, on motion, the resignation of Mr Parry was accepted and he [was] exonerated from the payment of all arrears due to the Society.

A letter from Enos Bronson was likewise read, resigning his right of membership and requesting that he might be exonerated from the payment of the amount he stood indebted to the Society and on motion the said letter was considered & the resignation accepted.

A motion was then made to exonerate Mr Bronson from the payment of his arrearages due the Society which on consideration was agreed to.

A letter of resignation was also received from Thomas A. Morgan whereupon, on motion, the resignation of Mr Morgan was accepted, he first paying the amount due from him to the Society.

Acting Committee Report – No Business

Mr Job Bacon, on behalf of the acting committee, made report stating, that the committee had had no occasion to disturb the funds of the Society since the last meeting, nor have the committee any subject of importance to lay before the meeting at this time.

Whereupon, on motion, the said report was accepted and ordered to be filed.

PART THREE

Organization: Committee Work and Illegal Detention of a Welsh Emigrant

Vice President Lewis laid before the meeting a letter from Mr Joseph Simons requesting to be released from further attendance on the committee appointed in January last, to whom had been referred the case of Bridget Williams illegally held a prisoner by John Whittall of Germantown and

On motion, Mr Simons was excused from further care of the case, & Mr John R. Griffith appointed to fill his place in said committee.

Mr John R. Griffith made report on behalf of the committee to whom was referred the case of Bridget Williams; and being read was adopted as follows: viz

A report of John R. Griffith & Thomas Evans who were appointed in January 1820 by the committee of the Welch Society to settle the case of Bridget Williams, an emigrant from Wales, who was then held prisoner under a false indenture by John Whittall of Germantown. They have attended to the business entrusted to them; got the girl cleared from prison & from John Whittall, through the medium of the court and recovered by law her wages & clothing due her. The expenses attending the above, paid for bail-piece, jail fees, court charges & other expenses amount to ten dollars & five cents, time of trouble not included (signed) John R. Griffith for himself & Thos Evans.

It was moved & seconded that an order to be drawn on the treasury for ten dollars & five cents in favor of John R. Griffith & Thomas Evans, the amount stated in the foregoing report which was agreed and an order was accordingly drawn for that sum signed and delivered to Mr Griffith.

Membership: New Member

Mr Reece Lewis proposed Mr Richard Wood as a member of the Society.

Finance

A motion was made by Mr J. Worrell & Mr Norris & read as follows

Resolved that the expense incurred during the time of transacting the business of this Society at the annual quarterly & special meetings thereof, be paid by the Treasurer out of the general fund.

Resolved that the fourth section of the By[e]-Laws be & the same is hereby repealed.

And, on motion the said resolutions were ordered to be on the table.

A motion was made by J. Worrell & Mr Norris, that the expenses of the present meeting be paid out of the funds of the Society by the Treasurer thereof

And on consideration the same was agreed to.

adjourned

(signed) Geo. Worrall Secretary

Welch Society

At a Quarterly Meeting of the Welch Society held at Peter Evan[s]'s Tavern, December 4th, 1820.

Present

Robert Wharton
Joseph S. Lewis
Thomas Morris
George Worrall
Job Bacon
Dr Thomas Parke
Benjamin R. Morgan
Reece Lewis

Joseph Huddell
Isaac R. Jones
Joseph Worrell
E. E. Maddock
Benjamin Thomas
Wm H. Morgan
Joseph O. Evans
Josiah Evans

Joseph Simons   Lewis Miles
John R. Griffith

Organization: Minutes of Previous Meeting

The roll having been called, the minutes of last meeting were read, and approved.

Acting Committee Report – No Business

The Register stated verbally that the acting committee had no report to make to this meeting.

Membership: Resignation

A letter from Jonathan Smith resigning his right of membership in the Society, which was read, and the resignation of Mr Smith accepted, on the usual condition of first paying all arrears due to the Society.

Community Interaction: Annual Dinners of Ethnic Societies

A letter was laid before the meeting from James Imbrie, Secretary of St Andrew's Society, communicating the proceedings of a joint meeting of the officers of the German, St George's, St Andrew's Hibernian and Welch Societies, relative to the propriety of relinquishing the practice of inviting the officers of their respective societies to their anniversary dinners. And after some time spent in consideration thereof, a motion was made to postpone the subject until the annual meeting on the first of March next; which was agreed to.

Finance: Expenses of Meetings

Mr J. Worrell called up for consideration, two resolutions offered by him & Mr Norris on 5 June last, on the subject of changing the mode of defraying the expenses of the meetings of the Society & for repealing the fourth section of the By[e]-Laws.

After various observations by the members present, it was agreed to postpone the same, until the annual meeting on the first of March next.

Membership: New Members

On motion of Mr Reece Lewis, the meeting proceeded to ballot for Mr Richard C. Wood, proposed as a candidate for membership by Mr Lewis, on 5th June last; which having been effected, the Tellers reported Mr Wood to be duly elected, & the Secretary was directed to give him notice thereof.

Robert W. Sykes was proposed by Mr Robert Wharton, as a member of the Society.

Community Interaction: Annual Dinners of Ethnic Societies

Mr Bacon, offered the following resolution, which was adopted *nem: con*:[43]

Resolved, that the proper officers be directed to make the necessary arrangements for the annual dinner on the first of March, and that they be instructed to invite the officers of other benevolent Societies usually present with us on the occasion, with such other guests, not exceeding eight in number, as in their judgement may contribute to the more perfect enjoyment of the day.

Adjourned.

signed Geo. Worrall Secretary

---

43   Unanimously or with no dissenting voices.

PART THREE

1821
Welch Society

At an Annual Meeting of the Welch Society held at the Mansion House Hotel on the First of March 1821.

Present

Robert Wharton
Joseph S. Lewis
Thomas Morris
Job Bacon
John Roberts
Dr Thomas Parke
Dr Thomas C. James
Benjamin R. Morgan
Joseph Simons
William E. Howell
John R. Griffith
Charles Dixey
Richard C. Wood
Joseph Huddell Jr
Benjamin Chew
Thomas Elliott
Josiah Evans

Samuel Evans
Joseph O. Evans
Caleb Griffith
John Hallowell
George Howell
William W. Howell
Isaac R. Jones
Ezekiel C. Maddock
Lewis Miles
Joseph P. Norris
John M. Price
William Parker
Zachariah Poulson
James Read Jr
Benjamin Stephens
Joseph Worrell
William P. Williams

Organization: Minutes of Previous Meeting

The roll having been called, the minutes of the last meetings were read & approved.

Membership: Resignations

Letters of Resignation

A letter was received from James Williams resigning his right of membership in the Society which was accepted on the usual condition of paying all arrearages due from him to the Society.

Also, from George Worrell resigning the office of Secretary which was accepted.

Community Interaction: Annual Dinners of Ethnic Societies

On motion of Mr Chew seconded by Mr Poulson it was agreed that the further consideration of the subject relative to the invitation of guests to our annual dinner, be postponed to the next quarterly meeting.

Acting Committee Report and Assistance to Welsh Emigrants

The acting committee submitted to the meeting their customary report

Since the meeting of the Society in June last an unusual number of emigrants from Wales have arrived in this city & have received the attention of the acting committee.

The committee have great satisfaction in stating that the greater number of these strangers were in a condition to shift for themselves; being possessed of some property & having had their plans of proceeding fully matured previous to arrival, they were not, as is too often the case with their fellow countrymen, at a loss in the commencement of their operation. It remained therefore for the committee only to offer them such advice as might prove serviceable & they are happy to say that their kind intentions appear to have been duly appreciated, & their advice cordially received.

It was necessary however to extend relief to two or three families who by some accident had been separated from their friends & were left entirely destitute. The committee considering that in all probability the Society would be burthened with the maintenance of these persons during the approaching winter, deemed it the most economical plan to furnish them with money to enable them to rejoin their friends who had gone to the Westward under highly favorable circumstances.

The committee are far from thinking it expedient, even if it were in the power of the Society, to supply with money to those who are in good health and able to earn their subsistence. On the contrary they would recommend a more strict adherence to the course formerly pursued & to appropriate the pecuniary means of the Society to the relief of those only who are unable to provide for themselves.

The cases above alluded to were those of John Francis, Samuel Reynolds, and David Davis. The committee considered them as objects peculiarly worthy of assistance from the Society, as they were separated from friends on whom they entirely relied for future success and their families consisted of very young children unaccustomed to the climate & consequently in danger of falling victims to the diseases prevalent in our city during the hot months. To these individuals, fourteen in number, sixty dollars were accordingly advanced, which with $11.40/^{100}$ dollars paid for printing & stationary constitute the amount of disbursements for the last quarter.

The committee appointed in the case of Bridget Williams having succeeded in obtaining from the person who held it, whatever property belonged to her, & in securing her from further molestation recommend to the Society to proceed no further in the business.

All which is respectfully submitted.

Job Bacon Register

Finance: Accounts and Investments

Philad^a, 31 August 1820

☞ The foregoing report was intended to have been laid before the September meeting, but no quorum was formed on the stated evening & at the ensuing meeting in December it was omitted.

To the proceeding report, the committee have not much to add –

	$
the calls upon the benevolence of the Society for the year past, having happily been few, compared with those of the year proceeding the expenditures on that account have only amounted to	121.01
leaving at this time in the hands of the Treasurer	363.88
from which is to be deducted a debt due the Trustees of the Washington Benevolent Society for the use of their rooms in the year 1818	75
	288.88

To which is to be added the fund of the Society

	$
in stock of Bank No. America 3 shares	1800
United States 6 p%	4129.72
City Water Loan	1500
	<u>7429.72</u>
making the amount of the funds of the association	<u>7718.60</u>

Discipline: Membership and Arrears

The committee take this opportunity of expressing their deep regret that all their exertions to procure from delinquent members the payment of arrearages due the Society have in great measure been ineffectual; they therefore again recommend the subject to the consideration of the meeting, that measures may be adopted to recover, at least a part of, the very heavy debt due the Society.

all which is respectfully submitted

Job Bacon Register

Philad^a March 1st 1821

The report was adopted & ordered to be entered on the minutes. On motion it was resolved that a committee be appointed again to make exertions to recover the outstanding debts due the Society; and the undernamed gentlemen were accordingly nominated to that service – to wit

Thomas Morris	William W. Howell
Joseph Simons	Richard C. Wood
Joseph Huddell	

Finance

The resolution offered by Mr Norris & Mr Worrell on 5 June last were called up for consideration, to wit

Resolved, that the expense incurred during the time of transacting the business of this Society at the annual, quarterly & special meetings thereof be paid by the Treasurer out of the "general fund".

And the question having been taken on each resolution separately they were both adopted without opposition.

Membership: New Member

Robert W. Sykes proposed for membership by Mr R. Wharton, at the last meeting, was duly elected & the Secretary instructed to give him notice thereof.

Assistance to Welsh Emigrants: Repayment to the Society

Mr Joseph Simons stated that he had received a letter from (one of those who had been assisted by the Society in emigrating to the Westward) enclosing a bank note for five dollars, & encouraging us to expect further remittances from our countrymen in that quarter.

Organization: Election of Officers

This being the day of annual election for officers the meeting proceeded thereto, when Zachariah Poulson was called to the Chair and Benjamin Chew and Benjamin R. Morgan appointed Tellers, who upon counting the votes declared the following gentlemen duly elected to their several offices for the ensuing year, to wit.

President	Robert Wharton
Vice President	Joseph S. Lewis
Treasurer	Thomas Morris
Secretary	Job Bacon
Register	John Roberts
Counsellors	Benjamin R. Morgan
	Charles Chauncey
Physicians	Dr Thomas Parke
	Dr Thomas C. James
Stewards	Richard Price
	William E. Howell
	Joseph Simons
	John R. Griffith
	Joseph Huddell
	Charles Dixey
	Richard C. Wood

Adjourned.

Welch Society

At a Quarterly Meeting of the Welch Society held at Peter Evans Tavern, George Street, June 4 1821.

Present

Robert Wharton	John Bevan
Joseph S. Lewis	Josiah Evans
Thomas Morris	Thomas Evans of P[eter]
Job Bacon	Peter Evans
John Roberts	Lewis Miles
Joseph Simons	John Morgan
John R. Griffith	Timothy Mount

Richard C. Wood
Dr Thomas Parke
Benjᵃ R. Morgan
William P. Williams

Benjamin Thomas
George Worrall
Joseph Worrell

Membership: Resignations

Letters of Resignation were received from several members, which were read & their resignations accepted on the usual conditions that any arrearages due the Society be first paid – to wit

From Robert Waln
      William T. Stockton
      George Vaux
      Richard L. Howell
      Redwood Fisher

Discipline: Membership and Arrears

The committee appointed at the last meeting to attend to the collection of outstanding debts, not being prepared to report, were continued.

Acting Committee Report – No Business

The Register stated verbally that the acting committee had no report to lay before the meeting.

Finance: Accounts and Investments

The Treasurer reported a cash balance of about two hundred dollars in his hands, which he was instructed in invest in such public securities as he may consider most advantageous to the Society.

Welsh Manufacturing and Good Relations with Welsh Settlers in Pittsburgh

The Vice-President, who has lately returned from a visit to Pittsburgh, informed the meeting, that he there met with a considerable number of our Welch brethren who were engaged in the manufactories of that neighbourhood.

The manner in which, he, as an officer of the Society was received by these settlers was of the most affectionate character; at the same time that he was highly gratified with the apparent prosperity of their situation. They seemed to entertain a grateful sense of the benefit conferred on them by the Society, by whose assistance a great number of them had been enabled to find their way to Pittsburgh and were evidently solicitous to repay the Society the sums advanced to them for that purpose. To effect this object, they, by the assistance of the V. Pres^t had made an arrangement with a mercantile house there, by whose friendly aid it is expected that the Society will gradually become repossessed of the monies disbursed on their account.

The present comfort & future prospect of these our countrymen afford much encouragement to the Society to persevere in their efforts to promote the emigration of Welchmen to that quarter, and confirm them in their previous conviction that such a course is best calculated to insure their future prosperity.

Adjourned.

Welch Society

At a Quarterly Meeting of the Welch Society held at Peter Evans Tavern, September 3 1821.

Present

Robert Wharton
Joseph S. Lewis
Job Bacon
John Roberts
Dr Thomas Parke
Joseph Huddell Jr
Richard C. Wood
John Bevan
Peter Evans

Josiah Evans
Joseph O. Evans
Thomas Evans of P[eter]
Lewis Miles
Wm W. Fisher
Robt W. Sykes
Wm Rawle Jr
Joseph Worrell
Lewis Walker

Membership: Resignation

Letter of resignation from Thomas R. Tunis was read & accepted on the usual condition.

Acting Committee Report and Assistance to Welsh Emigrants – Reverse Migration

Report of the acting committee

The acting committee of the Welch Society beg leave to report.

That since the last meeting of the Society they have been called upon to give aid to several natives of Wales, one of whom, William Prosser they assisted with twenty dollars to enable him to return to Wales, the other Enos Tobias (who has friends in the State of Indiana) and his family of seven small children they advanced forty dollars to, to enable him to transport his family to Pittsburgh; from both of whom they have taken receipts for the return thereof when in their power.

Finance: Sundry Expenses

They also report that in addition to the above sixty dollars, they have drawn orders on the Treasury for sundry expenses of printing &^{c} amounting to $9.65/^{100}

all which is respectfully submitted.

Friday 31 August 1821

(signed) John Roberts Register

Assistance to Welsh Emigrants – Letter to a Welsh Migrant at Pittsburgh

The Vice-President read a letter that he had written to one of the emigrants at Pittsburgh, relating to the monies due the Society, which was ordered to be put on file.

Adjourned.

Welch Society

At a Quarterly Meeting held at Peter Evans Tavern in George Street on Monday, December 3 1821.

Present

Joseph S. Lewis
Thomas Morris
John Roberts
Dr Thomas Parke
Joseph Simons
Richard C. Wood
John Bevan
Edward Davies
Peter Evans
Joseph O. Evans
George Worrall

Josiah Evans
John Hallowell
Isaac R. Jones
William H. Morgan
Timothy Mount
Joseph P. Norris
William Parker
Benjamin Thomas
Joseph Worrell
William P. Williams

Previous Meeting Minutes

The minutes of the last meeting were read & approved.

Membership: Resignation

Letter of resignation of membership was received from Lawrence Lewis and accepted on the usual condition.

Acting Committee Report and Assistance to Welsh Emigrants

The report of the acting committee was read and ordered to be entered on the minutes as follows.

The acting committee of the Welch Society beg leave to

Report

That since the last quarterly meeting of the Society but two cases of distress have come under their notice, for both of whom (being sick) they have procured admission to the Pennsylvania hospital, free of charge. One of them, David Davis, a man eighty-seven years of age, has since died there; and for the paying of his funeral expenses, an order has been drawn on the Treasurer for twenty dollars. The other, Lewis Lewis, had been struck with the palsy; he is at present in a state of recovery, & still there; the Vice-President has engaged to have him removed when required by the managers.

Finance: Sundry Expenses

In addition to the above order they have also drawn on the Treasurer for $1.62/^{100}$ for notices.

all which is respectfully submitted.

Friday, 30 Nov. 1821

John Roberts Register

Finance: Accounts and Investments

The Treasurer stated verbally that three hundred $ had been invested, since his last report, for account of the Society, in Government Stock.

Discipline: Membership and Arrears

The committee on outstanding debt, not being prepared to report, were continued; and it was on motion resolved that the Secretary be directed to request the committee to make exertion for collecting the sums due from delinquent members & be prepared to report, if practicable at the next meeting.

Relationship with Welsh migrants at Pittsburgh

The Vice-President informed the Society that since his last communication on the subject, he had been to Pittsburgh & had a second opportunity of meeting with Welch emigrants settled there & that he found them animated by the liveliest gratitude for the advice & assistance afforded them by the Society.

Membership: New Members

Thomas P. Roberts, and Thomas Shoemaker were proposed by the Treasurer as candidates for membership.

Annual Dinner

On motion of Mr Lewis it was resolved that the acting committee be directed to make the necessary arrangements for the annual dinner on the first of March & that they be instructed to invite the officers of such benevolent societies as reciprocate the compliment & such other guests, not exceeding six in number as in their judgement will contribute to the enjoyment of the day.

adjourned

Job Bacon Secr[y]

PART THREE

1822
Welch Society

At an Annual Meeting of the Welch Society held at Daniel Rubicam's on Sixth [Street] on the first of March 1822.

Present

Thomas Morris
Job Bacon
John Roberts
Dr Thomas Parke
Joseph Simons
Charles Dixey
Capt Thomas Morgan
Matt^w L. Bevan
Benjamin Chew
Edward Davies
Thomas Evans
Joseph O. Evans
Josiah Evans
Peter Evans
Wm W. Fisher
Caleb Griffith
Joseph Huddell Jr
John Halllowell

Isaac R Jones
Ez. E. Maddock
Timothy B. Mount
Wm H. Morgan
John Morgan
Joseph P. Norris
John M. Price
Richard Price
Zachariah Poulson
William Parker
William Rawle Jr
James Read Jr
Benjamin Stephens
Robert W. Sykes
Benjamin Thomas
George Worrall
Joseph Worrell
William P. Williams

Previous Meeting Minutes

The roll having been called the minutes of the last meeting were read and approved.

Acting Committee Report and Assistance to Welsh Emigrants

The acting committee submitted their quarterly report

That since the report made to the Society at their quarterly meeting in

December last, two cases requiring advice or assistance have come under their notice; the first the wife of David Jeffreys arrived here in December in the Ship *Tuscarora*, West Master from Liverpool, with five children one boy and four girls the youngest of whom is six years of age. On their arrival comfortable lodgdings [sic] were provided for them and they were in the course of a couple of weeks, sent on to Pittsburgh under the care of a careful waggoner, to the arms of an anxious husband and father who immediately wrote to the acting committee acknowledging his grateful thanks for the attention paid his family, it will be remembered that David Jeffreys arrived here about two years ago when advice and assistance were afforded him and that he had since that time remitted the amount advanced him.

The other case is that of Thomas Watkins who arrived in New York, in the Ship *William* from Liverpool with his wife and eight children in September 1819; he immediately proceeded on with the four youngest to Ebensburg (Cambria County) leaving the remaining four under the care of Mr Joseph Simons, who had benevolently offered to pay attention to them; he has since came on here to take three of them back with him; not having the means to procure any other conveyance they intended proceeding on foot; your committee thinking, that as the claims on the Society were not numerous, and the difficulty of three females the eldest but sixteen and the youngest twelve years of age walking so great a distance, in the inclement season of winter, have thought proper to advance them twenty dollars to enable them to procure a more eligible conveyance; for which the father, as well as two daughters (who all waited on the committee) expressed the most grateful thanks.

Finance: Accounts and Investments

Your committee have also examined the Treasurers accounts and compared the vouchers produced, and find that there is a cash balance of two hundred and six dollars and eighty-three cents in his hands and that the Society are in possession of seven thousand and seven hundred and twenty-nine $72/^{100}$ dollars of the following stocks

PART THREE

$
4429.72   six per cent United States Stock
1500   Water Loan of 1820 and
1800   three shares of Bank of North America Stock

All which is respectfully submitted.

J^{no} Roberts Register

February 19th 1822

which was read, adopted and ordered to be entered on the minutes.

Discipline: Membership and Arrears

The committee on collecting the outstanding debts reported progress therein and were continued.

Organization: Election of Officers

The period for the annual election of officers having come round Matthew L. Bevan and George Worrall were appointed Tellers who, after having received the votes and counted the same, reported the following gentlemen as duly elected officers for the ensuing year

President	Robert Wharton
Vice President	Joseph S. Lewis
Treasurer	Thomas Morris
Secretary	Job Bacon
Register	John Roberts
Physicians	Dr Thomas Parke
	Dr Thomas C. James
Counsellors	Charles Chauncey
	William Rawle Jr
Stewards	Richard Price
	Joseph Simons
	John R. Griffith
	Charles Dixey

Thomas Morgan
Thomas Elliott
Timothy B. Mount
Isaac R. Jones

Membership: New Members

Thomas P. Roberts proposed by Thomas Morris was duly elected a member of the Society.

Thomas Shoemaker also proposed by Mr Morris was in like manner elected and declared to be a member of the Welch Society and the Secretary was directed to give them official notice thereof.

Mr George Worrall proposed [by] Mr [forename not inserted] Hunt as a candidate for membership.

Adjourned

(signed) Job Bacon Secretary

Welch Society

At a Quarterly Meeting of the Welch Society held at Peter Evans in George Street, on Monday, June 3rd 1822.

Present

Robert Wharton
Joseph S. Lewis
John Roberts
Dr Thomas Parke
Joseph Simons
John Bevan
Peter Evans
Josiah Evans
George Worrall

Joseph O. Evans
Edmund Kinsey
Isaac R. Jones
Lewis Miles
Thomas P. Roberts
Thomas Shoemaker
Robert W. Sykes
Joseph Worrell and

PART THREE

Previous Meeting Minutes

The roll being called, the minutes of the last meeting were read and approved.

Membership: Death of Richard Price, a Steward

The death of Richard Price one of the Stewards of the Society was announced by the Vice President and on motion made and seconded it was resolved that a committee of three be appointed to prepare a memorial in testimony of the respect the Society held for him on which committee Mess[rs] Charles Chauncey, Dr Thomas Parke and Joseph S. Lewis were appointed and requested to report at the next meeting.

Discipline: Membership and Arrears

The committee on the collection of the outstanding debts not being present were continued.

Finance: Sundry Expenses

Solomon W. Conrads bill for $5 for printing was presented and an order for the amount drawn on the Treasurer.

Inter-Community Relations: Pennsylvania Infirmary of the Eye and Ear

A communication from James Gibson for the Pennsylvania Infirmary of the Eye and Ear was read and it was resolved that the President return to the managers of Pennsylvania Infirmary for the Eye and Ear the thanks of this Society for the friendly offer of the benefit of their institution.

Adjourned.

J[no] Roberts Register

Welch Society

At a Quarterly Meeting of the Welch Society held at Peter Evans in George Street on Monday, 2nd September 1822.

Present

Joseph S. Lewis
John Roberts
Dr Thos Parke
William Rawle Jr
John R. Griffith
Thomas Elliott
Isaac R. Jones
Joseph Simons
Thomas Morgan
Edward Davies
Richard C. Wood

Josiah Evans
Peter Evans
Joseph O. Evans
William W. Fisher
Lewis Miles
Thomas P. Roberts
Robert W. Sykes
Benjamin Thomas
Joseph Worrell
Thomas Evans and

Previous Meeting Minutes

The roll being called, the minutes of the last meeting were read and approved.

Membership: Testimony to Richard Price

The committee appointed to prepare a testimony of the respect of the Society to the memory of Richard Price made report which being amended by inserting the words 'who died at the advanced age of 86 years' was unanimously adopted in the following words

It is with unfeigned regret the Welch Society causes to be placed on its records the decease of Richard Price who died at the advanced aged of 86 years one of its founders and of its officers, and one of its most attentive and respected members. It is due to the memory of the deceased, to record, that he was a member of the St David's Society, before the Revolution, and continued so until its dissolution at some time during the war. When this benevolent association was afterward revived, under the name of the Welch Society, he was actively instrumental in organizing it and may be justly regarded as one of the founders of this institution. He was elected one of the first stewards of the Welch Society and continued to fill that office to the entire acceptance of his fellow officers and members until his death.

This lamented member of our Society was distinguished by activity and fidelity in the discharge of his duties, and by ardent devotion to the objects and interests of the institution.

The kindness of his affections, the mildness and serenity of his temper, and the cheerfulness which marked his social hilarity to the last period of a protracted life, will long be in remembrance and the anniversary of the Society will not return without the recollection, of its having been cheered, for so many revolutions, by the heartfelt joy which it always awakened in the breast of Mr Price.

Discipline: Membership and Arrears

The committee on the collection of the outstanding debts not having reported on motion of Mr Richard C. Wood, one of the committee, they were discharged from the duty.

On motion made and seconded resolved that the Register return to the Society at their next meeting a list of the debts due by the members.

Membership: Resignation

Letter of resignation from Dr William P. Dewees of his membership was received and accepted on the usual condition of the arrearages being paid.

Membership: Death of William P. Williams

The death of William P. Williams, a member of the Society was mentioned by Mr Joseph Simons and on motion made by Mr Simons and seconded the following testimony of their respect for his memory was unanimously agreed to.

Resolved that this Society truly regret the death of a worthy man whose philanthropy did him honour and whose services to his fellow countrymen and usefulness to this Society will not easily be replaced. The Society will always bear in mind that his peculiar services induced them to admit him as a member without the usual fees of admission and as a mark of their respect.

Adjourned

J^{no} Roberts Register

Welch Society

At the Quarterly Meeting of the Welch Society held at Peter Evans' in George Street on Monday, 2nd December 1822.

Present

Edward Davies
Peter Evans
Joseph O. Evans
John R. Griffith
Isaac R. Jones
Joseph S. Lewis
Thomas Morgan
Timothy B. Mount
William H. Morgan
Joseph P. Norris
and George Worrall

Dr Thomas Parke
William Parker
William Rawle Jr
Thomas P. Roberts
John Roberts
Joseph Simons
Thomas Shoemaker
Benjamin Thomas
Robert Wharton
Joseph Worrell

Previous Meeting Minutes

The minutes of the last quarterly meeting were read and approved of.

Discipline: Membership and Arrears

A list of the outstanding debts due the Society was received from the Register.

When on motion made and seconded it was resolved that a committee of three be appointed to prepare a list of and attend to the outstanding debts due to the Society on which committee Messrs Joseph S. Lewis, Timothy B. Mount and Joseph Worrell were appointed.

Acting Committee Report and Assistance to Welsh Emigrants, including the refusal to help in this matter

The acting committee made the following report which was read and ordered to be entered on the minutes

The acting committee of the Welch Society beg leave to report

That they have since their last report paid the necessary attention to the general business of the Society and afforded advice to such emigrants as stood in need of it as well as pecuniary assistance to several in distress, and have expended the following sums of money for the purpose viz

Forty dollars advanced Robert Jones (and his note taken therefor) he arrived here on the ship *Mary Ann* from Liverpool in August last with his wife and five children, three boys and two girls.

Twenty-five dollars to John Davis (from whom a note was also taken) he arrived with his wife and seven children (one boy and six girls) in the same vessel with Jones and both families intended to proceed to Delaware County, State of Ohio. Your committee also gave ten dollars to Richard Hughes a poor Welchman with a sick child who applied for aid; in addition to the pecuniary aid afforded as above your committee have also aided with their advice and assistance several other emigrant families, they are Mary Lewis who arrived here in the ship *Moss* from London with the children, she was assisted to proceed to her husband at Pittsburgh; and twenty one others that arrived in the ship *Liverpool Packet* in September last, in order to provide for the immediate necessities of whom Mrs Williams the widow of the late William P. Williams was called upon who accommodated them under her hospitable roof tho' greatly inconvenient to herself and family, but one of your committee urged her thereto on the assurance that she should sustain no loss in succouring these strangers. They resided with her eight or ten days when they proceeded to Ebensburg the place of their destination. None of them made any application for pecuniary aid, the only other known person who has applied for aid is John Evans, a distressed Welchman, who lost his wife of the yellow fever in Baltimore and came on here to obtain work but being unwell wished assistance to return to his poor family of seven children, but your committee considered his case such as did not come under the provisions of the Society.

Finance: Accounts and Investments

Your committee also report that the Treasurer has in his hands after paying the foregoing sums a balance of 412 78/^{100} dollars of which your committee have directed him to invest in stock the sum of three hundred dollars.

all which is respectfully submitted

J^{no} Roberts Register

Philadelphia

30 Novem^r 1822

Assistance to Welsh Emigrants: Remuneration to Mrs Williams

On motion made and seconded it was unanimously resolved that Mrs Williams widow of William P. Williams be presented with twenty dollars as a remuneration for the expense and trouble she was at in aiding and assisting a number of Welch emigrants as mentioned in the report of the acting committee and as a token of the respect and esteem in which the Society hold her and that the President be authorised to draw for that amount.

Annual Dinner

On motion made and seconded it was unanimously resolved, that the acting committee be directed to make the necessary arrangements for the annual dinner on the first of March next and that they be instructed to invite the officers of such other benevolent societies as reciprocate the compliment and other guests not exceeding six in number as in their judgement will contribute to the enjoyment of the day.

Membership: Request for Membership Withdrawn

The nomination of Mr Hunt for membership was withdrawn.

Finance: Investments

The Treasurer made report that he had invested by order of the acting committee $300 in the City Five per cent loan cost $306 25/^{100} and had a balance in his hands of $106 53$^{[/100]}$

Membership: New Members

The following gentlemen were proposed for membership

Edward Rawle	by Thomas Morris
Charles Marshall Jr (formerly a member)	by Thomas Morris
Charles Pritchett	by John Roberts

Adjourned

J^{no} Roberts Register

1823

Welch Society

At an Annual Meeting of the Welch Society held at Franklin House (Joseph Heads) corner of Walnut and Washington Streets on Saturday, the First of March 1823.

Present

Matthew L. Bevan
John Bevan
William Chancellor
Thomas Elliott
Josiah Evans
Thomas Evans
Joseph O. Evans
William W. Fisher
John R. Griffith
Caleb Griffith
Joseph Huddell Jr
George Howell
Isaac R. Jones
Joseph S. Lewis
Thomas Morris
Thomas Morgan
Timothy B. Mount

Lewis Miles
Joseph P. Norris
Dr Thomas Parke
William Parker
John M. Price
Zachariah Poulson
John Roberts
William Rawle Jr
Thomas P. Roberts
Joseph Simons
Robert W. Sykes
John R. Smith
Thomas Shoemaker
Benjamin Thomas
Samuel Wetherill
Joseph Worrell
Richard C. Wood

Minutes of Previous Meeting

The minutes of the last meeting were read and approved of.

Acting Committee Report and Assistance to Welsh Emigrants

The acting committee submitted their quarterly report.

The acting committee of the Welch Society beg leave to report that the only claim made on them since their last quarterly report is for a

PART THREE

poor distressed Welchman by the name of John Hughes who arrived in Boston in December last and since came on here, it has been referred to the Stewards of the Society with a discretionary power to aid him as far as thirty dollars.

Finance: Accounts and Investments

They also beg leave to report that they have examined the Treasurers account and the vouchers produced in support thereof and find a cash balance in his hands of $269 97/[100] and that the Society hold the following stocks

	$
Six per cent stock of the United States	4429.72
Water Loan at 5 per cent interest	1800
Three shares of Bank of North America stock at cost (par value $1200)	1800
D^{rs44}	8029.72

Organization: Consequences of Resignations etc

Before closing their report the committee would remark that from the great number of resignations and the lukewarmness evinced by many of the members they fear the income as well as the usefulness of the instution [*sic*] will be much curtailed, they therefore think it their duty to impress on the minds of the members the necessity of endeavouring to get gentlemen of Welch descent to join the Society.

all which is respectfully submitted

J^{no} Roberts Register

Saturday, 1st March 1823

which after being read was adopted and ordered to be entered on the minutes.

---

44   Dollars.

Discipline: Membership and Arrears

The committee appointed on the outstanding debts made the following report and submitted the resolutions subjoined thereto

The committee who were appointed on the second of December last to prepare a list and attend to the outstanding debts due the Society, beg leave respectfully to report

That they have carefully examined the minutes and the list of debts furnished by the collector amounting to 888.75/^{100} D^{rs} and find amongst them the names of several gentlemen who only require to be called on to discharge the amount due from them and they are therefore not brought forward on the present occasion, but amongst the list are the names of

Ward Griffin for	$50
Thomas S. Roberts	40.50

neither of whom have complied with the second article of the Charter and, of course, cannot be considered as members in relation to whom the following resolutions is recommended viz

Resolved that Ward Griffin and Thomas S. Roberts are not members of this Society.

Several names are also found on the list of persons who are deceased and of them who are not bound by the rules of the Society to pay fines and contributions which of course ought to be struck off the List of Outstanding Debts and in relation to them the following resolution is offered viz

Resolved that the names of the following persons be struck off the List of Outstanding Debts viz

		D^{rs}
Thomas Allibone	dec^d	25
Joshua Edwards	Honorary	43
Rowland Ellis	[Honorary]	49

Edward Gray	Honorary	35
Joshua Humphreys	[Honorary]	36. 50
Jonathan Jones	[Honorary]	39. 50
Samuel Nicholas	[Honorary]	10

The committee also find on the list the following names which, of course, ought not to appear on this list as their cases have already been acted on viz.

		D^{rs}
Jesse Waln	suspended	50
Daniel Thomas	exonerated & resigned	39. 50
Fishbourn Wharton	ditto	58
William Meredith	ditto	32

The last of whom is, however, by minute of 1st March 1820 held liable for 18½ D^{rs} and there remains

	D^{rs}
Edward Davies	44. 75
T. B. Freeman	18. 50
John Harrison	36. 50
Joseph Jones	30. 50
E. E. Maddock	21
David Meredith	17. 50
George Reinholdt	23. 50
Samuel Relf	18
William W. Smith	14. 50
Joseph Wildes	39. 50
Richard Ware	17. 50
T. B. Zantzinger	23. 50

respecting whom the following resolution is recommended

Resolved that they be informed by the Secretary of the amount respectively due from them and requesting payment thereof or of such part as they can conveniently pay, in which last case the Society will be pleased they should continue as members and exonerate them from the balance unpaid, or will accept their resignation if more desirable.

All which is respectfully submitted

Joseph S. Lewis
Joseph Worrell

To the Welch Society

Feb. 14 1823

The report was read and accepted.

The First resolution was adopted as submitted. The Second resolution was also adopted as submitted with the addition of the names of Samuel Relf and Richard Ware, both of whom are deceased and the Third resolution was passed with the alteration occasioned by the preceding resolution and the committee were discharged.

Membership: Resignation of Robert Wharton as President

A letter was read from Robert Wharton Esq[r] resigning the office of President.

Membership: New Members

The meeting then proceeded to the election of new members when Charles Pritchett proposed by John Roberts as also Charles Marshall Jr (formerly a member) proposed by Thomas Morris were both duly elected.

The name of Edward Rawle nominated at last meeting was withdrawn.

Organization: Election of Officers

This being the day for the annual election of officers of the Society, Matthew L. Bevan & William Parker were appointed Tellers who after having received all the votes and counted the same reported the following gentleman as duly elected officers for the ensuing year

President	Joseph S. Lewis
Vice President	Thomas Morris
Treasurer	Job Bacon
Secretary	John Roberts
Register	Joseph Simons
Stewards	John R. Griffith
	Charles Dixey
	Thomas Morgan,
	Thomas Elliott
	Timothy B. Mount
	Isaac R. Jones
	Thomas Shoemaker
Counsellors	William Rawle Jr
	Robert W. Sykes
Physicians	Dr Thomas Parke
	Dr Thomas C. James

Membership: Resignations

Letters of Resignation of membership from Charles Chauncey, Benjamin Stephens, George Worrall and Charles Foulke were received read and accepted on the usual condition of paying all arrearages.

Membership: New Member

John M. Read was proposed for membership by William Rawle Jr

Adjourned

J^{no} Roberts Register

Welch Society

At a Quarterly Meeting of the Welch Society held at Peter Evans' in George Street on Monday 2nd June 1823.

Present

Joseph S. Lewis   Presid^t

Thomas Morris   Peter Evans
Dr Thomas Parke   Josiah Evans
William Rawle Jr   Lewis Miles
Robert W. Sykes   Joseph P. Norris
John Roberts   Thomas P. Roberts
John R. Griffith   Thomas Shoemaker
Timothy B. Mount   Benjamin Thomas
Isaac R. Jones   Robert Wharton
Joseph Simons   Joseph Worrell and
Edward Davies   Richard C. Wood

Previous Meeting Minutes

The minutes of the last meeting were read and approved.

Acting Committee Report and Assistance to Welsh Emigrants

The acting committee presented their report

The acting committee for the Welch Society beg leave to report that they have attended to the benevolent purposes of the Society and have since the last meeting assisted John Hughes, the object stated at the annual meeting, with ten dollars; no other application having been made to them they have no business to report.

all which is respectfully submitted

Joseph Simons Register

Saturday, 31 May 1823

Membership: New Members

John M. Read proposed for membership by Wm Rawle Jr was duly elected.

The following gentlemen were proposed as members

David Z. Davis of Holmesburg by Joseph S. Lewis
James C. Biddle by John Roberts
Armon Davis
William M. Evans
Francis Perot by Thomas Morris

Adjourned

J^{no} Roberts Secretary

Welch Society

At a Quarterly Meeting of the Welch Society held at Peter Evans' in George Street on Monday 1st September 1823.

Present

Joseph S. Lewis Presid^t

Job Bacon	Josiah Evans
John Roberts	Peter Evans
Joseph Simons	Thomas Evans
Timothy B. Mount	William W. Fisher
Thomas Shoemaker	Lewis Miles
William Rawle Jr	William H. Morgan
Robert W. Sykes	Joseph P. Norris
Dr Thomas Parke	Charles Pritchett
Isaac R. Jones	Benjamin Thomas
John Bevan	Lewis Walker and
Joseph Worrell	

Previous Meeting Minutes

The minutes of the last meeting were read and approved of.

Acting Committee Report and Assistance to Welsh Emigrants

The acting committee submitted their quarterly report which being read as follows

The acting committee of the Welch Society beg leave to report that since the last meeting of the Society there have been several claims made for aid by emigrants from Wales principally by way of New York. Your committee immediately paid the necessary attention to their wants and have forwarded them on their journey to Pittsburgh where they all wished to proceed. Your committee have been compelled in doing this to incur a larger expense than they wished but considering that if they had not paid their carriage back to Pittsburgh they would in all probability have became [*sic*] a burthen to the Society by remaining in Philadelphia, where being unable to speak any but their native tongue it would have been difficult to obtain employ for them and as a large portion of them were young children the likelyhood [*sic*] of their becoming sick in the neighbourhood of a large city during the hot weather further induced them to go to this expense. The following is a statement of the persons relieved as also the amount laid out for each family.

	D^{rs}
Robert Rogers his wife one son and four daughters	30.73
Edward Nicholas his wife and daughters	22.84
Griffith Jones his wife three sons and a daughter	34
David Williams his wife two sons and a daughter	27.80
and William Breese	11
besides which sums they have paid sundry expenses for provisions, board and medicines for said families while here of	19.52

making the whole sum one hundred forty-five dollars and eighty-nine cents.

In addition to the above your committee have also been called upon to assist a distressed Welchman (Joseph Jennings who lies sick on the Ridge Road about two miles from the city) and his family they have procured for him a physician and such medicines as his disorder requires and have likewise taken the measures requisite for their future relief. All of them expressed the liveliest gratitude for the aid afforded them and from those to whom money was advanced. Their obligations were taken to refund the same when able.

all which is respectfully submitted

Joseph Simons Register

Friday, 29 August 1823

was accepted and ordered to be entered on the minutes.

Finances: Membership Arrears

The Secretary reported that he had notified the members mentioned in the third resolution passed on the First day of March last of the sums they respectively owed the Society and requesting payment.

Membership: New Members

The following gentlemen proposed at the last meeting were duly elected

David Z. Davis of Holmesburg	being proposed by Joseph S. Lewis
James C. Biddle	proposed by John Roberts
Armon Davis	ditto
William M. Evans	ditto
Francis Perot	proposed by Thomas Morris

Assistance to Welsh Emigrants

The President stated that since the meeting of the acting committee the family of Joseph Jenkins had all been attended to. The father had been admitted into the Pennsylvania Hospital, the mother had also been admitted in the lying-in department of that charitable institution and had been there delivered of a son and the children had been attended to as their necessities required.

Membership: Resignations

The resignation of William J. Jones, Paschall Hollingsworth and Edward Davies as members of the Society were received, read and accepted. The two first on the usual condition of paying the arrearages due by them and the last was accepted unconditionally.

Adjourned

J^{no} Roberts Secretary

Welch Society

At a Quarterly Meeting of the Welch Society held at Peter Evans' in George Street on Monday, 1st December 1823.

Present

Jos. S. Lewis	President
Thos Shoemaker	Lewis Miles
Jos. Simons	William Rawle Jr
J^{no} M. Price	Josiah Evans
Thos Parke	Thos P. Roberts
R. C. Wood	John Roberts
T. B. Mount	J^{no} R. Griffith
W. H. Morgan	Joseph Worrell
Armon Davis	Joseph P. Norris
Wm M. Evans	Peter Evans
Joseph Evans	

Previous Meeting Minutes

The minutes of the last meeting were read and approved of.

PART THREE

Acting Committee Report and Assistance to Welsh Emigrants

The acting committee presented their report which was read, adopted and ordered to be entered on the minutes.

The acting committee of the Welch Society, beg leave to report, that from circumstances that have occurred they are led to believe that the objects for which this association was form^d have become misunderstood in Wales and many persons emigrate to this country under an idea that on their arrival in Philadelphia they would be forwarded on to any place in the interior they thought proper to proceed to or be supported by the Society until they could procure employment, free from any expense to themselves. Your [committee] have therefore thought proper to address a circular letter (a copy of which is annexed) to influential persons in Wales explaining the purposes for which this Society associated and with a view to prevent persons emigrating to this country from coming here under the false impression that they can rely totally on the Society to forward their objects; Your President, at the request of the your committee, readily undertook the task of having them distributed at the least expense to the Society by sending them out by Capt. Dixey to his friends and correspondents in Liverpool with a desire they should be forwarded to the different towns in Wales directed to such clergymen and gentlemen as they considered would be most likely to give publicity to them; by which course we hope the demands lately made on the funds of the Society may be greatly diminished, thereby leaving us in a situation to assist the really sick and distressed descendants of St David in the hour of their necessity.

Assistance to Welsh Emigrants

Your committee have also to report that the only new demand made on them for pecuniary aid has been from an emigrant named John Thomas who arrived in New York with his wife and seven children in the Brig *Joseph* they are from Llanfillen,[45] Montgomeryshire. They have been assisted in proceeding to the West by your committee procuring them

---
45   Llanfyllin.

a passage in a wagon for which they paid forty-five dollars and took his obligation for the repayment of the same when able, they likewise paid Mrs Williams five dollars a[s] compensation for two weeks residence of them in her house.

The family of Joseph Jennings reported at the last meeting as also himself still remain under the care of your committee.

all which is respectfully submitted

signed Joseph Simons Register

Saturday 29 Novem^r 1823

Annual Dinner

On motion made and seconded, it was unanimously resolved that the acting committee be directed to make the usual arrangements necessary for the anniversary dinner in celebration of St Davids day and that they be instructed to invite the officers of such other benevolent society or societies as reciprocate with us and such other guests not exceeding six in number as they shall deem will best contribute to the enjoyment of the day.

Membership: New Members

The following gentlemen were proposed as candidates for membership

Saml Humphries   by Joseph Simons
James Gowen   by John Roberts
Saml P. Wetherill   by Joseph S. Lewis
J^{no} O. Wetherill   by Joseph Simons
J^{os} R. Hopkins   by John Roberts

Adjourned

signed John Roberts Sec^{ry}

PART THREE

1824

Welch Society

At an Annual Meeting of the Welch Society held at Franklin House (Joseph Heads) corner of Walnut & Washington Streets on Monday the First of March 1824.

Present

J^{os} S. Lewis   Presid^t

Matthew L. Bevan   Caleb Griffith
Francis Perot   John Bevan
John R. Griffith   Wm Rawle Jr
J. C. Biddle   John Huddell Jr
John Roberts   Wm Chancellor
George Howell   Thos P. Roberts
Charles Dixey   Wm W. Howell
J^{os} Simons   David Z. Davis
John Morgan   J^{no} R. Smith
Peter Evans   E. E. Maddock
R. W. Sykes   Thomas Evans
Wm H. Morgan   Thos Shoemaker
Joseph O. Evans   Lewis Miles
Benj. Thomas   Josiah Evans
John M. Price   Robert Wharton
Thomas Elliott   Thos Parke M.D.
Lewis Walker   Wm M. Evans
Zachariah Poulson   Saml Wetherill
John Watson   Wm Parker
Joseph Worrell   Richard C. Wood

Previous Meeting Minutes

The minutes of the last meeting were read and approved of.

Acting Committee Report and Assistance to Welsh Emigrants

The acting committee submitted their quarterly report with a resolution annexed. Ordered to be entered on the minutes.

The acting committee of the Welch Society beg leave to report that your committee since their report at the last quarterly meeting of the Society have attended to the duties enjoined on them and have relieved several Welch emigrants – viz

Richard Jenkins with ten dollars to assist him to proceed to Steubenville;[46] Evan Rees (who with his wife and four young children had arrived here from Wales by the way of New York) with fifteen dollars to enable them to proceed to Pittsburg[h], and David Hughes with ten dollars, being here sick and in distress; Joseph Jenkins (in the last report and minutes under the name of Joseph Jennings) who remained under the care of your committee at the last meeting of the Society has since recovered his health and has went into the country to procure a place to work, for the assistance and support of himself and family. They have had to draw orders on the Treasurer for ninety-five dollars and twenty-three cents; the above are all the claims made on the funds since their last report.

Your President has received a letter from his friends S. & T. Sherlock in Liverpool, to whom were sent for distribution the circular reported at the last meeting, stating the objects for which the association was

---

46 Approximately thirty-nine miles from Pittsburgh, Steubenville was a port town on the Ohio River, but it is now a city in Jefferson County, Ohio. Between 1786 and 1787 Fort Steuben was erected by soldiers of the 1st American Regiment and named after Baron Friedrich Wilhelm August Heinrich Ferdinand von Steuben (1730–94), a Prussian officer, and later a Major General and Inspector General of the Continental Army during the American Revolutionary War. The fort was established to assist government-appointed surveyors who were in the process of mapping the territory west of the Ohio River. For details of von Steuben, see John MacAuley Palmer, *General von Steuben* (New Haven, Mass: Yale University Press, 1937); Arnold Whitridge, 'Baron von Steuben, Washington's Drillmaster', *History Today*, 26/7 (July 1976), 429–36; Stephen C. Danckert, 'Baron von Steuben and the Training of Armies', *Military Review*, 74 (1994), 29–34.

formed, giving the information of their receipt and of their having been distributed at an expense of £ Stg 1.2.8 for postages and carriage, and that they had procured its insertion in several of the newspapers. These gentlemen having so very cheerfully undertaken the trouble and so promptly attended to the business your committee recommend the adoption of the annexed resolution and that the President be requested to forward a copy of the same to them.

Finance: Accounts – Lack of Scrutiny

The Vice President acting as Treasurer being absent from the city, your committee have been unable to examine a report on his accounts.

Membership: Purpose of Association

Your committee take this opportunity to state that during the preceding year several gentlemen of Welch descent have joined the Society and the resignations have diminished. They hope the members duly appreciate the objects for which they associated and that they will remember that social and convivial intercourse is a strong tie to hold them together they therefore would feel a great pleasure at finding a general attendance at the festive board this day.

all which is respectfully submitted

by your ob[edient] ser[vant]

Joseph Simons

Saturday 28 Feb. 1824

Assistance to Welsh Emigrants: Letter of Thanks to S. & T. Sherlock, Liverpool

Resolved that the thanks of the Welch Society at Philadelphia be given to Mess^r S. & T. Sherlock of Liverpool for the kind and prompt manner in which they attended to the distribution of a number of circular letters sent to them stating the object for which the Society associated and that the President be requested to forward the same to them.

The foregoing resolution was adopted.

Membership: New Members

The meeting then proceeded to the election of new members, when James Gowen, Saml Humphreys, Saml P. Wetherill, John P. Wetherill, & Joseph R. Hopkins were all duly elected.

Mordecai Lewis was proposed as a candidate for membership by Joseph S. Lewis.

Organization: Election of Officers

This being the day of the annual election of officers for the Society, Robert W. Sykes & T. P. Roberts were appointed Tellers who after having receiv'd all the votes offered, and counted the same reported the following gentlemen as duly elected for the ensuing year

President	Joseph S. Lewis
Vice President	Thomas Morris
Treasurer	Job Bacon
Secretary	John Roberts
Register	Joseph Simons
Stewards	John R. Griffith
	T. B. Mount
	Thos Elliott
	Charles Dixey
	Thomas Shoemaker
	Thomas P. Roberts
	Armon Davis
Counsellors	Wm Rawle Jr
	R. W. Sykes
Physicians	Dr Thos C. James
	Dr Thomas Parke

Membership: Resignations

The resignations of Thos Biddle & Wm W. Fisher were read & accepted on the usual condition of paying arrearages.

Membership: New Members

Stephen Lassall[e], by J. Simons, Wm H. Jones by J. Roberts & Dr Saml M. Fox by J. Simons were proposed for membership.

adjourned

(signed) J^{no} Roberts Sec^y

Welch Society

At a Quarterly Meeting of the Welch Society held at Peter Evans' in George Street, on Monday, 7th June 1824.

Present

John Roberts	Joseph Simons
Thos Shoemaker	Timothy B. Mount
Thos P. Roberts	Lewis Miles
Peter Evans	J^{no} Bevan
Wm Pritchett	Josiah Evans
Francis Perot	Thomas Evans

Organization: Meeting Not Quorate

There being no quorum, the Society adjourned, after reading the report of the acting committee as follows

Acting Committee Report and Assistance to Welsh Emigrants

The acting committee of the Welch Society, beg leave to report that your committee have since the annual meeting of the Society paid the necessary attentions to the duties entrusted to them and have relieved the wants and aided the exertions of such emigrants as have claimed the assistance of the Society.

The family of Joseph Jenkins mentioned in the last report have been advanced forty dollars to defray the expenses attendant on their removal to Pike Township Bradford County[47] and his note payable in 12 months taken for that amount. Thirty dollars and 7 cents have also been expended by your committee for the board of Mrs Jenkins and her two children and other expenses incurred by them; they have also assisted John Thomas, a poor distressed young Welchman, by procuring his admission into the Pennsylvania Hospital where he has died, and for the board and funeral expenses of whom they have had to incur an expense of.

Three other Welch families have likewise claimed the advice and assistance (tho' not pecuniary) of the Society, for one of which Edward Evans, employment has been procured; the others have receiv'd our advice as their cases needed.

all which is respectfully submitted

Friday, June 4 1824

signed J^{no} Roberts Sec^y

Welch Society

At a Quarterly Meeting of the Welch Society held at the House of Peter Evans in George Street, on Monday, 7th September 1824.

Present

Thomas Morris   Vice President

John Bevan   John R. Griffith
Job Bacon   Joseph R. Hopkins
Peter Evans   Saml Humphreys
Thos Evans   Lewis Miles
Wm M. Evans   Timothy B. Mount

---

47   Pike Township is in eastern Bradford County, north-eastern Pennsylvania.

Joseph O. Evans
Josiah Evans
Armon Davis
Francis Perot
John Roberts
Thos Shoemaker
Richard C. Wood

Mordecai Lewis Jr
Wm H. Morgan
Thomas Parke M.D.
Wm Rawle Junr
Joseph Simons
Benjamin Thomas

Previous Meeting Minutes

The minutes of the last meeting were read.

Acting Committee Report and Assistance to Welsh Emigrants

The Register made a verbal report, that the acting committee had attended to their duties and had assisted a number of emigrants with advice and to procure employment as also to shew them the best and cheapest methods of proceeding to their destinations, some of them were taken sick after their arrival, their wants were attended to, and Doctors Parke & James have paid unremitted attention to them. To Evan Evans they advanced twenty dollars to enable him to proceed with the family to Ohio – taking from him his obligation to repay the same if able, none of the others required pecuniary assistance.

Assistance to Family of Former Member and His Wife

The death of Mrs Williams, widow of the late Wm P. Williams was mentioned. When on motion made and seconded, it was resolv'd, that the acting committee be instructed to enquire into the situation in which the family of the widow of the late Wm P. Williams are left by her decease and to pay such attention to them as they may deem proper, as also to pay the funeral expenses if they think necessary.

Membership: Resignation

A letter of resignation from Benj. R. Morgan was read & accepted on the usual terms of paying all arrearages.

Membership: New Members

The following persons were unanimously elected as members.

Stephen B. Lassalle, proposed on the first of March by J^{os} Simons

Dr Saml M. Fox, proposed also by J. Simons and Wm H. Jones proposed by John Roberts at the last meeting.

adjourned

signed J^{no} Roberts Sec^y

Welch Society

At the Quarterly Meeting of the Welch Society held at Peter Evans in George Street on Monday, 6th December 1824.

Present

Joseph S. Lewis	President
Thomas Morris V.P.	Timothy B Mount
John R. Griffith	Wm H. Morgan
Mordecai Lewis Jr	Stephen B. Lassalle
John Roberts	Thomas Evans
Job Bacon	Armon Davis
J^{os} O. Evans	George Howell
Thos Shoemaker	Isaac R. Jones
Thos Parke M.D.	Saml Fox M.D.
J^{os} Simons	Peter Evans
Joseph Huddell	Wm M. Evans
R. W. Sykes	Thos P. Roberts
Chas Marshall Jr	Josiah Evans
John Watson	Wm Rawle Jr
John Bevan	Lewis Miles
Joseph P. Norris	Joseph Worrell

PART THREE

Previous Meeting Minutes

The minutes of the last meeting were read and approved of.

Organization: Absence of President

The President mentioned that his absence at the last meeting was occasioned by business of a public nature in the City of New York.

Acting Committee Report and Assistance to Welsh Emigrants

The report of the acting committee was read and ordered to be entered on the minutes.

The acting committee of the Welch Society beg leave to report that the only case that has come under the notice of your committee since their last report is that of Edward Jones who arrived here in August last in the Ship *Sarah Ralston* from Liverpool with his wife and eight children the eldest about 21 and the youngest 2½ years old since which time they have been afflicted with sickness and have spent the little they had to enable them to proceed to Bradford County (at which place they are going to settle). Your committee have advanced them $20 taking his obligation to refund the same when able, which from the character given him by Mr Thomas Mitchell on his property he is going to reside they have little doubt of his doing.

all which is respectfully submitted

Friday, 3rd December 1824

(signed) Joseph Simons Register

Assistance to Family of Former Member and His Wife

The acting committee not being prepared to report on the business of Mrs Williams were continued.

Annual Dinner

Resolved that the acting committee be directed to make the usual arrangements necessary for the anniversary dinner in celebration of St Davids day, and that they be instructed to invite the officers of such other benevolent Societies as reciprocate with us and such other guests not exceeding six in number as they shall deem will most contribute to the enjoyment of the day.

adjourned

signed John Roberts Secretary

PART THREE

1825
Welch Society

At an Annual Meeting of the Welch Society held at Franklin House (Joseph Heads corner of Walnut and Washington Streets) on Tuesday the first day of March 1825.

Present

Thomas Morris
Job Bacon
John Roberts
Joseph Simons
J^{no} R. Griffith
Thos Shoemaker
Armon Davis
Stephen B. Lassalle
Lewis Miles
Wm W. Howell
Francis Perot
John P. Wetherill
Josiah Evans
Joseph P. Norris
Isaac R. Jones
Thomas Evans
Mord. S. Lewis

Joseph Huddell
W. H. Morgan
Geo. Howell
Wm Parker
Richd C. Wood
W. Rawle Jr
Lewis Walker
John Bevan
Caleb Griffith
C. Marshall Jr
Saml P. Wetherill
John M. Price
Robert Wharton
Thomas Parke M.D.
Wm M. Evans
J^{no} R. Smith
Wm Chancellor

Previous Meeting Minutes

The minutes of the last meeting were read and approved of.

Acting Committee Report and Assistance to Welsh Emigrants

The acting committee submitted their annual report, which was read accepted and ordered to be entered on the minutes.

The acting committee of the Welch Society, beg leave to report that since the last meeting of the Society no claim has been made on them for pecuniary aid, advice and assistance had been bestowed on all emigrants who have stood in need of the same. It is with pleasure they have to mention the name of Evan Rees who has returned ten dollars part of a loan to him last summer of $15 to enable him to proceed to the Westward; the return of this amount shews a recollection of the benefits receiv'd from the Society and a desire to discharge the obligation due to it.

Finance: Accounts and Investments

Your committee have examined the Treasurers account and compared the same with the vouchers produced in support thereof and find a cash balance in his hands of Dollars 557 of which they have directed $400 to be invested in City Stock reimbursable at a long date conceiving that species of stock as the kind most for the interest of the institution the amount of stocks now held by the Society are as follows

	$
Six per cent United States Stock	4429.72
Water Loan 5 per cent interest	1800.00
3 shares of Bank of North America Stock	1800.00
amounting together to	8029.72

Assistance to Welsh Emigrants

It is with much gratification your committee have to remark that the amount required the past year from the funds of the Society for the relief of emigrants is not so great as that of preceding years from which circumstance they will be better enabled to grant relief if an unusual number should arrive here from Wales during the coming year.

Membership: Call for Membership

Before closing this report your committee would take the liberty to impress strongly on the members the necessity of increasing their numbers by inducing gentlemen to join the Society thereby adding to its sphere of usefulness and as social intercourse is a strong cement to hold us together they would express a hope to see a full and general attendance at the convivial board this day.

all which is respectfully submitted.

(signed) Jos. Simons Register

March 1 1825

Organization: Election of Officers

This being the day of the annual election of officers of the Society, Thomas Shoemaker & J. P. Wetherill were appointed Tellers who, after having receiv'd all the votes offer'd and counted the same, reported the following gentlemen as duly elected for the ensuing year

President	Joseph S. Lewis
Vice President	Thomas Morris
Treasurer	Job Bacon
Secretary	John Roberts
Register	Joseph Simons
Stewards	John R. Griffith
	Thos Elliott
	Charles Dixey
	Thos Shoemaker
	Timo. B. Mount
	Thos P. Roberts
	Armon Davis
Counsellors	Wm Rawle Junr
	Robt W. Sykes
Physicians	Thos C. James
	Saml M. Fox

Organization: No Fines for Non-Attendance at Meetings

Mr Simons offered the following resolution, which was laid on the table.

Resolv'd, that hereafter no fines shall be inflicted for non-attendance at any annual, quarterly, or special meeting provided that a quorum shall attend otherwise all absent to be fined as heretofore.

The following resolution was offered and adopted.

Resolv'd, that all fines due from the Physicians of the Society for non-attendance at the stated meetings be remitted.

adjourned

(signed) John Roberts Secretary

Welch Society

At a Quarterly Meeting of the Welch Society held at the House of Peter Evans in George Street on Monday, 6th June 1825.

Present

Joseph S. Lewis   President

Thomas Morris	Josiah Evans
Job Bacon	Saml M. Fox M. D.
John Roberts	George Howell
Joseph Simons	Wm H. Jones
Thomas Shoemaker	Stephen B. Lassalle
Thomas Elliott	Wm H. Morgan
John R. Griffith	Thomas Parke M.D.
Thos P. Roberts	Francis Perot
Armon Davis	Wm Rawle Jr
Peter Evans	Lewis Walker
Thomas Evans	Jos. Worrell
Jos. O. Evans	Richard C. Wood

Previous Meeting Minutes

The minutes of the last meeting were read and approved of.

Organization: No Fines for Non-Attendance at Meetings and its Legality

A resolution was offer'd altering the payments of fines, which after being discussed and contrary to the Constitution of the Society, it was on motion made by Mr Morris and seconded by John Roberts.

Resolv'd, that it be referr'd to the Counsellors of the Society with a request to report on the legality of the same.

Finance: Fines and Investments

The Treasurer reported that he had receiv'd from the collector $118 for fines and contributions, had invested $300 in City Stock and had a balance in his hands of about two hundred dollars.

Organization: No Further Business

The acting committee reported that no business had come before them.

adjourned

John Roberts Secretary

Welch Society

At a Quarterly Meeting of the Welch Society held at the House of Peter Evans, in George Street on Monday, 5th Sept[embe]r 1825.

Present

Joseph S. Lewis	President
Job Bacon	John Roberts
W. H. Jones	Thos Parke M.D.
Jos. Worrell	Wm H. Morgan
Armon Davis	Josiah Evans
Thos Evans	Francis Perot

Thos Morris
S. B. Lassalle
Wm Rawle Jr
Robt W. Sykes
Lewis Walker
Peter Evans

Timothy B. Mount
Richd C. Wood
John R. Griffith
Jos. R. Hopkins
Thos. P. Roberts

Previous Meeting Minutes

The minutes of the last meeting were read and approved of.

Finance: Investments

The Treasurer reported that he had invested $119, making with what had been invested since the annual meeting $475 – and leaving a balance in his hands of $154.

Acting Committee Report and Assistance to Welsh Emigrants

The acting committee made the following report

Since the last meeting there has nothing materially occurred worth reporting, there has been several of our countrymen arrived but none of them stood in need of pecuniary assistance, employment has been procured for those who required it, and others who came out with the intention of travelling on to the Westward, have been assisted with advise as to the cheapest way of proceeding to their place of destination.

signed Jos. Simons Register

Sep^t 7, 1825

Organization: No Fines for Non-Attendance and its Legality

The Counsellors who were instructed to report whether the Society have power to pass the following resolution – viz.

Resolv'd, that hereafter no fines shall be inflicted for non-attendance at any annual, quarterly or special meeting, provided that a quorum shall attend; otherwise all absent members to be fined as heretofore. And also whether the fines imposed by the Sixth Article of the Constitution and the Sixth Article of the Bye-Laws refer to the officers of the Society or to the members generally respectfully report,

That the language of the Sixth Article of the constitution is somewhat ambiguous, but the true construction of it in connection with other parts of the same instrument appears to be that the fines therein imposed refer as well to the members generally as to the Officers of the Society. The fourth article, provides for the annual and quarterly meetings of the Society, and attendance at these meetings, as well as at Special meetings is the duty not only of the officers, but of the members at large. The second clause of the sixth article, after authorising the election of temporary officers, in case of the absence of the regular officers of the Society, imposes in express terms a fine of fifty cents on every 'absent member' residing in the city of suburbs for 'each omission', which can only mean omission to attend the meetings of the Society, and a fine of one dollars for an omission to attend the annual meetings. But what must remove all doubt that the fines above notified are applicable to the members generally and not to the officers, is that in the very next sentence of the same clause a fine of one dollar is imposed on all the officers of the Society, except the Counsellors, Physicians, and Stewards, for non-attendance at special and quarterly meetings. If therefore the clause imposing the fine of fifty cents does not refer to the members generally, it can have nothing to operate on, but the Counsellors, Physicians and Stewards, which is inconsistent with the whole tenor of it. That it does not refer to the acting committee, is perfectly clear, because they are directed by the first clause of the Sixth Article to hold monthly meetings; and the clause imposing the fines applies in express words to annual meetings and by necessary implication to quarterly and special meetings.

With respect to the fines imposed by the Sixth Article of the Bye-Laws it does not admit of a doubt that they extend to the members of the Society generally as well as to the officers.

The Society have no power by resolution, to abrogate any of the Constitution, and consequently cannot do away the fines imposed by it. The only remedy is by an alteration of the Charter in the manner prescribed by law.

If the fines imposed by the Sixth Article of the Bye-Laws for non-attendance at special meetings, depended on the Bye-Laws alone, they might be annulled by the repeal of the Bye-Law in the mode pointed out by the Fourth Article of the Constitution. But fines for non-attendance at special meetings seem to be provided for by the Constitution itself, the Fifth Article of which authorises the President, at the request of two thirds of the acting committee present, to call extra meetings; and the Sixth Article as already shewn, inflicts fines for absence from the constitutional meetings of the Society.

For the reasons given above the Counsellors are of opinion that the fines imposed by the Sixth Article of the Constitution and the Sixth Article of the Bye-Laws are applicable to the members of the Society generally as well as to the officers, and that the Society have no right by resolution to annul those fines.

signed Wm Rawle Junr

R. W. Sykes

Septr 5, 1825

Organization: Annual Fees Discussed

Resolv'd, that the 8th Article of the Bye-Laws, which impose an annual contribution of two dollars to be paid by each member be repealed, provided this resolution shall not affect the contributions now due (laid on the table).

The foregoing resolution was offer'd by R. C. Wood & seconded by W. H. Rawle Jr.

PART THREE

Membership: Resignation

The resignation of Matthew L. Bevan was read & accepted on the usual terms.

adjourned

signed John Roberts Secretary

Welch Society

At a Quarterly Meeting of the Welch Society held at the House of Peter Evans Inn, on Monday Evening, 5th December 1825.

Present

Joseph S. Lewis	President
Thomas Morris V.P.	Stephen B. Lassalle
John Roberts Sec	John Morgan
Jos. Simons Reg.	William H. Morgan
James C. Biddle	Timothy B. Mount
Charles Dixey	Thomas Parke M.D.
Armon Davis	Francis Perot
Peter Evans	Wm Rawle Jr
Thomas Evans	Thos P. Roberts
Josiah Evans	John M. Read
John R. Griffith	Joseph Worrell
Joseph R. Hopkins	Thomas Shoemaker
William H. Jones	

Previous Meeting Minutes

The minutes of the last meeting were read and approved of.

Organization: Annual Fees

The resolution, with regard to repealing the Bye-Law imposing an annual contribution, was called up and continued until the next meeting.

Organization: No Business

The Register made a verbal report, that no business had come before the acting committee since the last meeting of the Society.

Annual Dinner

On motion and seconded, resolv'd, that the acting committee be directed to make the usual arrangements necessary for the anniversary dinner in celebration of St David's day and that they be instructed to invite the officers of such other benevolent societies as reciprocate with us, and such other guests not exceeding six in number as they shall deem will contribute to the enjoyment of the day.

Membership: New Members.

The following gentlemen were proposed as candidates for membership – James Glentworth & W[m] Craig by J[no] Roberts and Thomas W. Morris by Thomas Morris.

Adjourned

signed John Roberts Sec[y]

PART THREE

1826

Welch Society

At an Annual Meeting of the Welch Society held at the Washington Hotel / Daniel Rubicam's N°. 20 South Sixth Street[48] on Wednesday the first-day of March 1826.

Present

Job Bacon
James C. Biddle
Benj. Chew
David Z. Davis
Armon Davis
Peter Evans
Thomas Evans
Jos. O. Evans
Josiah Evans
Thomas Elliott
Saml M. Fox
Caleb Griffith
John R. Griffith
James Gowen
Joseph Huddell
George Howell
Isaac R. Jones
Stephen B. Lassalle
John Morgan

Thomas Morris
Wm H. Morgan
Timothy B. Mount
Charles Marshall Jr
Thomas Parke
Zachariah Poulson
Francis Perot
James Read Jr
John Roberts
Thomas P. Roberts
John M. Read
Joseph Simons
John R. Smith
Robert W. Sykes
Thomas Shoemaker
Lewis Walker
Saml Wetherill
Joseph Worrell
John P. Wetherill

Previous Meeting Minutes

The minutes of the last meeting were read and adopted.

---

48   See n.42.

Acting Committee Report and Assistance to Welsh Emigrants

The acting committee submitted their annual report, which was accepted and ordered to be entered on the minutes.

The acting committee of the Welch Society, beg leave to report,

That it is with much pleasure they have to state that no application has been made for pecuniary aid from the funds of the Society since their last quarterly meeting and that nothing material has occurr'd within the knowledge of your committee worth reporting.

Finance: Accounts and Investments

Your committee have examined the Treasurers' accounts and compared the same with the vouchers produced in support thereof and find a cash balance in his hands of $262 14/^{100}

The amount and species of stock held by the Society are as follows and to give a fair view of the same they state the par as also the market value thereof viz.

	par value	market value
Six per cent United States Stock	4029.75	4068.11
Six per cent City Stock	900.00	1068
Five per cent City Stock	1800.00	1920
Bank of N America Stock 3 shares	1200	1440
	7929.75	8496.11
Cash as above	262.14	
Dollars	8191.89	total funds

of the institution (exclusive of the above premium) of $566 36/^{100} or whatever advance may be received when the stock shall be sold.

Philanthropy: Purpose of the Society

As social intercourse expands the heart and opens the hands of charity it would afford much gratification to your committee to observe a full attendance at the festive board this day.

all which is respectfully submitted

Jos. Simons Register

Wednesday 1st March 1826.

Membership: New Members

James Glentworth Jr proposed by John Roberts was duly elected a member of the Society.

Thomas W. Morris proposed by Thomas Morris was duly elected a member of the Society.

William Craig (formerly a member) proposed by J^{no} Roberts was re-elected.

Organization: Annual Elections

This being the day for the annual election of officers of the Society, Thomas P. Roberts and Robt W. Sykes were appointed Tellers who made the following report

At an election for officers of the Welch Society held at Washington Hotel (Daniel Rubicam's), on St David's day, Wednesday the 1st March 1826

Thomas P. Roberts & Robt W. Sykes were appointed Tellers who after having receiv'd the votes offer'd reported the following persons elected to the offices affixed to their respective names for the ensuing year

President	Joseph S. Lewis
Vice President	Thomas Morris
Treasurer	Job Bacon
Secretary	John Roberts
Register	Joseph Simons
Stewards	John R. Griffith
	Charles Dixey

	Timothy B. Mount
	Tho[s] Elliott
	Tho[s] Shoemaker
	Tho[s] P. Roberts
	Armon Davies
Counsellors	Rob[t] W. Sykes
	W[m] Rawle Jr
Physicians	Dr Tho. C. James
	Dr Sam[l] M. Fox
Tellers	Thomas P. Roberts
	R. W. Sykes

Finance: Annual Contribution – Amendment to Bye-Law

The resolution with regard to the annual contribution which was continued at the last meeting was now called up and after some discussion was adopted with the following amendments provided this resolution shall not affect the contributions now due, the resolution as amended and adopted is as follows.

Resolv'd, that the Eighth Article of the Bye Laws which imposes an annual contribution of two dollars by each member be repealed, provided this resolution shall not affect the contributions now due.

Membership – Resignations

The resignations of Robert Wharton and Joseph R. Hopkins were read and accepted on the payment of all arrearages.

adjourned

signed John Roberts Secretary

PART THREE

Welch Society

At a Quarterly Meeting of the Welch Society held at the House of Thomas Evans in George Street on Monday 5th June 1826.

Present

Joseph S. Lewis	President

Thomas Morris V.P.	Stephen B. Lassalle
Job Bacon	Thomas Parke M.D.
Armon Davis	Francis Perot
Joseph O. Evans	John Roberts
Josiah Evans	Thomas P. Roberts
Saml M. Fox M.D.	Joseph Simons
John R. Griffith	Thomas Shoemaker
James Glentworth Jr	Lewis Walker
Joseph Worrell	

Previous Meeting Minutes

The minutes of the last meeting were read and adopted.

Membership: Resignations

The resignations of Joseph P. Norris and James Read Jr were read and accepted on the usual condition of paying all arrearages.

Acting Committee Report

The acting committee stated that nothing had occurred for them to report.

adjourned

signed John Roberts Secretary

Welch Society

At a Quarterly Meeting of the Welch Society held at the House of Thos Evans in George Street on Monday Sept[ember] 4 1826.

Present

Joseph S. Lewis	President
Thomas Morris	V.P.
Job Bacon	Tr
John Roberts	Sec^y

Timothy B. Mount	Armon Davis
Joseph Evans	Wm H. Morgan
Lewis Walker	Thomas Elliott
Robert W. Sykes	John R. Griffith
Thomas Parke M.D.	Joseph Worrell

Previous Meeting Minutes

The minutes of the last meeting were read and adopted.

Acting Committee Report and Assistance to Welsh Emigrants

The acting committee reported that the only assistance afforded by them since the last meeting of the Society was a donation of ten dollars to Elizabeth Lewis, the widow in distress of a poor Welchman who had died to the Westward, and that they had procured her the situation of a nurse.

Finance: Investments

The Treasurer reported that the stock of the Society which had been paid off, since the last meeting had been reinvested.

adjourned

signed John Roberts Secretary

PART THREE

Welch Society

At a Quarterly Meeting of the Welch Society held at the House of Thomas Evans in George Street on Monday December 4 1826.

Present

Joseph S. Lewis   President

Thomas Morris V.P.   Wm H. Morgan
John Roberts Sec^y John Morgan
Joseph Simons Reg^r Timothy B. Mount
William Craig   Charles Marshall Jr
Thomas Evans   Thomas Parke M.D.
Josiah Evans   Thomas W. Morris
Armon Davis   Francis Perot
Charles Dixey   Thomas P. Roberts
Saml M. Fox M.D.   William Rawle Junr
Caleb Griffith   Thomas Shoemaker
John R. Griffith   Lewis Walker
Isaac R. Jones   Saml P. Wetherill
Stephen B. Lasalle   Joseph Worrell

Previous Meeting Minutes

The minutes of the last meeting were read and adopted.

Acting Committee Report – No Business

The Register reported that the acting committee since the last meeting of the Society had nothing come before them necessary to report.

Annual Dinner

The following resolution offered by Thomas Shoemaker and seconded by Thomas Morris unanimously adopted.

Resolv'd, that the acting committee be directed to make the usual arrangements necessary for the Anniversary dinner in celebration of St David's day and that they be instructed to invite the officers of such other benevolent societies as reciprocate with us and such other guests not exceeding six in number as they shall deem will most contribute to the enjoyment of the day.

adjourn'd

signed John Roberts Secretary

PART THREE

1827
Welch Society

At an Annual Meeting of the Welch Society held at Washington Hotel (D. Rubicam's No.20 South Sixth Street) on Thursday the first day of March 1827.

Present

Joseph S. Lewis	President
Thomas Morris V.P.	Armon Davis
Thos. P. Robert Sec P.T.	Thos W. Morris
Joseph Simons Reg^r	Charles Marshall
Job Bacon Treas^r	Timothy B. Mount
Lewis Walker	Robert W. Sykes
John Bevan	Zach. Poulson
Wm H. Morgan	Benjn Chew Junr
Jos. O. Evans	Thomas Parke M.D.
Thos Shoemaker	George Howell
Caleb Griffith	John M. Read
Ja^s Glentworth Jr	Thomas Evans
Joseph Worrell	Josiah Evans
David Z. Davis	William Rawle Jr

Previous Meeting Minutes

The minutes of the last meeting were read and adopted.

Acting Committee Report and Assistance to Welsh Emigrants

The acting committee submitted their annual report, which was accepted and ordered to be entered on the minutes.

The acting committee of the Welch Society, report that since the last annual meeting the calls on the charities of the institution have happily been few, consisting only of relief afforded to Elizabeth Lewis, a widow, with 4 children $20.

Thomas Morris & wife an aged and respectable pair, too old for labour [$]20.

Mrs Lewis by the kind assistance of Dr Parke & Dr James has been provided with employment as a nurse and her two eldest children placed in suitable and comfortable situation with a prospect of doing well.

Finance: Accounts and Investments

The committee on the Treasurers accounts have carefully examined the same and report them to be correct. From thence it appears that the funds of the corporation consist of

		$
$900	City 6 per cent stock worth at present	1053
1800	City 5 per cent	1908
3600	Bank of N. America stock 9 shares	4356
1629.75	United States 6 per cent stock (16 million)	1629.75
7925.75		8946.75
120.75	cash in hands of the Treasurer	120.75
8050.50 Doll[ar]s		Doll[ar]s 9067.50

signed Joseph Simons
Register

Membership: Resignations

The resignation of Joseph Hemphill and Wm W. Howell were read and accepted upon the usual conditions.

Organization: Annual Elections

This being the day for the election of officers of the Society for the ensuing year J. Glentworth Jr & Thos Shoemaker were appointed Tellers, who made the following report

President   Joseph S. Lewis
Vice President   Thomas Morris

Treasurer	Job Bacon
Secretary	John Roberts
Register	Joseph Simons
Physicians	Thomas C. James
	Saml M. Fox
Stewards	Timothy B. Mount
	Thomas Shoemaker
	John R. Griffith
	Thomas P. Roberts
	Armon Davis
	Thomas Elliott
	Charles Dixey
Counsellors	William Rawle Jr
	Rob. W. Sykes

signed James Glentworth Jr
Thos Shoemaker
Tellers

adjourned

Thos P. Roberts Sec^y P.T.

Welch Society

At a Quarterly Meeting of the Welch Society held at the House of Thomas Evans in George Street on Monday June 4 1827.

Present

Joseph S. Lewis	President
Thomas Parke M.D.	John Bevan
Timothy B. Mount	Thomas Morris
Samuel M. Fox M.D.	John R. Griffith
Joseph Worrell	Josiah Evans

William H. Morgan
Joseph Simons
Stephen B. Lassalle
Francis Perot

Lewis Walker
Armon Davis
James Glentworth Jr
Thomas Evans

Acting Committee Report and Assistance to Welsh Emigrants

The acting committee of the Welch Society report, that they have attended to the benevolent purposes of the Society and have since the last meeting (March 1st) expended four dollars in relieving Robert and John Owen (father & son), the former upwards of sixty and the latter in his nineteenth year. They arrived in the Ship *Ann* Captain Bartleson on the 2nd inst from Liverpool, and on the same day sat off for Birmingham Mills, New Jersey.[49]

The above is all the communication the committee have to make at present.

all which is respectfully submitted

signed Joseph Simons Register

adjourn'd

Welch Society

At a Quarterly Meeting of the Welch Society held at the House of Thomas Evans in George Street on Monday Septr 3rd 1827.

Present

Joseph S. Lewis   President

Job Bacon
Joseph O. Evans
Thomas Evans
Josiah Evans

Thomas P Roberts
Joseph Simons
Robert W. Sykes
Joseph Worrell

---

49 Now in Pemberton Township, Burlington County.

Stephen B. Laselle
John R. Griffith
Thomas Morris
Timothy B. Mount

William Rawle Jr
Samuel Evans
Thomas W. Morris
Thomas Parke M.D.

Acting Committee Report and Assistance to Welsh Emigrants

The quarterly report of the acting committee was submitted from which it appeared that the calls on the benevolence of the institution since the last quarterly meeting have been very inconsiderable.

Membership and Benevolence: Death of the Society's Former Secretary and Assistance to his Wife and Family

The acting committee in making their quarterly report to the Society have to regret the decease of their worthy Secretary John Roberts, whose zealous services, and strong attachment to the interest of the Society, connected with the urbanity of his manners and the humanity displayed in his conduct to our distressed Welch brethren entitle him to our fondest recollection and our warmest regret. Cut off in the meridian of his life by a lingering disease which has anticipated a provision for his amiable wife and large family who are left in destitute circumstances, the committee are of it would be proper for the society to appropriate a portion of its funds as a donation to his wife in consideration of his faithful services. The committee therefore offer the following resolution

Resolv'd, that the President be authorised to draw an order on the Treasurer for two hundred dollars, which he be directed to present to Mrs Roberts in the name of the Society accompanied by a copy of this minute.

Membership: Death of a Steward

The committee have also to lament the decease of their fellow member Thomas Elliott whose conduct as a Steward and benevolence and philanthropy of character entitle him to the grateful remembrance of the Society.

Benevolence of the Society

The committee have paid their usual attention to the objects and interest of the Society, and the sums paid which are but small, will be found in the annual accounts of the Treasurer.

Organization: Election of New Officers

By the Rules of the Society, it becomes their duty to elect members to fill the vacancy by the decease of an officer.

all which is respectfully submitted.

The foregoing preamble and resolution were unanimously adopted.

The death of Mr John Roberts which deprived the Society of his valuable services having left the office of Secretary vacant, the meeting proceeded to the election of an officer to supply his place. When upon counting the ballots it appeared that Thomas P. Roberts was duly elected.

The death of Thomas Elliott and the election of T. P. Roberts to the office of Secretary, having also left vacancies in the list of Stewards – the meeting proceeded to the election to supply their places – when on counting the ballots Mess[rs] Caleb Griffith & Thomas W. Morris were declared to be duly chosen to supply their places.

Membership: New Members

Mr John C. Tillinghast and Mr Horace Mann were proposed by Thomas Morris, as candidates for membership.

Organization: Records of the Society

The President produced at the meeting, the books and papers of the Society lately in possession of our Secretary, which were delivered to the charge of Secretary elect, Tho[s] P. Roberts.

adjourn'd.

PART THREE

Welch Society

At a Quarterly Meeting of the Welch Society held at the Washington Inn, in George Street on Monday December 3rd 1827.

Present

Joseph S. Lewis	President

John Bevan	Thomas Parke M.D.
Charles Dixey	Francis Perot
Thomas Evans	Thomas P. Roberts
John R. Griffith	William Rawle Jr
Stephen B. Lasalle	Joseph Simmons
Thomas Morris	Thomas Shoemaker
Timothy B. Mount	Lewis Walker
Thomas W. Morris	Joseph Worrell
Joseph Huddell	Armon Davis

Previous Meeting Minutes

The minutes of the last meeting were read and approved.

Acting Committee Report and Assistance to Welsh Emigrants

The acting committee of the Welch Society report, that they have attended to the benevolent duties of the Society, and with great satisfaction they inform, that they have had no calls upon them for any pecuniary assistance since the last meeting of the Society

which is respectfully submitted.

signed Joseph Simons Regs.

Decr 3rd 1827.

Benevolence : Assistance to the Former Secretary's Wife and Family

The President reported, that in compliance with the resolution of the

Society passed at the last meeting, he had presented to Mrs Hannah Roberts, in the name of the Society, a check for two hundred dollars, and a copy of the minute of the acting committee.

Membership: Resignation

A letter of resignation was read from William Craig, which was accepted upon the usual conditions.

Annual Dinner

Resolv'd, that the acting committee be directed to make the usual arrangements necessary for the anniversary dinner in celebration of St David's day, and that they be instructed to invite the officers of such other benevolent Societies as reciprocate with us, and such other guests not exceeding six in number, as they shall deem best calculated to promote the enjoyment of the day.

adjourn'd

Tho[s] P. Roberts Secretary

Membership: New Member

Sansom Perot proposed for membership by T. Shoemaker.

PART THREE

1828

Welch Society

At an Annual Meeting of the Welch Society held at the Mansion House South Third Street, on Saturday the first of March 1828.

Present

Joseph S. Lewis   President

Job Bacon	Zachariah Poulson
John Bevan	William Parker
James C. Biddle	Francis Perot
Benjamin Chew	Williams Rawle Jr
David Z. Davis	Thomas P. Roberts
Armon Davis	John M. Read
Thomas Evans	Robert W. Sykes
Joseph O. Evans	Thomas Shoemaker
Josiah Evans	Lewis Walker
William M. Evans	Samuel Wetherill
James Gowen	Joseph Worrell
James Glentworth Jr	Richard C. Wood
Joseph Huddell	Samuel P. Wetherill
George Howell	John P. Wetherill
Thomas Morris	Timothy B. Mount
Thomas W. Morris	Thomas Parke

Previous Meeting Minutes

The minutes of the last meeting were read and approved.

Acting Committee Report and Assistance to Welsh Emigrants

The acting committee submitted their annual report, which was read and ordered to be entered on the minutes.

The acting committee of the Welch Society report, that since our last quarterly meeting, no application has been made for pecuniary assistance from the funds of the Society.

Finance: Treasurer's Accounts and Investments

The accounts of the Treasurer for the past year, have been examined and compared with the vouchers produced in support thereof, and the balance of cash in the hands of the Treasurer amounts to three hundred and eighty-six dollars and sixty-three cents.

The funds of the Society as stated by the Treasurer consists of

		$
City Stock of 1840	6 per ct at par 400 value	460.00
City Stock of 1840	5 per ct at par 300	322.50
City Stock of 1846	6 per ct at par 500	590.00
City Stock of 1846	5 per ct at par 1500	1627.50
North American Bank	12 Shares 4800	6000.00
	Doll[ar]s 7500	9000
	Cash	386.63
Cash value	Dollars	9386.63

Membership: New Members

John C. Tillinghast and Horace Mann proposed by Thomas Morris on the 3rd September last were duly elected members of the Society.

Sansom Perot proposed at the last meeting by Thomas Shoemaker was also duly elected a member.

Organization: Election of Officers

This being the day for the annual election of officers of the Society, James C. Biddle and Saml P. Wetherill were appointed Tellers, who after having receiv'd all the votes offer'd and counted the same, reported the following gentlemen, as duly elected for the ensuing year

President   Joseph S. Lewis
Vice President   Thomas Morris
Treasurer   Job Bacon
Secretary   Thomas P. Roberts
Register   Joseph Simons
Physicians   Thomas C. James &
                    Saml. M. Fox
Stewards   Timothy B. Mount
                    Thomas Shoemaker
                    John R. Griffith
                    Armon Davis
                    Charles Dixey
                    Thomas W. Morris and
                    James Glentworth Jr
Counsellors   William Rawle Jr
                    Robert W. Sykes

signed March 1 1828

James C Biddle
Saml. P. Wetherill
Judges

adjourn'd

Thos P. Roberts Secretary

Welch Society

At a Quarterly Meeting of the Welch Society held at the House of Thomas Evans June 2nd 1828.

Present

Joseph S. Lewis	President
Thomas Morris V.P.	Charles Marshall
Job Bacon Tr.	Thomas P. Roberts
Armon Davis	Joseph Simons
Thomas Evans	Thomas Shoemaker
Jos. O. Evans	John C. Tillinghast
Josiah Evans	Lewis Walker
James Glentworth Jr	Joseph Worrell
John R. Griffith	Richard C. Wood
Sansom Perot	Thomas Parke M.D.

Previous Meeting Minutes

The minutes of the last meeting were read and approved.

Acting Committee Report and Assistance to Welsh Emigrants

The acting committee beg leave to report, that they have had no application for pecuniary assistance, or any other business before them since the last quarterly meeting necessary to be laid before the Society.

Excepting in the case of Mr John Jones, lately from Montgomeryshire, who solicited the aid of the Society to procure him a situation as an assistant apothecary.

Your committee attended to that duty and are happy in saying with their assistance a situation has been procured suitable to his wishes.

signed Joseph Simons Register

Philad. June 2nd 1828

adjourn'd

Thos P. Roberts Sec^y

PART THREE

Welch Society

At a Quarterly Meeting of the Welch Society held at the House of Thomas Evans September 1st 1828.

Present

Thomas Morris   Vice President

Thomas Evans   Joseph Simons
Josiah Evans   Thomas Shoemaker
Wm M. Evans   Lewis Walker
Thomas Parke   Joseph Worrell
William Rawle Jr   Thomas P. Roberts

Previous Meeting Minutes

The minutes of the last meeting were read and approved.

Acting Committee Report and Assistance to Welsh Emigrants

The acting committee beg leave to report, that since the last quarterly meeting one case only has come before them requiring assistance. A poor widow, Ann Comey, from Llanfehangelgenerglyn,[50] Montgomery Shire, in great distress, with three small children, having lost her husband about three months ago, supposed to be drown'd, he left home in an open boat along with the intention (as he had often done before) of going to Kingston about 15 miles from Poughkepsie,[51] the boat was found, but he had not been heard of. Having inform'd a cousin who lives in Pittsburg [*sic*] of her situation he invited her to come on with her little ones. On her arrival in Philadelphia, she became short of funds to proceed. Through Mr Richard North she applied to the Welch Society; the Stewards after some consultation agreed to advance her 10 dollars and accordingly an order was drawn on the Treasurer for that amount.

50   Llanfihangel Genau'r Glyn, Cardiganshire. About five miles from Aberystwyth.
51   Kingston is the county seat of Ulster County, New York State, and Poughkeepsie is a town in Dutchess County, New York State.

signed Joseph Simons Register

Sept 1 1828.

Membership: New Members

John J. Griffith and Saml Jenkins were proposed by John R. Griffith as candidates for membership.

adjourn'd

Thos P. Roberts Sec^y.

Welch Society

At a Quarterly Meeting of the Welch Society held at the House of Thomas Evans December 1st, 1828.

Present

Joseph S. Lewis   President

Job Bacon   Stephen B. Lassalle
John Bevan   Thomas Morris
Armon Davis   Thomas W. Morris
Thomas Evans   William H. Morgan
Joseph O. Evans   Francis Perot
William M. Evans   Samson Perot
Josiah Evans   Thomas Shoemaker
Caleb Griffith   Joseph Simons
John R. Griffith   Lewis Walker
James Glentworth Jr

Previous Meeting Minutes

The minutes of the last meeting were read and approved.

PART THREE

Acting Committee Report and Assistance to Welsh Emigrants

The acting committee report, that since the last meeting of the Society, the attention of the committee has been called, to visit a Welch family on the ridge road, namely John Evans Rogers, wife and seven children from Montgomery Shire, whom they found in the greatest distress, all sick, without any nurse, and scarcely strength in either to assist the other to a glass of water. The poor woman inform'd one of the committee, that had it not been for a Mrs Clarke, who resides some little distance from them, they must have perished; she very kindly administered greatly to their wants, by sending soup and a few other necessaries daily.

It was considered to advance them ten dollars and accordingly an order was drawn on the Treasurer for that amount.

Philad Decr 1 1828

signed Joseph Simons Register

Annual Dinner

On motion, resolv'd, that the acting committee be directed to make the usual arrangements necessary for the anniversary dinner in celebration of St David's day and that they be instructed to invite the officers of such benevolent societies as reciprocate with us and such other guests not exceeding six in number as they shall deem best calculated to contribute to the enjoyment of the day.

adjourn'd.

Thos P. Roberts Secretary

1829

Welch Society

At an Annual Meeting of the Welch Society held at the Mansion House South Third Street, on Monday the 2nd of March 1829.

Present

Joseph S. Lewis — President

Job Bacon
John Bevan
Armon Davis
D. Z. Davis
Thomas Evans
Wm M. Evans
Josiah Evans
John R. Griffith
James Glentworth Jr
John J. Griffith
Caleb Griffith

Thos W. Morris
Joseph Simmons
Thomas Parke MD.
William Parker
Sansom Perot
Francis Perot
Thomas P. Roberts
William Rawle Jr

Previous Meeting Minutes

The minutes of the last meeting were read and approved.

Acting Committee Report and Assistance to Welsh Emigrants

The acting committee submitted their annual report, which was read, accepted and ordered to be entered on the minutes.

The acting committee of the Welsh Society, report that since the last annual report, the calls upon the benevolence of the Society, have been few in number, and the amount advanced for relief, has not exceeded forty-five dollars. The Treasurer's accounts have been examined, and compared with the vouchers produced in support thereof, and the balance of cash in the Treasurer's hands amounts to one hundred and eighty-nine dollars ninety-four cents.

Finance: Accounts and Investments

The funds of the Society as stated by the Treasurer consists of

		$
500 dollars City Stock of 1860	5 p^r c^t worth 105½	527.50
300 dollars City Stock of 1840	5 p^r c^t worth 104	312.00
1500 dollars City Stock of 1846	5 p^r c^t worth 104½	1567.50
400 dollars City Stock of 1840	6 p^r c^t worth 112	448.00
500 dollars City Stock of 1860	5 p^r c^t worth 105½	580
North American Bank	12 Shares 107	5136
	Doll[ar]s	8571
	Cash	189.94
	Doll[ar]s	8760.94

Philad^a March 2nd 1829

signed Jos. Simons Register

Membership: New Members

John J. Griffith was duly elected a member and being informed thereof, was introduced to the Society.

Samuel Jenkins was also duly elected a member of the Society.

Finance: Treasurer's Accounts and Investments

The Treasurer's account was presented and approved of as stated in the report of the acting committee.

Organization: Election of Officers

The Society then proceeded to the election of officers for the ensuing year. Wm Rawle Jr & James Glentworth Jr were appointed Tellers, who having receiv'd and counted all the votes report, the following gentlemen, as duly elected for the ensuing year.

President   Joseph S. Lewis
Vice President   Thomas Morris
Treasurer   Job Bacon
Secretary   Thomas P. Roberts
Register   Joseph Simons
Physicians   Thos C. James
   Saml M. Fox
Stewards   Timothy B. Mount
   Thomas Shoemaker
   John R. Griffith
   Armon Davis
   Charles Dixey
   Thomas W. Morris
   James Glentworth Jr
Counsellors   William Rawle Jr
   Robert W. Sykes

The Society then adjourn'd

Thos P. Roberts Secretary

Welch Society

At a Quarterly Meeting of the Welsh Society held at the House of Thomas Evans, June 1st 1829.

Present

Joseph S. Lewis   President

Job Bacon   Stephen B. Lassalle
John Bevan   Thomas Morris
Armon Davis   Thomas Parke M.D.
Thomas Evans   Sansom Perot
Josiah Evans   Thomas P. Roberts
William M. Evans   William Rawle Jr

John R. Griffith
James Glentworth Jr
John Hallowell
Samuel Jenkins

Joseph Simons
Thomas Shoemaker
Joseph Worrell

Previous Meeting Minutes

The minutes of the last meeting were read and approved.

Acting Committee Report and Assistance to Welsh Emigrants – Problems Relating to Misinformation

The acting committee of the Welsh Society report, that since the last meeting two persons only have come under their notice that required any pecuniary assistance viz Hannah Lewis, a young widow, and a little girl just turned of five years of age from Swansea, South Wales. They arrived in the Ship *Alexander*, Capt Baldwin on Sunday 17 May – Mrs Lewis spoke very highly of Capt Baldwin's kind treatment to her and her child. Mrs Lewis came at the solicitation of her brother and sister who are well settled in Lawrenceburg, Indiana.[52]

The following is an extract from her sister's letter.

If possible enter a vessel to Philadelphia, if you are scarce of money and as there is a provision made at Philad. to help the Welsh people to any part of the United States, you must enquire for some Welsh family and they will tell you what to do, as there is money there to help the Welsh people on their way.

Your committee lost no time in informing the writer of the above how erroneous it was to give such information to her connections in Wales, observing that such misrepresentations would have a tendency to mislead a number of persons to come over, only to be disappointed at the same time pointing out such as came under the notice of the Society.

---

52 Founded in 1802, Lawrenceburg is now a city in Dearborn County, Indiana. It was strategically placed as an important trading centre for riverboats on the Ohio River.

A meeting of the acting committee was called on Monday and they met according to appointment at the Treasurer's office in Ches[t]nut Street, after some deliberation concluded to assist her with forty dollars, and took the following receipt.

Receiv'd of the Welsh Society forty dollars (as a Loan) which I promise to return, whenever it is in my power to do.

The committee took charge of the mother and child conveyed them safe to the Pittsburg[h] Stage Office, agreed for their passage and on Tuesday morning at 3 o' Clock they started for their place of destination.

June 1 1829

signed Jos. Simons Register

Discipline: Fines for Non-Attendance

The fines of Joseph Worrell for absence at the last two stated meetings were remitted.

Organization: Appointments to a Committee for the Relief of Emigrants

The following preamble and resolution were offer'd by Joseph Worrell and being seconded, was carried, and the following members were appointed to the committee viz Joseph Worrell, Job Bacon, T. P. Roberts, William Rawle Jr and Thomas Morris.

This Society having been for many years since established by the Sons of St David in the City of Philadelphia, and its vicinity for the humane and benevolent purposes of dispensing advice and assistance to Welshmen in distress – and they having long since obtained an act of incorporation under the title of the Welch Society since which time they have so increased in number and in pecuniary concerns that will enable them to extend their benevolence to the widow and offspring of Welchmen, but more especially to those of this Society should any of them stand in need. Therefore resolv'd, that a committee of five be appointed to take the above subject into consideration and report their opinion in form of Bye-Law or otherwise to carry the same into effect.

Membership: New Members

Nathan R. Potts was proposed as a candidate for membership by Thomas P. Roberts.

Doctor Erasmus Thomas was proposed by Joseph Simons as a candidate for membership.

adjourn'd

Thos P. Roberts Sec^y

Welch Society

At a Quarterly Meeting of the Welch Society held at the House of Thomas Evans, September 7 1829.

Present

Joseph S. Lewis   President

Job Bacon   Thomas W. Morris
John Bevan   Horatio Mann
Thomas Evans   Thomas Parke M.D.
William M. Evans   William Rawle Jr
John R. Griffith   John M. Read
Joseph Huddell   Thomas Shoemaker
William H. Morgan   John C. Tillinghast
Charles Marshall

Previous Meeting Minutes

The minutes of the last meeting were read and approved.

Organization: Appointments to a Committee for the Relief of Emigrants

The committee appointed at the last meeting, to report upon the resolution offer'd by Joseph Worrell, being unprepared to report were continued.

Acting Committee Report and Assistance to Welsh Emigrants

The acting committee made the following report, which was read and accepted.

Since the last quarterly meeting, one case only requiring assistance has come under their notice, namely George Williams, from Carnarvonshire. A young man about 21 years of age, brought up to the conveyancing business. Your committee endeavoured to procure employment for him, but finding it impossible, advanced him ten dollars towards paying his board, as well as to defray his expenses to New York. A letter has been receiv'd from him acknowledging his gratitude to the Society and informing them that he was fortunate in getting immediate employment on his arrival. Several others have receiv'd the attention and advise of your committee for which they were very thankful.

all which is respectfully submitted

signed Joseph Simons, Register

Organization: Resignation as Steward

The resignation of Timothy B. Mount as Steward was read & accepted.

Membership: New Members

Nathan R. Potts and Erasmus Thomas M.D. were elected members of the Society.

Dr Benj[n] Rush Rhees was proposed as a candidate for membership.

adjourned

Tho[s] P. Roberts Secretary

PART THREE

Welsh Society[53]

At a Meeting of the Welsh Society held at the House of Thomas Evans, December 7th 1829.

Present

Thomas Morris   Vice President

John Bevan   Charles Marshall Jr
Charles Dixey   Thomas Parke
Thomas Evans   Sansom Perot
William M. Evans   Nathan R. Potts
John R. Griffith   Thomas P. Roberts
John Bevan   Charles Marshall Jr
James Glentworth Jr   John M. Read
Stephen B. Lasalle   Joseph Simons
Timothy B. Mount   Erasmus Thomas
Joseph Worrell

Previous Meeting Minutes

The minutes of the last meeting were read and approved.

Acting Committee Report and Assistance to Welsh Emigrants – Problems Retrieving Luggage etc

The acting committee of the Welsh Society, beg leave to report, that since the report made to the Society at their last quarterly meeting in September last, the following cases requiring advice or assistance have come under their notice.

Viz – Eliza Jones a distressed widow, to whom fifteen dollars was awarded towards assisting her on her journey to the Westward.

John Davis, wife and three children; this family in company with about sixty others, arrived in the Ship *Washington* Captain Willis on the 6th

---

53   Note change of spelling from 'Welch Society'.

September last from Liverpool, the Captain refused to let them have their clothes, or any part of their baggage until they had paid him $3.75/^{100} per head (say for man, woman, & child) for what he called hospital money. The above, John Davis received information of your committee called upon them, they lost no time in waiting on Mr Robert W. Sykes, who promptly came, and met the Captain and owner at Mr Binns office on Saturday afternoon 12th September, and succeeded in defeating the Captain, as far as concerned the Welsh, and obtained all we could wish; procured an order immediately from the Captain before he left the Office, to have everything belonging to them on shore. This was the only family who stood in need of any pecuniary assistance the committee granted them $20 and took their receipt – procured an introduction for them, as well as others from Messr^s Lippincott & Richards to their agent at Mount Carbon.[54]

Your committee waited on Mr Stoddard who gave his permission for their going up free of expense, in the companies boats. A letter has been receiv'd by the committee from John Davis acknowledging his grateful thanks as well for himself as all the others for the attention paid to his, and their families, and gives the committee pleasure to inform the Society that they all had full employment and are much satisfied with their situation.

The next is Elizabeth Garrett, a poor widow and son about 15 years of age in a very bad state of health. She was recommended by Mr John Vaughan as being worthy of our assistance and assured the committee that the money (say $30) advanced to her, will be faithfully returned, he having a knowledge of her family and connections in the western country, whence she and her son intend going. Mr V[aughan] assisted in procuring a wagon as well as supplying her with necessaries for the journey.

---

54 Mount Carbon is in Schuylkill County, Pennsylvania. In 1828 the small settlement comprised six houses, a store, a warehouse, and the collector's office. For further details see, Anon., *History of Schuylkill County, Pa.: with Illustrations and Biographical Sketches of Some of Its Prominent Men and Pioneers* (New York: W. W. Munsell & Co., 1881), pp. 250–1.

PART THREE

Thomas Jones's wife and three children, fellow passengers of Mrs Garrett, in the absence of the husband (who went to Mount Carbon in search of employment) your committee being informed of the distressed situation of the woman, waited upon her; found her with an infant at her breast, and a very interesting girl about 12 years of age with a diseased hip. Your committee procured a good situation for the eldest who is in her 15th year, took the crippled child to Dr Physick,[55] who pronounced her curable and recommended that she should be taken to the hospital.

Your committee made the necessary enquiry and in a few days obtained permission for her to be admitted a patient in that excellent institution. They have frequently called to see her, and are happy to say, that she is doing well. The committee drew an order on the Treasurer for ten dollars in favor of Mrs Jones, since which the husband returned with the intention of taking up all his family with him, with a prospect of having constant employment, but his wife and infant only accompanied him, expressing great satisfaction as well as his grateful sense of the attention and kindness shewn to his wife and family during his absence, and those he has left behind he feels perfectly satisfied will be taken care of.

The last John Morris' wife and three children who arrived in New York from Liverpool in the Ship *Minerva* Capt Putman on the 2nd November. The children consisted of one boy 11 years of age and two girls one 6 and the other 4 years of age. They were desirous to proceed to Pittsburg[h] where John Morris's father resides, but were destitute of funds to convey them there, in consideration of which the acting committee (on the recommendation of Mr John R. Griffith) loaned the said Morris 25 dollars, for which they took his promissory note, payable on demand.

---

55   Dr Philip Syng Physick (1768–1837), is acknowledged as a pioneer of American surgery and famed for his determination to treat the sick in Philadelphia during the yellow fever epidemic of 1793. See Jacob Randolph, *A Memoir on the Life and Character of Philip Syng Physick, M.D.* (Philadelphia: T. K. & P. G. Collins, 1839); Luis Horacio Toledo-Pereyra, *Vignettes on Surgery, History and Humanities* (Baco Raton, Fl.: CRC Press, 2018), pp. 53–4.

John Morris and his family came from Montgomeryshire North Wales. Morris produced a certificate from Evan Price, John Jones and Morris James, ministers of the Baptist church, certifying that he and his wife being members and of their good standing in society.

Finance: Treasurer's Accounts – Expenditure

The following is reported by the Treasurer as being expended since the 1st September last as follows.

		$
September 1st	Elizabeth Jones	15
16th	John Davis	20
October 6	Eliza Garrett	30
November 1	Ann Jones	10
13	John Morris	<u>25</u>
	Doll[ar]s	100

all which is respectfully submitted

Philad^a Decr 1 1829

signed, Joseph Simons Register

Organization: Appointments to a Committee for the Relief of Emigrants

The committee appointed on the first of June last upon the resolution then offer'd by Mr J. Worrell, being unprepared to report were continued.

Membership: New Members

Doctor Benjn Rush Reese was duly elected a member of the Society.

John Evans was proposed as a candidate for membership by Joseph Simons.

Annual Dinner

On motion and seconded, it was resolved, that the acting committee be directed to make the customary arrangements, necessary for the anniversary dinner in celebration of St Davids' day and that they be requested to invite the officers of such benevolent societies as reciprocate with us and such other guests not exceeding six in number as they shall deem best calculated to contribute to the enjoyment of the day.

adjourn'd

Thos P. Roberts Sec^y

1830
Welch Society

At an Annual meeting of the Welch Society held at the House of D. Rubicam N°. 20 South 6th Street on Monday the first of March 1830.

Present

Joseph S. Lewis	President
Thomas Morris	Vice President
Thomas P. Roberts	Secretary
Joseph Simons	Register

Joseph E. Bloomfield	Joseph Huddell
John Bevan	Thomas Parke M.D.
David Z. Davis	Zachariah Poulson
Armon Davis	William Parker
Thomas Evans	Sansom Perot
William M. Evans	Nathan R. Potts
Caleb Griffith	John M. Read
John R. Griffith	Erazmus Thomas M.D.
James Glentworth Jr	Lewis Walker
John J. Griffith	Joseph Worrell
	John P. Wetherill

Previous Meeting Minutes

The minutes of the last meeting were read and approved.

Assistance to Welsh Emigrants – Conditional Support

The committee to whom was referr'd a preamble and resolution relative to extending the benevolence of this Society 'to the widows and offspring of Welchmen or such of its members as may stand in need' having considered the subject, are of opinion that under existing circumstances it would be inexpedient to extend its benevolence any farther than is now the practice (that is to Welch emigrants in distress) – they therefore offer the following, Resolv'd, that the committee be discharged.

Adopted.

Acting Committee Report and Assistance to Welsh Emigrants

The acting committee of the Welch Society beg leave to report, that there has been several emigrants arrived since our last report, but none who required much assistance from the Society. They were advised in regard to the best mode of traveling and a few single young men who preferr'd remaining in the city found employment without difficulty.

There was however one distressing case [which] came within the notice of the Committee. Robert Humphrey's wife and four children from Denbig[h]] Shire North Wales, who arrived in the Ship *Mary* Capt Noyes bound to New York, when within two days sail of that port, the ship was blown off, and after enduring a violent hurricane, which lasted upwards of two weeks they made Boston Harbour on the 16th of October 1829 in a wretched state and quite dismasted, the vessel a perfect wreck. They lost all their clothes, books and in fact every thing that was valuable to them. Mrs Humphreys was unfortunately far advanced in pregnancy.

They were treated kindly at Boston, were provided with clothing, their passages paid to Philadelphia, when they arrived in the Brig *Pilot* on the 30 November 1829.

It was the intention of R. Humphreys to proceed with his family to the State of Ohio, but the indisposition of Mrs Humphreys and her youngest child prevented it. In ten days after their arrival here, the child died.

Dr Benj. Rush Rhees faithfully attended to the mother and child during their illness.

The committee attended as much as possible to their several necessities, provided them with a more commodious room, at less rent than they were paying.

Application was made to the managers of the Pennsylvania Hospital for the admission of Mrs Humphreys. She was visited by Doctor James who found her a proper patient, and gave a certificate to that effect, and she was admitted.

The children have been placed in comfortable situations, a girl about eleven years of age with Mrs Morgan J. Rhees, and two boys with Mr Sam[l] Jenkins, from whence they go to school every day.

Mr Humphrey's has gone to Pottsville[56] with letters of recommendation from Mr Warder with a prospect of being employed immediately. The committee became responsible for the rent of the room as well as a few other incidental expenses attending the child's funeral &c.

John Price, a young man from North Wales, arrived at Alexandria in the Ship *Julian* from Liverpool in November last, came to this city about the 23rd was employed at his trade (a painter) until the winter, when he went to work as a labourer on board of a shallop[57] near Smiths Island[58] where he met with a severe accident having his hand badly bruised so as to render him incapable of doing any kind of work; his landlord, threatened to discharge him, and the committee drew an order on the Treasurer for ten dollars and took a receipt to be returned when in his power to do.

all which is respectfully submitted

March 1 1830

signed Joseph Simons Register

---

56   Pottsville was a town (now a city) in Schuylkill County, Pennsylvania. From 1790 onwards anthracite coal was mined there and in 1829 the brewery D. G. Yuengling & Son was established.
57   A small sailboat used for coastal fishing.
58   Presumably this is Smith Island on the Chesapeake Bay, Maryland.

Membership: Resignations

Letters of resignation were read from Francis Perot, Horatio Mann, & Charles Marshall, which were accepted upon their compliance with the usual conditions, of all dues being paid.

Finance: Treasurer's Accounts and Investments

The Treasurer's account for the past year was presented, as examined by a committee appointed for that purpose, and accepted. It appears that the funds of the Society are invested as follows viz.

300 dollars	of City Stock of 1840 (five's worth)	315
1500	[of City Stock of] 1846 [five's worth]	1590
500	[of City Stock of] 1860 [five's worth]	540
400	[of City Stock of] 1840 [six's worth]	444
500	[of City Stock of] 1846 [six's worth]	565
4800	Bank of North America (12 Shares)	4910
550	Sch. Navigation Loan	550
103 32/^{100}	Cash on hand	103.32
$8653.32	Dollars	9017.32

Membership: New Members

David Thomas was proposed by John J. Griffith as a candidate for membership.

Revd Morgan J. Reese & Charles Humphreys were proposed as candidates for membership by Joseph Simons.

Organization: Election of Officers

The Society then proceeded to the election of officers for the ensuing year.

Nathan R. Potts and Sansom Perot were appointed Tellers, who having receiv'd and counted the votes – Report, the following gentlemen as duly elected to serve the ensuing year

President   Joseph S. Lewis
Vice President   Thomas Morris
Treasurer   Job Bacon
Secretary   Thomas P. Roberts
Register   Joseph Simons
Physicians   Thomas C. James M.D.
                      Benjamin Rush Rhees M.D.
Stewards   Thomas Shoemaker
                      John R. Griffith
                      Armon Davis
                      Charles Dixey
                      Thomas W. Morris
                      James Glentworth Jr
                      Sansom Perot
Counsellors   William Rawle Jr
                      Robert W. Sykes

adjourned

Thos P. Roberts Secretary

Welch Society

At a Quarterly Meeting of the Welch Society held at the House of Thomas Evans June 7 1830.

Present

Thomas Morris   Vice President
Thomas P. Roberts   Secretary

Thomas Parke M.D.
John M. Read
Thomas Shoemaker
James Glentworth Jr
Lewis Walker

PART THREE

Organization: Meeting Not Quorate

No quorum appearing, adjourned

Thos P. Roberts Secretary

Welch Society

At a Quarterly Meeting of the Welch Society held at the House of Thomas Evans, September 6 1830.

Present

Joseph S. Lewis	President
Thomas Morris	Vice President
Job Bacon	Treasurer
Thomas P. Roberts	Sec^y
John Bevan	Wm H. Morgan
Armon Davis	Sansom Perot
Thomas Evans	Zach^h Poulson
James Glentworth Jr	Nathan R. Potts
Thomas Evans	Thos Shoemaker
John R. Griffith	John M. Read
Joseph Worrell	

Acting Committee Report and Assistance to Welsh Emigrants

The acting committee made the two following reports, which were approved.

The acting committee of the Welch Society beg leave to report, that they have since the last report paid the necessary attention to the general business of the Society, and afforded advice and assistance to such emigrants as stood in need, one only as regarded pecuniary assistance, namely William Tegan a young man who arrived in the Ship *Bainbridge* from Liverpool. He applied to your committee for a small relief, and they advanc'd him ten dollars, for which they drew an order on the

Treasurer and took the usual receipt to be return'd as soon as he had it in his power so to do.

all which is respectfully submitted.

June 2nd 1830

signed Joseph Simons Register

They also report, that since the quarterly meeting in June last, the committee have had many applications for assistance and advice from indigent Welch emigrants, and have paid the following sums, and taken the usual promissory notes for the return of the money, when they shall be enabled so to do.

Organization: Absence of Register

Owing to the unavoidable absence of the Register, the committee are unable to make as full a report as could be wished, but hope to do so, previously to the annual meeting in March next.

Assistance to Welsh Emigrants Details

Orders paid by the Treasurer since the annual meeting in March last

		$
March 1	To William Tegan	20
	David Davis	20
30	Wm Meredith	10
	Thos Williams family	12
April 6	Wm Williams	5
	Wm Davis & family	10
June 10	Richd Evans	15
	Thos Davis & family	26.32
25	Thos Llewellyn & family	50
	Mary Williams	28
26	T. Rees, J. Anthony & J. Phelps	20
	Wm Jones (deaf & dumb)	7

July 3	J. Reese & Fanny Griffith	40
6	Reese Evans & family	20
6	J^{no} Reese & family	15

altogether amounting to two hundred ninety-eight dollars and thirty-two cents.

Membership: Resignation

A letter of resignation was read from William Rawle Jr Esqr which was accepted.

adjourn'd

Thos P. Roberts Secretary

Welch Society

At a Quarterly Meeting of the Welch Society held at the House of Thomas Evans in George Street, December 6 1830.

Present

Thomas Morris V. P.
Thomas Parke
Thomas Shoemaker
Thomas Evans
Charles Dixey
Robert W. Sykes
John R. Griffith
Isaac R. Jones
Nathan R. Potts
James Glentworth Jr
Sansom Perot

Job Bacon
Thomas P. Roberts
Thomas W. Morris
William M. Evans
Samuel P. Wetherill
William H. Morgan
James Gowen
Joseph Worrell
James C. Biddle
Jos. O. Evans

Previous Meeting Minutes

The minutes of the last meeting were read and approv'd.

Membership: New Members

David Thomas proposed on the 1st of March last was duly elected a member of the Society.

Reverend Morgan J. Reese also proposed on the first of March was duly elected a member of the Society.

Charles Humphreys proposed on the first of March was duly elected a member of the Society.

Acting Committee Report and Assistance to Welsh Emigrants

The acting report, that since the last quarterly meeting, they have afforded relief to the following persons

	$
Ann Richards and Elizabeth Vaughan	22.00
James Ewing, E. Hitchens & R. Hawkins	23.00
C. O'Donnell, board of A. Richards & E. Vaughan	6.25
Henry James 8 & Robert Popkins 10. E Vaughan 6.	24.00
Dec' 6. 1830	$75.25

Membership: New Member

Jeremiah James was proposed by Thomas P. Roberts as a candidate for membership.

Annual Dinner

On motion and seconded, resolv'd that the acting committee be directed to make the customary arrangements for the anniversary dinner in celebration of St David's day, and that they be instructed to invite the officers of the German & St George's Society, and such other guests (not exceeding six in number) as they deem best calculated to promote the enjoyment of the day.

Membership: New Members

James M. Broome was proposed by R. W. Sykes and Robert O. Wharton by J. S. Lewis as candidates for membership.

Annual Dinner: Additional Guests

On motion and seconded, resolv'd that any member may be allowed the privilege of inviting a friend to the annual dinner provided he becomes responsible for his dues, and due notice be given to the acting committee.

adjourn'd

Tho[s] P. Roberts Secretary

1831
Welsh Society

At an Annual Meeting of the Welsh Society held at the House of J. Head N⁰. 122 South 3ʳᵈ Street on Tuesday the First of March 1831.

Present

Joseph S. Lewis President
Thomas Morris V. President
Thomas P. Roberts Secʸ
Job Bacon Treasʳ
R. W. Sykes
Thoˢ Shoemaker
Thoˢ W. Morris
N. R. Potts
Z. Poulson
Thoˢ Evans
Joseph Huddell
Armon Davis
Caleb Griffith

Chˢ Humphreys
Thoˢ Parke M.D.
Lewis Walker
Sansom Perot
David Z. Davis
J. R. Griffith
David Thomas
John Bevan
Samˡ Jenkins
Jⁿᵒ M. Read
Wᵐ M. Evans

Previous Meeting Minutes

The minutes of the last meeting were read and approv'd.

Acting Committee Report and Assistance to Welsh Emigrants – Drain on Resources

The following report of the acting committee was read and adopted.

The acting committee report the names of the following persons to whom relief has been afforded from the funds of the Society amounting as per Treasurer's report to $475 50/¹⁰⁰

Wᵐ Meredith
Eliza Hitchens

Thoˢ Williams & wife
Wᵐ Williams

Wm Davis wife & 3 children
Richard Evans
E Vaughan [board]
Mary Williams & 5 [children]
Thos Rees & others
Robert Popkin
Ann Richards & 3 children
Rees Evans wife & child
Mary Walter[59]
James Elway

A. Richards (board)
Thos Davis wife & 4 [children]
Thos Llewelyn
Henry James
Wm Jones deaf & dumb
J. Rees & J. Griffith
Eliza Vaughan
Eliza Vaughan & 3 [children]
David Davis & 5 children
Catherine Morgan

It will be perceiv'd by the foregoing list that the calls on the funds of the Society have been unusually numerous, and from the Treasurer's report that the relief afforded equally great, occasioned by many applications for support whilst in the city and the heavy expenses incurr'd by the removal of applicants – of whom a considerable number were sent to Pottsville, and there established under the guidance and advice of our benevolent fellow member and true hearted Welshman Jos^h Simmons.

The expenditures of the past year having exceeded the income, it became necessary to encroach on the capital, of which one hundred & fifty dollars 5 per cent Schuylkill Navigation loan unconvertible was sold by and with the advice and consent of the President at 103 per cent.

It becomes the duty of the acting committee to lay before the Society a particular statement of the case of Elizabeth Vaughan and her three children who arrived here from Liverpool in the month of September last in the Barque *Huskinson* with every reasonable expectation of meeting her husband, either in this city or at Pottsville. He had written for her and stated that he was settled at Pottsville and that she and her children must join him at that place, so soon as she could raise a sufficient sum to defray the expense of their passages – this was accomplished with great difficulty, and on her arrival she had the mortification and

---

59 The writing is particularly unhelpful concerning this emigrant. It might be Mary Waller, but a Mary Walters of Monmouthshire was assisted in 1832.

disappointment to learn that he had return'd to Wales, without leaving for her either the means for her support or return. The committee advised her to remain with her friends until her husband could be heard from and advanced her money for her board and the passage of herself and children to Pottsville where her friends resided. After remaining there a few weeks she received a letter from her husband, expressing his determination to remain in Wales, and directing her to return as soon as possible without however having provided funds for the payment of necessary expenses. She returned to this city forthwith and applied to your committee for the means of returning to Wales; after due deliberation the committee determined that it would be advisable to send her home, in preference to being at the expense of the maintenance of herself and her children during the winter. Accordingly, a contract was enter'd into with Capt Dixey for the passage of herself and children to Liverpool for the sum of $45 – he to find every necessary for their comfort and support during the passage. In so doing the committee believe they have somewhat exceeded their legitimate authority, but believe that they have acted in conformity with the true interests of the Society. And therefore hope their act will meet their approbation.

The committed appointed to examine the Treasurer's accounts have reported the same correct.

Thomas W. Morris Register pro tem

Finance: Investments

The funds of the Society consist of

City Stock of 1840	five per cent par Doll[ar]s	300
[City Stock of] 1846	[five per cent par Dollars]	1500
[City Stock of] 1860	[five per cent par Dollars]	500
[City Stock of] 1840	[five per cent par Dollars]	400
[City Stock of] 1846	six per c^t [par Dollars]	400
Stock of Bank of North America	12 Shares	4800
Sch[uylkil]l Navigation Loan		550
	Doll[ar]s	<u>8550</u>

Annual Dinner

The committee appointed to procure a dinner for the Society report, that they have agreed with Mr Head of the Mansion House at the rate of four dollars for each person.

Membership – Resignation

Letter of resignation was read from T. B. Mount which was accepted on the usual conditions.

Membership – Membership: New Members

Jeremiah James, proposed at the last quarterly meeting, was duly elected a member of the Society.

James M. Broome was likewise elected a member of the Society.

Robert O. Wharton was also duly elected a member of the Society.

Organization: Election of Officers

The Society then proceeded to the election of officers for the ensuing year.

William M. Evans and Nathan R. Potts were appointed judges of the election.

The election being concluded, the judges reported the following persons as duly elected

President	Joseph S. Lewis
Vice President	Thomas Morris
Treasurer	Job Bacon
Secretary	Thos P. Roberts
Register	Sansom Perot
Physicians	Thomas C. James MD.
	Benjn Rush Reese
Stewards	Thomas Shoemaker
	Armon Davis

John R. Griffith
James Glentworth Jr
James Gowen
Counsellors

Charles Dixey
John P. Wetherill

Robert W. Sykes
Thomas W. Morris

adjourn'd

Thos P. Roberts Secretary

Welch Society

At a Quarterly Meeting of the Welch Society held at the House of Thomas Evans in George Street, June 6 1831.

Present

Thomas Morris   V. President

Job Bacon Treas^r Thos. P. Roberts Sec^y
Thomas Evans   Isaac R. Jones
John R. Griffith   Thomas Parke
Wm H. Morgan   Thomas Shoemaker
James M. Broome   Lewis Walker
David Thomas

Previous Meeting Minutes

The minutes of the last meeting were read and approv'd.

Acting Committee Report – No Business

The acting committee being unprepared to report, and no further business before the meeting.

adjourned

Thos P. Roberts Secretary

PART THREE

Welch Society

At a Quarterly Meeting of the Welch Society held at the House of Thos Evans in George Street on Monday, 5th September 1831.

Present

Joseph S. Lewis	President
Thos Parke M.D.	Wm M. Evans
S. B. Lassalle	J^{no} M. Read
Ja^s. Glentworth	Thos P. Roberts Sec^y
Wm H. Morgan	Thos Morris V.P.
Thomas Shoemaker	Nathan R. Potts
Thomas Evans	Job Bacon Tr.
Lewis Walker	J^{no} R. Griffith
Sansom Perot	

Previous Meeting Minutes

The minutes of the last meeting were read and approved.

Acting Committee Report and Assistance to Welsh Emigrants

The acting committee made the two following reports, which were approved.

The acting committee report, that since the annual meeting in March last, the applications for pecuniary assistance have been few in number.

On the 2nd March, relief to the amount of $5 was afforded to Ellis Roberts, a native of Balla Manora,[60] North Wales, sufficient to enable him to get to Pottsville.

On the 3rd March to Elizabeth Edwards and Eliza Jones $10 each both natives of Anglisie [*sic*] North Wales, and on the 25th May twelve dollars to Mary Watters.

---

60   Presumably Bala in Gwynedd, but it could also refer to Bala Cynwyd in Pennsylvania, which was settled in the 1680s.

June 6 1831

signed Sansom Perot, Register

The acting committee further report, that Edward and Richard Roberts (two lads who were desirous to go to Pottsville to see their brother) are the only persons who have applied for relief since the last quarterly meeting – two dollars were allowed them. One man asked advice, which was given him, and for which he appeared thankful.

Sept 5 1831

signed Sansom Perot, Register

The Society then adjourned.

Thos P. Roberts Sec^y

Welch Society

At a Quarterly Meeting of the Welch Society held at the House of Thomas Evans in George Street on Monday Decr 5 1831.

Present

Thomas Morris	Vice President
Job Bacon	Treasurer
James Gowen	Thomas W. Morris
J^{no} R. Griffith	Thomas Parke
Lewis Walker	Ja^s Glentworth Jr
Sansom Perot	Samuel Jenkins
David Thomas	Thomas Evans

Previous Meeting Minutes

The minutes of the last meeting were read and approved.

PART THREE

Acting Committee Report and Assistance to Welsh Emigrants, including recovering costs

The acting committee made the following report, which was read and approved.

The acting committee report, that since the last quarterly meeting, relief has been afforded to the following persons – viz

	Doll[ars]
to Thomas Thomas	10.00
David Walton & family	15.00
Evan Harries	15.00
Thomas Roberts	10.00

Evan Harries has a claim of $309 against Burge and Laval[61] – the business is under the charge of Robert W. Sykes Esqr who is of opinion that most of it will be recovered, in which event the Society will get refunded, the amount of the loan they made him.

signed Sansom Perot Register

Decr 5 1832[62]

Membership: Resignation

The resignation of Armon Davis was read and accepted upon the payment of whatever arrearages may be due from him.

Annual Dinner

On motion and seconded, resolv'd, that the acting committee be directed to make the usual preparations, for celebrating the anniversary of St David, by a dinner, and that they be requested to invite the officers of such benevolent societies as reciprocate with us, and such other guests not exceeding 6 in number, as they may think best calculated to contribute to the enjoyment of the day.

---

61   No further information has been found. This might nevertheless relate to the development of Steubenville in Ohio.
62   Clearly there was a mistake recording the year; it should read 1831.

Membership: New Members

Jenkins S. Jenkins &
E^d W. Roberts

were proposed as candidates for membership, the former by S. Jenkins & the latter by Thos Morris

Joseph Worrell Jr

by Sansom Perot.

Samuel N. Gray

was proposed by James Glentworth Jr

adjourn'd

Thos P. Roberts Secretary

PART THREE

1832
Welch Society

At the Annual Meeting of the Welsh Society held at the House of Daniel Saint in 6th Street March 1st 1832.

Present

Joseph S. Lewis	President
Thomas P. Roberts	Secretary
Z. Poulson	Sansom Perot Regr.
J. Glentworth Jr	Saml Jenkins
Ja^s M. Broome	Caleb Griffith
J^{no} P. Wetherill	Charles Humphries
Joseph Worrell	Thomas W. Morris
Joseph Huddell	Robert W. Sykes
John R. Griffith	David Z. Davis
David Thomas	John J. Griffith
John M. Read	Thomas Evans

Previous Meeting Minutes

The minutes of the last meeting were read and approv'd.

Acting committee Report and Assistance to Welsh Emigrants

The acting committee made the following report, which was read and approv'd.

The acting committee report, that since the last annual meeting of the Society, they have expended the sum of $174 50/^{100} in loans for the relief of poor Welsh persons and annex a list of the names of those to whom pecuniary assistance was afforded, amounting to 19[63] adults and 19 children – viz.

---

63 Although twenty-three were recorded in the assessment given below.

385

$			adults	children
5	2 Mar	to Ellis Roberts of Balla Manora North Wales	2	1
10	3 [Mar]	to Elizabeth Edward of Anglesea [North Wales]		2
10	[3 Mar]	to Eliza Jones [of Anglesea, North Wales]	2	
12	25 May	To Mary Walters of Monmouthshire	2	6
10	6 Aug	Thomas Thomas of Aberyshire [sic][64]	3	1
2	24 Aug	Edward & Richard Roberts Denbrickshire[65]	2	
15	15 Oct	To David Walton, [G]Lamorganshire	1	
10	8 Nov	Thomas Roberts of Denby shire	2	3
25	[8 Nov]	Evan Harris of Merthy[r] tyd[66]	2	1
50	12 Dec	Ambrose Ambrose of Monmouthshire	2	7
10.50	1 Feb 1832	To Saml Jenkins by direction of the Com[mitte]^e for Board of Wm Davis	1	
15	28 Feb	to John R. Griffith by direction of [the committee] $10 for account of Thomas Morgan & [$]5 to John Jones	2	
174.50			23.19	

Although the amount loaned the past year appears large, yet the committee are of opinion that it has been the means of doing much good. They have been particular in examining into all applications for relief and when advice has been asked, it has been freely afforded.

---

64 It is unclear which county is being referred to.
65 Denbighshire.
66 Merthyr Tydfil.

all which is respectfully submitted.

Sansom Perot Register

Finance: Accounts and Investments

The Treasurer presented a statement of his receipts, and expenditures for the past year showing a balance in his hands amounting to $260 78/^{100} which was directed to be entered on the minutes:

City Stock of 1840 five per cents par Doll[ar]s	300
City [Stock of] 1846 [five per cents par Dollars]	1500
City [Stock of] 1860 [five per cents par Dollars]	500
City [Stock of] 1840 six per cents [par Dollars]	400
City [Stock of] 1846 [six per cents par Dollars]	500
Bank North America 12 Shares at par [Dollars]	4800
Schuylkill Navigation 5 pr ct Loan	400
	8400
Cash in the Treasury	260.78
Doll[ar]s	8660.78

Membership: Resignations

The resignation of Doctor Thomas Parke was read, and accepted by the Society with great regret.

Membership: Honorary Member

On motion and seconded, it was resolv'd, that Doctor Thomas Parke be placed on the list of honorary members, and that the Secretary be directed to notify him thereof.

Membership: New Members

The meeting then proceeded to the election of new members, and accordingly,

Jenkins S. Jenkins	proposed by Saml Jenkins
Edward W. Roberts	proposed by Thomas Morris

Joseph Worrell Junr   proposed by Sansom Perot
Saml N. Gray   proposed by Jas. Glentworth Jr

were duly elected members of the Society.

Organization: Election of Officers

The Society next proceeded to the election of officers for the ensuing year. David Z. Davis & John J. Griffith were appointed Tellers, who reported that the following gentlemen were duly elected to serve the ensuing year

President	Joseph S. Lewis
Vice President	Thomas Morris
Treasurer	Job Bacon
Secretary	Thomas P. Roberts
Register	Sansom Perot
Physicians	Thomas C. James
	Erasmus Thomas
Stewards	Thomas Shoemaker
	John R. Griffith
	James Glentworth Jr
	James Gowen
	Charles Dixey
	John P. Wetherill
	Charles Humphries
Counsellors	Robert W. Sykes
	Thomas W. Morris

The Society then adjourn'd.

PART THREE

Welsh Society

At a Quarterly Meeting of the Welsh Society held at the House of Thomas Evans, June 4 1832.

Present

Thomas Morris   Vice President

Job Bacon, Treas^r William Parker
Ja^s M. Broome   Sansom Perot
C. Dixey   Nathan R. Potts
Thos Evans   R. W. Sykes
Ja^s Gowen   Er^s Thomas[67]
J^{no} R. Griffith   Lewis Walker
Ja^s Glentworth Jr   Jos. Worrell Jr
Saml N. Gray
Thos P. Roberts

Previous Meeting Minutes

The minutes of the last meeting were read and approved.

Acting Committee Report and Assistance to Welsh Emigrants

The acting committee report the following, as the only cases in which relief has been afforded since the last annual meeting of the Society – viz

$
10   to Rachel Daniel
10   to Evan Ashton
10   to Hannah Harries

respectfully submitted

Sansom Perot

---
67   Erasmus.

Membership: Resignation

The resignation of David Thomas was receiv'd, read, and accepted.

Membership: New Members

The following gentlemen were proposed as candidates for membership by Sansom Perot viz.

William W. Fisher, Dr Wm Wetherill & Chas Wetherill.

Membership: Death of a Member

The President reported to the Society the death of Thomas Shoemaker, a member of this Society.

Whereupon, it was on motion of James M. Broome Esqr resolv'd, that this Society have learned with deep regret the death of one, who by his long and faithful services rendered himself as useful to the Society as he was endeared to its members by the uniform kindness and benevolence of his character.

The Society then adjourned

Thos P. Roberts Sec^y

Welsh Society

At a Meeting of the We[l]sh Society held at the House of Thomas Evans September 3 1832.

Present

Joseph S. Lewis	President
Thos Morris, V.P.	Wm H. Morgan
Thos P. Roberts Secr	Saml N. Gray
Nathan R. Potts	E^d W. Roberts
J^{no} R. Griffith	R. W. Sykes
Jos. Worrell Jr	Thomas Evans
Ja^s Glentworth Jr	Erasmus Thomas

PART THREE

Previous Meeting Minutes

The minutes of the last meeting were read and approved.

Acting Committee Report and Assistance to Welsh Emigrants – Large Number of Cases and the Society's Restrictions

The Treasurer on behalf of the Register made the following report which was accepted.

Report, that since the last meeting of the Society, an unusually large number of emigrants from Wales have arrived in this city, many of them penniless and in distress and all in need of advice.

The committee have extended toward them that assistance which it is the object of the Society to afford and have satisfaction in expressing the belief that the relief has been timely and effectual and that the emigrants are in a way to do well – they appear to be generally persons of decent and respectable standing. Some indeed are well provided with funds and only required advice as to the best mode of making use of them. The number of individuals to whom the charity of the Society has been extended amounts to 31 adults and 52 children & the sum expended to Dollars 274.12.

Some applications have been made to the committee by persons long resident in the country – these applications, one instance only excepted, the committee felt bound to deny, considering themselves unauthorized to dispose of the funds intended solely for the relief of emigrants directly from Wales, for the purpose of assisting those who are domiciliated in the country – which they trust will meet the approbation of the Society.

All which is respectfully submitted.

pro register

Job Bacon Treasurer Sept 3, 1832

Discipline: Non-Payment of Admission Fee

On motion and seconded, it was resolv'd that the Secretary notify

Samuel Jenkins, that unless he complies with the rules and regulations of the Society in regard to the payment of his admission fee, previously to the next stated meeting, that his name will be stricken from the roll.

adjourn'd

Thos P. Roberts Secretary

Welch Society

At a Quarterly Meeting of the Society held at the House of Thomas Evans December 3rd 1832.

Present

Joseph S. Lewis	President
Thomas Morris V.P.	Charles Dixey
Job Bacon Tr.	Wm H. Morgan
Saml Perot Reg	Lewis Walker
Thos P. Roberts Sec^y	Jos Worrell Jr
Nathan R. Potts	James Glentworth Jr

Previous Meeting Minutes

The minutes of the last meeting were read and approv'd.

Discipline: Non-Payment of Admission Fee

The collector of the Society reported that he had receiv'd the admission fee from Samuel Jenkins.

Assistance to Welsh Emigrants – Correspondence

A letter was read from Saml Jenkins in relation to Welsh Emigrants.

Acting Committee Report and Assistance to Welsh Emigrants

The acting committee made the following report viz.

That since the last quarterly meeting they have loaned the following sums viz

To Barbara Davis	15
[To] Elizabeth Lloyd	10
[To] John Jones	10
[To] Jane Morris	20
[To] David Davis	5
Doll[ar]s	60

The case of John Jones was very interesting – his wife had just be[en] confined, was entirely destitute of every article necessary in her situation and the committee who visited her are of opinion, that both her and the child would have perished, had no relief been afforded them – the husband was too sick to do any work.

respectfully submitted

signed Sansom Perot Register

Decr 3 1832

Membership: New Member

Sansom Perot proposed Geo. W. Jones, as a candidate for membership.

Annual Dinner

Resolv'd, that the acting committee be requested to make its customary arrangements for the celebration of St David's day and that they be authorized to invite the officers of such benevolent institutions as reciprocate with us, and such other guests not exceeding six in number, as they shall deem best calculated to promote the festivity of the day.

Membership: New Member

Saml Grice and Samuel Chew proposed as candidates by

Thos P. Roberts

Sec^y

adjourn'd

1833
Welch Society

At the Annual Meeting of the Society held at the Mansion House, March 1 1833.

Present

Joseph S. Lewis	President
Thomas Morris	Vice Pres^t
Z. Poulson	W. H. Morgan
J. Glentworth Jr	J. P. Wetherill
S. N. Gray	Jos. Huddell
L. Walker	N. R. Potts
J. Worrell Junr	Jos. O. Evans
C. Dixey	D. Z. Davis
R. W. Sykes	T. W. Morris
J. Gowen	C. Humphries
S. Perot	C. Griffith
E. W. Roberts	Thos Evans
S. Jenkins	Wm Parker

Previous Meeting Minutes

The minutes of the last meeting were read and approved.

Acting Committee Report and Assistance to Welsh Emigrants

The acting committee made the following report, which was adopted.

The acting committee report, that since the last annual meeting of the Society they have extended relief in the shape of loans, to 38 adults and 47 children, the whole sum amounting to $297 50/^{100}

The demands on the Society this year, far exceed those of the last – this has been caused principally by the arrival of a much larger number of

394

poor emigrants than in former years. The committee however feel a satisfaction in reporting their belief, that in many instances (and they think in most) the loans made by the Society have been of essential service to deserving newcomers. There possibly may have been an instance or two, where the relief afforded has not been deserved, and the committee recommend caution, on the part of the members of the Society, when they are applied to, for pecuniary assistance, by persons who represent themselves as Welsh.

all which is respectfully submitted.

Samson Perot Register

March 1 1833

Finance: Accounts and Investments

The Treasurer presented a statement of his receipts and expenditures for the past year, from which it appears that the Society have a balance in the hands of the Treasurer amounting to $238.29

The funds of the Society consist of

City 5 per cent Stock	Doll[ar]s	2300.00
City 6 per cent Stock		900.00
Bank North America 12 Shares		4800.00
Schuylkill Navigation Loan 5 p^r c^t		400.00
Cash		238.29
Par Value	Doll[ar]s	8,638.29

Assistance to Welsh Emigrants – Correspondence to Wales

On motion and seconded, it was resolv'd, that [blank space] copies of a letter addressed to Welsh emigrants dated Sept. 27 1823 be printed, the date being altered to correspond with the present year, and that they be forwarded to such places in Wales as the acting committee may direct.

Membership: New Members

The Society then proceeded to ballot for new members.

Wm W. Fisher	proposed by Sansom Perot
William Wetherill	[proposed by Sansom Perot]
Charles Wetherill	[proposed by Sansom Perot]
George W. Jones	[proposed by Sansom Perot]
Samuel Grice	proposed by Thomas P. Roberts
Samuel Chew	[proposed by Thomas P. Roberts]

were duly elected members of the Society.

Assistance to Welsh Emigrants: Correspondence Regarding Assistance

A letter was read from R. W. Jones in relation to Welch emigrants &c. whereupon it was resolv'd, that the Secretary be requested to inform Mr Jones, that the Society decline entering into his views in regard to the plan proposed by him.

Organization: Election of Officers

The Society next proceeded to the election of officers for the ensuing year. S. N. Gray & N. R. Potts were appointed Tellers, who having counted the votes, reported the following were elected for the ensuing year

President	Jos. S. Lewis
Vice President	Thomas Morris
Treas^r	Job Bacon
Secretary	Thomas P. Roberts
Register	Sansom Perot
Stewards	Chas Dixey
	J. Glentworth Jr
	J^{no} P. Wetherill
	J. Gowen
	Charles Humphries

Physicians

Counsellors

Thos P. Roberts Sec^y

Saml N. Gray
Jos. Worrell Junr
Thos C. James
E. Thomas
R. W. Sykes
T. W. Morris

Welch Society

At a Quarterly Meeting of the Welsh Society held at the House of Thomas Evans on the 3rd day of June 1833.

Present

William Parker	who acted as chairman
Thomas W. Morris	Edward R. Roberts
Saml N. Gray	Robert W. Sykes
James Glentworth Jr	Wm H. Morgan
Nathan R. Potts	Thomas Evans
Thomas P. Roberts	Secretary

Previous Meeting Minutes

The minutes of the annual meeting were read and approved.

Assistance to Welsh Emigrants: Correspondence Regarding Assistance

The Secretary reported that in compliance with the resolution of the Society passed on the 1st March last, he had replied to the letter of R. W. Jones and stated therein the substance of the resolution.

The Society then adjourned

Thos P. Roberts Sec^y

Welch Society

At a Quarterly Meeting of the Welch Society held at the House of Thomas Evans September 2nd 1833.

Present

Joseph S. Lewis Pres^t
Thomas Morris V.P.

James M. Broome Thos W. Morris
James Glentworth Jr Sansom Perot
Edward W. Roberts Nathan R. Potts
Joseph Worrell Jr Lewis Walker
W. H. Morgan Saml Jenkins
S. N. Gray J^{no} P. Wetherill
Thomas Evans Thos P. Roberts

Previous Meeting Minutes

The minutes of the last meeting were read.

No Business Transacted

No further business, the Society adjourned.

Thos P. Roberts Secretary

Welch Society

At a Quarterly Meeting of the Welch Society held at the House of Thomas Evans December 2nd 1833.

Present

Joseph S. Lewis President

James M. Broome S. B. Lasalle
S. N. Gray W. H. Morgan
Saml Grice Wm Parker

398

James Gowen
Thomas Evans
Thomas P. Roberts
Nathan R. Potts

Jos. Worrell
Sam[l] P. Wetherill
Secretary

Previous Meeting Minutes

The minutes of the last meeting were read and approv'd.

Acting Committee Report and Assistance to Welsh Emigrants

The acting committee made the following report that since the last quarterly meeting, the Society has rendered assistance to several Welch persons, both in money and advice. Pecuniary assistance has been afforded <u>only</u> to such as were considered by the committee, objects of charity and coming within the view of the Society.

signed Sansom Perot Register

Finance: Accounts and Investments

The Treasurer reported that the balance of cash in his hands to the credit of the Society amounted to $73 54/^{100}.

On motion and seconded, it was resolved, that the acting committee be authorised to make the customary arrangements for the celebration of St David's day, by providing a dinner & that they be requested to invite the officers of such benevolent societies as reciprocate with us, and such other guests, as they may think best calculated to promote the pleasures of the day.

Membership: New Members

Thomas Morgan & James Bryan were proposed as candidates for membership by John J. Griffiths & Edward Jones by R. W. Sykes.

adjourned

Tho[s] P. Roberts
Secretary

1834

Welch Society

At the Annual Meeting of the Society held at the House of Daniel Saint[68] on the First Day of March 1834

Present

Joseph S. Lewis	President
Thomas Morris	Vice President
Sansom Perot	Register
Charles Dixey	Charles Humphreys
David Z. Davis	Samuel Jenkins
Thomas Evans	Thos W. Morris
Wm M. Evans	Wm H. Morgan
Caleb Griffith	Zach. Poulson
James Glentworth Jr	Nathan R. Potts
John J. Griffith	John M. Read
Samuel N. Gray	Edward W. Roberts
Samuel Grice	Robert W. Sykes
Jos. Huddell	Lewis Walker
Joseph Worrell Junr	

Previous Meeting Minutes

The minutes of the last quarterly meeting were read and approved.

Acting Committee Report and Assistance to Welsh Emigrants

The acting committee then made their report as follows

---

68 He was the proprietor of the Congress Hall Hotel on 27 South 3rd Street (c.1828) and the American Hotel, 20 South 6th Street (c.1835–6). See Robert DeSilver (ed.), *DeSilver's Philadelphia Directory and Stranger's Guide, 1828* (Philadelphia: Robert DeSilver, 1828), p. 71, and Robert DeSilver (ed.), *DeSilver's Philadelphia Directory and Stranger's Guide, 1835–6* (Philadelphia: Robert DeSilver, 1835), p. 157.

The acting committee report, that during the past year $254 50/^{100} had been loaned to the following emigrants from Wales

	Adults	Children	$
Charles Edwards	2	2	10
Watkins Prosser	2	4	10
Mashach Jones	1	0	7
Shadrach Jones	2	3	15
Thomas Morgan	2	2	10
Jane James	1	3	30
William Evans	1	1	30
David Griffith	2	3	9
Daniel Williams	7	3	20
Elizabeth Jones	1	4	10
Joseph Jones	2	1	6
Daniel Pask	2	0	5
Sarah Williams	2	2	10
Jocai Jones	2	0	15
C. Lowrie	2	2	3.50
Robert Williams	2	2	20
Sarah Williams	2	2	5
Thomas Franks	1	1	5
Frederick David	2	7	24
Charles Lewis	2	3	10
	40 adults	45 children	254.50

In submitting their report to the Society at its annual meeting, the committee feel gratified in being able to state their belief, that the amount expended, has been productive of much good.

signed Sansom Perot Register

March 1 1834

Finance: Accounts and Investments

The committee appointed to examine the Treasurer's accounts, report they have examined the statements of the Treasurer, and compared them with the vouchers, and found them correct, shewing a balance of cash in his hands on the 27th of February 1834 of $273.54

They further state that the funds of the Society consists of

		[$]
City Stock of 1840	five per cents	300
Same 1846	[five per cents]	1500
Same 1860	[five per cents]	500
Same 1840	six per cents	400
Same 1846	[six per cents]	500
Bank North America	12 Shares @ per cents	4800
Schuylkill Navigation	5 pr. ct Loan	400
		8400
Cash in the Treasury		273.54
		8673.54

signed Thomas P. Roberts

Thomas W. Morris

committee

Membership: New Members

Thomas Morgan proposed by John J. Griffith was duly elected a member of the Society.

James Bryan proposed by John J. Griffith was duly elected a member of the Society.

Edward Jones proposed by Robert W. Sykes was duly elected a member.

Membership: Resignation

The resignation of Capt Thomas Morgan was read & accepted.

Welsh Burial Ground – Repairs

The committee to whom was referred the proposition of John J. Griffith and others, made a report which was read and laid on the table, and the acting committee were authorized to take such order and make such repairs to the wall &c. of the burial ground as may at this time be deemed necessary.

Membership: New Members

Benjamin W. Richards was proposed as a candidate for membership by Samuel Grice.

The Society then proceeded to elect officers for the ensuing year. Edward W. Roberts and David Z. Davis were appointed Tellers, who reported the following gentlemen as duly elected

President	Joseph S. Lewis
Vice President	Thomas Morris
Secretary	Thomas P. Roberts
Treasurer	Job Bacon
Register	Sansom Perot
Counsellors	Robert W. Sykes
	Thomas W. Morris
Stewards	James Glentworth Jr
	Joseph Worrell Jr
	John P. Wetherill
	George W. Jones
	Charles Humphries
	Samuel N. Gray
Physicians	Thomas C. James
	Erasmus Thomas

The Society then Adjourned.

Thos P. Roberts

Secretary

Welch Society

At a Quarterly Meeting of the Society held at the House of Thomas Evans in George Street June 2nd 1834.

Present

Thomas Morris	Vice President
Thos Evans	Jeremiah James
Jas Glentworth Jr	Sansom Perot Register
J^{no} J. Griffith	Thos P. Roberts Sec^y
Saml N. Gray	Lewis Walker
Saml Grice	Joseph Worrell
Saml Jenkins	Saml P. Wetherill
S. B. Lassalle	J^{no} P. Wetherill
Thos Morris	Joseph Worrell Junr

Previous Meeting Minutes

The minutes of the last meeting were read and approved.

Membership: New Members

Benjamin W. Richards proposed at the last meeting by Samuel Grice was duly elected a member of the Society.

Welsh Burial Ground

The acting committee made the following report and accompanied thereto was a report of a sub-committee in relation to the enclosure of the burial ground lately convey'd to this Society by the remaining members or trustees of St David's Society, which was directed to the entered on the minutes.

Assistance to Welsh Emigrants

The acting committee report, that since the last quarterly meeting, there have been but few calls on the Society – two persons receiv'd five dollars each.

PART THREE

Welsh Burial Ground

The subject referr'd to them at the annual meeting in March last, respecting the burial ground, convey'd to the Society the surviving trustees of St David's Society, has engaged their especial attention.

They submit to the Society the enclosed report, which contains the proposition or offers which they have received, for erecting different kinds of wooden fences, or a stone wall around the grave.

signed Sansom Perot Register

June 2 1834

At a meeting of the acting committee of the Welch Society held on Saturday evening 24th day of May 1834 –the following resolution was adopted – viz –

That Saml N. Gray, J. Glentworth Jr, Joseph Worrell Jr, J. P. Wetherill & S. Perot be a committee to take into consideration the proposal for enclosing the burial ground at Hamilton Village.

In pursuance of the foregoing resolution your committee report, that they have visited the ground and examined the proposals – and as the latter may exceed in amount the sum contemplated by the Society – are of opinion that the same should be laid before the Society at the next quarterly meeting, for the purpose of ascertaining whether the Society are prepared to incur the expenditure necessary for enclosing the ground with stone to which the proposals above refer – and therefore offer the annexed resolution.

signed

Saml N. Gray
Ja^s Glentworth
Jos. Worrell Jr

on behalf of [the] Committee

Resolved, that the proposals for enclosing the burial ground of the

Society at Hamilton Village, with a stone wall be laid before the members at their next quarterly meeting for the purpose of obtaining the sense of the Society in relation to the same.

On motion of Joseph Worrell Senior, it was resolv'd that the burial ground be enclosed with a stone wall and that a committee of three be appointed to contract with a suitable person to construct the stone wall upon the best terms they can obtain, and with authority to draw upon the Treasurer for such sums as may be required for the completion of the same.

The committee consists of Jos. Worrell Senr, Saml N. Gray and J^{no} P. Wetherill.

Thos P. Roberts

Secretary

Welch Society

At a Quarterly Meeting of the Society held at Evans's 1st September 1834.

Present

Joseph S. Lewis	President
Thomas Morris	Vice President
Samuel Chew	Wm H. Morgan
Thos Evans	Thos W. Morris
Caleb Griffith	Thomas Morgan
Ja^s Glentworth Jr	Sansom Perot Register
Saml N. Gray	Nathan R. Potts
Edward Jones	Lewis Walker
S. B. Lassalle	Joseph Worrell Jr

Previous Meeting Minutes

The minutes of the last meeting were read and approved.

PART THREE

Acting Committee Report and Assistance to Welsh Emigrants

The acting committee report that since the last quarterly meeting they have expended $44. $14 of which was loaned to two girls – Sarah and Elizabeth Owens 15 & 12 years of age who had lost both parents by the cholera and wished to go to Pittsburg[h] where their brother resides – they were interesting children and the committee believe the loan made them will be returned by their brother.

Sept. 1 1834

signed Sansom Perot Register

Welsh Burial Ground

The burial ground committee, reported progress and were continued.

On motion, it was resolved, that the acting committee have charge of the burial ground, and make all regulations as to the depth and arrangement of the graves, to appoint a person to have the care of the same with such reasonable compensation as they may deem proper, to fix the price of interment and generally to make such rules and regulations, as they may deem adviseable, and submit a copy of the whole of their proceedings to the Society.

adjourned

Secretary protem.

Welch Society

At a Quarterly Meeting of the Society held at the House of Thomas Evans December 1 1834.

Present

Jos. S. Lewis	President
James Bryan	Stephen B. Lasalle
Thomas Evans	Thos W. Morris

J^no J. Griffith
Saml N. Gray
Jos. Huddell
Saml Jenkins
Jeremiah James
Edward Jones
Charles Humphries

Wm Parker
Nathl R. Potts
Thos P. Roberts
Edw. W. Roberts
John P. Wetherill
Jos. Worrell Junr

Previous Meeting Minutes

The minutes of the last meeting were read and approved.

Finance: Accounts

A report was read from the Treasurer, stating that the balance in his hands on 29th November amounted to sixty-seven dollars 24/^{100}.

Welsh Burial Ground

The President on behalf of the acting committee stated that they were unprepared to report upon the rules and regulations, relative to the burial ground, and were on motion continued.

The committee appointed for the purpose of erecting a stone wall around the burial ground of the Welsh Society in Hamiltonville beg leave to report,

That after as little delay as possible they fulfilled the intention of their appointment in having the same built and furnished in a workmanlike manner and durable, and in a very neat and tasteful style.

The committee are induced from all the information they could obtain, to believe the cost of erecting the wall is as low as it possibly could be done for.

They present herewith the bill, for materials and placing the same, with the contracts made with the different persons employed

		Doll[ar]s	
John Wright for laying stone, lime and sand, and digging as per bill		210.30	
Robert Coopers' bill for gates		11.00	
Richard Hardings bill for stone & half measuring as per contract	$184.65		
less a donation 5 per cent per perch	11.40	173.25	
Dolls		<u>394.55</u>	

signed,

Sam[l] N. Gray
J[no] P. Wetherill

Committee

Annual Dinner

On motion of J. P. Wetherill, it was resolved, that the acting committee be authorized and requested to make the usual arrangements for the celebration of St David's day, issue notes of invitation to the officers of such benevolent societies as reciprocate with us, and such other guests as are calculated to promote the enjoyment of the day.

Membership: New Members

Griffith J. Griffith was proposed as a candidate for membership by John J. Griffith.

William Vincent was also proposed by the J[no] J. Griffith.

Adjourned

Tho[s] P. Roberts Secretary

1835

Welch Society

At the Annual Meeting of the Welch Society held at the House of Daniel Saint, February 28 1835 were present

Joseph S. Lewis — President

James Bryan
T. P. Roberts
Sam¹ Jenkins
David Z. Davis
Lewis Walker
Thomas Morgan
Thoˢ Evans
Joseph Worrell Jr
Wᵐ Parker
Sanᵐ Perot
N. R. Potts

Ed^d Jones
James M. Broome
Ed. W. Roberts
S. B. Lasalle
Jos. O. Evans
Joseph Worrell
Zach. Poulson
James Glentworth Jr
John J. Griffith
Chaˢ Humphries

Previous Meeting Minutes

The minutes of the last meeting were read and approved.

Finance: Accounts and Investments

A statement of the receipts and disbursements of the Treasurer was laid before the board by the committee of accounts, showing a balance in his hands on this day of $379 24/^{100} and annexed also a statement of the stock, held by the Society as follows – viz

	$
City 6 per cent Stock par	900
City 5 per cent Stock [par]	2,300
Bank North America 12 Sh[are]s	4,800
Sch. Navigation Loan 5%	400
Cash	<u>379.24</u>
Dolls	<u>8,779.24</u>

Welsh Burial Ground

The Register on behalf of the acting committee made the following report, which was approved and the rules and regulations submitted in relation to the burial ground were adopted.

Acting Committee Report and Assistance to Welsh Emigrants

The acting committee report, that since the last annual meeting 18 adults and 33 children have received pecuniary assistance from the Society – the amount loaned during the year is $89. They believe the amount loaned, has been of much service to many and are only surprised that so few calls have been made, particularly when the unusual inclemency of the present winter, is taken into consideration – this fact does credit to Welchmen and their descendants.

Welsh Burial Ground

The following rules for the Welsh burial ground were adopted and the blanks were left to be filled by the Society – viz

Rule 1st That no person be interred therein unless known to be of Welsh descent.

2nd That no person be interred unless by a written order from at least one of those persons to be appointed by the acting committee, from time to time for that purpose.

3rd That the burial ground shall be divided in the center by a walk, extending from the north to the south, in width not less than six feet and that the graves shall be dug east and west, commencing at the north corner and the first row, extend next the wall, from north to south.

Membership: New Members

Griffith J. Griffith proposed by John J. Griffith was duly elected a member of the Society.

William Vincent was also duly elected a member.

Membership: Resignation

A letter of resignation was read and accepted from Job Bacon Esqr

Organization: Election of Officers

On motion the Society proceeded to the election of officers for the ensuing year – Messrs Huddell & Griffith were appointed Tellers – the election being closed, they reported the following gentlemen as elected.

President	Joseph S. Lewis
Vice President	Thomas Morris
Treasurer	Sansom Perot
Secretary	Thomas P. Roberts
Register	James Glentworth Jr
Counsellors	Robert W. Sykes
	Thos W. Morris
Stewards	J^{no} P. Wetherill
	Jos. Worrell Jr
	Chas Humphries
	Ed. W. Roberts
	Saml N. Gray
	Thomas Morgan
Physicians	Thomas C. James
	James Bryan

The Society then adjourned

Thos P. Roberts Secretary

Welch Society

At a Quarterly Meeting of the Welch Society held at the House of Thomas Evans in George Street, June 1st 1835.

Present

Thomas Morris   Vice President

Thomas Evans
Ja^s Glentworth Junr
Jer^h James
Edward Jones

Wm H. Morgan
Thos P. Roberts Sec^y
Joseph Worrell
S. B. Lasalle

Organization: Meeting Not Quorate

There being no quorum, the Society adjourned.

Welch Society

At a Quarterly Meeting of the Welch Society held at the House of Thomas Evans in Arch Street on the [blank] of September 1835.

Present

Thomas Morris   Vice President

James Bryan   Stephen B. Lassalle
Thomas Evans   Wm Morgan
James Glentworth Jr   Wm Parker
Saml N. Gray   Wm Vincent
Samuel Grice   Lewis Walker

Organization: Meeting Not Quorate

There being no quorum the Society adjourned.

Welch Society

At a Quarterly Meeting of the Society held at the House of Thomas Evans in George Street, December 7, 1835.

Present

James Bryan   Thos W. Morris
Thos Evans   Nath R. Potts

J. Glentworth Jr
S. N. Gray
C. Humphries
Edward Jones
Stephen B. Lassalle

Thos P. Roberts
Lewis Walker
Joseph Worrell
Joseph Worrell Junr

Acting Committee Report and Assistance to Welsh Emigrants

The acting committee report, that no applications had been made for relief during the last quarter.

Signed Ja^s Glentworth Register

Membership: New Member

Thomas Read of Montgomery was proposed as a candidate for membership by Joseph S. Lewis.

Membership: Resignation

The resignation of Thomas Cadwalader was read and accepted.

Annual Dinner

On motion of Thomas W. Morris, it was resolved that the acting committee be authorised and requested to make the usual arrangements for the celebration of St David's day on the first of March next and that they be requested to invite to the dinner the officers of such benevolent societies as reciprocate with us, and such other guests as they may deem best calculated to promote the enjoyment of the day.

Membership: New Member

Frederick H. Roberts was proposed by Joseph Worrell Jr

The Society then adjourned.

Thos. P Roberts Secretary

PART THREE

1836
Welch Society

At an Annual Meeting of the Welch Society held at the House of Thomas Evans in George Street, March 1. 1836 were present

Thomas Morris — Vice President
Sansom Perot — Treasurer
Thomas P. Roberts — Secretary

James Bryan
Saml Chew
Thomas Evans
J^{no} J. Griffith
Charles Humphries
Jeremiah James
Edward Jones
Jos. O. Evans
Caleb Griffith
Samuel Jenkins

James Glentworth Jr Register
William H. Morgan
Thomas Morgan
Zachariah Poulson
Nathan R. Potts
Robert W. Sykes
William Vincent
Lewis Walker
J^{no} P. Wetherill
Joseph Worrell Junr

Previous Meeting Minutes

The minutes of the last quarterly meeting were read & approv'd.

Membership: New Members

Thomas Read of Montgomery proposed by Joseph S. Lewis was duly elected a member.

Frederick A. Roberts proposed by Joseph Worrell Jr was also duly elected a member.

Finance: Accounts and Investments

The Treasurer presented a statement of his receipts and expenditures, as examined and approved by the acting committee, shewing a balance in his hands of five hundred and twenty-nine dollars 49/^{100}.

The funds of the Society consists of

	$
City 5 pr ct loan redeemable in 1840	300
City [5 pr ct loan redeemable in] 1846	1500
City [5 pr ct loan redeemable in] 1860	500
City 6 pr ct loan redeemable in 1840	400
City [6 pr ct loan redeemable in] 1846	500
Bank N. America 12 Shares at par	4800
Schuylkill Navigation Comp^y loan 5 pr ct	_400_
	8400
Balance of Cash in Treasury	_529.49_
Doll[ar]s	8929.49

Acting Committee Report and Assistance to Welsh Emigrants

The acting committee made the following report, that since the last annual meeting of the Society, they have extended relief in the shape of loans to seven adults and twenty one children, the whole sum expended amounting to $127 46/^{100}.

The demands on the Society for the past year have been considerably less than former years – The committee however feel a satisfaction in reporting their belief, that in every instance the loans made by the Society have been of essential service to deserving Welsh people.

The committee recommend caution on the part of the members of the Society, when they are applied to for pecuniary assistance by persons who represent themselves as Welsh.

all which is respectfully submitted

signed James Glentworth Jr Register

March 1, 1836.

Organization: Election of Officers

The Society proceeded to the election of officers for the ensuing year.

Mess. J. P. Wetherill and Charles Humphries were appointed Tellers – the polls being closed, it appeared the following gentlemen were unanimously elected

President — Joseph S. Lewis
Vice President — Thomas Morris
Treasurer — Sansom Perot
Secretary — Thomas P. Roberts
Counsellers — Robert W. Sykes
Thos W. Morris
Physicians — James Bryan
William Wetherill
Register — James Glentworth Jr
Acting Committee
J^{no} P. Wetherill
Charles Humphries — Joseph Worrell Jr
Samuel N. Gray — Edward W. Roberts
Thos P. Roberts Secretary — Thomas Morgan

Welsh Society

At a Quarterly Meeting of the Welsh Society held at the House of Thomas Evans in George Street on Monday June 6 1836.

Present

Thomas Morris — Vice President

James M. Broome — James Glentworth Junr
James Bryan — Saml N. Gray
T. Evans — Saml Grice
Jerem^h James — Edward Jones
Stephen B. Lasalle — Wm H. Morgan
Thomas W. Morris — Wm Parker
Sansom Perot — Joseph Worrell
Jos. Worrell Junr

Previous Meeting Minutes

The minutes of the last meeting were read and approved.

Acting Committee Report and Assistance to Welsh Emigrants

The Register on behalf of the acting committee reports that since the last quarterly meeting of the Society, the acting committee have drawn orders on the Treasurer for one hundred and twelve dollars, being the amount loaned to 9 adults and 18 children poor and deserving Welsh people, most of whom had just arrived in this country and were desirous of going to their families and relatives in Pottsville & Pittsburg[h].

May 28, 1836

signed James Glentworth Jr Register

Adjourned

Thos P. Roberts Secretary

Welsh Society

At a Quarterly Meeting of the Welsh Society held at the House of Thomas Evans, George Street, Sept. 5 1836.

Present

Thomas Morris	Vice President
James Bryan	Saml Jenkins
Thomas Evans	Jer^h James
James Glentworth Jr	Wm H. Morgan
Charles Humphries	Thomas Morgan
Thos P. Roberts	Robt W. Sykes
Lewis Walker	

Previous Meeting Minutes

The minutes of the last meeting were read and approv[ed].

Acting Committee Report and Assistance to Welsh Emigrants

The acting committee made the following report that during the last quarter the acting comm[ittee] have loaned to 8 adults and 11 children the sum of fifty-three dollars to poor and deserving emigrants from Wales.

signed James Glentworth Jr Register

Sept 3 1836

Membership: New Members

Mr Anthony Morris and Mr John Tolbert were proposed as candidates for membership by T. P. Roberts.

Adjourned

Thos P. Roberts Secretary

Welsh Society

At a Quarterly Meeting of the Welsh Society held at the House of Thomas Evans, George Street, on Monday Evening, Decr 5 1836.

Present

Thomas Morris	Vice President
Edward Jones	Charles Humphries
William Vincent	Thomas Evans
William Morgan	Samuel Jenkins
John J. Griffiths	Joseph Worrell Junr
Thomas Morgan	Nathan R. Potts
Thomas P. Roberts	

Previous Meeting Minutes

The minutes of the last meeting were read and approved.

Membership: New Members

Anthony Morris and John Tolbert proposed as candidates for membership at the last stated meeting were unanimously elected members of the Society.

Annual Dinner

On motion of Mr Gray, it was resolved, that the acting committee be requested to make the customary arrangements for the celebration of St David's day, and that they be authorised to invite the officers of such benevolent societies as reciprocate with us, and such other guests, as they may deem best calculated to promote the festivities of the day.

Membership: New Members

Benjamin Chew Jun[r] was proposed for membership by R. W. Sykes.

Charles Thompson Jones nominated by Doctor Bryan as a candidate for membership.

Adj[d]

Tho[s] P. Roberts Secretary

PART THREE

1837
Welch Society

At an Annual Meeting of the Welsh Society held at the House of Thomas Evans, George Street, on Wednesday, March 1 1837.

Present

Sansom Perot   Treasurer

C. Humphries   S. B. Lasalle
J. Glentworth Junr Register   Jos. Worrell
R. W. Sykes   Jos. Worrell Junr
Edward P. Jones   R. Huddell
Anthony Morris   Ed. W. Roberts
Jer^h James   Ja^s Bryan M.D.
Saml N. Gray   Wm Parker
Wm M. Evans   Wm H. Morgan
John Tolbert   Caleb Griffith
N. R. Potts   Zach. Poulson
Thos Evans   Thomas Morgan
Griffith J. Griffiths   Lewis Walker
George W. Jones   John J. Griffiths
Thos W. Morris   Samuel Jenkins
John M. Read   Thomas P. Roberts

Previous Meeting Minutes

The minutes of the last meeting were read and approved.

Membership: New Members

Benjamin Chew Jr and Charles Thompson Jones were duly elected members of the Society.

Acting Committee Report and Assistance to Welsh Emigrants

The acting committee made the following report

The acting committee report that since the last annual meeting of the Society orders have been drawn on the Treasurer for two hundred and thirty-five dollars, loaned to twenty-three adults and thirty-three children, poor and destitute families from Wales viz

	A[dults]	C[hildren]	$
Joseph Simons	1	-	50.00
Lucy Kelly	1	2	5
Eliza Thomas	1	1	15
John Jones	2	2	10
Henry Harris	2	5	15
Eliza Williams	1	6	12
Lucy Kelly	1	2	5
Philip Daniel	2	1	14
Daniel J. Morgan	2	3	6
Sarah Canver	1	4	8
Henry Walters	2	1	8
Mary Cann	1	4	8
Marg^t Aaron	1	-	5
Sarah Morgan	1	-	10
Jos^h Simons[69]	1	-	50
Lucy Kelly	1	2	5
David Thomas	1	-	6
Wm Reese	1	-	3

signed on behalf of the acting committee

Ja^s Glentworth Jr

Assistance to a Former Member

The loan mentioned in the report of the acting committee, as made to Joseph Simons deceased (late an active member of the Society) being considered a deviation from the usual course of proceeding. Messrs Morris & Sykes on behalf of the committee explained the nature of

---
69   Former member.

the case. Mr Morris, then offered the following resolutions which were unanimously adopted.

Resolved, that the loans or donations to Joseph Simons late a member of the Society now deceased be approved in consideration of his misfortunes, and many important services rendered by him to the Society.

Resolv'd, that the Society have heard with deep regret of the death of our late fellow member Joseph Simons which took place three days after the receipt of the last remittance.

Finance: Accounts and Investments

The Treasurer presented his account current for the past year as examined and approved by a committee appointed by the acting committee for that purpose, showing a balance in his hands of 637 dollars and thirty-seven cents.

The funds of the Society as stated in the report of the Treasurer which accompanied his account are as follows viz

City 6 per cent	Doll[ar]s 900
City 5 [per cent]	2300
Bank N. America (par)	4800
Schuylkill Nav^n Loan	400
Cash on hand	637.37
	Doll[ar]s 9037.37

Organization: Election of Officers

On motion of Mr Gray, it was resolved, that the Society proceed to the elections of officers, to serve the ensuing year. The Society on motion then adjourned for ten minutes for the purpose of preparing tickets for the election.

Messrs G. W. Jones and Nathan R. Potts being appointed Tellers, the election took place, and they reported the following named gentlemen as duly elected

President   Thomas Morris
Vice President   Thomas P. Roberts
Secretary   James Glentworth Jr
Treasurer   Sansom Perot
Register   Saml N. Gray
Counsellors   R. W. Sykes,
                    T. W. Morris
Physicians   Wm Wetherill,
                    Ja^s Bryan
Stewards   J. P. Wetherill
                    T. Morgan
                    Jos. Worrell Jr
                    E. W. Roberts
                    C. Humphries
                    Chas Dixey
                    George W. Jones

Adj^d

Thos P. Roberts Sec^y

Welsh Society

At a Quarterly Meeting of the Welsh Society held at the House of Thomas Evans, George Street on Monday Evening, June 5, 1837.

Present

Thomas P. Roberts   Vice President

Stephen B. Lassalle   James M. Broom
William H. Morgan   Thomas Evans
John Tolbert   Samuel N. Gray
William Vincent   Charles Humphreys
Lewis Walker   Jeremiah James
Joseph Worrell Jr   Charles Thomson Jones
Samuel Jenkins   James Glentworth Jr

PART THREE

Previous Meeting Minutes

The minutes of the last meeting were read and approved.

Acting Committee Report and Assistance to Welsh Emigrants

The acting committee report that during the last quarter they have drawn orders on the Treasurer for $27.00 loaned to 7 adults and 2 children.

signed Samuel N. Gray Register

June 3 1837

adj^d.

James Glentworth Jr Secretary

Welsh Society

At a Quarterly Meeting of the Welch Society held at the House of Thomas Evans September 4, 1837 – Thos P. Roberts acted as Secretary.

Present

Thomas Morris   President

James Bryan   Jeremiah James
Anthony Morris   Thomas Evans
Edward P. Jones   Nathan R. Potts
Charles Humphries   Charles T. Jones
Thos P. Roberts   Samuel Jenkins
William H. Morgan   Lewis Walker

Finance: Legacy

Nathan R. Potts offered the following preamble resolution which was read and adopted. Whereas this Society has been informed that they are entitled to a portion of the estate of Peter A. Blenon[70] dec^d under his will. Therefore resolved that the President of this Society be requested to make the proper application for and take the necessary steps to obtain said legacy.

Adjourned.

Thos. P Roberts

Secretary pro tem

Welch Society

At a Quarterly Meeting of the Welsh Society held at the House of Thomas Evans, George Street on Monday evening December 4, 1837.

Present

Thomas Morris	President
Thomas Evans	Jeremiah James
William Parker	William Vincent
James Glentworth Jr	Edward P. Jones
Sansom Perot	Joseph Worrell Jr
Charles Humphreys	Charles Thomson Jones
Thomas P. Roberts	John J. Griffith
Samuel Jenkins	Stephen B. Lassalle
Robert W. Sykes	Joseph Huddell

---

70 Dr Pierre Antione (Peter Anthony) Blénon of Hamilton Village, west Philadelphia was a doctor and druggist. He was born in 1766 in Sens, Burgundy, northern France, but took American citizenship in 1798. He died on 23 June 1836 and left a portion of his estate to charitable institutions, including the Welsh Society. For further details of his estate see Library Company of Philadelphia, McA MSS 028, Christian Godfrey Weber Papers, Series II, Documents (1802–1844).

PART THREE

Previous Meeting Minutes

The minutes of the last meeting were read and approved.

Finance: Legacy

The President reported, that he has made the necessary application to the Executors of the estate of Peter A. Blenon, deceased, as requested at the last meeting.

Annual Dinner

On motion of Joseph Worrell Jr it was resolved that the acting committee be requested to make the customary arrangements for the celebration of St Davids day, & that they be authorized to invite the officers of such benevolent societies as reciprocate with us, & such other guests as they may deem best calculated to promote the festivities of the day.

Membership: New Member

Theodore Evans was proposed for membership by Sansom Perot.

Membership: Resignation

The resignation of Judge John Hallowell, in consequence of ill health & not being able to attend the meetings of the Society was accepted.

Acting Committee Report and Assistance to Welsh Emigrants

The acting committee report that during the last two quarters they have loaned $94.00 to 18 adults & 28 children, poor & distressed Welsh.

Welsh Burial Ground: Rights to Ownership Contested

A letter was read from St George Campbell Esq on behalf of Dennis Sweeny & James Gasory surviving executors of Hugh Sweeny deceased, addressed to Messrs Sykes & Morris, the Solicitors of the Society, and claiming the burial ground in Hamilton Village, whereupon it was on motion resolved that the matter be referred to the acting committee with directions to take such measures through the solicitors, as the committee may deem proper, to contest the claim and maintain the title of the Society to their said lot, or burial grounds.

Membership: New Members

Judge John R. Jones proposed by John M. Read & Richard Griffith by Thomas Evans.

S. Morris Lynn & John P. Owens by C. Thomson Jones.

adjourned

James Glentworth Jr Secretary

PART THREE

1838
Welch Society

At the Annual Meeting of the Welch Society held at the House of Thomas Evans, George Street, on Thursday, March 1, 1838.

Present

Thomas Morris   President

James M. Broome   Benjamin Jones
Sansom Perot   Samuel Chew
Samuel Jenkins   Thomas P. Roberts
Charles Dixey   Jeremiah James
John M. Read   David Z. Davis
C. Thomson Jones   Thomas Read
Thomas Evans   Stephen B. Lassalle
William Vincent   Joseph O. Evans
William H. Morgan   Lewis Walker
William M. Evans   Thomas W. Morris
Joseph Worrall   James Glentworth Jr
Thomas Morgan   John P. Wetherill
John J. Griffith   Anthony H. Morris
Joseph Worrell Jr.   Griffith J. Griffith
Zachariah Poulson   Charles Humphreys
William Parker

Previous Meeting Minutes

The minutes of the last meeting were read and approved.

Membership: New Members

Theodore Evans, John R. Jones, Richard Griffith, S. Morris Lynn and John P. Owens were duly elected members of the Society.

Acting Committee Report and Assistance to Welsh Emigrants

The acting committee made the following report – That since the last annual meeting of the Society, orders have been drawn on the Treasurer for one hundred & thirty-eight dollars, loaned to twenty-nine adults and thirty-two children, poor and destitute families from Wales, viz.

	$	A[dults]	C[hildren]
Isaac Woods	5.00	2	
Richard Davis	5.00	2	
John Williams	7.00	2	2
James Roberts	10.00	1	
John Smith	6.00	2	4
John Davis	10.00	2	7
Jonah Reese	7.00	2	4
Ann Jones	10.00	2	3
Mary Lewis	12.00	1	5
Evan Baynes	5.00	2	1
David Haily	15.00	2	1
Mary James	15.00	2	1
Henry Harris	10.00	2	3
David Jones	4.00	1	
Frederick Davis	5.00	2	2
Mary Howells	5.00	1	
Mary Howard	7.00	1	

signed on behalf of the acting committee

James Glentworth Jr Acting Register

Finance: Accounts and Investments

The Treasurer presented his account current for the past year, as examined and approved by a committee appointed by the acting committee for that purpose shewing a balance in his hands of seven hundred and ninety-two dollars and seventy-five cents.

PART THREE

The funds of the Society as stated in the report of the Treasurer which accompanied his accounts are as follows

	$
City Six per cents	900
City Five per cents	2300
Twelve Shares Bank of North America	4800
Schuylkill Navigation Loan	400
Cash on hand	792.75
	<u>9192.75</u>

Organization: Election of Officers

On motion of John M. Read it was resolved, that the Society proceed to the election of officers to serve the ensuing year. The Society on motion adjourned for ten minutes for the purpose of preparing tickets for the election. Messrs John M. Read and Stephen B. Lassalle being appointed Tellers, the election took place and they reported the following named gentlemen as duly elected

President	Thomas Morris
Vice [President]	Thomas P. Roberts
Secretary	James Glentworth Jr
Treasurer	Sansom Perot
Register	Charles Thomson Jones
Physicians	William Wetherill
	James Bryan
Counsellors	Thomas W. Morris
	Samuel Chew
Stewards	Charles Humphreys
	Joseph Worrell Jr
	Stephen B. Lassalle
	Thomas Morgan
	Anthony H. Morris
	Robert W. Sykes
	Charles Dixey

Organization: Rules and Regulations

On motion of Thomas P. Roberts, it was resolved that the Secretary be authorized and directed to have two hundred and fifty copies of the Charter and Bye-Laws of the Society printed in a pamphlet form for the use of the members of the Society.

Welsh Burial Ground

Resolved that the Treasurer be directed to pay Thomas Betterton twenty-five dollars for his superintendence of the burial ground & that he be discharged, and that a suitable person be selected by the acting committee to supply the vacancy.

adjourned

James Glentworth Jr Secretary

Welch Society

At a Quarterly Meeting of the Welch Society held at the House of Thomas Evans, George Street, on Monday June 4, 1838.

Present

Thomas Morris	President
Charles Dixey	Jeremiah Evans
William Parker	Thomas Evans
Edward P. Jones	Sansom Perot
Theodore Evans	Charles Thomson Jones
Thomas P. Roberts	James Glentworth Jr
Stephen B. Lassalle	William Vincent
Richard Griffith	S. Morris Lynn
Joseph Worrell Jr	Charles Humphreys
Anthony H. Morris	Samuel Jenkins
Lewis Walker	

Previous Meeting Minutes

The minutes of the last meeting were read and approved.

Acting Committee Report – No Report

The report of the acting committee was laid over until the next meeting.

Welsh Burial Ground

A communication was received from William M. Evans, with an estimate for raising the wall of the burial ground in Hamiltonville, which was referred to the acting committee.

adjourned

James Glentworth Jr

Secretary

Welch Society

At a Quarterly Meeting of the Welch Society held at the House of Thomas Evans, George Street, on Monday September 3, 1838.

Present

Thomas Morris	President
Thomas Evans	Stephen B. Lassalle
Thomas P. Roberts	James Glentworth Jr
S. Morris Lynn	Lewis Walker
John J. Griffith	William H. Morgan
Joseph Worrell	Samuel Grice
Anthony H. Morris	Joseph Worrell Jr
Jeremiah James	John P. Owens
Samuel Jenkins	William Parker

Previous Meeting Minutes

The minutes of the preceding meeting were read & approved.

Acting Committee Report – No Report

In consequence of the absence of the Register, the acting committee have not reported for the two previous quarters.

adjourned

James Glentworth Jr

Secretary

Welch Society

At a Quarterly Meeting of the Welch Society held at the House of Thomas Evans, George Street, December 3, 1838.

Present

Thomas Morris	President
Thomas Evans	Samuel Jenkins
Anthony H. Morris	Theodore Evans
Jeremiah James	Nathan R. Potts
James Glentworth Jr	Edward P. Jones
Thomas P. Roberts	John J. Griffith
Stephen B. Lassalle	William Vincent
Joseph Huddell	S. Morris Lynn
Joseph Worrell Jr	Charles Humphreys
Wm H. Morgan	

Previous Meeting Minutes

The minutes of the preceding meeting were read and approved.

Acting Committee Report – No Report

The Register being absent no report has been received from the acting committee since the last annual meeting.

Annual Dinner

On motion of Thomas P. Roberts, it was resolved, that the acting committee be requested to make the customary arrangements for the celebration of St David's day & that they be authorized to invite the officers of such benevolent societies as reciprocate with us & such other guests as they may deem best calculated to promote the festivities of the day.

Membership: Resignations

The resignations of Dr Samuel M. Fox & Jenkins S. Jenkins were accepted.

Membership: Deaths

During the last eighteen months the Society have to regret the decease of John Tolbert, Samuel N. Gray, William W. Fisher, Caleb Griffith, James C. Biddle & Charles Wetherill, active & efficient members of the Society.

Membership: New Members

James Jones	was proposed as a candidate for membership by Wm Vincent.
Samuel J. Griffith	[was proposed as a candidate for membership] by John J. Griffith
William Thomas	[was proposed as a candidate for membership] by [John J. Griffith]
Algernon R. Roberts	[was proposed as a candidate for membership by] Charles Thomson Jones
James Hall Bready	[was proposed as a candidate for membership by] Thomas P. Roberts
Thomas Cadwalader Jr	[was proposed as a candidate for membership by] John M. Read

Adjourned

James Glentworth Jr Secretary

1839
Welch Society

At the Annual Meeting of the Welch Society held at the House of Thomas Evans, George Street, on Friday March 1 1839.

Present

Thomas Morris	President
Samuel Chew	Samuel Jenkins
Nathan R. Potts	David Z. Davis
Jeremiah James	Thomas P. Roberts
Thomas Evans	C. Thomson Jones
John M. Read	Joseph O. Evans
Stephen B. Lassalle	Robert W. Sykes
William M. Evans	William H. Morgan
Lewis Walker	Theodore Evans
Thomas Morgan	Joseph Worrell
James Glentworth	Anthony H. Morris
John P. Wetherill	John J. Griffith
Zachariah Poulson	Joseph Worrell Jr
Joseph Huddell	William Parker
Charles Humphreys	Sansom Perot

Previous Meeting Minutes

The minutes of the last meeting were read and approved.

Membership: New Members

Samuel S. Griffith, William Thomas, Algernon S. Roberts, James Hall Bready and Thomas Cadwalader Jr, were duly elected members of the Society.

Acting Committee Report and Assistance to Welsh Emigrants

The acting committee made the following report, that during the past year the Society has afforded relief to thirteen adults and twenty-two children, emigrants from Wales, in sums varying from five to thirty dollars & amounting in the total to the sum of one hundred and four dollars.

	$
David Griffith	15.00
David Davis	10.00
Evan Jones	30.00
David James	5.00
Sarah James	10.00
John Jones	5.00
David James &c.	10.00
Margaret Lewis	14.00
William Vincent	5.00
Total	104.00

signed, Charles Thomson Jones, Register

Finance: Accounts and Investments

The Treasurer presented his account current for the past year as examined by Thomas P. Roberts & Charles Humphreys, a committee appointed by the acting committee for that purpose, shewing a balance in his hands of one thousand & twenty-three dollars & seventy- five cents.

The funds of the Society as stated in the report of the Treasurer which accompanied his accounts are as follows

	$
City 6 per cents	900
City 5 per cents	2300
Twelve Shares B^k of N. America	4800
Schuylkill Nav. Loan	400
Cash on hand	1023.75
	9423.75

On motion of Zachariah Poulson, it was resolved that the acting committee, with the Treasurer, are hereby authorized and directed to invest such funds, as are now & may be hereafter in the Treasurer's hands, as they may deem necessary, in good & sufficient securities.

Organization: Election of Officers

On motion of James Glentworth it was resolved, that the Society proceed to the election of officers to serve the ensuing year. The Society on motion adjourned for ten minutes for the purpose of preparing tickets for the election. Charles Thomson Jones & Stephen B. Lassalle were appointed Tellers, the election took place & they reported the following named gentlemen as duly elected

President	Thomas Morris
Vice Pres^t	Thomas P. Roberts
Treasurer	Sansom Perot
Secretary	James Glentworth
Register	Charles Thomson Jones
Physicians	William Wetherill
	James Bryan
Counsellors	Thomas W. Morris
	Samuel Chew
Stewards	Charles Humphreys
	Robert W. Sykes
	Charles Dixey
	Joseph Worrell Jr
	Thomas Morgan
	Stephen B. Lassalle
	Anthony H. Morris

Welsh Burial Ground

On motion of John Price Wetherill it was resolved that the Stewards of the Society, be and they are hereby authorized and directed to repair and keep in order the burial ground and walls enclosing it, in Hamilton Village, and that they report at the annual meeting of the Society the number of internments during the year, with the names of the persons so interred.

Membership: Death

Since the last meeting, the Society have to regret the loss of Samuel P. Wetherill, an active and efficient member.

adjourned

James Glentworth Secretary

Welsh Society

At a Quarterly Meeting of the Welch Society held at the House of Thomas Evans, George Street on Monday June 3, 1839.

Present

Thomas P. Roberts	Vice President
Samuel Chew	Edward P. Jones
William Parker	Thomas Evans
Stephen B. Lassalle	Thomas Reed
James Glentworth	S. Morris Lynn
Nathan R. Potts	Charles Humphreys
Wm H. Morgan	William Vincent
Samuel Jenkins	Thomas Morgan
James Bryan	Jeremiah James
Anthony H. Morris	John J. Griffith
Griffith J. Griffith	

Previous Meeting Minutes

The minutes of the preceding meeting were read and approved.

Acting Committee Report – No Report

The acting committee were not prepared to report.

Membership: New Member

Owen Thomas proposed by John J. Griffith.

adjourned

James Glentworth Secretary

Welsh Society

At a Quarterly Meeting of the Welsh Society held at the House of Thomas Evans, George Street, on Monday September 2, 1839.

Present

Thomas P. Roberts	Vice President
Samuel Grice	Theodore Evans
Joseph Worrell Jr	Anthony H. Morris
Nathan R. Potts	S. Morris Lynn
William H. Morgan	James Glentworth
William Vincent	Stephen B. Lassalle
	Thomas Evans

Membership: Death

The Society have to regret the death of Capt Charles Dixey, one of the acting committee & a worthy and efficient member of the Society.

Organization: Meeting Not Quorate

No quorum being present the meeting adjourned

James Glentworth Secretary

Welsh Society

At a Quarterly Meeting of the Welsh Society, held at the House of Thomas Evans, George Street, on Monday, the 2nd Day of December 1839.

Present

Thomas Morris	President
Samuel Chew	Samuel Jenkins
William H. Morgan	Thomas Evans

PART THREE

Jeremiah James
Theodore Evans
Anthony H. Morris
S. Morris Lynn
Lewis Walker

Thomas Morgan
Stephen B. Lassalle
James Glentworth
Thomas P. Roberts
Joseph Worrell

Previous Meeting Minutes

The minutes of the preceding meetings were read and approved.

Annual Dinner

On motion of Thomas P. Roberts it was resolved that the acting committee be requested to make the customary arrangements for the celebration of St David's Day & that they be authorized to invite the officers of such benevolent societies as reciprocate with us, and such other guests as they may deem best calculated to promote the festivities of the day.

Acting Committee Report – No Report

The Register being absent, no report has been received from the acting committee since the last annual meeting.

Membership: Resignation

The resignation of Robert W. Sykes was read and accepted.

Membership: New Members

John Thomas   proposed by Charles Humphreys
John Sidney Jones   [proposed by] Charles Thomson Jones

Adjourned

James Glentworth Secretary

See Next Book

441

Plate 10. 'Congress Hall and New Theatre, in Chestnut Street, Philadelphia', c.1800.[71]

---

71   Birch and Son, *The City of Philadelphia*, plate 20.

PART FOUR

Select Biographies of Early Members and Associates

A

Allibone, Thomas

Thomas Allibone was a merchant who, in 1802, was located at 98 North Fourth Street, Philadelphia. Two additional entries might provide extra information about his business: Allibone T. and Son, merchants, were located next to 109 Water Street, while Allibone and Stephenson, curriers, were located at 216 North Second Street, Philadelphia.[1]

B

Bacon, Job (1786–c.1855)

Job Bacon was born on 15 January 1786, and was the son of Job and Mary Lownes, Quakers.[2] In 1800 he lived in the High Street Ward, in 1810 Middle Ward, and in 1830 he lived in a property in the Chestnut Ward, Philadelphia.[3] In 1831 he was the secretary of the American Fire Insurance Company located at 101 Chestnut Street, Philadelphia.[4]

---

1   James Robinson (ed.), *The Philadelphia Directory... 1802* (Philadelphia: William W. Woodward, 1802), p.16.
2   HC, PhM.P455.01a.001, Philadelphia Monthly Meeting, Births, Deaths and Burials, 1688–1826, p. 33.
3   1800 Census. High Street Ward, Philadelphia, M32, Roll 43, pp. 96, 97; 1810 Census. Middle Ward, Philadelphia, Roll 55, p. 537; 1830 Census. Chestnut Ward, Philadelphia, M19, Roll 159, p. 494.
4   Robert DeSilver (ed.), *DeSilver's Philadelphia Directory and Strangers Guide... 1831* (Philadelphia: Robert DeSilver, 1831), p. 3.

He died on 7 September 1855 and his burial in Christ Church burial ground was recorded as follows:

Black cloth coffin, Eng[rave]d plate, lined with flannel and red cedar case	$40
Laying out, shaving and dressing $5, ice & box $3	$8
Hearse from Mandry, 3 Kennedy, 3 Conway	$16
Interment $9.25. Flannel dress $4, ribbon 40 c[en]ts	$13.35
18 yds made at 87½. $15.75. Crape 3⅞ yds 56½ cts $2.18	$17.93
7 pair hosking gloves at $1.87. 4 pair interline 1 at 45 cts $1.80	$8.80
Paid	**$104.38**[5]

Bacon, John

In 1831, John Bacon lived at 117 Sassafras Street, Philadelphia.[6]

Ball, Joseph (c.1755 –1821)

Joseph Ball was born c.1755 and he was a Philadelphia merchant and industrialist. In 1778 he purchased the Batsto Ironworks in Burlington County, New Jersey. In an agreement of 5 June 1784 William Richards purchased the Batsto Ironworks from Joseph, his nephew, but Ball (and Charles Pettit) each retained one-third of the property. During the American Revolution he supplied the Continental Army with munitions and post-war he, along with Robert Morris and others, risked his fortune in the attempt to restore public credit. He was also the first director and president (1798–9) of the Insurance Company of North America. In 1790 it was recorded at the Gwynedd Meeting that he manumitted 'my negro woman named Charity wife of Benjamin a negro set free by Joseph Saltar'.[7] Three years later he was recorded as

---

5   HSP, Historic Pennsylvania Church and Town Records, Reel 98. R.R. Bringhurst & Co, Inc.
6   DeSilver (ed.), *DeSilver's Philadelphia Directory and Strangers Guide... 1831*, p. 3.
7   HC, PhM.P455.04.047, Philadelphia Manumissions Book, 1772–86 (although the dates covered are 1765–99), fol. 193.

'one of the aldermen of the City' and living at 96 North Water Street. He died on 29 April 1821.[8]

Biddle, Clement (1740–1814)

Clement Biddle was born in Philadelphia on 10 May 1740 and was the son of John Biddle (1707–89) and Sarah Owen (1711–73), Quakers. He was the brother of Sarah Penrose/Shaw/Tellier (1748–94), Colonel Owen Biddle (1737–99), Ann Owen Wilkinson (1742–1807), and Lydia Hutchinson (1753–85). He was married twice. First to Mary Richardson (6 June 1764) and later to Rebekah Cornell (1755–1831), the daughter of Gideon Cornell, the Chief Justice of Rhode Island. He was a merchant in his father's business but, in 1764, he helped coordinate the activities of a militia company to protect friendly Indians from the Paxton Boys. The next year he was involved in the non-importation agreement and would take a significant part in the revolution, especially the establishment of the 'Quaker Blues', a volunteer militia company. On 8 July 1776 he was appointed by Congress as lieutenant colonel of the volunteer Flying Camp and, in the winter of that year, he became aide-de-camp to General Nathanael Greene and fought at the battles of Princeton, Brandywine, Trenton, Germantown and Monmouth. He was the Commissary General at Valley Forge under George Washington. In October 1780 he resigned from the Continental Army and the following month the Pennsylvania Executive Council appointed him as Marshal of the Court of Admiralty while, on 11 September 1781, he became the quartermaster and colonel of the Pennsylvania militia. He was the first

---

8   James Hardie (ed.), *The Philadelphia Directory and Register... 1793* (Philadelphia: T. Dobson, 1793), p. 6; 'Penn People: Joseph Ball', Pennsylvania University Archives and Records Center, https://archives.upenn.edu/exhibits/penn-people/biography/joseph-ball [accessed 4 July 2021]; 'Industry in the Pines: The Story of Batsto Village', and provided at: https://www.thehistorygirl.com/2013/03/industry-in-pines-story-of-batsto.html [accessed 8 July 2021]; Philadelphia City Archives, Death Records: Philadelphia City Death Certificates, 1803–1915, Index. For further details of Joseph Ball, other family members, and his business transactions see HSP, Collection 0028, Ball Families Papers, 1672–1917.

United States Marshal (1789–93) for Pennsylvania. He later returned to his mercantile business and died in Philadelphia. He died on 14 July 1814, aged seventy-four, and was buried at Friends Arch Street Meeting House Burial Ground, Philadelphia.[9]

Biddle, George (1779–1812)

George Washington Biddle was born in 1779 and was the son of Clement Biddle. He died in 1812.

Biddle, James C. (1795–1838)

James Cornell Biddle was born in 1795 and was the son of Clement Biddle. He died in 1838.

Biddle, Thomas (1766–1857)

Thomas A. Biddle was born on 4 June 1776 and was the son of Clement Biddle (1740–1814) and Rebekah Cornell Biddle (1755–1831). He died, aged eighty, on 3 June 1857, and is buried in Laurel Hill Cemetery, Philadelphia.

Binney, Horace (1780–1875)

Horace Binney was born in Philadelphia on 4 January 1780 and was the son of Dr Barnabas Binney (1751–87), a prominent Philadelphia lawyer. He was educated in Bordentown, New Jersey. In 1797 he graduated from Harvard University where he had studied law under Jared Ingersoll and was a founding member of the Hasty Pudding Club, which is still in existence.[10] On 31 March 1800, Binney was admitted to

---

9   Clement Biddle, 'Selections from the Correspondence of Colonel Clement Biddle', *Pennsylvania Magazine of History and Biography (hereafter PMHB)*, 42 (1918), 310–42; 43 (1919), 53–76, 143–62, 193–207; https://www.usmarshals.gov/history/firstmarshals/biddle450.jpg [accessed 4 July 2021]. Also, see HSP, MSS. 1792, Biddle Family Papers, 1683–1954; https://www.hsp.org/sites/default/files/legacy_files/migrated/findingaid1792biddle.pdf [accessed 4 July 2021].
10 https://hastypudding.org/ [accessed 1 July 2021].

the bar in Philadelphia.[11]

He was a founding member of the Law Library Company of the City of Philadelphia and its director 1805–19 and 1821–7. Between 1806 and 1807 he was a member of the Pennsylvania Assembly. For the next seven years he compiled six volumes of the reported decisions of the Supreme Court of Pennsylvania. Among his other roles he was the first director of the United States Bank (1808), president of the City of Philadelphia, Common Council (1810–12) and, between 1816 and 1819, a member of the Select Council, City of Philadelphia. In 1821 he helped to establish the Apprentices' Library and was the Vice Chancellor of the Associated Members of the Bar of Philadelphia. From 1827 until 1836 he was the Vice Chancellor of the Law Association of Philadelphia, and later (1852–4) its Chancellor. In 1832 he was President of the Law Academy. From 4 March 1833 until 3 March 1835, Binney was a Congressman (anti-Jacksonian). He died on 12 August 1875 in Philadelphia and is buried in St James the Less Cemetery, Falls of the Schuylkill, Pennsylvania.[12]

Birchall, Caleb (?–1817)

Caleb Birchall was a hatter and, in 1802, he worked at 46 North Third Street, Philadelphia.[13] He died in 1817 and his will was proved on 16

---

11 It has been suggested that his practice was located close to 74 Walnut Street, Philadelphia. See James Robinson (ed.), *The Philadelphia Directory... 1804* (Philadelphia: John H. Oswald, 1804), p. 35.

12 See Horace Binney, *The Leaders of the Old Bar of Philadelphia* (Philadelphia: privately printed, 1866); William Strong, *An Eulogium on the Life and Character of Horace Binney* (Philadelphia: McCalla & Stavely Printers, 1876); Charles Chauncey Binney, *Life of Horace Binney, with Selections from His Letters* (Philadelphia: Lippincott, 1903); 'Horace Binney, 1780–1875', *Biographical Directory of the United States Congress* and provided at: https://bioguide.congress.gov/search/bio/B000475 [accessed 4 July 2021]. For details of his papers see HSP, 1505, Horace Binney Papers (11 volumes) which includes a travel journal (1836–7), commonplace book (1858), autobiography, essays, and genealogical notes; HSP, Amb.175, executor's accounts of Horace Binney's estate, 1875–8.

13 Robinson (ed.), *Philadelphia Directory... 1802*, p. 30.

January 1817.[14]

Bloomfield, Joseph E. (1787–1872)

Joseph Ellis Broomfield, a merchant, was born to Samuel and Abigail (Ellis) Bloomfield on 16 December 1787. He worked for a Philadelphia mercantile house in Cadiz, Spain, and later had an appointment as a consular official. Returning to America, he lived in New Jersey and later New York, and became involved in canal improvements. Consequently, he relocated to Oneida County, New York, and lived in Utica as a miller, and then in Tagerg, New York, where he became involved in railway expansion. On 24 September 1819 he married Mary Frances Barbarous (1801–81) in Burlington, New Jersey, and they later lived in Oswego, New Jersey. Joseph died on 29 June 1872.[15]

Brooke, Reese

In 1803 he was recorded as a flaxfeed merchant of Brookes Court, Philadelphia.[16]

Broom(e), Jacob (?–1810)

Jacob Broom was an honorary member of the Welsh Society. He was born in Wilmington, Delaware, and was the son of a blacksmith who became a wealthy farmer. He was educated at Wilmington's Old Academy, and became a successful farmer, surveyor and businessman. He soon sought public service as a borough assessor and president of the city's 'street regulators'.[17] He was also a magistrate in New Castle County and he was elected as assistant burgess (vice-mayor) of Wilmington in 1776, winning re-election several times as well as becoming chief burgess four times.

14 HSP, Will Book, Part C. 6.386. Will of Caleb Birchall, Philadelphia, 16 January 1817.
15 For further details see https://www.genealogy.com/ftm/f/o/w/Joyce-A-Fowler-WV/GENE6-0010.html – notes for Joseph Ellis Bloomfield, no. 52 [accessed 17 November 2021].
16 James Robinson (ed.), *The Philadelphia Directory... 1803* (Philadelphia: William W. Woodward, 1803), p. 38.
17 Responsible for the city's waste etc.

PART FOUR

During the revolution, Broom used his surveying skills for the benefit of the Continental Army, especially in the provision of detailed maps used before the battle of Brandywine. After the war he was elected as a state representative to the legislature between 1784 and 1786 and again in 1788. He promoted strong central government and a robust legal framework of governance. He was a delegate to the U.S. Constitutional Convention of 1787 and he was a signer of the United States Constitution. He played an important role in the reorganisation of the College of Wilmington and served on the college's first Board of Trustees. He died on 25 April 1810 in Philadelphia and was buried in Christ Church Burial Ground, Philadelphia.[18]

Bronson, Enos (1774–1823)

Enos Bronson was a writer and newspaper publisher. He was born on 31 March 1774 and died in 1823. He was the son of Eli and Mehitable (Atwater) Bronson, and the son-in-law of the Episcopal Bishop William White. The Bronson family were from Hartford and Farmington, Connecticut, where the line can be traced back to 1636. On 10 September 1798 Enos graduated from Yale College and before relocating to Philadelphia he was appointed as the first Preceptor of the Deerfield Academy, Massachusetts, a position he held for one year in 1799. It is unclear exactly when he moved to Philadelphia, but once there he was in the company of notable Federalists, including Thomas Biddle, Horace Binney, Dr Nathaniel Chapman, and Charles Chauncey.[19] In 1800, alongside Caleb P. Wayne, he was editing the *Gazette of the United*

---

18 Rev. William W. Campbell, *Life and Character of Jacob Broom* (Wilmington: Delaware Historical Society, 1909); 'Jacob Broom, Delaware' and provided at: https://history.army.mil/books/RevWar/ss/broom.htm [accessed 1 March 2021].
19 The Bronson family were originally from Hartford and Farmington (Connecticut) and their line has been traced back to 1636. See Burton Alva Konkle, 'Enos Bronson, 1774–1823', *PMHB*, 57 (1933), 355–8 (355); Richard C. Allen, '"There Burst a Noble Heart": Enos Bronson (1774–1823), Federalist and Editor of the *Gazette of the United States*', (forthcoming).

States, a paper he purchased on 2 November 1801,[20] and the following year he was joined in running the paper by Elihu Chauncey. From 1804 to 1818 they also published the semi-weekly *United States' Gazette for the Country*. According to Burton Alva Konkle, Bronson was 'the most forceful editor in American Federalism from 1801 to 1819', while Jerry Knudson has observed that he was 'one of the forgotten figures of American journalism'.[21] He has rarely received attention by historians and there is no mention of him in the *Dictionary of American Biography*. As such, as Knudson observes, Bronson was 'truely one of those powerful but faceless "twilight shadowes" of Federalism'.[22]

Brown, Abiah

The *Philadelphia Directory* in 1802 recorded that Abiah Brown was a shipbuilder located at 15 Vine Street, Philadelphia.[23]

Bryan, James (1810–81)

James Bryan was a physician in Philadelphia who lectured on 17 March 1851 to the Philadelphia College of Medicine (subsequently published) on the progress of medicine in the nineteenth century.[24] He also published on several other medical topics.[25]

---

20 Jerry W. Knudson, *Jefferson and the Press: Crucible of Liberty* (Columbia, SC: University of South Carolina Press, 2006), p. 27. At the time of taking over the newspaper its circulation had dropped to 800 from the previous 3,000 subscriptions.
21 See Konkle, 'Enos Bronson', 355; Knudson, *Jefferson and the Press*, p. 27.
22 Knudson, *Jefferson and the Press*, p. 27.
23 Robinson (ed.), *The Philadelphia Directory... 1802*, p. 39.
24 James Bryan, *Progress of Medicine During the First Half of the Nineteenth Century... Introductory Lecture to the Spring Session in the Philadelphia College of Medicine* (Philadelphia: Grattan & M'Lean, 1851).
25 For example, James Bryan, *A Treatise on the Anatomy, Physiology and Diseases of the Human Ear* (Philadelphia: privately published, 1851); *An Essay on Hernia* (Philadelphia: F. J. Pilliner, 1860).

C

Cadwallader, John (1762–?)

Possibly the son of Isaac Cadwallader and Elizabeth Michener. John was born on 27 March 1762 in Moreland Township, Pennsylvania.

Cadwallader, Joseph (1773–?)

Possibly the son of Isaac Cadwallader and Elizabeth Michener. Joseph was born on 3 September 1773 in Moreland Township, Pennsylvania.

Cadwal[l]ader, Lambert (1742–1823)

Lambert Cadwallader was born in Trenton, New Jersey, in December 1742 and was the son of Dr Thomas and Hannah (*née* Lambert) Cadwallader. The family had returned to Philadelphia by c.1750 and Lambert was educated at Dr Allison's Academy. In 1757 he matriculated at the College of Philadelphia (University of Pennsylvania), but he did not graduate; instead, he sought a merchant career with his brother John Cadwallader (1742–86). Both men signed the non-importation agreement in 1765, which sought to boycott English merchants, while Lambert opposed the Stamp Act. In 1774, he was elected to the Provincial Assembly and appointed to Philadelphia's Committee of Correspondence.

He was a Captain of one of the companies raised in Philadelphia (c.1775) and the following year promoted Pennsylvania's engagement in a Constitutional Convention. His promotion to Lieutenant Colonel of the Third Pennsylvania Battalion of the Continental Army (January 1776) led to immediate action in defence of New York and his involvement in the Battle of Brooklyn. He also defended Fort Washington, but was taken prisoner by the British but quickly released. In 1777 as a Colonel he was the commander of the Fourth Pennsylvania Regiment, but the condition of his parole meant that an exchange prisoner was required. This was not forthcoming and on 29 January 1777 George Washington accepted his resignation and he withdrew to his Greenwood Estate, Trenton, New Jersey.

He returned to political life and between 1784 and 1787 he was a delegate for New Jersey to the Continental Congress. He stood as a Federalist in the U.S. Congress (1788 and 1794). In 1793 he married Mary McCall (1764–1848), the daughter of Archibald and Judith (*née* Kemble) McCall. Apart from his association with the Welsh Society he was elected (c.1768) to the American Philosophical Society.

He died on 13 September 1823 in Greenwood and was buried in the Friends Burying Ground, Trenton.[26]

Chauncey, Charles (1777–1849)

Charles Chauncey was born in 1777 in New Haven, Connecticut, and he was the son of Judge Chauncey. He studied at Yale College (graduated c.1792) and entered the legal profession. He was admitted to the New Haven Bar in 1798 and Philadelphia Bar in 1799 where he served with distinction for fifty years. He was an original founder of the Philadelphia Academy of Fine Arts.[27]

Chauncey, Elihu (1779–1847)

Elihu Chauncey, the second son of Charles and Abigail Chauncey, was born on Friday, 15 January 1779. He died at Philadelphia on Thursday, 8 April 1847 leaving two daughters, Henrietta Chauncey and Sarah C. Savage surviving him. His remains were removed to

---

26 William Henry Rawle, *Colonel Lambert Cadwalader, of Trenton, New Jersey* (Philadelphia, n.p., 1878); Whitfield J. Bell and Charles Greifenstein, *Patriot-Improvers: Biographical Sketches of Members of the American Philosophical Society* (3 vols. Philadelphia: American Philosophical Society, 1997), II, pp. 256–60. For his papers and correspondence see American Philosophical Society Archives, Philadelphia, MSS. B.C625.1, Lambert Cadwalader Papers, 1779–98; Philadelphia, Record Group IIb APS.Archives.IIb, 1807–25.

27 In 1833 his portrait 'for his students' was engraved by John Sartain and belongs to the Law Association of Philadelphia. See Charles Henry Hart, *A Register of Portraits Painted by Thomas Sully, 1801–1871...* (Philadelphia: s.n., 1909), p. 42.

PART FOUR

Burlington, New Jersey, on 13 April 1847.[28] He, along with Enos Bronson, was from 1804 to 1818 the publisher of the semi-weekly *United States' Gazette for the Country*.[29]

Chew, Benjamin (1722–1810)

Benjamin Chew was born on 19 November 1722 on his father's Maidstone plantation, Anne Arundel County, Maryland. He was the son of Samuel Chew, a physician and first Chief Justice of Delaware, and Mary Galloway Chew (1697–1734). Chew relocated to Philadelphia in 1754 and turned his attention to a legal career and he represented various members of the Penn family. Subsequently he became the head of the Pennsylvania Judiciary System and Chief Justice of the Supreme Court of the Province of Pennsylvania. He was a lifelong friend of George Washington. His legal knowledge was invaluable in the construction of the Constitution and Bill of Rights. He died at Cliveden on 20 January 1810, and he is buried at St Peter's Churchyard, Philadelphia.[30]

Clarke, Samuel

Two Samuel Clarkes are recorded in the 1802 *Philadelphia Directory*. The first was a merchant, located on 227 South Front, and the second was a 'gentleman' who lived on 38 North Fifth Street.[31]

---

28   See Jeannie F-J. Robison and Henrietta C. Bartlett (eds), *Genealogical Records. Manuscript Entries of Births, Deaths and Marriages, taken from Family Bibles 1581–1917* (New York: The Colonial Dames of the State of New York, 1917), pp. 37–8.
29   Knudson, *Jefferson and the Press*, p. 27. A bust of Elihu Chauncey 'for Mr Dillingham' was commissioned in 1834. See Hart, *A Register of Portraits Painted by Thomas Sully*, p. 42.
30   For further details see Burton Alva Konkle, *Benjamin Chew 1722–1810: Head of the Pennsylvania Judiciary System under Colony and Commonwealth* (Philadelphia: University of Pennsylvania Press, 1932). For his family's papers see HSP, MSS. 2050, Chew Family Papers.
31   Robinson (ed.), *The Philadelphia Directory... 1802*, p. 53.

Clifton, John

The *Philadelphia Directory* in 1802 recorded two entries for John Clifton. The first was for a merchant on 82 Swanson Street, and the second, a carpenter, on 106 North Eight Street, Philadelphia.[32]

Clymer, George (1739–1813)

George Clymer was born in Philadelphia on 16 March 1739. He was orphaned when a year old and taken into the care of his uncle, William Coleman, a confidante of Benjamin Franklin, who would provide the means for Clymer to become a successful merchant. He was initially a clerk but later a partner in his uncle's mercantile business, which he inherited after Coleman died. In 1765 he married Elizabeth Meredith, the daughter of Reece Meredith, and would merge his business interests with that of his in-laws to form the prominent Meredith-Clymer merchant house in Philadelphia. His advantageous connections also brought Clymer to the attention of George Washington and other leading patriots. In 1773 he vigorously opposed the Tea and Stamp Acts in Philadelphia, which ultimately resulted in the resignation of Philadelphia tea consignees selected by Parliament under the Tea Act. He was a commander of a company of Associators, Philadelphia's volunteer militia, but never saw active duty during the revolutionary war. In the same year, Clymer was appointed to the Philadelphia Committee of Safety,[33] and, as an advocate of complete independence, was later to sign the Declaration of Independence.

Clymer was elected to the Continental Congress and served between 1776 and 1777. During this period he inspected the north army (*c.*fall 1776) and remained in Philadelphia during Sir Henry Clinton's occupation, but his prominent position made him the target for reprisals. After the Battle of Brandywine in 1777 the British troops destroyed his family residence in Chester County. Along with his

---

32 Robinson (ed.), *The Philadelphia Directory... 1802*, p. 54.
33 This was an executive body that was established by the legislature to administer Pennsylvania when the legislature was not in session.

son, Meredith Clymer, he nevertheless was able to salvage his business and increased his wealth during and after the war, particularly trading with St Eustatius in the Caribbean. Clymer was twice elected to the Pennsylvania Legislature (1780 and 1784). In 1782 he was appointed to inspect the southern states in order to recover subscriptions owed to the government. From 1787 he represented the State at the Constitutional Convention before his election to the United States Congress two years later and, alongside Michael Hillegas, acted as treasurer of the Continental Congress.

Apart from these responsibilities, Clymer was later appointed as the President of Philadelphia Bank, the Pennsylvania Academy of Fine Arts, and as vice-president of the Philadelphia Agricultural Society. He was also negotiated a treaty with the Creek Indian confederacy at Coleraine, Georgia (29 June 1796) and he was the first President of the Pennsylvania Society for the Abolition of Slavery. He died on 23 January 1813 at Sommerseat, his estate near Morrisville, New Jersey. He was interred at the Friends Burying Ground in Trenton, New Jersey.[34]

Cruckshank,[35] James

James Cruckshank was a bookseller and, in 1802, he was located at 87 High Street, Philadelphia.[36]

Cumpston, Thomas (c.1752–1820)

Thomas Cumpston was born c.1752 and was a shopkeeper in Philadelphia. In 1791 his business was located at 74 High Street, Philadelphia.[37] In 1797 a watercolour portrait was painted by James

---

34   For studies of Clymer's life see Jerry Grundfest, 'George Clymer, Philadelphia Revolutionary, 1739–1813', University of Columbia, Ph.D. thesis, 1973; Robert K. Wright, Jr. and Morris J. MacGregor, Jr. *Soldier-Statesmen of the Constitution* (Washington, DC: Center of Military History, U.S. Army, 1987), pp. 153–4.
35   Various spellings of the last name: Cruickshank, Cruckshanks etc.
36   Robinson (ed.), *The Philadelphia Directory... 1802*, p. 64.
37   'Market (or High) Street', http://philahistory.net/market.html [accessed 4 July 2021].

Peale. Cumpson was also one of the two commissioners appointed to oversee the bankruptcy proceedings of Robert Morris, signer of the Declaration of Independence, who was in a debtor's prison for three years for failure to pay back a promissory note of $4000 (see Morris, Robert). He died on 19 July 1820 in Philadelphia.[38]

D

Dewees, William P. (1768–1841)

William Potts Dewees was born in 1768 in Pottsgrove, Pennsylvania, and would later become a Professor of Obstetrics at the University of Pennsylvania providing advice on child rearing. He wrote *A Comprehensive System of Midwifery* (1824); *Treatise on the Physical and Medical Treatment of Children* (1825); *Treatise on the Diseases of Females* (1826); and *Practice of Medicine* (1830).[39] On 12 February 1805 he was also elected cashier of the Trenton Banking Company and his salary was fixed at $1,300 per year. He further served as the First President of the Musical Fund Society (1820–1835). He died in 1841.[40]

---

38 Philadelphia City Archives, Death Records: Philadelphia City Death Certificates, 1803–1915, Index. For his portrait see 'Thomas Cumpston', 1797. Worcester Art Museum, Worcester, Maine. Alexander and Caroline DeWitt Fund, 1983.2.
39 For additional information see G. J. Barker-Benfield, *Male Attitudes toward Women and Sexuality in Nineteenth Century America; The Horrors of the Half-Known Life* (London: Routledge, 2000), p. 31.
40 'No. 174. William Potts Dewees, M. D., (1768–1841)', in Pennsylvania Academy of Fine Arts, *Catalogue of the Memorial Exhibition of Portraits by Thomas Sully* (2nd edn. Philadelphia: s.n., 1922), p. 130; John H. Sines, 'History of the Trenton Banking Company', in Trenton Historical Society, *A History of Trenton, 1679–1929: Two Hundred and Fifty Years of a Notable Town...* (Princeton: Princeton University Press, 1929), chap. XI, and available at http://trentonhistory.org/His/banks.html [accessed 4 November 2020].

PART FOUR

Dickinson, Philemon (1739–1809)

Philemon Dickinson was the son of Samuel Dickinson and brother of Samuel and John. He was born on 5 April 1739 at Crosia-dore, near Trappe, Talbot County, Maryland. He relocated to Dover, Delaware with his parents in 1740 and was privately tutored before graduating at the University of Pennsylvania at Philadelphia in 1759. He proceeded to take charge of his father's estate and studied law in Philadelphia. Although he was admitted to the bar, he never practised. On 14 July 1767 he married Mary Cadwallader (1746–1781), his first cousin. They had two children: Mary (1768–1822) and Samuel (1770–1837). In the same year he relocated to Trenton, New Jersey, and in 1776 Dickinson was a delegate to the New Jersey Provincial Congress. He was a commissioned as a brigadier general in 1776, and a year later was major General in the Continental Army during the Revolutionary War commanding the New Jersey Militia. Between 1782 and 1783 he was a delegate to the Continental Congress from Delaware, and vice president of the Council of New Jersey from 1783 to 1784. From 23 November 1790 until 3 March 1793 he was a U.S. Senator from New Jersey. He died on 4 February 1809 at his home (The Hermitage), near Trenton, Mercer County, New Jersey. His body was interred at Friends Meeting House Burial Ground, Trenton.[41]

Drury/Drewry, Spafford (1770–c.1802)

In his will, dated 3 February 1802, Spafford Drewry was recorded as being of Charlestown, South Carolina, as well as a merchant in Philadelphia. He was born on 26 April 1770 in Philadelphia and was the son of William Drewry, a ship chandler. In 1799 he was listed in the *Philadelphia Directory* as living at 22 Arch Street, Philadelphia.[42] In his will he left provision for his uncle, George Drewry; an apprentice, John Dayton; and funds for the education of poor children that belonged to

---

41 'Philemon Dickinson: Major-General: New Jersey Militia-Revolutionary Service', *Magazine of American History*, 7 (December 1881), 420–7.
42 Cornelius William Stafford (ed.), *The Philadelphia Directory... 1799* (Philadelphia: William W. Woodward, 1799), p. 45.

the Third Presbyterian Church at Arch Street, Philadelphia.[43]

E

Ellis, David

In 1802 David Ellis was listed in the *Philadelphia Directory* as a merchant located above 16 Stampers Alley, Philadelphia.[44]

Evans, Cadwallader

In 1802 two Cadwallader Evans were listed in the *Philadelphia Directory*. The first was the owner of a boarding house located at 107 North Second Street, while the second was a merchant located at 80 North Eighth Street, and 23 Chestnut Street, Philadelphia.[45]

Evans, Cadwallader Jr (1762–1841)

Cadwallader Evans Jr was the son of John and Margaret, and was born at Gwynedd on 25 December 1762. He relocated to Philadelphia in 1812 and died there in 1841. After receiving a good education he embarked on a career as a surveyor. He was elected to the Legislature in 1790 and was chosen for Montgomery County between 1790 and 1798. In 1798 he was unanimously chosen to be Speaker of the House. He was again elected to serve Montgomery County in 1802 and 1805, and in 1814 represented Philadelphia as one of the city members.

In 1813 he sought the construction of a canal along the Schuylkill and was elected the first president of the Schuylkill Navigation Company. In 1816 he became a local director of the Bank of the United States. As a tribute to Evans, Joseph Foulke remarked that he began 'his distinguished career about the 18th or 19th year of his age... He was a man of quick and clear perception, of ready utterance, and a powerful

---

43   Historical Society of Pennsylvania, *Philadelphia County Wills, 1682–1819* (Philadelphia: Historical Society of Pennsylvania, 1900).
44   Robinson (ed.), *The Philadelphia Directory... 1802*, p. 81.
45   Robinson (ed.), *The Philadelphia Directory... 1802*, p. 83.

disputant; he was eminently gifted in conveyancing, and in drawing instruments of writing.'[46]

Evans, Peter

Peter Evans was the proprietor of several taverns in Philadelphia. In 1808 he was located at the corner of Schuylkill High and Front Streets, while in 1817 he was recorded as occupying the City Hotel on the N. W. corner of Chestnut and Seventh Streets, Philadelphia.[47]

F

Foulke, Caleb

Caleb Foulke was a merchant (c.1791) who was located at 293 High Street, Philadelphia. He was again recorded in the 1798 directory at the same address.[48]

Foulke, Caleb Jun[r]

In the 1798 *Philadelphia Directory*, Caleb and Owen Foulke are recorded as merchants located at 125 High Street, Philadelphia.[49]

Foulke, Charles

In the 1817 *Philadelphia Directory*, Charles Foulke is specified as a merchant located at 8 Sansom Street, Philadelphia.[50]

---

46 See Howard M. Jenkins, *Historical Collections Relating to Gwynedd, Pennsylvania* (Philadelphia: Ferris Brothers, 1884), chap. 27.
47 Robinson (ed.), *The Philadelphia Directory... 1808*, unpaginated; Robinson (ed.), *Robinson's Original Annual Directory... 1817*, p. 162.
48 Clement Biddle (ed.), *The Philadelphia Directory ... 1791* (Philadelphia: James & Johnson, 1791), p. 42; Cornelius W. Stafford (ed.), *The Philadelphia Directory... 1798* (Philadelphia: William W. Woodward, 1798), p. 57.
49 Stafford (ed.), *The Philadelphia Directory... 1798*, p. 57.
50 Robinson (ed.), *Robinson's Original Annual Directory... 1817*, p. 174.

Foulke, Owen

In the 1798 *Philadelphia Directory*, Caleb and Owen Foulke are recorded as merchants located at 125 High Street, Philadelphia.[51]

Freeman, Tristram B.

Tristram B. Freeman was an auctioneer and, in 1795, settled in Philadelphia. In this year John Nicholson, a revolutionary war financier, became a business partner in T. B. Freeman & Company. In 1800 the Company began retailing and wholesaling from 136 Market Street, Philadelphia.[52]

G

Garrigues, Benjamin F. (1761–1845)

Benjamin Franklin Garrigues was born c.1761 in Philadelphia, and he was the son of Samuel and Mary. On 4 August 1784 he married Elizabeth Emslie. He was recorded as a chocolate maker c. 1791 with a property at 133 South Second Street, Philadelphia, and simply a merchant (c.1808) with a property on 11 Pine Street, Philadelphia. He died on 5 January 1845.[53]

Gibson, Thomas

In 1802 Thomas Gibson was listed in the *Philadelphia Directory* as a fruiterer located at Tapers Alley, Philadelphia.[54]

---

51 Stafford (ed.), *The Philadelphia Directory... 1798*, p. 57.
52 For details of T. B. Freeman & Company see http://www.freemansauction.com/timeline.asp [accessed 9 July 2021].
53 HC, PhM.P466.01.009, Philadelphia Monthly Meeting, Southern District Marriages, 1773–1846, p. 15; HC, PhM.P466.01.007, Philadelphia Monthly Meeting, Southern District Record of Interments, Vol. 2, 1807–72, p. 69; Biddle (ed.), *The Philadelphia Directory ... 1791*, p. 45; James Robinson (ed.), *The Philadelphia Directory ... 1808* (Philadelphia: William W. Woodward, 1808), unpaginated.
54 Robinson (ed.), *The Philadelphia Directory... 1802*, p. 98.

Gillaspy, George

George Gillaspy, a surgeon to the Second Infantry (c.1797), was appointed by the War Department as one of the first American naval physicians and, in the autumn of 1797, he was a surgeon onboard the frigate, *United States*. Returning to Philadelphia he established a medical practice with Joseph C. Strong, but he was kept on by the Navy as he supplied them with medical equipment until his discharge in April 1801.[55]

Glentworth, James

In 1817 he was recorded in the *Philadelphia Directory* as port surveyor located on the south-east corner of Dock and Walnut Streets, Philadelphia.[56]

Glentworth, James Jr

In 1817 he was recorded in the *Philadelphia Directory* as being located on the south-east corner of Dock and Walnut Streets, Philadelphia.[57]

Grice, Samuel

In 1831 the *Philadelphia Directory* recorded Samuel Grice as a ship builder located on Penn near Marsh.[58]

Griffith, Elijah

Elijah Griffith was a physician who, in 1802, was located at 48 North

---

55 Harold Langley, *A History of Medicine in the Early U. S. Navy* (Baltimore, MD: Johns Hopkins Press, 1995), chap. 2; André B. Sobocinski, 'The Formative Years of the U.S. Navy Medical Corps, 1798–1871', provided at: https://www.history.navy.mil/content/history/nhhc/browse-by-topic/communities/navy-medicine/navy-med-history.html#56 [accessed 18 April 2021].
56 Robinson (ed.), *Robinson's Original Annual Directory... 1817*, p. 196.
57 Robinson (ed.), *Robinson's Original Annual Directory... 1817*, p. 196.
58 DeSilver (ed.), *DeSilver's Philadelphia Directory and Strangers Guide... 1831*, p. 83.

Second Street, Philadelphia.[59] For his Doctor of Medicine thesis (obtained c.1804) he outlined the condition known as ophthalmia.[60]

H

Haines, John

In 1802 there were two entries for John Haines, an innkeeper. The first located on Little Seventh Street, and the second 62 North Fourth Street, Philadelphia.[61]

Hallowell, John (1768–1839)

John Hallowell was born on 10 September 1768 and was the son of Israel and Mary, Quakers. He was educated at the Friends' Academy in Philadelphia and the University of Pennsylvania, but he did not graduate. He studied law under Miers Fisher in Philadelphia and on 17 March 1788 he was admitted to the Bar. Initially he was an attorney in the Court of Common Pleas in Philadelphia and between 1816 and 1817 he was a member of the state House of Representatives in Harrisburg. He was later (c. January 1820) President and Judge of the Court of Common Pleas of Philadelphia, and five years later was appointed as a Judge of the District Court of Pennsylvania (22 April 1825). Apart from his membership of the Welsh Society, he was the Treasurer of the Managers Committee for the Friends' Asylum for the Insane in Frankford, Pennsylvania. He resigned his membership of the Welsh Society in 1837 due to ill-health and died from a second stroke on 17 January 1839.[62]

---

59 Robinson (ed.), *The Philadelphia Directory... 1802*, p. 105. Also, see HSP, Amb.3825. Elijah Griffith Ledger 1801–14 which offers an insight into the patients he treated, the treatments used, and his fees.
60 Elijah Griffith, *An Essay on Ophthalmia or Inflammation of the Eyes. Dissertation for the Degree of Doctor of Medicine* (Philadelphia: H. Maxwell, 1804).
61 Robinson (ed.), *The Philadelphia Directory... 1802*, p. 105
62 www.findagrave.com/memorial/161284612/john-hallowell [accessed 16 July 2021].

Hamilton, James (1752-1819)

James Hamilton was born in 1752 in Ireland, but emigrated to America and settled in Carlisle, Cumberland County, Pennsylvania (c. 1780), where he was part of Robert Magaw's legal team. Hamilton later took over the practice. He was a Constitutionalist and Jeffersonian Republican, and, in 1802, he was appointed by President Jefferson as the deputy-attorney general for Western Pennsylvania. He was also President Judge of Pennsylvania's Ninth Judicial District and a trustee of Dickinson College.[63] He died in 1819.

Hamilton, William (1745-1813)

An honorary member of the Welsh Society of Philadelphia, William Hamilton was the grandson of Andrew Hamilton (c.1676-1741), a Philadelphian lawyer and political figure in the first half of the eighteenth century. William was a significant landholder whose estate 'stretched from the Schuylkill River on the east to present-day Forty-Third Street on the west, and from present-day Market Street on the north to the present-day Woodlands Cemetery on the south'. In 1808 he produced plans to subdivide his estate and establish 'Hamilton Village'.[64] He died in 1813.

Higbee, Joseph

In 1802 Joseph Higbee is recorded as merchant located at 64 South Fifth Street, and another entry suggests a partnership (Higbee and Milnor, merchants) located at 57 South Wharves, Philadelphia.[65]

---

63 Hamilton's papers and legal correspondence with leading eighteenth-century Americans are housed at HSP, MS. 1612, James Hamilton Collection. See https://hsp.org/sites/default/files/legacy_files/migrated/findingaid1612hamilton.pdf [accessed 1 June 2021].

64 For full details of Hamilton, his estate, including the plans for Hamilton Village, and his wider family see West Philadelphia Community History Center, 'West Philadelphia: The History – Pre-History to 1854', https://westphillyhistory.archives.upenn.edu/history/chapter-1 [accessed 4 June 2021)].

65 Robinson (ed.), *The Philadelphia Directory... 1802*, p. 117.

Hollingsworth, Paschall (c.1773–1852)

Paschall Hollingsworth was born c.1773. In 1817 he was recorded in the *Philadelphia Directory* as a merchant located at 120 Spruce Street.[66] He died in Philadelphia on 17 May 1852.

Hopkinson, Joseph (1770–1842)

Joseph Hopkinson was born in Philadelphia on 12 November 1770, and he was the son of Francis Hopkinson, a signer of the Declaration of Independence, a member of the Continental Congress and the first United States District Judge for Pennsylvania. He was educated at the University of Pennsylvania and was admitted to the bar and practiced in Philadelphia and Easton, Pennsylvania, from 1791 to 1814. In 1794 Joseph married Emily, the daughter of Governor of Pennsylvania Thomas Mifflin. In 1802 Joseph Hopkinson is recorded as an attorney at law located at Chestnut Street above Fourth Street, Philadelphia. He was elected as a Federalist to the Fourteenth Congress and re-elected to the succeeding Congress (4 March 1815 to 3 March 1819), and he was a United States District Judge of the United States District Court for the Eastern District of Pennsylvania (1828–42). Among his many public roles, Joseph was President of the Pennsylvania Academy of the Fine Arts and Vice-President of the American Philosophical Society (elected in 1815). He wrote the anthem *Hail, Columbia* in 1798. He died in Philadelphia on 15 January 1842 and was buried in the old Borden-Hopkinson Burial Ground, Bordentown, New Jersey.[67]

Huddell, Joseph (1764–1842)

Joseph Huddell Jr was born on 29 May 1764 and was a lumber merchant

---

66   Robinson (ed.), *Robinson's Original Annual Directory... 1817*, p. 223.
67   Burton Alva Konkle, *Joseph Hopkinson, 1770–1842, Jurist-Scholar-Inspirer of the Arts* (Philadelphia: University of Pennsylvania Press, 1931); National Portrait Gallery, NPG.84.108, Smithsonian Institution, Washington, D.C. John Sartain, 'Joseph Hopkinson, c.1832–5'; 'Hopkinson, Joseph, 1770–1842', Biographical Directory of the United States Congress and provided at: https://bioguide.congress.gov/search/bio/H000784 [accessed 4 July 2021]; Robinson (ed.), *The Philadelphia Directory... 1802*, p. 121.

who owned property in c.1802 on 362 South Front Street, Philadelphia. He died, aged 77, on 19 April 1842.[68]

Humphreys, Clement

Clement Humphreys was the head inspector and measurer of lumber. In 1802 he was located at 48 Spruce Street, Philadelphia.[69]

Humphreys, Joshua (1751–1838)

Joshua Humphreys was born in Haverford, Delaware County, Pennsylvania, on 17 June 1751. His grandfather, Daniel Humphreys, was a Quaker emigrant who settled in Haverford in 1682. Joshua was apprenticed as a ship carpenter in Philadelphia, but he was forced to take over the business upon the untimely death of his mentor. He was quickly recognised for his talents and was regarded as the foremost naval architect in America. With the need to construct a navy after the adoption of the Constitution of the United States, Humphreys was regularly in correspondence with Robert Morris and General Henry Knox, the secretary of war, who accepted his proposal for new ships on 6 January 1793. He thereby built six frigates of the United States Navy and is recognised as the father of the American navy. He died in Philadelphia on 12 January 1838.[70]

---

68 Robinson (ed.), *The Philadelphia Directory... 1802*, p. 123.
69 Robinson (ed.), *The Philadelphia Directory... 1802*, p. 124.
70 Humphreys's papers are extant and they are housed at HSP, MSS. 0306, Joshua Humphreys Papers, 1660–1931. For further details see Anon., 'Letters from the Joshua Humphreys Collection of the Historical Society of Pennsylvania', *PMHB*, 30 (1906), 376–8, 503; Henry H. Humphreys, 'Who Built the First United States Navy?', *Journal of American History*, 10 (1916), 49–89; James J. Farley, '"To Commit Ourselves to Our Own Ingenuity and Industry": Joshua Humphreys and the Construction of the United States, 1794–1799', *Explorations in Early American Culture*, 5 (2001), 288–327. Farley has also written a lengthy online biography of Humphreys, see '"To Commit Ourselves to Our Own Ingenuity: Joshua Humphreys – Early Philadelphia Ship Building', [accessed 15 July 2021].

Humphreys, Samuel

In 1817 Samuel Humphreys was recorded in the *Philadelphia Directory* as a shipbuilder located at 240 Swanson Street, Philadelphia.[71]

Humphreys, Thomas

In 1817 a Thomas Humphreys is recorded as being a shipwright located at Cherry near Queen, Philadelphia.[72]

Hunt, Pearson

Pearson Hunt was a merchant who, in 1802, was located at 57 South Wharves, 62 South Fifth Street, Philadelphia.[73]

Hunt, Wilson

Wilson Hunt was a merchant who, in 1802, was located at 16 South Front Street, Philadelphia.[74]

J

James, Thomas Chalkley (1766–1835)

Thomas Chalkley James was the son of Abel, a successful Welsh emigrant Quaker merchant, and Rebecca James, the daughter of Thomas Chalkley, the Quaker preacher. He was born in Philadelphia on 31 August 1766 and in 1802 married Hannah Morris. He was educated in Friends' schools, notably at Robert Proud's school, and studied medicine under Dr Adam Kuhn. In 1787 James received his M.B. from the University of the State of Pennsylvania and in 1811 his M.D. from the Medical Department of the University of Pennsylvania. Between 1788 and 1790 he was Ship's Surgeon on a voyage to the Cape of Good

---

71   Robinson (ed.), *Robinson's Original Annual Directory... 1817*, p. 232.
72   Robinson (ed.), *Robinson's Original Annual Directory... 1817*, p. 233.
73   Robinson (ed.), *The Philadelphia Directory... 1802*, p. 124.
74   Robinson (ed.), *The Philadelphia Directory... 1802*, p. 125.

Hope and thereafter completed his studies in the United Kingdom, notably in London at St George's Hospital and the Story Street lying-in hospital. At the latter he studied obstetrics under Dr Thomas Osborne and Dr John Hunter, FRS. A year before returning to Philadelphia in 1793 he went to the University of Edinburgh and attended a series of chemistry lectures given by Joseph Black. The following year, after a military expedition to the West, he established his own practice.

Along with John Church, in 1802 he began to lecture on midwifery in the Philadelphia Almshouse, and between 1807 and 1808 was assisted by Nathaniel Chapman. These lectures were the foundation of a lecture course on midwifery at the University of Pennsylvania given between 1810 and 1834. James also set up the lying-in ward at the Almshouse and was a physician to the Pennsylvania Hospital between 1807 and 1810, and from 1810 until his death the obstetric physician. He was elected to the Fellowship of the College of Physicians of Philadelphia on 6 October 1795, and was their secretary between 1796 and 1802, Treasurer between 1809 and 1826, Vice-President from 1826 to 1835, and just prior to his death, he was President of the College. Alongside his many medical pursuits he penned several anonymous poems and essays, and between 1811 and 1822 he was the editor of the *Eclectic Repertory*. This was a publication that sought out and published abstracts and articles from foreign medical journals. James was also the founder of the Historical Society of Pennsylvania. He died on 5 July 1835 in Philadelphia.[75]

Jones, Israel

In 1802 the *Philadelphia Directory* recorded that Israel Jones & David were grocers on 4 South Fifth Street, Philadelphia.[76]

---

75 The above information is largely derived from Hugh L. Hodge, *A Memoir of Thomas C. James, M.D. Read Before the College of Physicians of Philadelphia* (Philadelphia: T. K. and P. G. Collins, 1843).
76 Robinson (ed.), *The Philadelphia Directory... 1802*, p. 132.

Jones, Richard C. (c.1767–1809)

Richard C. Jones was born c.1767. He was a Philadelphian merchant of Bickleys Wharf and a steward/secretary of the Welsh Society who had a lengthy testimony written upon his death in 1809. He was instrumental in helping the sick during the Yellow Fever epidemic in the late 1790s. He died after a short illness on 9 January 1809. His will (proved 12 January 1809) stated that he wanted all his estate, real and personal, to be looked after by Thomas Cumpston and Joseph S. Lewis, two members of the Welsh Society, in trust for his brother William J. Jones.[77]

Jones, William

In 1802 the *Philadelphia Directory* recorded several William Joneses, but the merchant located at 144 South Fourth Street, Philadelphia, is the most likely entry.[78]

K

Kinsey, Edmund

Edmund Kinsey was a saddler with a business in 1799 located at 19 Carter's Alley, Philadelphia. In 1817 he was the leader of the Philadelphia Society for the Promotion of American Manufacturers.[79]

L

Lassalle, Stephen B. (1796–1854)

Stephen Beasley Lassalle was born in Philadelphia in 1796, and in c.1831 was the owner of an iron foundry located on High East of

---

77 Robinson (ed.), *The Philadelphia Directory... 1802*, p. 133; Historical Society of Pennsylvania, *Philadelphia County Wills, 1682–1819*.
78 Robinson (ed.), *The Philadelphia Directory... 1802*, p. 133.
79 Stafford (ed.), *The Philadelphia Directory... 1799*, p. 81. For details of the Society see Mathew Carey, *National Interests and Domestic Manufactures: Addresses of the Philadelphia Society for the Promotion of Domestic Industry, to the Citizens of the United States* (Boston: William W. Clapp, 1819).

Schuylkill on Seventh Street and had a dwelling house on 51 South Thirteenth Street, Philadelphia. He died, aged 58, on 8 March 1854 in Philadelphia.[80]

Lewis, Joseph Saunders (1778–1836)

Joseph S. Lewis was the son of Mordecai Lewis. He was Chairman of the Schuylkill Navigation Company and the Fairmount Water Works. He presided over the project of converting to waterpower at Fairmount, which led to the building of a dam and water works on the Schuylkill river at Fairmount. This dam was the main source of water supply for Philadelphia for many years. A monument to his memory, erected at Laurel Hill, stated:

> Erected, by Grateful Fellow-Citizens and Friends, To the Memory of JOSEPH S. LEWIS, Who long and faithfully presided over The Schuylkill Navigation Company, And the Fairmount Water Works. He originated the latter, and by his persevering and disinterested exertions, brought to a completion that great Public Work, which, for magnificence of conception, simplicity and solidity of execution, and unmixed character of beneficence, is worthy of being placed amongst the noblest achievements of enlightened Civic Enterprise. His remains fitly repose in this spot, on the River rendered by his labors a source of Prosperity, Health and Safety to his Native City. Born, May 9th, 1778. Died, March 13th, 1836.[81]

Lewis, Mordecai (1748–99)

Mordecai Lewis was born in Philadelphia on 21 September 1748 and died on 13 March 1799. His great-grandfather was William Lewis, a

---

80 Philadelphia City Archives, Death Records: Philadelphia City Death Certificates, 1803–1915, Index; DeSilver (ed.), *DeSilver's Philadelphia Directory... 1831*, p. 117.
81 For details see Thomas Gilpin, 'Fairmount Dam and Water Works, Philadelphia', *PMHB*, 37/4 (1913), 471–9.

Quaker from Glamorgan in Wales (?-1707) who emigrated in 1686 and purchased land in Newton Township, Chester County. Mordecai's grandfather was Evan Lewis (?-1734), another well-known Quaker who acted as a representative of the Newtown meeting to the Philadelphia Yearly Meeting. Mordecai's father, Jonathan, was the younger of Evan's two sons, and settled in Philadelphia as a merchant in 1747, but died young. Jonathan's widow was Rachel, the daughter of John Breintnall, who continued to look after her son and two daughters. Mordecai was a model student and, among other academic subjects, was proficient in Latin. He was offered a position in Samuel Neave's counting-house and later joined forces with Neave and Jacob Harman to form Neave, Harman and Lewis, ship-owners and importers. Eventually, along with William Bingham, he established Lewis and Company and was engaged in the East India trade.

In 1772 he travelled to Europe and, upon his return, he married Hannah, daughter of Joseph Saunders, a merchant, of Philadelphia, on 7 January 1773 with whom he had seven children. From a Quaker background he was decidedly uneasy about the growing tension concerning British governance of the Colonies. In 1775 he was a volunteer in the military company organised in Philadelphia, but never entered active service. Prior to this his name was emblazoned on Provincial paper money as well as on Continental currency sanctioned by Congress in February 1776. Like many others members of the Welsh Society he was active in other public arenas, including the Philadelphia Library Company, Treasurer of the Pennsylvania Hospital, a directorship of the Bank of North America and the Philadelphia Contributionship for the Insurance of Houses from Loss by Fire. Upon his death in 1799 the executors of his will (Thomas Morris, Samuel Coates, and Joseph Morris) wrote a letter on 27 March 1799 to his business associates in London stating his 'general character for integrity as a merchant, in his very extensive commercial concerns, his unobtrusive benevolence to those who stood in need of his advice or assistance, and the dedication of his time and his valuable talents, in most of our public institutions of merit, as well as his application of them to the benefit of individuals in the settlement of intricate subjects of dispute, have left on the public mind a sense of loss sustained, such as has rarely occurred in our observation. Among his friends who had a more intimate knowledge of him in the private walks of life, his death has left a void more easily imagined than described.'[82]

Lewis, Samuel N. (1785–1841)

Samuel Neave Lewis was born in 1785 in Philadelphia, and he was the son of Mordecai and Hannah (Saunders) Lewis, Quakers. He became a well-known Philadelphia merchant, ship owner, and white lead manufacturer. He was later a Treasurer of the Pennsylvania Hospital and Treasurer of the State in Schuylkill. He died in 1841.[83]

M

Maddock, Ezekiel C.

In 1802 the *Philadelphia Directory* recorded Ezekiel Maddock as a merchant of 313 High Street, Philadelphia.[84]

Maddock, William L.

In 1802 the *Philadelphia Directory* recorded William Maddock as a grocer of 51 Spruce Street, Philadelphia.[85]

Maris, Richard (1772–1817)

Richard Maris was a son of Jesse and Margaret (Edwards) Maris, Quakers, and born on 19 December 1772 at 'Home House', Springfield, Chester County (now Delaware County). On 3 October 1793 the

---

82 For the business records of Mordecai and his family see HSP, MSS. 1735, Leonard T. Beale Collection, 1746–1892. See also Frank Cousins and Phil M. Riley, *The Colonial Architecture of Philadelphia* (Boston: Little, Brown, and Company, 1920), p. 45.
83 'No. 151. Mrs Samuel Neave Lewis, 1790–1866, and her daughter, Martha S. 1810–1877', in Pennsylvania Academy of Fine Arts, *Catalogue of the Memorial Exhibition of Portraits*, p. 103.
84 Robinson (ed.), *The Philadelphia Directory... 1802*, p. 162.
85 Robinson (ed.), *The Philadelphia Directory... 1802*, p. 162.

Darby Meeting of Friends drew up a certificate of removal for Richard Maris, an apprentice, to remove to Philadelphia. On 29 November 1804 he married Rachel Ross (23 March 1782–5 July 1875) of West Chester. After leaving the Darby Meeting, he later became a prosperous merchant in Philadelphia. Maris died on 5 February 1817.[86]

Meredith, Samuel (1741–1817)

Samuel Meredith, the son of Rhys (Reese), a Welsh Quaker from Radnorshire who became a Philadelphian merchant, and Martha (Carpenter) Meredith. Samuel was born in Philadelphia in 1741 and studied at Dr Allison's Academy before joining the family business. In later life he became a prosperous merchant and land speculator. This enterprise was expanded in the 1760s when he entered into partnership with his brother-in-law George Clymer,[87] notably in Delaware, eastern Kentucky, New York, northeastern Pennsylvania, and western Virginia. On 19 May 1772 Samuel married Margaret Cadwallader and they had six children.

He became more involved in public life when he signed the non-importation resolutions in Philadelphia in 1765, and in 1775 was a Philadelphian deputy at the Provincial Convention. As a close confidant of George Washington, he financially supported the war effort from 1776. In the War of Independence, he was as an officer of the 3rd Battalion of Associators (the 'Silk Stocking Company'), and later became a General in the Continental Army and fought at Trenton, Princeton, Brandywine and Germantown. On 5 April 1777 he was promoted to brigadier-general of the Pennsylvania militia. The following year he resigned his command and returned to his mercantile business.

---

86   See Agnes Longstreth Taylor, *The Longstreth Family Records* (Philadelphia: Press of Ferris & Leach, 1909), p. 132; 'No. 81 Mrs Richard Maris, 1782–1875 and son, George G. Maris, 1810–1887', in Pennsylvania Academy of Fine Arts, *Catalogue of the Memorial Exhibition of Portraits*, p. 56. His portrait was painted by Charles Balthazar Julien Févret de Saint-Mémin (1770–1852).
87   Clymer married Elizabeth Meredith in 1765.

Meredith was a member of the Pennsylvania Colonial Assembly three times (1778–83) as well as a Member of the Continental Congress between 1786 and 1788. He was also briefly the surveyor of the Port of Philadelphia, before accepting Washington's appointment as the first United States Treasurer under the new Constitution, a position he held from 11 September 1789 until his resignation on 31 October 1801. During this period Meredith loaned the government a sum in advance of $100,000 which was never repaid. He relocated on a number of occasions, living in Northeastern Pennsylvania, and residing in Carbondale Township in Lackawanna County. He died on 10 February 1817 on his estate, Belmont Manor, near Pleasant Mount in Wayne County, and is interred in a private cemetery.[88]

Meredith, William (1772–1844)

William Tuckey Meredith was born in 1772 and was the son of Jonathan and Elizabeth (Tuckey) Meredith. In 1795 he married the poet Gertrude Gouverneur Ogden (1777–1828). He was a lawyer in Philadelphia and died in 1844.[89]

Miles, Samuel (1740–1805)

Samuel Miles was born at Whitemarsh, Montgomery County, Pennsylvania, on 11 March 1739. He was the son of James Miles II and Hannah Miles (*née* Pugh). He was part of Isaac Wayne's company during the French and Indian War. Although wounded at the Battle of Fort Ligonier, he later commanded the garrison there. In his second

---

88 See *Dictionary of American Biography* (New York: Charles Scribner's Sons, 1961), *Vol. 6* (entry: Meredith, Samuel); Richard C. Allen, 'Samuel Meredith (1741–1817): American Patriot and Welsh Philanthropist', in Maurice Jackson and Susan Kozel (eds), *Quakers and their Allies in the Abolitionist Cause, 1754–1808* (London: Routledge, 2015), pp. 73–84, 167–75.

89 His papers (mixed with those of his son, William Morris Meredith 1799–1873, Secretary of the Treasury, 1849–50 and Attorney General of Pennsylvania, 1861–7) are housed at HSP, MSS. 3302, William Meredith Legal Papers. Also, see HSP, MSS. 1509, Meredith Family Papers, 1756–1964.

enlistment he joined Thomas Lloyd's company as a sergeant before being promoted to captain-lieutenant during the expedition to Fort Duquesne. In 1760 he was a captain commanding the garrison on Presque Isle (now Erie), Pennsylvania. A successful career beckoned as a wine merchant after the war ended, while he also turned his attention to political matters. In 1772 he was elected to the House of Assembly and would promote the cause for independence. During this period, he married Catherine Wister, a daughter of John Wister of Grumblethorpe, Philadelphia.

During the revolution, he raised a militia and was promoted to Colonel of the Pennsylvania State Rifle Regiment but was captured at the Battle of Long Island. During his incarceration he was promoted to Brigadier General of Pennsylvania troops and was released in April 1778 during a prisoner swap whereby he had to swear not to take up arms. Accepting this as a matter of honour, he turned his attention to equipping the army and became Quartermaster for the State of Pennsylvania.

After the war ended Miles turned his attention to his business interests and, in 1783, he owned a sugar refinery on 77 Vine Street, Philadelphia, with Colonel Jacob Morgan. Alongside Robert Morris he helped finance the voyage of the *Empress of China* to mainland China – the first American vessel to visit the country. From the 1790s onwards Miles was active in the political arena and in public service. Between 1790 and 1791 he was a Judge of the High Court of Errors and Appeals in 1783 and was Mayor of Philadelphia (1790). He was re-elected again as mayor but declined to serve in this office. He ran for Congress twice (1798) as a Democratic-Republican, but he lost to the Federalist Robert Waln.

Miles was also a trustee of the University of Pennsylvania, a member of the American Philosophical Society and a zealous member of the First Baptist Church of Philadelphia. Milesburg in Centre County, Pennsylvania, was named after him as he helped to establish the Centre Furnace Iron Works, along with Colonel John Patton and John Dunlop. He died on 29 December 1805 and was buried in the First Baptist

Church, Philadelphia.[90]

Morgan, Benjamin Rawle (1765–1840)

Benjamin Rawle Morgan was born in Gloucester County, New Jersey, in 1765, but relocated to Philadelphia. He was a lawyer and was admitted to the Bar in 1785 and in 1821 he was a judge on the District Court. He was also a candidate for the Pennsylvania state senate. He was well-known and respected for his philanthropic and political endeavours, including acting as a trustee of the University of Pennsylvania from 1797 until his death in 1840. He also served as a secretary of the Library Company from 1792 to 1825 and as a director between 1825 and 1840. In 1805 he was among the founders of the Pennsylvania Academy of the Fine Arts. In 1819, along with John C. Smith, he was assignee to Robert Waln and Gideon Hill Wells's Eagle Factory in New Jersey. His portrait was painted by Jacob Eichholtz (1776–1842) in 1823. It is among the collections of the Library Company of Philadelphia.[91]

Morgan, Jacob (1742–1802)

Jacob Morgan was born in Caernarvon township, Berks County, in 1742 to Jacob Morgan Senior. He was an Ensign in the British army during the French and Indian War (1754–1763) and was later promoted to the rank of Lieutenant in the 2nd Battalion of Regulators. Like many of the early members of the Society he was an active participant in the revolution. On 4 December 1776 he was appointed by the Philadelphia Executive Council as a Colonel and commander of the First Battalion of Associators of the City of Philadelphia and Northern Liberties, and subsequently Colonel of the Third Battalion of Philadelphia

---

90 American Philosophical Society, MSS. B.M589, Samuel Miles Papers, 1776–1802; 'Colonel Samuel Miles', *Centinel* (Gettysburg, Pennsylvania), 5 February 1805, p. 3; 'Auto-Biographical Sketch of Col. Samuel Miles', *American Historical Record*, 2 (1873), 49–53, 114–18. In 1860 Miles may have been reinterred at Mount Moriah Cemetery, Philadelphia.

91 For details of his business dealings see HSP, MSS. 1628, Smith and Waln family papers, 1774–1891; HSP, Am.9415, Benjamin R. Morgan Letterbook, 1830–40.

Associators in the Continental Army. He fought in the Battles of Princeton and Monmouth and was promoted to a General. In 1780 he was appointed as Superintendent of the Commissioners of Purchases for the Continental Army and was the Wagon-Master for the State of Pennsylvania. These two posts he retained until the end of the war. After the war, he developed a sugar refinery business with his son-in-law, Alexander Douglass. He was Vice-President of the Welsh Society between 1798 and 1800. He died in Philadelphia on 18 September 1802.[92]

Morris, Richard Hill (1762–1841)

Richard Hill Morris, the son of William and Margaret (Moore) Hill, was born on 5 September 1762 in Philadelphia. On 17 March 1786, Richard Hill Morris married Mary Mifflin and after her death he married his second wife Mary Smith on 25 October 1798. A successful businessman,[93] in 1818 he was appointed as President of the Philadelphia Stock Exchange. He died on 6 December 1841 in the city.

Morris, Robert (1734–1806)

Robert Morris, a merchant, was the son of Robert Morris Sr and Elizabeth Murphet, and was born in Liverpool, England, on 20 January 1734. Along with his family, Morris emigrated to America when he was fourteen. Thereafter he joined his father's firm, before becoming a partner in a mercantile firm: Willing, Morris and Company. As a patriot, Morris has been recognised as helping to finance the War for American Independence and signed the Declaration of Independence, the Articles of Confederation, and the United States Constitution. He was a delegate to the Continental Congress and chaired secret committees

---

92   See Morton Luther Montgomery, *History of Berks County, Pennsylvania: in the Revolution, from 1774 to 1783* (Reading, Pa.: C. F. Haage, 1894); 'Philadelphia City Revolutionary War Militia', provided at https://www.phmc.pa.gov/Archives/Research-Online/Pages/Revolutionary-War-Militia-Philadelphia-City.aspx [accessed 4 July 2021].

93   For example, in 1804 he owned a sugar refinery at 13 Church Alley, Philadelphia. See *United States' Gazette*, 17 March 1804, p. 3.

on trade and correspondence. This committee secured military supplies for the war. Although declared a bankrupt by Congress in 1781, he helped finance General Washington's troops and after the war, he issued 'Morris Notes' and repaid his debts. He established the United States first bank and helped finance the transition to a national currency. He was also involved in revising the Pennsylvania Constitution and was a delegate both to the State and as a U.S. Senator from 1789 to 1795. Between 1781 and 1784 Morris was the Superintendent of Finance of the United States and recognised as the 'Financier of the Revolution'. His later years, however, were controversial as he was imprisoned for three and half years due to his debts (c. 1798–1801). He died on 8 May 1806 and is buried in Christ Church graveyard in Philadelphia.[94]

Morris, Thomas (1774–1841)

Thomas Morris was born in 1774 in Philadelphia and was the son of Thomas and Mary (Saunders) Morris. He was descended from a Quaker family and became a brewer in the city. In 1797 he married Sarah Marshall, daughter of Charles and Patience, at Philadelphia Friends' Meeting. He was a member of the State in Schuylkill, manager of the Pennsylvania Hospital, and Treasurer of the Library Company of Philadelphia.[95]

Murdock, Robert

Robert Murdock was in c.1817 a merchant with a property located at 279 South Front Street, Philadelphia.[96]

---

94 For further information see Clarence L. Ver Steeg, *Robert Morris: Revolutionary Financier* (Philadelphia: University of Pennsylvania Press, 1954); James Ferguson (ed.), *The Papers of Robert Morris 1781–1784* (9 vols. Pittsburgh: University of Pittsburgh Press, 1978); Gordon S. Wood, *Empire of Liberty: A History of the Early Republic, 1789–1815* (Oxford: Oxford University Press, 2009); Charles Rappleye, *Robert Morris: Financier of the American Revolution* (London: Simon & Schuster, 2010).
95 'No. 58 Thomas Morris, 1774–1841', in Pennsylvania Academy of Fine Arts, *Catalogue of the Memorial Exhibition of Portraits*, p. 37.
96 Robinson (ed.), *Robinson's Original Annual Directory... 1817*, p. 5.

N

Nichols, William

In the 1802 *Philadelphia Directory* there are two entries for William Nichols. The first is for a merchant located at 117 Sassafras Street, Philadelphia, and the other, a shipwright, at 414 South Second Street, Philadelphia.[97]

Norris, Joseph P. (?–1841)

Joseph Parker Norris was the son of Charles and Mary [Parker] Norris of Philadelphia. He married Elizabeth Hill Fox and had fourteen children. In the 1802 *Philadelphia Directory* there are two entries for Joseph Norris. The first, a gentleman resided at 140 Chestnut Street, Philadelphia, while another was a shipwright located at 157 North Front Street, Philadelphia.[98] He died on 22 June 1841.

North, Joseph

In the 1802 *Philadelphia Directory* there are two entries for Joseph North. The first is for a shopkeeper located at 66 Sassafras North Street, and the other, a chandler, of 86 Union Street, Philadelphia.[99]

O

Ogden, William

William Ogden was an innkeeper whose tavern was used by the Welsh Society in the late 1790s/early 1800s. This was located at 86 Chestnut Street, Philadelphia.[100]

---

97 Robinson (ed.), *The Philadelphia Directory... 1802*, p. 182.
98 Robinson (ed.), *The Philadelphia Directory... 1802*, p. 183.
99 Robinson (ed.), *The Philadelphia Directory... 1802*, p. 183.
100 See Pennsylvania Historical and Museum Commission, Harrisburg, Pa. Records of the House of Representatives; Records of the General Assembly, Record Group 7. Septennial Census Returns, 1779–1863. Box 1026, p. 136 (no. 262). For some contemporary information regarding drinking habits in Philadelphia see Peter Thompson, '"The Friendly Glass": Drink and Gentility in Colonial Philadelphia', *PMHB*, 113/4 (October 1989), 549–73.

PART FOUR

Otto, Jacob S. (?–1826)

From 1821 until his death in 1826 Otto was a local agent for the Holland Land Company. While attending the celebrations for the opening of the Grand Canal in Lockport on 26 October 26 1825 he caught a severe chill and died on 2 May 1826. The town of Otto in Cattaraugus County bears his name.[101]

P

Palmer, John

In the 1802 *Philadelphia Directory* there are two entries for John Palmer. The first is for a merchant located at 76 South Eighth Street, and the other, a shipwright, of 45 Budd Street, Philadelphia.[102]

Parke, Thomas (1749–1835)

Thomas Parke was born in 1749 in Chester County, Pennsylvania, and he was a student under the tutelage of Robert Proud, the historian, before studying medicine under Dr Calwalader Evans. He graduated in 1770 from the College of Philadelphia. In 1771 he toured Europe before returning to Philadelphia in 1773. He was a prominent physician and the founder of the Philadelphia College of Physicians as well as a curator of the American Philosophical Society. He was a director of The Library Company of Philadelphia from 1778 until his death. He died in 1835.[103]

Parrish, Samuel

In 1798 Samuel Parrish was recorded in the *Philadelphia Directory* as a

---

101 See William Chazanof, *Joseph Ellicott and the Holland Land Company* (Syrcause: Syracuse University Press, 1970), pp. 205–6.
102 Robinson (ed.), *The Philadelphia Directory... 1802*, p. 187.
103 For further details see Whitfield J. Bell, 'Thomas Parke, Physician and Friend' in his *The Colonial Physician* (New York: Neale Watson Academic, 1975). For a portrait see 'No. 63 Thomas Parke, M.D. 1749–1835', in Pennsylvania Academy of Fine Arts, *Catalogue of the Memorial Exhibition of Portraits*, p. 42.

merchant located at 17 North Second Street, Philadelphia.[104]

Parry, John J.

In the 1802 John J. Parry was recorded in the *Philadelphia Directory* as a clock and watch maker, located on 58 South Second Street, Philadelphia.[105] He was also the nephew of Hannah Jacobs, the wife of Dr David Rittenhouse. Upon Rittenhouse's death, Parry inherited the instruments of the master clock maker. He was in business between c.1794 and 1835, and had shops on Second Street, High Street, and North Sixth Street.[106]

Perot, Sansom

In 1831 Sansom Perot was recorded in the *Philadelphia Directory* as a merchant located at 41 North Water Street with a dwelling house at 299 High Street, Philadelphia.[107]

Peters, Richard (1744–1828)

Richard Peters was born on 22 June 1744 at Belmont (now Philadelphia's Fairmount Park), and he was the son of William Henry Peters of Liverpool and Mary Breintnall. Between 1776 and 1781 he served as secretary of the Continental Board of War and uncovered Benedict Arnold's appropriation of funds. Consequently, he challenged Arnold to a duel. In 1780 he provided $25,000 to the Bank of Pennsylvania for

---

104 Stafford (ed.), *The Philadelphia Directory... 1798*, p. 110. For further details of the Parrish family see HSP, MSS. 0154, Cox–Parrish–Wharton Family Papers, 1700–1900, including Samuel Parrish's trade records from the 1760s to early 1800s; Swarthmore College Library, Pennsylvania, RG5/229. Parrish Family Papers, 1780–1966. See also Susanna Parrish Wharton, *The Parrish Family...* (Philadelphia: George H. Buchanan, 1925).
105 Robinson (ed.), *The Philadelphia Directory... 1802*, p. 188.
106 Further details extracted from 'John J. Parry, Philadelphia c.1825 Twin Fusee Mahogany Bracket Clock' – advertising the sale in auction. https://adamsbrown.com/wordpress1/antique-clocks-for-sale/shelf-clocks/john-j-parry-philadelphia-c-1820-twin-fusee-mahogany-bracket-clock/ [accessed 10 July 2021].
107 DeSilver (ed.), *DeSilver's Philadelphia Directory... 1831*, p. 166.

the provisioning of the Continental Army as well as serving as a member of Continental Congress (1782–3) and Pennsylvania General Assembly (1787–90). As Speaker of this Assembly, he was an ex officio trustee of the University of the State of Pennsylvania (now the University of Pennsylvania). In 1791 he was elected as Speaker of the Pennsylvania Senate and a judge for the United States District Court of Pennsylvania. This position he held from 1792 to 1828. It was noted that he was 'a kind friend, liberal host, excellent conversationalist, and considerable wit'. He died, aged 84, on 22 August 1828 in Philadelphia.[108]

Potts, Nathan R.

In 1831 Nathan R. Potts was an attorney at law located at 97 Mulberry Street, Philadelphia.[109]

Poulson, Zachariah (1761–1844)

Zachariah Poulson was the son of a Danish immigrant. He was born in Philadelphia on 5 September 1761 and died there on 31 July 1844. He learned his trade as a printer from Christopher Sower in Germantown, Pennsylvania, and was the state printer for a considerable period. On 1 October 1800 until its discontinuance on 28 December 1838 he edited and published the first daily newspaper in America – the *American Daily Advertiser*. From 1789 to 1801 he published *Poulson's Town and Country Almanac*, Robert Proud's *History of Pennsylvania* between 1797 and 1798, the works of William Gerar de Brain, and other texts. Alongside his membership of the Welsh Society, he was a member of several other literary and charitable associations, including being the founding member and President of the Philadelphia Society for Ameliorating the Miseries of Public Prisons (known as the Pennsylvania Prison Society), the Society for Promoting the Abolition of Slavery, and the Pennsylvania Hospital. He was also a member of the

---

108 'Penn People: Richard Peters, 1743–1828', Pennsylvania University Archives and Records Center; https://archives.upenn.edu/exhibits/penn-people/biography/richard-peters-2 [accessed 8 July 2021].
109 DeSilver (ed.), *DeSilver's Philadelphia Directory... 1831*, p. 169.

Library Company of Philadelphia for fifty-eight years. In the latter he was a director for thirty-two years, librarian for twenty-one years, and treasurer for six years.[110]

Preston, William

In the *Philadelphia Directory* for 1802 there are several entries for William Preston. The first was for a shipwright located at 480 South Second Street; the next a boat builder located at 32 Artillery Lane; the third a bricklayer, located next to 229 South Fifth Street; and the final entry was for a carpenter located at 26 Elfriths Alley, Philadelphia.[111]

Price, Chandler (1766–1827)

Chandler Price was born on 22 February 1766 in Trenton, New Jersey. The 1817 *Philadelphia Directory* records him as a merchant of 96 South Front, Philadelphia, with a countinghouse at 41 Dock Street, Philadelphia.[112] He had previously married Helen ('Ellen') Matlack at Christ Church, Philadelphia, on 8 March 1800. He died on 27 December 1827.[113]

Price, John M. (?–c.1828)

The 1817 *Philadelphia Directory* records John M. Price as a merchant

---

110 For further details of Poulson's career see Susan E. Klepp, 'The Demographic Characteristics of Philadelphia, 1788–1801: Zachariah Poulson's Bills of Mortality', *Pennsylvania History*, 53/3 (July, 1986), 201–21. For his portrait see 'No. 221. Zachariah Poulson, 1761–1844', in Pennsylvania Academy of Fine Arts, Catalogue of the Memorial Exhibition of Portraits, p. 171. His portrait, commissioned by the Library Company of Philadelphia in 1843, was painted by Thomas Sully.
111 Robinson (ed.), *The Philadelphia Directory... 1802*, p. 196.
112 Robinson (ed.), *Robinson's Original Annual Directory... 1817*, p. 354; George Norbury Mackenzie and Nelson Osgood Rhoades (eds), *Colonial Families of the United States of America* (7 vols. New York; Boston; Baltimore: Grafton Press; Seaforth Press 1907–1920), VI (1912), p. 383.
113 Anon., *Marriage Record of Christ Church, Philadelphia, 1709–1806* (2 vols. Harrisburg, Pennsylvania: C. M. Busch, 1896), I, p. 207.

of 143 High Street, Philadelphia.[114] He died intestate in 1828.[115]

Price, Joseph

In the 1802 *Philadelphia Directory* there are two Joseph Prices listed. One was a wood sawer located on 41 Cable Lane, the other was a hatter located on 79 High Street, Philadelphia.[116]

Price, Samuel

In 1802 Samuel Price was recorded in the *Philadelphia Directory* as a merchant located on 36 South Front Street, Philadelphia.[117]

R

Randall, Matthew

In 1817 Matthew Randall was recorded in the *Philadelphia Directory* as a recorder of deeds located on 80 Walnut Street, Philadelphia. It is possible that this was Judge Randall who sat on the Philadelphia Court of Common Pleas.[118]

Read, Collinson (1741–1815)

Collinson Read was born in 1741. He was a lawyer in Philadelphia and compiled various legal texts. In 1802 he was located at 125 Saffaras, Philadelphia. He died on 2 March 1815 and is buried at the Charles Evans Cemetery, Reading, Berks County, Pennsylvania.[119]

---

114 Robinson (ed.), *Robinson's Original Annual Directory... 1817*, p. 354.
115 Philadelphia (Pennsylvania). Register of Wills, Book N, No. 55, pp. 184–98. Administration of John M. Price, 1828.
116 Robinson (ed.), *The Philadelphia Directory... 1802*, p. 196.
117 Robinson (ed.), *The Philadelphia Directory... 1802*, p. 197.
118 Robinson (ed.), *Robinson's Original Annual Directory... 1817*, p. 358.
119 Robinson (ed.), *The Philadelphia Directory... 1802*, p. 200; Collinson Read, *An Abridgment of the Laws of Pennsylvania...* (Philadelphia: privately printed, 1801); Collinson Read, *The American Pleader's Assistant: Being a Collection of Approved Declarations, Writs, Returns, and Proceedings in... the United States...* (Philadelphia: Hugh Maxwell; New York: I. Riley & Co., 1806).

Read, James

According to the 1802 *Philadelphia Directory*, James Read was a merchant who lived at 1 North Alley, Philadelphia.[120]

Read, James Jr

Presumably, the son of James Read, the merchant of Philadelphia (above).

Read, John Jr

According to the 1802 *Philadelphia Directory*, John Read was an attorney at law on 36 North Fourth Street, Philadelphia.[121]

Read, William

There are two entries cited in the *1802 Philadelphia Directory*. The first was a merchant located at 135 South Front, Philadelphia, and the other, another merchant, located at 190 South Second Street, Philadelphia.[122]

Relf, Samuel (1776–1823)

Samuel Relf, the son of John Relf and Ann King, was born in Virginia on 22 March 1776. Along with his mother he came to Philadelphia as a child and is best known as the editor and owner (until 1819) of the *National Gazette*. Apart from his journalistic skills, he was an accomplished writer and he was author of a novel. He died on 14 February 1823.[123]

Renshaw, William (1771–1824)

William Renshaw was born on 1 May 1771 in London, England. He had emigrated to Philadelphia in August 1804 and initially opened the Exchange Coffee House (c.1806) on the corner of Third and Spruce

---

120 Robinson (ed.), *The Philadelphia Directory... 1802*, p. 200.
121 Robinson (ed.), *The Philadelphia Directory... 1802*, p. 200.
122 Robinson (ed.), *The Philadelphia Directory... 1802*, p. 200.
123 Samuel Relf, *Infidelity; or, the Victims of Sentiment. A Novel, in a Series of Letters* (Philadelphia: W. W. Woodward, 1797); Sarah Knott, *Sensibility and the American Revolution* (Chapel Hill: University of North Carolina Press, 2009), pp. 297–306, 309–10.

Streets, Philadelphia. He was persuaded to opened the Mansion House Hotel in 1807, located at 122 Third Street, between Walnut and Spruce Streets, Philadelphia. It was, according to the reports of the period, a very fashionable house. In 1812 Renshaw moved to a new location on Eleventh and Market Streets, but he returned to the former residence in 1814. His second property was known as Washington Hall Hotel (122 South Third Street, Philadelphia) until it was destroyed by fire. He died on 14 March 1824 in Long Branch, Monmouth, New Jersey.[124]

Rhees/Rhys, Morgan John (1760–1804)

John Morgan Rhys (Rhees) was born on 8 December 1760 and was the fourth son of John and Elizabeth Rhys. He initially lived at 'Graddfa', a farm-house, near Llanbradach in Glamorganshire. He was educated at a school kept by David Williams (1709–84) and later at Carmarthen. Between 1780 and 1786 he taught at Llanbradach and joined the Baptists at Hengoed, becoming a minister. He furthered his studies at the Baptist Academy in Bristol and between October 1787 and June 1791 he ministered to the congregation at Pen-y-Garn, near Pontypool. In February 1793 he established the short-lived *Y Cylchgrawn Cymraeg* (The Welsh Magazine) and expressed his views on a host of social, political and religious concerns including the abolition of the slave trade, the missionary movement, disestablishment, Sunday schools and day schools. Influenced by the French Revolution, he 'advocated the reform of Parliament and the abolition of class privileges, oppressive taxes, and the waste of public money by wars and bribery'. He established 'The Welsh Treasury', a body which attacked the immorality of the church and state before emigrating to America. On 12 October 1794 he disembarked in New York where he met Dr Rodgers, the provost of the University of Pennsylvania. During this period, he married Ann, the daughter of Colonel Benjamin Loxley, and had five children. He initially

---

124   Robinson (ed.), *The Philadelphia Directory... 1808,* unpaginated; Robinson (ed.), *Robinson's Original Annual Directory... 1817,* p. 364; William H. Ukers (ed.), *All About Coffee* (New York: Tea and Coffee Trade Journal Company, 1922), p. 130.

settled in Philadelphia (c.1796) and while there he campaigned for the abolition of slavery.[125] In 1798 he purchased a sizable tract of land in the Alleghany mountains for his followers which he called 'Cambria' and named his capital 'Beulah'. Here he published *The Western Sky*, founded a library and a missionary society, promoted the rights of indigenous Americans, and established the Church of Christ. In 1799 he relocated to Somerset, Somerset County, Pennsylvania, and died there on 7 September 1804.[126]

Richards, Benjamin W. (1797-1851)

Benjamin Wood Richards was the son of Colonel William Richards and his wife Mary, and was born on 12 November 1797 in Batsto, New Jersey. He was the son of an iron foundry entrepreneur, and graduated from Princeton University, New Jersey, in 1815. In 1821 he married Sarah Ann, the daughter of Joshua Lippincott of Philadelphia. Benjamin practiced law in Philadelphia for many years and was an able politician. In 1826 he was elected to the Pennsylvania State Legislature and served the General Assembly from 1827 to 1829. Richards was the Democrat mayor of Philadelphia in 1829, 1831 and 1832. In the 1830s he was a director of Girard College, and in 1836 he founded the Girard Life Insurance, Annuity and Trust Company (later Girard Bank). He was a member of the American Philosophical Society and was a patron of the Asylum for the Blind, and one of the managers of the Deaf and

---

125 *Gazette of the United States & Philadelphia Daily Advertiser*, 12 January 1796, p. 2.

126 John James Evans, 'Rhys, Morgan John', *Y Bywgraffiadur Cymraeg hyd at 1940* (Dictionary of Welsh Biography before 1940) (London: Honourable Society of Cymmrodorion, 1953; 1959 English version), p. 795; G. A. Williams, *The Search for Beulah Land: The Welsh and the Atlantic Revolution* (London: Croom Helm, 1979); H. M. Davies, '"Very Different Springs of Uneasiness": Emigration from Wales to the United States of America during the 1790s', *Welsh History Review*, 15/3 (1991), 368–98; E. Wyn James, '"Seren Wib Olau": Gweledigaeth a Chenhadaeth Morgan John Rhys (1760–1804)', *Trafodion Cymdeithas Hanes y Bedyddwyr* (2007), 5–37. His private papers and diaries are housed at Columbia University, New York, Rare Book & Manuscript Library, MS#1066, Morgan J. Rhees papers, 1794–1968.

Dumb Asylum. He died on 12 July 1851 in Philadelphia.[127]

Roberts, Edward

According to the 1798 *Philadelphia Directory*, Edward Roberts was located at 145, South Third Street, but no occupation is recorded. In the 1802 publication of the directory there is an entry for Edward Roberts, a corder, located at the Drawbridge, 147 South Third Street.[128]

Roberts, Joseph

Joseph Roberts was in 1802 a merchant located at 16 North Front Street, Philadelphia.[129]

Roberts, Josiah

In 1802 Josiah Roberts was recorded in the *Pennsylvania Directory* as merchant, located at 212 South Third Street, Philadelphia.[130]

Roberts, Michael

Michael Roberts was a jeweller and stationer (c.1791–6), and also classified as the owner of a 'fancy & ironmonger store', 87 Chestnut Street, Philadelphia.[131]

Rolph, James

According to the *Philadelphia Directory* of 1802, James Rolph was a grocer, aged 67, who lived on Shippen Street (later renamed as Bainbridge Street), Southwark, Philadelphia.[132] He was expelled from

---

127 Jordan John Woolf, *Colonial Families of Philadelphia* (2 vols. New York: Lewis Publishers, 1911), II, pp. 1585–6 (and portrait).
128 Stafford (ed.), *The Philadelphia Directory... 1798*, p. 120; Robinson (ed.), *The Philadelphia Directory... 1802*, p. 206.
129 Robinson (ed.), *The Philadelphia Directory... 1802*, p. 206.
130 Robinson (ed.), *The Philadelphia Directory... 1802*, p. 206.
131 Winterthur Museum, Garden and Library, Delaware, Card File of American Craftspeople, 1600–1995; Robinson (ed.), *The Philadelphia Directory... 1802*, p. 207.
132 Robinson (ed.), *The Philadelphia Directory... 1802*, p. 209.

the Society in 1821.[133]

S

Sharpless, Jesse (1759–1832)

Jesse Sharpless was born in 1759 and he was the son of Jacob and Ann Blakey Sharpless, Quakers. In 1784 he married Joanna Townsend and they had ten children, eight surviving to maturity. Jesse was initially a saddler and then became a Philadelphia merchant located at 48 High Street, Philadelphia (c.1802). He died in 1832.[134]

Shaw, William A. (?–c.1816)

William A. Shaw was a merchant in Philadelphia. Formerly a Quaker in 1805 he married Anna M. outside of the Philadelphia Meeting of Friends. His will was dated 5 May 1816.[135]

Shoemaker, Thomas (1772–1832)

Thomas Shoemaker was born in 1772 but few details have been found concerning his life. According to *DeSilver's Philadelphia Directory and Strangers Guide* in 1831 he was located at 'bottling cellar' on the corner of Fifth Street and Library. He died on 19 May 1832 and was buried at Friends Western Burial Ground. The following year the Welsh Society paid tribute to 'one, who by his long and faithful services rendered himself as useful to the Society as he was endeared to its members by the uniform kindness and benevolence of his character'.[136]

---

133 This might be James Rolf (1768–1825). See Philadelphia City Archives, Death Records: Philadelphia City Death Certificates, 1803–1915, Index.
134 Robinson (ed.), *The Philadelphia Directory... 1808*, no pagination. For the Sharpless family records see Friends Historical Library of Swarthmore College, Swarthmore, SFHL-MSS-040, Sharpless Family Papers, 1792–1892.
135 HC, PhM.P455.02.014; PhM.P455.02.015, Philadelphia Monthly Meeting minutes, 1795–1801, 1801–7 (testimony of disownment, 1806); Historical Society of Pennsylvania, *Philadelphia County Wills, 1682–1819*.
136 DeSilver (ed.), *DeSilver's Philadelphia Directory... 1831*, p. 192; HC, MC-1186, Vol. 1, 4 June 1832.

PART FOUR

Simons/Simmons, Joseph (1771–1821)

Joseph Simmons was born in Philadelphia on 17 July 1771 and was the son of Captain Leeson Simmons and Hannah Watkins. In the 1802 Philadelphia Directory Joseph was recorded as an ironmonger of 91 High Street, Philadelphia. He died on 6 February 1821.[137]

Smith, Daniel (1755–1836)

Daniel Smith was the son of Richard and Hannah (Somers) Smith. At the start of the revolution, Smith was employed at the counting-house of Francis Gurney in Philadelphia and established a partnership with his employer. Active in the war he was appointed as a Lieutenant of Marines, but he was captured and imprisoned in a British prison-ship at Providence, Rhode Island. Post-war, Smith was a director of the Bank of North America (1800–33) and a vestryman of Christ Church (1798–1831). In 1780 he married Elizabeth Shute, daughter of William Shute, a merchant. He died in 1836.[138]

Snowden, Joseph

According to the *Philadelphia Directory* of 1802 Joseph Snowden was a ship chandler located at 88 South Fifth Street, Philadelphia.[139]

Stockton, William T. (?– 1823)

William T. Stockton was a proprietor of the New York and Baltimore stagecoach company. He was involved in the Farmers and Mechanics Bank in early nineteenth century Philadelphia.[140] He died intestate in 1823 in Roxborough, Philadelphia, and an inventory was made of his

---

137 HSP, Historic Pennsylvania Church and Town Records, Reel 179; Robinson (ed.), *The Philadelphia Directory... 1802*, p. 221.
138 'No. 80 Daniel Smith, 1755–1836', in Pennsylvania Academy of Fine Arts, *Catalogue of the Memorial Exhibition of Portraits*, p. 56.
139 Robinson (ed.), *The Philadelphia Directory... 1802*, p. 227.
140 American Philosophical Society, Philadelphia, MSS. B.St66. William T. Stockton Notebook, 1813–17.

property which amounted to over $12,693 alongside $1421 that he was owed.[141]

Strawbridge, John (1780–1858)

John Strawbridge was born in Elkton, Maryland, on 25 April 1780. He was the son of John and Hannah, the daughter of George Evans, a miller on the Brandywine. Three years later the family moved to Third Street below Market, Philadelphia, and his father had a store on Walnut Street wharf. In 1793 his father, aged forty-four, died of yellow fever. John recorded the episode in the following graphic terms:

> I may mention here as the evidence of the alarm and distress then prevailing in Phila. that in six hours, my good father was hurried to the grave. My uncle and two negroes alone attending him to our Arch St. ground... For nearly five weeks after his decease, we were shut up, and nearly starved, such was the difficulty in procuring provisions. No one came near us, at last George Evans our grandfather took us to Newark, Delaware where we lived six months, then removed to Wilmington where my mother ended her days. My father had few close city friends but they were highly respectable.

Despite a serious downturn in the family's fortunes, John was able to secure the patronage of some leading Philadelphians and attended Princeton College in 1797 and later secured a position as a merchant with the support of Robert Ralston. He gained valuable experience of global trade while travelling twice to India in 1802. Two years later he married Elizabeth Stockton and they had two sons, Stockton and John Ralston Strawbridge. Unfortunately, Elizabeth died in 1807, and three years later John married Frances Taylor. They had eight children. He

---

141 Philadelphia City Archives, Pennsylvania County, District and Probate Courts, City of Philadelphia, Administration Files No. 239–309, Administration and Inventory etc of William T. Stockton, 1823.

died at Germantown, Pennsylvania, on Easter Sunday, 4 April 1858.[142]

Strong, Joseph (1770–1812)

Joseph Strong was born on 10 March 1770 in Coventry, Tolland County, Connecticut. A graduate of Yale College in 1788 he received training under the guidance of Dr Lemuel Hopkins between 1788 and 1790 in Hartford, Connecticut, and trained as a physician under Dr Benjamin Rush at the University of Pennsylvania in Philadelphia (1791–2). He was a physician in 1792 in Middletown, Connecticut, and later served in the military (1792–6) as a surgeon. He is accredited with several inventions, including the axle tourniquet (29 January 1801) and an early version of the bicycle. Apart from his membership of the Welsh Society of Philadelphia, Strong supported the Philadelphia Society for the Encouragement of Domestic Manufacturers. He died of yellow fever on 24 April 1812.[143]

Sykes, Robert W. (1796–1875)

Robert Wharton Sykes was the son of William and Mary (Wharton) Sykes and was born on 26 July 1796. He trained as a lawyer in Philadelphia and owned considerable land and property in Philadelphia and New Jersey. He died in Germantown on 13 September 1875.[144]

T

Thomas, Evan

An honorary member of the Welsh Society who resided in New Castle, Pennsylvania.

---

142 'Autobiography of John Strawbridge', written in Philadelphia in April 1843. See http://www.users.interport.net/a/s/aswhite/JSFULBIO.html [accessed 1 July 2021].
143 Lockwood Barr, *Biography of Dr. Joseph Strong, 1770–1812* (Pelham Manor, NY: privately printed, 1940).
144 For further details see William L. Clements Library, University of Michigan, Lamb-Sykes Family Papers, 1680–1947, 1819–1911.

Thompson, Edward

Edward Thompson was shipwright who, according to the 1802 Philadelphia Directory, lived at Christian above Third Street, Philadelphia.[145]

Thompson, George

In the 1802 *Philadelphia Directory*, a George Thompson was recorded as an 'oak cooper', located at 11 and 13 Little Water, [45 Penn], Philadelphia.[146]

Tilghman, Edward (1750–1815)

Edward was the son of Edward Tilghman Snr (1713–1785), a representative of Queen Anne's County (Maryland) in the General Assembly, a colonel in the militia, and a member of the Stamp Act Congress. His mother was Elizabeth Chew-Tilghman. Edward Jr was born in Wye (East Maryland) in 1750. He was educated at the Academy of Philadelphia (c.1761) and graduated from the College of Philadelphia (the present-day University of Pennsylvania) in 1761. He then proceeded to study as a lawyer at the Middle Temple in London before practising law in Philadelphia. He married his second cousin, Elizabeth, the daughter of the Hon. Benjamin Chew in 1774, and enlisted as a private with the Philadelphia Associators. Within the year he acted as brigade major at the Battle of Long Island. A distinguished and well-respected lawyer he refused the position of chief justice of Pennsylvania Supreme Court in 1806. From 1794 until his resignation in 1807 he was a trustee of the University of Pennsylvania. He died in Philadelphia in 1815.[147]

---

145 Robinson (ed.), *The Philadelphia Directory... 1802*, p. 242.
146 Robinson (ed.), *The Philadelphia Directory... 1802*, p. 242.
147 For additional details of the Tilghman family see Jennifer A. Bryan, 'The Tilghmans of Maryland's Eastern Shore, 1660–1793', University of Maryland, Ph.D. thesis, 1999; Robinson (ed.), *The Philadelphia Directory... 1802*, p. 243 states that he was located at 116 Chestnut Street.

PART FOUR

Tilghman, William (1756-1827)

William Tilghman was born in Talbot County, Maryland, on 12 August 1756. He was educated at the College of Philadelphia and received his degree in 1772 and Master of Arts before reading law (c.1783) and practicing in Maryland between 1783 and 1788. He was a delegate to the Maryland State Convention (c.1788), a representative of the Maryland House of Delegates (1788-90) and Maryland Senate (1791-3). He then practiced law between 1794 and 1801. He was appointed as a Judge to the United States Circuit Court for the Third Circuit (1801-2) and Chief Justice of the Supreme Court of Pennsylvania (1806-27). Although he emancipated slaves on his planation in Maryland and passed legal judgments concerning the abolition of slavery, his efforts were nonetheless not fully acknowledged. He died on 29 April 1827.[148]

V

Vaux, George

In 1817 the *Philadelphia Directory* recorded that George Vaux was an attorney at law located at 39 South Street, Philadelphia.[149]

Vaux, Roberts (1786-1836)

Roberts Vaux was the eldest son of Richard and Ann (Roberts) Vaux, and he was born in Philadelphia in 1786. He was descended from English

---

148 Horace Binney, 'Life of Chief Justice Tilghman', *American Law Magazine* (April 1843), 1-31. For his papers and correspondence etc see American Philosophical Society, Philadelphia, MSS. B.T45, William Tilghman papers, 1771-1838; HSP, Philadelphia, MSS. 0659, William Tilghman Correspondence, 1772-1827, and Am.9262-3, William Tilghman (and wife) Ledgers, 1785-1835; David M. Rubenstein Rare Book and Manuscript Library, Duke University, Durham, North Carolina, RL.10093, William Tilghman Papers, 1671-1876.
149 Robinson (ed.), *Robinson's Original Annual Directory... 1817*, p. 444.

Quakers. His father, Richard (1751–90)[150] emigrated to Philadelphia in 1768 and became an apprentice in the mercantile firm of Samuel Sansom in Philadelphia, before establishing a prosperous mercantile business of his own. Roberts served an apprenticeship with the Philadelphian firm of Cooke & Co. before setting up his own business. He was to become renowned for his philanthropic endeavours, and, according to Edward Digby Baltzell, associated with 'almost every worthy public and private social welfare activity' in the city, and most notably with prison reform and education.[151] In 1817 the *Philadelphia Directory* recorded that Roberts Vaux was located at 79 Mulberry, Philadelphia. He died in 1836.[152]

Vincent, William

In 1817 the *Philadelphia Directory* recorded that William Vincent was a shoemaker, located near 117 North Tenth Street, Philadelphia.[153]

W

Walker, Lewis

In 1802 the *Philadelphia Directory* recorded that Lewis Walker was an ironmonger, located at 148 High Street, Philadelphia.[154]

Waln, Jesse (? –1848)

Jesse Waln was a merchant who traded, with his cousin Robert, in the

---

150 Richard Vaux was born on 29 November 1751 to George and Frances (Owen) Vaux, a London Quaker family.
151 Edward Digby Baltzell, *Philadelphia Gentlemen: The Making of a National Upper Class* (Glencoe, Ill.: Free Press, 1958), p. 139. Records of the family 1739–1923 are housed at HSP, MSS. 0684, Vaux Family Papers.
152 Robinson (ed.), *Robinson's Original Annual Directory... 1817*, p. 444. For a portrait see Albert Newsam, 'Roberts Vaux' c.1840. National Portrait Gallery, Smithsonian Institution, Washington, DC. NPG.97.231 [accessed 1 July 2021].
153 Robinson (ed.), *Robinson's Original Annual Directory... 1817*, p. 445.
154 Robinson (ed.), *The Philadelphia Directory... 1802*, p. 251.

East Indies and China. Their business was located at Waln's wharf, near Spruce Street, Philadelphia. Jesse died in 1848.[155]

Waln, Robert (1765–1836)

Robert Waln was born in Philadelphia on 22 February 1765. With a basic education he pursued career as a merchant in the East Indies and China with his cousin, Jesse (see above). He was later to turn his attention to politics and was a member of the Pennsylvania Legislature and city council, acting as president of the select council. As a Federalist, he was elected to serve the Fifth Congress and subsequently was re-elected to the Sixth Congress (3 December 1798 to 3 March 1801). He also took an interest in the production of cotton and, in 1812, he established a factory in Trenton, New Jersey. Public service always loomed large, particularly as a trustee of the University of Pennsylvania. He died on 24 January 1836 in Philadelphia and was buried in Arch Street Friends Meeting House Burial Ground in the city.[156]

Wayne, Isaac (1772–1852)

Isaac Wayne was born near Paoli, Chester County, Pennsylvania, in 1772 and was the son of General Anthony Wayne. He was educated in the local schools and graduated with a law degree from Dickinson College, Carlisle, Pennsylvania. In 1795 he was admitted to the Chester County Bar in 1795. Between 1799 and 1801 (and in 1806) he was a member of the State House of Representatives and, in 1810, he served

---

155 See notes to 'To James Madison from Jesse Waln, 23 April 1810', Founders Online, National Archives [America], https://founders.archives.gov/documents/Madison/03-02-02-0391 [accessed 13 July 2021]; J. C. A. Stagg, Jeanne Kerr Cross and Susan Holbrook Perdue (eds), *The Papers of James Madison, Presidential Series*, vol. 2, 1 October 1809–2 November 1810 (Charlottesville: University Press of Virginia, 1992), pp. 322–3, and citing Thomas J. Scharf and Thompson Westcott, *History of Philadelphia, 1609–1884* (3 vols. Philadelphia: L. H. Everts & Co., 1884), II, pp. 2213, 2215.
156 'Waln, Robert, 1765–1836', *Biographical Directory of the United States Congress* and provided at: https://bioguide.congress.gov/search/bio/W000094 [accessed 4 July 2021].

in the State Senate. Wayne was captain of a troop of Pennsylvania Horse Cavalry during the War of 1812 and was later promoted to Colonel of the Second Regiment, Pennsylvania Volunteer Infantry. He was unsuccessful in his attempt to become Governor of the State in 1814 but he was elected to the Eighteenth Congress, which he served from 4 March 4 1823 until 3 March 1825. He died on 25 October 1852 in Chester County, Pennsylvania, and was buried in St David's Episcopal Church Cemetery, Radnor, Pennsylvania.[157]

Wells, Gideon H. (1765–1827)

Gideon Hill Wells was the son of Richard and Rachel (Hill) Wells, and he was born on 25 September 1765 in Philadelphia. He married Hannah, daughter of Robert Waln, on 5 November 1790 and died on 26 March 1827 in Philadelphia. As a result of his marriage Wells became involved in cotton manufacturing in Trenton, New Jersey. The business, however, was not a great success and by 1803 Wells was bankrupt. The rights to his mill were assigned to his brother-in-law, Robert Waln. Despite this he was, with Robert Waln, able to establish the Eagle Factory in Trenton, New Jersey, in 1814. By the end of the decade Wells was under severe financial pressure and between May and September 1819 he was being pursued in court by the Trenton Banking Company after his defaulting on a mortgage of $22,000 for his share of the mill property. The factory was put up for sale in the November of that year, but he failed to attract any interest. It was eventually sold to Robert's son, Lewis, for $15,000.[158]

157 'Isaac Wayne – Biography', Pennsylvania State Senate and provided at https://www.legis.state.pa.us/cfdocs/legis/BiosHistory/MemBio.cfm?ID=5026&body=S [accessed 1 July 2021].

158 Details of Wells' family are provided in Bell and Greifenstein, *Patriot Improvers,* I, pp. 440–6 ('Richard Wells (1734–1801): American Society (Corresponding Member), 26 February 1768'). For details of Wells' business interest see Richard W. Hunter, Nadine Sergejeff and Damon Tvaryanas, 'On The Eagle's Wings: Textiles, Trenton, and a First Taste of the Industrial Revolution', particularly pp. 65, 67, 71, 77–8. It is available at: https://njh.libraries.rutgers.edu/index.php/njh/article/view/991 [accessed 9 July 2021]. Also, see HSP, MSS. 1628, Smith and Waln Family Papers, 1774–1891.

PART FOUR

Wetherill, John Price (1794-1853)

John Price Wetherill was born in 1794 and was the son of Samuel Wetherill and grandson of Samuel Wetherill, the leader of the 'Free Quakers'. He had a successful business as a chemical and white lead manufacturer in Philadelphia. He married Maria Kane Lawrence in 1817 and in the same year the *Philadelphia Directory* recorded that he was an oil and colourman[159] located on the south-west corner of Front and Arch Street with a dwelling house on 291 Sassafras Street, Philadelphia.[160] He was a public servant and in 1829 he was a member of Common Council and served the City Council for over twenty-three years. He was Vice-president for many years of the Academy of Natural Science, and was active in numerous learned, scientific and social organizations. He served as a director of the Girard Bank and was President of the Schuylkill Bank. He died in 1853.[161]

Wetherill, Samuel P.

In 1817 the *Philadelphia Directory* recorded that Samuel P. Wetherill was an oil and colourman located on 65 North Front Street with a dwelling house on 76 North Front Street, Philadelphia.[162]

Wharton, Fishbourne (1778-1846)

Fishbourne Wharton, a merchant, was born on 10 August 1778, and

---

159 An oil and colourman was someone employed in the paint manufacturing trade.
160 Robinson (ed.), *Robinson's Original Annual Directory... 1817*, p. 459.
161 'No. 215. John Price Wetherill, 1794-1853', in Pennsylvania Academy of Fine Arts, *Catalogue of the Memorial Exhibition of Portraits*, p. 165.
162 Robinson (ed.), *Robinson's Original Annual Directory... 1817*, p. 459.
For further details of the Wetherill family and their business see Van Pelt Library, University of Pennsylvania, Wetherill Papers; Miriam Hussey, *From Merchants to 'Colour Men': Five Generations of Samuel Wetherill's White Lead Business* (Philadelphia: University of Pennsylvania Press, 1956); Joshua Lisowski, 'Wetherill & Son's White Lead Factory', *The Encyclopaedia of Greater Philadelphia* and provided at: https://philadelphiaencyclopedia.org/wetherill-2/ [accessed 13 July 2013].

he was the son of Thomas Wharton Jr, the first President (Governor) of Philadelphia. On 10 May 1804 he married Susan Shoemaker who died in November 1821. He subsequently married her sister, Mary Ann Shoemaker, on 20 January 1832. He died in 1846.[163]

Wharton, Franklin (1767–1818)

Franklin Wharton was born on 23 July 1767 in Philadelphia and he was the son of Joseph Wharton I and Hannah Owen. He received his first commission as a Captain of Marines in August 1798. On 6 March 1804, aged 36, he became Lieutenant Colonel and third Commandant of the Marine Corps. He saw active service in the War of 1812. He died on 1 September 1818 in New York and was buried in Old Trinity Church Yard.[164]

Wharton, Peregrine H. (1765–1811)

Peregrine Hogg Wharton was born on 14 February 1765 and married Jane, daughter of Benjamin Brown, on St Valentine's Day 1765 and they had ten children. In 1802 he was recorded in the *Philadelphia Directory* as a merchant at 180 South Front Street, Philadelphia. He died in Philadelphia on 27 May 1811.[165]

Wharton, Robert (1757–1834)

Robert Wharton was born in Southwark, Philadelphia, on 12 January 1757, and he was the son of Joseph Wharton, a Philadelphian merchant. In December 1789 Wharton married Salome Chancellor. At a relatively

---

163 Anne Hollingsworth Wharton, *Genealogy of the Wharton Family of Philadelphia, 1664 to 1880* (Philadelphia: privately published, 1880), p. 27.
164 Wharton, *Genealogy of the Wharton Family of Philadelphia*, pp. 23–4; 'Lieutenant Colonel Franklin Wharton, SMC (Deceased)', Marine Cops University, and provided at https://www.usmcu.edu/Research/Marine-Corps-History-Division/People/Whos-Who-in-Marine-Corps-History/Vandegrift-Worley/Lieutenant-Colonel-Franklin-Wharton/ [accessed 8 July 2021].
In 1802 he was located at North Eleventh Street, Philadelphia. See Robinson (ed.), *The Philadelphia Directory... 1802*, p. 257.
165 Wharton, *Genealogy of the Wharton Family of Philadelphia*, pp. 18–28; Robinson (ed.), *The Philadelphia Directory... 1802*, p. 257.

early age he abandoned his education and was apprenticed to a hatter, later joining the counting-house of Samuel, his brother, a merchant of Philadelphia. From 1792 until 1795, Wharton was member of the city council, while in 1796 he was appointed as an alderman. During that year he was forced to crush a sailors' demonstration for higher wages. The riot act was read requiring them to disperse. With their refusal to do so, he ordered his troops to capture the protestors and imprison them. In 1798 he was a member of the First Troop Philadelphia City Cavalry and quashed the Walnut Street prison riot, while between 1803 and 1811 he was their captain. Wharton was the longest-serving Mayor of Philadelphia, a position he held sixteen times between 1798 and 1824. These included: 1798–1800, 1806–8 and 1810–11. He was re-elected in 1811, but he declined to serve. During his mayoralty in 1810 the six troops of cavalry in Philadelphia became a regiment of which Wharton was elected as Colonel, and he was later to become the elected Brigadier-General of the state militia. He returned to politics in 1814 and served as mayor between 1814 and 1819, and 1820 and 1824).

Apart from his commitment to the Welsh Society, Wharton was vice-president and one of the founder members of the Washington Benevolent Society. He enjoyed outdoor sports, and until 1818 was President of the famous Fox-Hunting Club of Gloucester, New Jersey (est. 1766). In 1790 he became a member of the Schuylkill Fishing Company, acting as President between 1812 and 1828. He died in Philadelphia on 7 March 1834.[166]

Wheeler, John J.

In 1803 the *Philadelphia Directory* recorded an entry for John Wheeler as a tailor who was located on 17 Strawberry Street. There was also a J. Wheeler, tavern keeper and grocer of 1 Butlers Court.[167]

---

166 For full details and portrait see Wharton, *Genealogy of the Wharton Family of Philadelphia*, pp. 18–28.
167 Robinson (ed.), *The Philadelphia Directory... 1803*, p. 270.

Wheeler, Samuel

In 1802 the *Philadelphia Directory* recorded an entry for Samuel Wheeler as a black and white smith who was located on 99 Vine Street, Philadelphia.[168]

Wildes, Joseph

In 1817 the *Philadelphia Directory* recorded an entry for Joseph Wildes as a merchant tailor who was located on 37 North Third Street, Philadelphia.[169]

Willett, John Stephenson (1787–1818)

John Stephenson Willett, the son of Esther Lewis and Captain John S. Willett, was born on 7 August 1787 in Philadelphia. He died on 16 October 1818 in Camden, Kershaw County, South Carolina.

Worrell, Joseph (c.1769–1840)

Joseph Worrell was the son of Ezekiel and Ann (King) Worrell. In 1788 he was apprenticed as a carpenter to James Pearson and he would later become Company Secretary of the Carpenters' Company between 1801 and 1803, Vice President (1818–20), and its President (1821–3, 1827–9). There are no details of his work apart from a business that he set up with Isaac Forsyth located at 7 Little George Street, Philadelphia. He served on the Select Council of the City of Philadelphia and as a committee member oversaw the construction of Girard College.[170]

---

168 Robinson (ed.), *The Philadelphia Directory... 1802*, p. 14 (this was part of the removals and omissions section of the directory).
169 Robinson (ed.), *Robinson's Original Annual Directory... 1817*, p. 466.
170 Roger W. Moss, 'Worrell, Joseph (c.1769–1840), master builder', and provided at American Architects and Buildings database: https://www.americanbuildings.org/pab/app/ar_display.cfm/23275 [accessed 12 December 2019]; Carpenters' Company Digital Archive & Museum, Philadelphia, ccccp 91.1.01. Jacob Eichholtz (?), 'Oil on Canvas Portrait of Joseph Worrell', c.1821. https://archive.carpentershall.org/items/show/22601 [accessed 13 July 2021].

PART FOUR

Y

Yeatman, Charleton

In 1798 Charleton Yeatman was recorded in the *Philadelphia Directory* as a physician located on the south-east corner of Lombard and Second Street, Philadelphia.[171]

Z

Zantzinger, Thomas B. (1776–1821)

Thomas Barton Zantzinger was a merchant. He was the son of Paul and Esther Barton Zantzinger, and was born in Lancaster, Pennsylvania, on 5 January 1776 between 1 and 2 o'clock in the morning, and was baptized by the Rev. Helmuth. He graduated from the University of Pennsylvania in 1793 and, in 1805, married Susanna Sheaff (17 January 1783–2 April 1831) and they had seven children. Little is known about his life apart from a few references, including his purchase in 1811 of the *Mirror of Taste and Dramatic Censor* which he published at Shakespeare Buildings at Sixth and Chestnut Streets, Philadelphia. He died on 21 December 1847.[172]

---

171 Stafford (ed.), *The Philadelphia Directory... 1798*, p. 157.
172 Brief details are available from the Historical Society of Pennsylvania, MF Reel 1079: Historic Pennsylvania Church and Town Records for St Stephen's Episcopal Church; Albert Smyth, *The Philadelphia Magazines and their Contributors 1741–1850* (Philadelphia: Robert M. Lindsay, 1892), p. 173; Daniel Kolb Cassel, *The Family Record of David Rittenhouse, including his sisters Esther, Anne and Eleanor, also Benjamin Rittenhouse and Margaret Rittenhouse Morgan* (Norristown, Pa.: Herald printing, 1897), pp. 31–2.

Plate 11. 'The City & Port of Philadelphia, on the River Delaware from Kensington', c.1800.[173]

---

173 Birch and Son, *The City of Philadelphia*, plate 2 (frontispiece).

BIBLIOGRAPHY

Primary Sources

American Philosophical Society, Philadelphia

MSS. B.C625.1, Lambert Cadwalader Papers, 1779–98

MSS. B.M589, Samuel Miles Papers, 1776–1802

MSS. B.St66, William T. Stockton notebook, 1813–17

MSS.B.T45, William Tilghman papers, 1771–1838

Record Group IIb APS.Archives.IIb, 1807–25

Columbia University, New York, Rare Book & Manuscript Library

MSS. 1066, Morgan J. Rhees papers, 1794–1968

David M. Rubenstein Rare Book and Manuscript Library, Duke University, Durham, North Carolina

RL.10093, William Tilghman Papers, 1671–1876

Friends Historical Library of Swarthmore College, Swarthmore, Pennsylvania

RG5/229, Parrish Family Papers, 1780–1966

SFHL-MSS-040, Sharpless Family Papers, 1792–1892

Historical Society of Pennsylvania, Philadelphia

Am. MS. 9415, Benjamin R. Morgan Letterbook, 1830–40

Am. MSS. 9262–3, William Tilghman (and wife) Ledgers, 1785–1835

Amb. MS. 175, Executor's Accounts of Horace Binney's Estate, 1875–8

Amb. MS. 3825, Elijah Griffith Ledger 1801–14

Historic Pennsylvania Church and Town Records, Microfilm Reels 98, 179, 1079

MSS. 0028, Ball Families Papers, 1672–1917

MSS. 0154, Cox–Parrish–Wharton Family Papers, 1700–1900

MSS. 0306, Joshua Humphreys Papers, 1660–1931

MSS. 0659, William Tilghman Correspondence, 1772–1827

MSS. 0684, Vaux Family Papers, 1739–1923

MSS. 1454, Series VIII. Cadwallader Collection. Box 22. Folder 4. Morris Family

MSS. 1505, Horace Binney Papers

MSS. 1509, Meredith Family Papers, 1756–1964

MSS. 1612, James Hamilton Collection

MSS. 1628, Smith and Waln Family Papers, 1774–1891

MSS. 1735, Leonard T. Beale Collection, 1746–1892

MSS. 1792, Biddle Family Papers, 1683–1954

MSS. 2050, Chew Family Papers

MSS. 3302, William Meredith Legal Papers

Will Book Part C. 6.386. Will of Caleb Birchall, Philadelphia, 16 January 1817

Library of the Society of Friends, London

unpublished Dictionary of Quaker Biography

Lutnick Library Quaker and Special Collections, Haverford College, Haverford, Pennsylvania.

MC-1186. Vol 1. Unpaginated Minute Book of the Records of the Welsh Society of Philadelphia (4 June 1798–2 December 1839); Copy of the Original Association, 1 March 1798; First Constitution and Rules; Second Constitution and Rules; Bye-Laws; Supplemental Rules and Regulations

MC-1186. Box 2. Attendance Records, 1814–70

MC-1186. Box 5. Dues and Fines Record, 1810–15

MC-1186. Box 5. Dues and Fines Record, 1814–35

MC-1186. Box 5. Dues and Fines Record, 1834–68

PhM.P455.01a.001, Philadelphia Monthly Meeting, Births, Deaths and Burials, 1688–1826

PhM.P455.02.014, Philadelphia Monthly Meeting minutes, 1795–1801

PhM.P455.02.015, Philadelphia Monthly Meeting minutes, 1801–1807

PhM.P455.04.047, Philadelphia Manumissions Book, 1772–86 (although dates covered are 1765–99)

PhM.P466.01.009, Philadelphia Monthly Meeting, Southern District Marriages, 1773–1846

PhM.P466.01.007, Philadelphia Monthly Meeting, Southern District Record of Interments, Vol 2, 1807–72

National Library of Wales, Aberystwyth

MS. 2703F, 'Crynwyr Cymru ac UDA' – enclosed James Jones Levick, 'The Ancient Britons spoken at the Annual Dinner of the Welsh Society of Philadelphia... March 1st 1890'

MS. 14094D, The Rev. George Roberts of Ebensburg (1769–1853) to Evan, his father, and mother, Llanbrynmair, Montgomeryshire, 13 October, 1801 (in Welsh)

Philadelphia City Archives

Death Records: Philadelphia City Death Certificates, 1803–1915, Index.

Pennsylvania County, District and Probate Courts, City of Philadelphia, Administration Files No. 239–309, Administration and Inventory etc of William T. Stockton, 1823

Pennsylvania Historical and Museum Commission, Harrisburg

Records of the House of Representatives

Records of the General Assembly, Record Group 7. Septennial Census Returns, 1779–1863 (Box 1026).

Van Pelt Library, University of Pennsylvania

Wetherill Papers

William L. Clements Library, University of Michigan

Lamb-Sykes Family Papers, 1680–1947, 1819–1911

BIBLIOGRAPHY

Winterthur Museum, Garden and Library, Delaware

Card File of American Craftspeople, 1600–1995

Portraits

Carpenters' Company Digital Archive & Museum, Philadelphia

ccccp 91.1.01. Jacob Eichholtz (?), 'Oil on Canvas Portrait of Joseph Worrell', c.1821

National Portrait Gallery, Smithsonian Institution, Washington, D.C.

NPG.84.108, John Sartain, 'Joseph Hopkinson, c.1832–5'

NPG.97.231, Albert Newsam, 'Roberts Vaux' c.1840'

Worcester Art Museum, Worcester, Maine

1983.2, 'Thomas Cumpston', 1797. Alexander and Caroline DeWitt Fund

Printed Sources

Historical Society of Pennsylvania, *Philadelphia County Wills, 1682–1819* (Philadelphia: Historical Society of Pennsylvania, 1900)

Pugh, Ellis, *Annerch ir Cymru, iw galw oddiwrth y llawer o bethau at yr un peth angenrheidiol er mwyn cadwedigaeth eu heneidiau* (Philadelphia: Andrew Bradford, 1721)

Pugh, Ellis, *A Salutation to the Britons: to call them from the many things, to the one thing needful for the saving of their souls: Especially, to the poor unlearned tradesmen, plowmen and shepherds, those that are of a low degree like myself... Translated from the British language by Rowland Ellis, revised and corrected by David Lloyd* (Philadelphia: S. Keimer, 1727)

Scots Thistle Society of Philadelphia, *Constitution of the Scots Thistle Society of Philadelphia* (Philadelphia: John Bioren, 1799)

Society of the Sons of St George, *List of the Members of the Society of the Sons of St George, Established at Philadelphia/Revised and Corrected the 23rd of April, 1802* (Philadelphia: James Humphreys, 1802)

Works of Reference

[i] **Dictionaries of Biography**

Dictionary of American Biography (New York: Charles Scribner's Sons, 1961)

Y Bywgraffiadur Cymraeg hyd at 1940 (Dictionary of Welsh Biography before 1940) (London: Honourable Society of Cymmrodorion, 1953; 1959 English version)

[ii] **Trade Directories (in year of appearance)**

Biddle, Clement (ed.), *The Philadelphia Directory* (Philadelphia: James & Johnson, 1791)

Hardie, James (ed.), *The Philadelphia Directory and Register, 1793* (Philadelphia: T. Dobson, 1793)

Stafford, Cornelius W. (ed.), *The Philadelphia Directory... 1798* (Philadelphia: William W. Woodward, 1798)

Stafford, Cornelius W. (ed.), *The Philadelphia Directory... 1799* (Philadelphia: William W. Woodward, 1799)

BIBLIOGRAPHY

Robinson, James (ed.), *The Philadelphia Directory... 1802* (Philadelphia: William W. Woodward 1802)

Robinson, James (ed.), *The Philadelphia Directory... 1803* (Philadelphia: William W. Woodward, 1803)

Robinson, James (ed.), *The Philadelphia Directory... 1804* (Philadelphia: John H. Oswald, 1804)

Robinson, James (ed.), *The Philadelphia Directory... 1808* (Philadelphia: William Woodhouse, 1808)

Robinson, James (ed.), *The Philadelphia Directory... 1810* (Philadelphia: William Woodhouse, 1810)

Robinson, James (ed.), *Robinson's Original Annual Directory... 1817* (Philadelphia: James Robinson, 1817)

DeSilver, Robert (ed.), *DeSilver's Philadelphia Directory and Stranger's Guide, 1828* (Philadelphia: Robert DeSilver, 1828)

DeSilver, Robert (ed.), *DeSilver's Philadelphia Directory and Strangers Guide, 1831* (Philadelphia: Robert DeSilver, 1831)

DeSilver, Robert (ed.), *DeSilver's Philadelphia Directory and Stranger's Guide, 1835–6* (Philadelphia: Robert DeSilver, 1835)

[iii] Censuses

1800 Census. High Street Ward, Philadelphia, M32, Roll 43

1810 Census. Middle Ward, Philadelphia, Roll 55

1830 Census. Chestnut Ward, Philadelphia, M19, Roll 159

Newspapers

American Weekly Mercury, 528 (Tuesday, 10 February–Thursday, 19 February 1729/30), 530 (3 March 1730)

Centinel (Gettysburg, Pennsylvania), 'Colonel Samuel Miles', 5 February 1805

Gazette of the United States & Philadelphia Daily Advertiser, 12 January 1796, 27 February 1799, 5 March 1799

London Gazette, 12 February 1714/15

Pennsylvania Gazette, 25 February 1729, 1 March 1729, 16 February 1731, 4 March 1731, 5 March 1741

United States' Gazette, 17 March 1804

Secondary Sources

Allen, Joan and Allen, Richard C., '"Competing identities": Irish and Welsh Migration and the North-East of England', in A. J. Pollard and A. G. Green (eds), *Regional Identities in North-East England 1300–2000* (Woodford: Boydell and Brewer, 2007)

Allen, Richard C., '"In Search of a New Jerusalem". A Preliminary Investigation into Welsh Quaker Emigration to North America c.1660–1750', *Quaker Studies*, 9/1 (September 2004), 31–53

Allen, Richard C., *Quaker Communities in Early Modern Wales: From Resistance to Respectability* (Cardiff: University of Wales Press, 2007)

Allen, Richard C., 'The Making of a Holy Christian Community: Welsh Quaker Emigrants to Pennsylvania, c.1680–1750', in Tim Kirk and Luda Klusáková (eds), *Cultural Conquests, 1500–2000* (Prague: Philosophica et Historica, Studia Historica, 2009)

Allen, Richard C., 'The Origins and Development of Welsh Associational Life in Eighteenth-Century Philadelphia', *Transactions of the Honourable Society of Cymmrodorion: Trafodion Anrhydeddus Gymdeithas y Cymmrodorion*, New Series, 15, 2008 (2009), 105–26

Allen, Richard C., 'Samuel Meredith (1741–1817): American Patriot and Welsh Philanthropist', in Maurice Jackson and Susan Kozel (eds), *Quakers and their Allies in the Abolitionist Cause, 1754–1808* (London: Routledge, 2015)

Anon., *An Historical Sketch of the Origin and Progress of the Society of the Sons of St George* (Philadelphia: W. W. Bates & Co., 1872)

Anon., 'Auto-Biographical Sketch of Col. Samuel Miles', *American Historical Record*, 2 (1873), 49–53, 114–18

Anon., *History of Schuylkill County, Pa.: with Illustrations and Biographical Sketches of Some of Its Prominent Men and Pioneers* (New York: W. W. Munsell & Co., 1881)

Anon., 'Philemon Dickinson: Major-General: New Jersey Militia-Revolutionary Service', *Magazine of American History*, 7 (December 1881), 420–7

Anon., 'John Roberts of Merion', *Pennsylvania Magazine of History and Biography*, 19 (1895), 262–3

Anon., *Marriage Record of Christ Church, Philadelphia, 1709–1806* (2 vols. Harrisburg, Pennsylvania: C. M. Busch, 1896)

Anon., 'Letters from the Joshua Humphreys Collection of the Historical Society of Pennsylvania', *Pennsylvania Magazine of History and Biography*, 30 (1906), 376–8, 503

Anon., 'John *Jones to Hugh Jones, c.1725*', in A. C. Myers (ed.), *Narratives of Pennsylvania, West New Jersey and Delaware, 1630–1707* (New York: Charles Scribner's Sons, 1912; rept. New York: Barnes & Noble, 1967)

Armitage, David and Braddick, Michael J. (eds), *British Atlantic World, 1500–1800* (Basingstoke: Palgrave Macmillan, 2002)

Ashton, E. T., *The Welsh in the United States* (Hove: Caldra House, 1984)

Baltzell, E. D., *Philadelphia Gentlemen: The Making of a National Upper Class* (Philadelphia: University of Pennsylvania Press, 1979)

Barker-Benfield, G. J., *Male Attitudes toward Women and Sexuality in Nineteenth Century America; The Horrors of the Half-Known Life* (London: Routledge, 2000)

Barr, Lockwood, *Biography of Dr. Joseph Strong, 1770–1812* (Pelham Manor, NY: Privately printed, 1940)

Bell, Whitfield J., *The Colonial Physician* (New York: Neale Watson Academic, 1975)

Bell, Whitfield Jenks and Greifenstein, Charles, *Patriot Improvers: Biographical Sketches of Members of the American Philosophical Society* (3 vols. Philadelphia: American Philosophical Society, 1997)

Biddle, Clement, 'Selections from the Correspondence of Colonel Clement Biddle', *Pennsylvania Magazine of History and Biography*, 42 (1918), 310–42; 43 (1919), 53–76, 143–62, 193–207

Biddle, Henry D., *A Sketch of Owen Biddle... A List of His Descendants* (Philadelphia: privately published, 1892)

Binney, Charles Chauncey, *Life of Horace Binney, with Selections from His Letters* (Philadelphia: Lippincott, 1903)

Binney, Horace, 'Life of Chief Justice Tilghman', *American Law Magazine* (April 1843), 1–31

Binney, Horace, *The Leaders of the Old Bar of Philadelphia* (Philadelphia: privately published, 1866)

Birch, W. and Son, *The City of Philadelphia, in the State of Pennsylvania North America; As it Appeared in the Year 1800: Consisting of Twenty-Eight Plates* (Philadelphia: W. Birch, 1800)

Bourque, Monique, 'Populating the Poorhouse: A Reassessment of Poor Relief in the Antebellum Delaware Valley', *Pennsylvania History:*

BIBLIOGRAPHY

A Journal of Mid-Atlantic Studies, 70/3 (Summer 2003), 235–67

Bowen, H. V. (ed.), *Wales and the British Overseas Empire: Interactions and Influences, 1650–1830* (Manchester: Manchester University Press, 2012)

Bronner, Edwin B., 'Village into Town, 1701–1746', in Russell F. Weighley, Nicholas B. Wainwright, Edwin B. Wolf, Joseph E. Illick and Thomas Wendel (eds), *Philadelphia: A 300-Year History* (New York and London: W. W. Norton & Co., 1982)

Browning, C. S., *The Welsh Settlement of Pennsylvania* (Philadelphia: W. J. Campbell, 1912)

Bryan, James, *Progress of Medicine During the First Half of the Nineteenth Century... Introductory Lecture to the Spring Session in the Philadelphia College of Medicine* (Philadelphia: Grattan & M'Lean, 1851)

Bryan, James, *A Treatise on the Anatomy, Physiology and Diseases of the Human Ear* (Philadelphia: privately published, 1851)

Bryan, James, *An Essay on Hernia* (Philadelphia: F. J. Pilliner, 1860

Bueltmann, Tanja, *Clubbing Together: Ethnicity, Civility and Formal Sociability in the Scottish Diaspora to 1930* (Liverpool: Liverpool University Press, 2014)

Bueltmann, Tanja and MacRaild, Donald, *The English Diaspora in North America: Migration, Ethnicity and Association, 1730s–1950s* (Manchester: Manchester University Press, 2017)

Campbell, John H., *History of the Friendly Sons of St Patrick and of the Hibernian Society for the Relief of Emigrants from Ireland: March 17, 1771–March 17, 1892* (Philadelphia: Hibernian Society, 1892)

Campbell, Rev. William W., *Life and Character of Jacob Broom* (Wilmington: Delaware Historical Society, 1909)

Carey, Mathew, *National Interests and Domestic Manufactures: Addresses of the Philadelphia Society for the Promotion of Domestic Industry, to the Citizens of the United States* (Boston: William W. Clapp 1819)

Cassel, Daniel Kolb, *The Family Record of David Rittenhouse, including his sisters Esther, Anne and Eleanor, also Benjamin Rittenhouse and Margaret Rittenhouse Morgan* (Norristown, Pa.: Herald Press, 1897)

Chazanof, William, *Joseph Ellicott and the Holland Land Company* (Syrcause: Syracuse University Press, 1970)

Clark, Peter, *British Clubs and Societies 1580–1800: The Origins of an Associational World* (Oxford: Clarendon Press, 2000)

Clement, Priscilla Ferguson, *Welfare and the Poor in the Nineteenth-Century City: Philadelphia, 1800–1854* (Fairleigh: Dickinson University Press, 1985)

Conway, Alan, 'Welsh Emigration to the United States', in Donald Fleming and Bernard Bailyn (eds), *Dislocation and Emigration: The Social Background of American Immigration, Perspectives in American History* 7 (Cambridge, MA: Harvard University Press, 1974)

Conway, Alan, *The Welsh in America: Letters from the Immigrants* (Cardiff: University of Wales Press, 1961)

Cousins, Frank and Riley, Phil M., *The Colonial Architecture of Philadelphia* (Boston: Little, Brown, and Company, 1920)

Davies, H. M., '"Very Different Springs of Uneasiness": Emigration from Wales to the United States of America during the 1790s', *Welsh History Review*, 15/3 (1991), 368–98

Davis, Allen and Haller, Mark (eds), *The Peoples of Philadelphia: A History of Ethnic Groups and Lower-Class Life, 1790–1940* (Philadelphia: University of Pennsylvania Press, 1973)

Davis, Susan G., '"Making Night Hideous": Christmas Revelry and Public Order in Nineteenth-Century Philadelphia', *American Quarterly*, 34/2 (1982), 185–99

DeClue Anita and Smith, Billy G., 'Wrestling the "Pale Faced Messenger": The Diary of Edward Garrigues during the 1798 Philadelphia Yellow Fever Epidemic', *Pennsylvania History: A Journal of Mid-Atlantic Studies*, 65, Special Supplemental Issue (1998), 243–68

Dodd, A. H. (ed.), 'Letters from Cambria County, 1800–1823', *Pennsylvania History: A Journal of Mid-Atlantic Studies*, 22/2 (April 1955), 134–45

Dodd, A. H., 'The Background of the Welsh Quaker Migration to Pennsylvania', *Journal of the Merioneth Historical and Record Society*, 3/2 (1958), 111–27

Dunaway, W. F., 'Early Welsh Settlers of Pennsylvania', *Pennsylvania History: A Journal of Mid-Atlantic Studies*, 12 (1945), 252–3

Dunn, Mary Maples and Dunn, Richard S., 'The Founding, 1681–1701', in Russell F. Weighley, Nicholas B. Wainwright, Edwin B. Wolf, Joseph E. Illick and Thomas Wendel (eds), *Philadelphia: A 300-Year History* (New York and London: W. W. Norton & Co., 1982)

Erikson, Charlotte, *Leaving England: Essays on British Emigration in the Nineteenth Century* (Ithaca and London: Cornell University Press, 1994)

Farley, James J., '"To Commit Ourselves to Our Own Ingenuity and Industry": Joshua Humphreys and the Construction of the United States, 1794–1799', *Explorations in Early American Culture*, 5 (2001), 288–327.

Ferguson, James (ed.), *The Papers of Robert Morris 1781–1784* (9 vols. Pittsburgh: University of Pittsburgh Press, 1978)

Finger, Simon, *The Contagious City: The Politics of Public Health in Early Philadelphia* (Ithaca: Cornell University Press, 2012)

Fischer, David Hacket, *Albion's Seed: Four British Folkways in America* (Oxford: Oxford University Press, 1989)

Frost, J. W., *A Perfect Freedom: Religious Liberty in Pennsylvania* (University Park, Pa.: Pennsylvania State University Press, 1993)

Gilpin, Thomas, 'Fairmount Dam and Water Works, Philadelphia', *Pennsylvania Magazine of History and Biography*, 37/4 (1913), 471–9

Glenn, T. A., *Merion in the Welsh Tract* (Norristown: Herald Press, 1896)

Griffith, Elijah, *An Essay on Ophthalmia or Inflammation of the Eyes. Dissertation for the Degree of Doctor of Medicine* (Philadelphia: privately printed, 1804)

Hart, Charles Henry, *A Register of Portraits Painted by Thomas Sully, 1801–1871...* (Philadelphia: s.n., 1909)

Hodge, Hugh L,. *A Memoir of Thomas C. James, M.D. Read Before the College of Physicians of Philadelphia* (Philadelphia, T. K. and P. G. Collins, 1843)

Hughes, Heather, '"How the Welsh became White in South Africa": Immigration, Identity and Economic Transformation from the 1860s to the 1930s', *Transactions of the Honourable Society of Cymmrodorion: Trafodion Anrhydeddus Gymdeithas y Cymmrodorion*, New series, 7 (2001), 112–27

Humphreys, Henry H., 'Who Built the First United States Navy?', *Journal of American History*, 10 (1916), 49–89

Hussey, David, *Coastal and River Trade in pre-Industrial England: Bristol and its Region, 1680–1730* (Exeter: University of Exeter Press, 2000)

BIBLIOGRAPHY

Hussey, Miriam, *From Merchants to 'Colour Men': Five Generations of Samuel Wetherill's White Lead Business* (Philadelphia: University of Pennsylvania Press, 1956)

James, E. Wyn, 'Morgan John Rhys a Chaethwasiaeth Americanaidd', in D. G Williams (Ed.), *Canu Caeth: Y Cymry a'r Affro-Americaniaid* (Llandysul: Gwasg Gomer, 2010)

Jenkins, G. H., 'From Ysgeifiog to Pennsylvania: The Rise of Thomas Wynne, Quaker Barber-Surgeon', *Flintshire Historical Society Journal*, 28 (1977–8), 39–61

Jenkins, Howard M., 'The Welsh Settlement at Gwynedd', *Pennsylvania Magazine of History and Biography*, 8 (1884), 175–6

Jenkins, Howard M., *Historical Collections Relating to Gwynedd, Pennsylvania* (Philadelphia: Ferris Brothers, 1884; 2nd edn. Philadelphia: privately published, 1897)

Jenkins, R. T. and Rammage, Helen M., *The History of the Honourable Society of Cymmrodorion, 1751–1951* (London: The Honourable Society of Cymmrodorion, 1951)

Jewell, Wilson, *Historical Sketches of Quarantine: Address, Delivered before the Philadelphia County Medical Society, January 28, 1857* (Philadelphia: T. K. and P. G. Collins, 1857)

Jones, Aled and Jones, Bill, *Welsh Reflections: Y Drych and America, 1851–2001* (Llandysul: Gomer Press, 2001)

Jones, Bill, 'Desiring and Maintaining a Welsh Australia: The Cambrian Society of Victoria in the 1830s and 1940s', *Australia Studies*, 19/1 (Summer 2004), 113–46

Jones, Emrys, 'A Concise History of the Society', *Transactions of the Honourable Society of Cymmrodorion: Trafodion Anrhydeddus Gymdeithas y Cymmrodorion*, New Series, 9 (2003), 4–28

Jones, Horatio Gates, *Welsh Society Charter and Bye Laws* (Philadelphia: William Mann, 1880)

Jones, Maldwyn A., 'From the Old Country to the New: The Welsh in Nineteenth Century America', *Flintshire Historical Society*, 27 (1975–6), 85–100

Jones, William D., *Wales in America: Scranton and the Welsh 1860–1920* (Cardiff: University of Wales Press; Scranton, Pa.: University of Scranton Press, 1993)

Jones, W. D., 'The Welsh Language and Welsh Identity in a Pennsylvanian Community', in G. H. Jenkins (Ed.), *Language and Community in the Nineteenth Century: A Social History of the Welsh Language* (Cardiff: University of Wales Press, 1998)

Kidd, Colin, *British Identities Before Nationalism: Ethnicity and Nationhood in the Atlantic World, 1600–1800* (Cambridge; New York: Cambridge University Press, 1999)

Klepp, Susan E., 'The Demographic Characteristics of Philadelphia, 1788–1801: Zachariah Poulson's Bills of Mortality', *Pennsylvania History: A Journal of Mid-Atlantic Studies*, 53/3 (July 1986), 201–21

Klepp, Susan E., 'Demography in Early Philadelphia, 1690–1860', *Proceedings of the American Philosophical Society*, 133/2 (1989), 85–111

Klepp, Susan E., *'The Swift Progress of Population': A Documentary and Bibliographic Study of Philadelphia's Growth, 1600–1859* (Philadelphia: American Philosophical Society, 1989)

Konkle, Burton Alva, *Joseph Hopkinson, 1770-1842, Jurist-Scholar-Inspirer of the Arts* (Philadelphia: University of Pennsylvania Press, 1931)

Konkle, Burton Alva, *Benjamin Chew, 1722–1810: Head of the Pennsylvania Judiciary System under Colony and Commonwealth* (Philadelphia: University of Pennsylvania Press, 1932)

Konkle, Burton Alva, 'Enos Bronson, 1774–1823', *Pennsylvania Magazine of History and Biography*, 57 (1933), 355–8

Knott, Sarah, *Sensibility and the American Revolution* (Chapel Hill: University of North Carolina Press, 2009)

Knowles, Anne Kelly, 'Immigrant Trajectories through the Rural-Industrial Transition in Wales and the United States 1759–1850', *Annals of the Association of American Geographers*, 85/2 (1995), 246–66

Knowles, Anne Kelly, *Calvinists Incorporated: Welsh Immigrants in Ohio's Industrial Frontier* (Chicago: Chicago University Press, 1997)

Knudson, Jerry W., *Jefferson and the Press: Crucible of Liberty* (Columbia, SC: University of South Carolina Press, 2006)

Lambert, William Rees, *Drink and Sobriety in Victorian Wales, c.1820–c.1895* (Cardiff: University of Wales Press, 1980)

Landes, Jordan, *London Quakers in the Trans-Atlantic World: The Creation of an Early Modern Community* (Basingstoke: Palgrave Macmillan; 2015)

Langley, Harold, *A History of Medicine in the Early U. S. Navy* (Baltimore, MD: Johns Hopkins Press 1995)

Leathart, W. D., *The Origin and Progress of the Gwyneddigion Society of London, instituted MDCCLXX* (London: Hugh Pierce Hughes, 1831)

Levy, Barry, *Quakers and the American Family* (Cambridge: Cambridge University Press, 1988)

Lewis, Ronald, *Welsh Americans: A History of Assimilation in the Coalfields* (Chapel Hill: University of North Carolina Press, 2009)

Mackenzie, George Norbury and Rhoades, Nelson Osgood (eds), *Colonial Families of the United States of America* (7 vols. New York; Boston; Baltimore: Grafton Press; Seaforth Press 1907–1920)

MacRaild, Donald, Bueltmann, Tanya and Clarke, J. C. D. (eds), *British and Irish Diasporas: Societies, Cultures and Ideologies* (Manchester: Manchester University Press, 2019)

Miller, Randall M. and Pencak, William (eds), *Pennsylvania: A History of the Commonwealth* (University Park: Pennsylvania State University Press; Harrisburg, Pa.: Pennsylvania Historical and Museum Commission, 2002)

Morton Luther Montgomery, *History of Berks County, Pennsylvania: in the Revolution, from 1774 to 1783* (Reading, Pa.: C. F. Haage, 1894)

Morgan, Prys, *The Eighteenth Century Renaissance* (Llandybïe: Christopher Davies, 1981)

Morgan, Prys, 'From a Death to a View: The Hunt for the Welsh Past in the Romantic Period', in Eric Hobsbawm and Terence Ranger (eds), *The Invention of Tradition* (Cambridge: Cambridge University Press, 1983)

Morton, Thomas G. and Woodbury, Frank, *The History of the Pennsylvania Hospital 1751–1895* (Philadelphia: Times Printing House, 1895)

Nash, Gary B., 'Poverty and Poor Relief in Pre-Revolutionary Philadelphia', *William and Mary Quarterly*, Third Series, 33/1 (January 1976), 3–30

Nash, Gary B., *First City: Philadelphia and the Forging of Historical Memory* (Philadelphia: University of Pennsylvania Press, 2002)

O'Leary, Paul, 'Power and Modernity: Transnational Wales, c.1780–1939', *Llafur: Journal of Welsh People's History/Clychgrawn Hanes Pobl Cymru*, 12/4 (2019/20), 33–55

Packard, Francis R. and Greim, Florence M., *Some Account of the Pennsylvania Hospital from 1751 to 1938* (2nd edn. Philadelphia: Pennsylvania Hospital, 1957)

Payton, P., *The Cornish Overseas* (Fowey: Cornwall Editions, 1999)

Pennsylvania Academy of Fine Arts, *Catalogue of the Memorial Exhibition of Portraits by Thomas Sully* (2nd edn. Philadelphia: s.n.,

1922)

Pfleger, B., *Ethnicity Matters: A History of the German Society of Pennsylvania* (Washington DC: German Historical Institute, 2006)

Pullin, Naomi, *Female Friends and the Making of Transatlantic Quakerism, 1650–1750* (Cambridge: Cambridge University Press, 2018)

Rappleye, Charles, *Robert Morris: Financier of the American Revolution* (London: Simon & Schuster, 2010)

Rawle, William Henry, *Colonel Lambert Cadwalader, of Trenton, New Jersey* (Philadelphia, privately published, 1878)

Rees, Thomas Mardy, *A History of the Quakers in Wales and their Emigration to North America* (Carmarthen: W. Spurrell & Son, 1925)

Richards, Eric, *Britannia's Children: Emigration from England, Scotland, Wales and Ireland since 1600* (London and New York: Hambledon, 2004)

Richardson, Edgar P., 'The Athens of America, 1800–1825', in Russell F. Weighley, Nicholas B. Wainwright, Edwin B. Wolf, Joseph E. Illick and Thomas Wendel (eds), *Philadelphia: A 300-Year History* (New York and London: W. W. Norton & Co., 1982)

Robison, Jeannie F-J. and Bartlett, Henrietta C. (eds), *Genealogical Records. Manuscript Entries of Births, Deaths and Marriages, taken from Family Bibles 1581-1917* (New York: The Colonial Dames of the State of New York, 1917)

Roney, Jessica Choppin, *Governed by a Spirit of Opposition: The Origins of American Political Practice in Colonial Philadelphia* (Baltimore, MD: Johns Hopkins University Press, 2014)

Sacks, D. H., *The Widening Gate: Bristol and the Atlantic Economy, 1540–1700* (Berkeley and Oxford: University of California Press, 1991)

Sahle, Esther, *Quakers in the British Atlantic World, c.1660–1800* (Woodbridge: Boydell Press, 2021)

Scharf, Thomas J. and Westcott, Thompson, *History of Philadelphia, 1609–1884*, 3 vols. (Philadelphia: L. H. Everts & Co., 1884)

Schlenther, Boyd S., 'The English is Swallowing up Their Language': Welsh Ethnic Ambivalence in Colonial Pennsylvania and the Experience of David Evans', *Pennsylvania Magazine of History and Biography*, 114 (1990), 202–28

Schwartz, Sally, '*A Mixed Multitude*': *The Struggle for Toleration in Colonial Pennsylvania* (New York and London: New York University Press, 1987)

Shafer, Henry Burnell, 'Medicine in Old Philadelphia', *Pennsylvania History: A Journal of Mid-Atlantic Studies*, 4/1 (January 1937), 21–31

Simmons, R. C., *The American Colonies: From Settlement to Independence* (New York: D. McKay Co., 1976)

Smiles, S., *The Image of Antiquity: Ancient Britain and the Romantic Imagination* (New Haven and London: Yale University Press, 1994)

Smith, B., 'Death and Life in a Colonial Immigrant City: A Demographic Analysis of Philadelphia', *Journal of Economic History*, 37/4 (1977), 863–88

Smith, Samuel S., *Lewis Morris: Anglo-American Statesman, ca.1613–1691* (Atlantic Highland, New Jersey: Humanities Press, 1983)

Smyth, Albert, *The Philadelphia Magazines and their Contributors 1741–1850* (Philadelphia: Robert M. Lindsay, 1892)

Society of the Sons of St George, Philadelphia, *History of the Society of the Sons of St George, Philadelphia* (Philadelphia: T. C. Knauff, 1923)

Stagg, J. C. A., Cross, Jeanne Kerr and Perdue, Susan Holbrook (eds), *The Papers of James Madison, Presidential Series, Vol. 2, 1 October*

1809–2 November 1810 (Charlottesville: University Press of Virginia, 1992)

Strong, William, *An Eulogium on the Life and Character of Horace Binney* (Philadelphia: McCalla & Stavely, Printers, 1876)

Sullivan, Aaron, '"That Charity which begins at Home": Ethnic Societies and Benevolence in Eighteenth-Century Philadelphia', *Pennsylvania Magazine of History and Biography*, 134/4 (October 2010), 305–37

Taylor, Agnes Longstreth, *The Longstreth Family Records* (Philadelphia, Press of Ferris & Leach, 1909)

Thompson, Peter, *Rum Punch and Revolution: Taverngoing and Public Life in Eighteenth-Century* (Philadelphia: University of Pennsylvania Press, 1998)

Thompson, Peter, '"The Friendly Glass": Drink and Gentility in Colonial Philadelphia', *Pennsylvania Magazine of History and Biography*, 113/4 (October, 1989), 549–73

Tinkcom, Harry M., 'Town into City, 1746–1765', in Russell F. Weighley, Nicholas B. Wainwright, Edwin B. Wolf, Joseph E. Illick and Thomas Wendel (eds), *Philadelphia: A 300-Year History* (New York and London: W. W. Norton & Co., 1982)

Trenton Historical Society, *A History of Trenton, 1679–1929: Two Hundred and Fifty Years of a Notable Town...* (Princeton: Princeton University Press, 1929)

Tyler, Robert Ll., *The Welsh in an Australian Gold Town: Ballarat, Victoria, 1850–1900* (Cardiff: University of Wales Press, 2010)

Tyler, Robert Ll., *Wales and the American Dream* (Newcastle: Cambridge Scholars Publishing, 2015)

Tyler, Robert Ll., 'Migrant Identity and Culture Maintenance:

The Welsh in Clearfield County, Pennsylvania, USA, 1880–1920', *Immigrants and Minorities*, 38/3 (2020), 205–32

Tyler, Robert Ll., 'Culture Maintenance in an Immigrant Community: The Welsh in Seattle, Washington 1890–1940', *Pacific Northwest Quarterly*, 111/4 (2020), 134–48

Tyler, Robert Ll., 'Migrant Culture Maintenance: The Welsh in Silver Bow County, Montana, 1890–1930', *Montana: Magazine of Western History*, 68/4, (Winter 2018), 20–35

Tyler, Robert Ll., 'Migrant Culture Maintenance: The Welsh Experience in Martins Ferry, Belmont County, Ohio, 1900–1940', *Ohio History*, 125/1 (Spring 2018), 70–94

Tyler, Robert Ll., 'Migrant Culture Maintenance: The Welsh in Granville, Washington County, New York, 1880–1930', *New York History*, 99/1 (Winter 2018), 99–120

Tyler, Robert Ll., 'Culture Maintenance, Occupational Change, and Social Status: The Welsh in San Francisco, 1880–1930', *California History*, 94/1 (Spring 2017), 6–25

Tyler, Robert Ll., 'Culture Maintenance, Occupational Mobility and Social Status: The Welsh in a Pennsylvania Slate Town 1900–1930', *Welsh History Review*, 28/1 (July 2016), 115–45

Tyler, Robert Ll., 'Occupational Mobility and Social Status: The Welsh Experience in Sharon, Pennsylvania 1880–1930', *Pennsylvania History: A Journal of Mid-Atlantic Studies*, 83/1 (Winter 2016), 1–27

Tyler, Robert Ll., 'Identity, Culture Maintenance and Social Mobility: The Welsh in Emporia, Lyon County, 1870–1930', *Kansas History: A Journal of the Central Plains*, 38/2 (Summer 2015), 65–78

Tyler, Robert Ll., 'Migrant Culture Maintenance: The Welsh Experience in Poultney, Rutland County 1900–1940', *Vermont History*, 83/1 (Winter/ Spring 2015), 19–42

BIBLIOGRAPHY

Tyler, Robert Ll., 'Occupational Change, Culture Maintenance and Social Status: The Welsh in a Missouri Coal Town, 1870–1930', *Missouri Historical Review*, 109/1 (October 2014), 18–40

Ukers, William H. (ed.), *All About Coffee* (New York: Tea and Coffee Trade Journal Company, 1922)

Van Vugt, William E., 'Welsh Emigration to the United States during the Mid-Nineteenth Century', *Welsh History Review*, 15/4 (December 1991), 545–61

Ver Steeg, Clarence L., *Robert Morris: Revolutionary Financier* (Philadelphia: University of Pennsylvania Press, 1954)

Wainwright, Nicholas B., 'The Age of Nicholas Biddle, 1825–1841', in Russell F. Weighley, Nicholas B. Wainwright, Edwin B. Wolf, Joseph E. Illick and Thomas Wendel (eds), *Philadelphia: A 300-Year History* (New York and London: W. W. Norton & Co., 1982)

Wharton, Anne Hollingsworth, *Genealogy of the Wharton Family of Philadelphia, 1664 to 1880* (Philadelphia: privately published, 1880)

Wharton, Susanna Parrish, *The Parrish Family [Philadelphia, Pennsylvania], including the related families of Cox–Dillwyn–Roberts–Chandler–Mitchell–Painter–Pusey by Dillwyn Parrish, 1809–1886, with special reference to Joseph Parker, M.D., 1779–1840, with sketches of his children, by members of the family and others* (Philadelphia: George H. Buchanan, 1925).

Williams, Glanmor, 'A Prospect of Paradise? Wales and the United States, 1776–1914', in G. Williams, *Religion, Language and Nationality in Wales* (Cardiff: University of Wales Press, 1979)

Williams, Gwyn A., *When Was Wales?* (pbk edn. London: Penguin, 1985)

Williams, Gwyn A., *The Search for Beulah Land: The Welsh and the Atlantic Revolution* (London: Croom Helm, 1979)

Williams, William H., *America's First Hospital: The Pennsylvania Hospital, 1751–1841* (Wayne, Pa: Haverford House, 1976)

Woolf, Jordan John, *Colonial Families of Philadelphia* (2 vols. New York: Lewis Publishers, 1911)

Wood, Gordon S., *Empire of Liberty: A History of the Early Republic, 1789-1815* (Oxford: Oxford University Press, 2009)

Wright, Robert K. Jr. and MacGregor, Morris J. Jr., *Soldier-Statesmen of the Constitution* (Washington, DC: Center of Military History, U.S. Army, 1987)

Unpublished Works

[i] Theses

Bryan, Jennifer A., 'The Tilghmans of Maryland's Eastern Shore, 1660–1793', University of Maryland, Ph.D. thesis, 1999

Gilbert, Daniel R., 'Patterns of Organization and Membership in Colonial Philadelphia Club Life, 1725–1755', University of Pennsylvania, Ph.D. thesis, 1952

Grundfest, Jerry, 'George Clymer, Philadelphia Revolutionary, 1739–1813', University of Columbia, Ph.D. thesis, 1973

Taylor, Sean, '"We Live in the Midst of Death": Yellow Fever, Moral Economy, and Public Health in Philadelphia, 1793–1805', Northern Illinois University, Ph.D. thesis, 2001

[ii] Electronic Studies

Ball, Joseph: 'Penn People: Joseph Ball', Pennsylvania University Archives and Records Center, *https://archives.upenn.edu/exhibits/penn-people/biography/joseph-ball*

Basto Village: 'Industry in the Pines: The Story of Batsto Village', *https://www.thehistorygirl.com/2013/03/industry-in-pines-story-of-batsto.html*

BIBLIOGRAPHY

Binney, Horace: 'Horace Binney, 1780–1875', *Biographical Directory of the United States Congress,* https://bioguide.congress.gov/search/bio/B000475

Bloom, Joseph: 'Jacob Broom, Delaware', https://history.army.mil/books/RevWar/ss/broom.htm

Blumfield family, https://www.genealogy.com/ftm/f/o/w/Joyce-A-Fowler-WV/GENE6-0010.html – notes for Joseph Ellis Bloomfield, no. 52

Farley, James, 'To Commit Ourselves to Our Own Ingenuity: Joshua Humphreys – Early Philadelphia Ship Building', https://earlyphiladelphiashipbuilding.wordpress.com/

Freeman, T. B. & Company, http://www.freemansauction.com/timeline.asp

Hallowell, John, www.findagrave.com/memorial/161284612/john-hallowell

Hasty Pudding Club, https://hastypudding.org/

'Hopkinson, Joseph, 1770–1842', Biographical Directory of the United States Congress, https://bioguide.congress.gov/search/bio/H000784

Hunter, Richard W., Sergejeff, Nadine and Tvaryanas, Damon, 'On The Eagle's Wings: Textiles, Trenton, and a First Taste of the Industrial Revolution', https://njh.libraries.rutgers.edu/index.php/njh/article/view/991

Jones, Bill, '"Raising the Wind": Emigrating from Wales to the USA in the late nineteenth and early twentieth centuries', Canolfan Uwchefrydiau Cymry America, Prifysgol Caerdydd / The Cardiff Centre for Welsh American Studies, Cardiff University, Annual Public Lecture for 2003, http://orca.cf.ac.uk/48163/1/RaisingTheWind.pdf

Lisowski, Joshua, 'Wetherill & Son's White Lead Factory',

The Encyclopaedia of Greater Philadelphia, *https:// philadelphiaencyclopedia.org/wetherill-2/*

Market Street: 'Market (or High) Street', *http://philahistory.net/ market.html*

Moss, Roger W., 'Worrell, Joseph (c.1769–1840), master builder; American Architects and Buildings database, *https://www. americanbuildings.org/pab/app/ar_display.cfm/23275*

'Penn People: Richard Peters, 1743–1828', Pennsylvania University Archives and Records Center, *https://archives.upenn.edu/exhibits/ penn-people/biography/richard-peters-2*

Philadelphia City Revolutionary War Militia, *https://www.phmc. pa.gov/Archives/Research-Online/Pages/Revolutionary-War-Militia-Philadelphia-City.aspx*

Sobocinski, André B., 'The Formative Years of the U.S. Navy Medical Corps, 1798–1871', *https://www.history.navy.mil/content/history/ nhhc/browse-by-topic/communities/ navy-medicine/navy-med-history. html#56*

Soderlund, Jean R., 'Colonial Era' in 'The Encyclopedia of Greater Philadelphia'. *https://philadelphiaencyclopedia.org/archive/colonial-philadelphia/*

Strawbridge, John: 'Autobiography of John Strawbridge', written in Philadelphia in April 1843, *http://www.users.interport.net/a/s/aswhite/ JSFULBIO.html*

Trenton Historical Society: *http://trentonhistory.org/His/banks.htm*

US First Marshals, *https://www.usmarshals.gov/history/firstmarshals/ biddle450.jpg*

Waln, Jesse: 'To James Madison from Jesse Waln, 23 April 1810', Founders Online, National Archives [America], *https://founders. archives.gov/documents/Madison/03-02-02-0391*

BIBLIOGRAPHY

Waln, Robert: 'Waln, Robert, 1765–1836', Biographical Directory of the United States Congress, *https://bioguide.congress.gov/search/bio/W000094*

Wayne, Isaac: 'Isaac Wayne – Biography', Pennsylvania State Senate; *https://www.legis.state.pa.us/cfdocs/legis/BiosHistory/MemBio.cfm?ID=5026&body=S*

Wenzel, Charles D., 'The Mount Moriah Cemetery of the Welsh Society of Philadelphia', *https://www.peoplescollection.wales/sites/default/files/Mt.%20Moriah.pdf*

West Philadelphia Community History Center, 'West Philadelphia: The History – Pre-History to 1854', *https://westphillyhistory.archives.upenn.edu/history/chapter-1*

Wharton, Franklin: 'Lieutenant Colonel Franklin Wharton, SMC (Deceased)', Marine Corps University, *https://www.usmcu.edu/Research/Marine-Corps-History-Division/People/Whos-Who-in-Marine-Corps-History/Vandegrift-Worley/Lieutenant-Colonel-Franklin-Wharton/*

INDEX OF ASSISTED WELSH EMIGRANTS

Aaron, Margaret 422
Ambrose, Ambrose (Monmouthshire) 386
Anthony, J. 52, 372
Ashton, Evan 389
Baynes, Evan (& family) 430
Bowen, Henry 243
Bowen, John 243
Breese, William 306
Cann, Mary (& family) 422
Canver, Sarah (& family) 422
Comey, Ann (widow, Llanfihangel Genau'r-Glyn, Cardiganshire) 46, 351–2
Daniel, Philip (& family) 422
Daniel, Rachel 389
David, Frederick (& family) 401
Davies, David (& family) 46, 48, 372, 377
Davis,[1] Barbara 393
Davis, David 44, 52, 253, 277, 284–5, 393, 437
Davis, Edward 243
Davis, Frederick (& family) 430
Davis, John (& family), Delaware County, Ohio 295
Davis, John (& family), Ebensburg, Cambria County 296
Davis, John (& family) 361–2, 364, 430
Davis, Owen 241

Davis, Richard (and wife) 430
Davis, Thomas (& family) 52, 372, 377
Davis, William (& family) 52, 372, 377, 386
Edward(s), Elizabeth (Anglesey) 381, 386
Edwards, Charles (& family) 401
Edwards, Daniel 243
Elway, James 377
Evans, Evan (& family), Ohio 42n, 317
Evans, Evan 44, 251, 253
Evans, John (& family), Baltimore 48, 296
Evans, Reese (& family) 52, 373, 377
Evans, Richard 52, 372, 377
Evans, Williams (& family) 401
Ewing, James 53, 374
Francis, John 48, 277
Franks, Thomas (& family) 401
Garrett, Elizabeth (widow & son) 50, 362, 364
Griffith, David 437
Griffith, David (& family) 401
Griffith, Fanny 52, 373
Griffith, J. 377
Griffith, John R. 386
Haily, David (& family) 430
Haines, David 243
Harries, Hannah 389

---

1 Many of these emigrants recorded as Davis would have had the last name Davies.

INDEX OF ASSISTED WELSH EMIGRANTS

Harris/Harries, Evan (Merthyr Tydfil) 383, 386
Harris, Henry (& family) 422, 430
Harris, Thomas (child/apprentice house carpenter) 39, 140–1, 173, 178
Hawkins, R. 53, 374
Hitchens, E. 53, 374, 376
Howard, Mary 430
Howell, Owen (apprentice) 173
Howells, Mary 430
Hughes, David 312
Hughes, Edward 44, 253
Hughes, John, Boston 299, 304
Hughes, Richard (and child) 295
Humphreys, Robert (& family), Denbighshire/Pottsville, Schuylkill County 50–1, 367–8
James, David (& family) 437
James, Henry 53, 374, 377
James, Jane (& family) 401
James, Mary (& family) 430
James, Sarah 437
Jeffreys, David (& family) 45, 288
Jenkins/Jennings, Joseph (& family), Pike Township, Bradford County, Pennsylvania 45&n, 307, 310, 316&n
Jenkins, Reese (& wife) 44, 251, 253
Jenkins, Richard, Steubenville, Ohio 42n, 312
Jones, Ann (& daughter) 50, 364
Jones, Ann (& family) 430
Jones, David 430
Jones, Edward (& family), Bradford County, Pennsylvania 319
Jones, Eliza (widow) 361, 364
Jones, Eliza (Anglesey) 381, 386
Jones, Elizabeth (& family) 50, 401
Jones, Evan 243, 437

Jones, Griffith 306
Jones, Howell (orphan) 190
Jones, James 251
Jones, Jocai 401
Jones, John (Montgomeryshire), apothecary 37, 350
Jones, John (amputee) 40, 185
Jones, John (child) 39, 140–1
Jones, John 386, 437
Jones, John (& family) 393, 422
Jones, Joseph (& family) 401
Jones, Mashach 401
Jones, Richard (child) 39, 140–1
Jones, Richard (children) 121
Jones, Shadrach (& family) 401
Jones, Thomas 44, 251, 253
Jones, Thomas 243
Jones, Thomas (& family) 363
Jones, William (deaf & dumb) 52, 372, 377
Jones, William (wife & family) 251
Kelly, Lucy (& family) 422
Lewis, Charles 401
Lewis, Elizabeth ('distressed widow' & family) 46, 50, 336, 339–40
Lewis, Hannah (& daughter), Swansea, Glamorganshire 49
Lewis, Margaret 437
Lewis, Mary (joined husband in Pittsburgh) 295
Lewis, Mary (& family) 430
Lewis, Richard, Baltimore 38–9
Lewis, Samuel 243
Lewis, William Jr 44, 251, 253
Lewis, William Sr 44, 251, 253
Llewellyn, Thomas (& family) 52, 372, 377
Lloyd, Elizabeth 393
Lowrie, C. (& family) 401
Meredith, William 52, 372, 376

Miles, Lewis 38, 104
Morgan, Catherine 377
Morgan, Daniel J. (& family) 422
Morgan, John (letter of gratitude) 43n, 250
Morgan, Sarah 422
Morgan, Thomas 251
Morgan, Thomas (& family) 44, 251, 253
Morgan, Thomas 386
Morgan, Thomas (& family) 401
Morris, Jane 393
Morris, John (& family, Montgomeryshire), Pittsburgh 50n, 363–4
Morris, Thomas (& wife) 45, 340
Nicholas, Edward (& family) 306
O'Brien (widow & family) 44, 253
O'Donnell, C. 53, 374
Owen, Elizabeth (widow of John & family) 37–8, 101–2, 104
Owen, Robert (& John, his son), Birmingham Mils, New Jersey 45, 342
Owens, Elizabeth (orphan) 407
Owens, Sarah (orphan) 407
Pask, Daniel 401
Pearce, Mrs 201, 204
Phelps, J. 52, 372
Popkins, Robert 53, 374, 377
Price, Edward, passage to West Indies 41, 131
Price, John (painter, North Wales), Smith Island, Maryland 41, 368&n
Prichard, Thomas (& family) 42n, 243
Pritchet (Prichard), Mary 46, 157
Prosser, Watkins (& family) 401
Prosser, William (returned to Wales) 48, 283
Rees, Evan (& family), New York /

Pittsburgh 43n, 312 return of his loan 322
Rees, T[homas] 52, 372, 377
Reese, Elias (Susan, his wife & family) 251
Reese, J. 52, 373, 377
Reese, John (& family) 52, 373
Reese, Jonah (& family) 430
Reese, William 422
Reynolds, Samuel 48, 277
Richards, Ann 53, 374, 377
Richards, Evan (widow of & family) 104
Roberts, Edward (Denbighshire), Pottsville 382, 386
Roberts, Ellis ('Balla Manora'), Pottsville 381, 386
Roberts, Evan 251
Roberts, George, Ebensburg, Cambria County 38
Roberts, James 430
Roberts, John (Hannah, his wife & family) 40–1, 47, 211, 212–13, 215
Roberts, Richard (Denbighshire), Pottsville 382, 386
Roberts, Thomas (Denbighshire) 383, 386
Robinson, Elizabeth 46
Rogers, John Evans (& family, Montgomeryshire) 353
Rogers, Robert (& family, Montgomeryshire) 45, 306
Smith, John (& family) 430
Sylvanus, Joshua (lunatic) 40, 125
Tegan, William 52, 371–2
Thomas, David 422
Thomas, Eliza (& family) 422
Thomas, John 46n, 316
Thomas, John (& family, Llanfyllin, Montgomeryshire) 48n, 309–10

Thomas, Thomas 131
Thomas, Thomas 243
Thomas, Thomas ('Aberyshire') 383, 386
Thomas, William 247
Tobias, Enos (& family), Indiana 283
Vaughan, Elizabeth (& family and unspecified husband), Pottsville 52, 53, 374, 377-8
Vincent, William 437
Waller/Walter/Watters, Mary, Monmouthshire 377, 386
Walters, Henry (& family) 422
Walton, David (& family, Glamorganshire) 383, 386
Watkins, George 44, 253
Watkins, Jacob 44, 253
Watkins, Thomas (& family), Ebensburg, Cambria County 45, 288
Wilkins, Edward 44, 253
Williams, Bridget 47, 271, 277
Williams, Daniel (& family) 401
Williams, David 306
Williams, Eliza (& family) 422
Williams, George (Caernarfonshire) 37, 360
Williams, John 243
Williams, John (& family) 430
Williams, Mary (& family) 52, 372, 377&n
Williams, Robert (& family) 401
Williams, Sarah (& family) 401
Williams, Thomas (& family) 52, 372, 376
Williams, William 52, 372, 376
Williams, William 243
Williams, William Jr 243
Woods, Isaac (& wife) 430

INDEX

Allibone, Thomas 443
American Revolution / War of
  Independence 15–16, 31–3
  Continental Army 32, 444, 445, 449, 451, 457, 472, 476, 481
  Continental Congresses 15, 31, 33, 452, 454, 455, 457, 464, 473, 476, 481
  Declaration of Independence 15
ap Evan, Thomas 5
ap John, William 5
associational life 1–2&n, 10–13, 26&n
  Academy of Natural Science 497
  American Philosophical Society 15, 452, 464, 474, 479, 486
  Caradogion 26
  celtic revivalism 11
  Cymdeithas Cymreigyddion y Fenni 26
  Cymreigyddion 26
  Gwyneddigion 26
  ethnic societies (English, Scottish, Irish & German) 27&n, *passim*
  Fox-Hunting Club of Gloucester, New Jersey 32, 499
  Honourable and Loyal Society of Ancient Britons, London (later Hon. Soc of Cymmrodorion) 10–11, 26
  Library Company of Philadelphia 15, 470, 477, 479, 482
  Pennsylvania Academy of Fine Arts 31

Saint David's day festivities 24–6, 92
Saint David's Society, Philadelphia 17, 31
Schuylkill Fishing Company 32, 499
Society of the Sons of Ancient Britons, Philadelphia (also see Welsh Society of Philadelphia) 2, 8–10, 13–14, 16, 54
Washington Benevolent Society 32, 499
Bacon, Job 443–4
Bacon, John 444
Ball, Joseph 444–5
  industrialist (see businesses, Basto Ironworks); public life
Biddle, Clement 33, 445–6
  family; military and political career
Biddle, George 446
Biddle, James C. 446
Biddle, Owen 33
Biddle, Thomas A. 18, 446
Binney, Horace 446–7
  education; Hasty Pudding Club, Harvard University, founder of; legal, political career; public life
Birchall, Caleb 447–8
Blénon, Pierre Antoine / Peter Anthony 22, 425–6&n, 427
  medical career; bequest
Bloomfield, Joseph E. 448
  canal and railway construction,

INDEX

involvement with; mercantile career
Bronson, Enos 18, 23, 34n, 449–50
  education (Yale College); early
  career (Deerfield Academy,
  Massachusetts); *Gazette of the
  United States / United States
  Gazette for the Country*, editor and
  proprietor of; Federalist
Brooke, Reese 448
Broome, Jacob (Wilmington,
  Delaware) 39, 109, 448–9
  education and career; involvement
  in American Revolution; political
  career; United States Constitution,
  signer of; Constitutional
  Convention, delegate to
Brown, Abiah 450
Bryan, James
  medical career 450
burial grounds (Welsh)
  conditions of interment 411
  contested ownership of 427–8
  Hamilton's estate, part of 28–9,
    405–6
  Mount Moriah cemetery 29&n,
    189&n
  ownership of 403–6
  maintenance and superintendence
    of 403, 405–6, 407, 408–9, 411,
    432, 433, 438
  St David's Society, discussions with
    189&n, 190, 192–3, 195
businesses
  Allibone and Stephenson, curriers,
    Philadelphia 443
  Allibone, T. and Son, merchants,
    Philadelphia 443
  American Fire Insurance Company
    443
  Bank of North America 470, 489

Bank of the United States 458
Basto Ironworks, Burlington
  County, New Jersey 444
Birmingham Mills, New Jersey 45
Centre Furnace Ironworks,
  Milesburg, Centre County,
  Pennsylvania 474
Cooke and Company (merchants)
  494
Eagle Factory, Trenton, New Jersey
  475, 496
Fairmount Water Works 469
Farmers and Mechanics Bank 489
Freeman, T. B. & Company 460
Girard Life Insurance, Annuity and
  Trust Company (Girard Bank)
  486, 497
Holland Land Company 479
Insurance Company of North
  America 444
Lewis and Company (merchants)
  470
Neave, Harman and Lewis
  (shipowners and importers) 470
New York and Baltimore
  Stagecoach Company 489
Philadelphia Bank 31
Samuel Sansom (merchant) 494
Schuylkill Bank 497
Schuylkill Navigation Company
  52, 458, 469
Trenton Banking Company 456
Willing, Morris and Company 476
Cadwallader, Gen. John (Pres. of St
  David's Society) 25
Cadwallader, John 451
Cadwallader, Joseph 451
Cadwallader, Lambert 451–2
  education Dr Allison's Academy,
  College of Philadelphia; family;

535

political and military career;
American Philosophical Society,
election to; Carpenters' Company
500
Chauncey, Charles 452&n
 family; education (Yale College);
 legal career; Philadelphia Academy
 of Fine Arts, founder of; portrait
 of
Chauncey, Elihu 18, 452
 *United States' Gazette for the
 Country*, co-publisher of
Chauncey, Thomas 18
Chew, Benjamin 453&n
 early life; legal career; Bill of Rights,
 involvement with; bust of
Clark, Samuel 453
Clifton, John 454
Clymer, George 31, 454–5
 family and early life; business
 interests; political career; public life
Cruckshank, James 455
Cumpston, Thomas 19, 238, 455–6&n
 Treasurer of the Welsh Society;
 bankruptcy of Robert Morris, role
 in; portrait of
Davis, John 19
Dewees, William Potts 456&n
 medical career; public activities;
 portrait of
Dickinson, Philemon 457
 family; education (University of
 Pennsylvania); political and military
 career
disease
 cholera 407
 infant mortality 50, 367
 yellow fever 30&n, 48, 103n, 296, 363n, 490, 491

Dixey, Captain Charles 52, 309, 378
Drury / Drewry, Spafford 457–8
 philanthropic activities; public life
Elliott, Thomas 343
Ellis, David 458
emigration
 seventeenth century
  causes and settlements (Welsh
  Tract) 3–7
  self-government 4–5
  Susquehanna Land Company 5
 nineteenth century
  behaviour of migrants 43, 246–8
  conditions in Pennsylvania 40–1, 43
  costs of travel 52
  dangers of sea passage 38–9, 50, 367
  historiography 36–7
  numbers, increase in 49–50
Evan, Griffith 18n
Evans, Cadwallader 458
Evans, Cadwallader Jr 458–9
 political career; public life
Evans, John 19
Evans, Peter 459
Foulke, Caleb 459
Foulke, Caleb Jr 459
Foulke, Charles 459
Foulke, Owen 18, 460
Franklin, Benjamin 454
Freeman, Tristram B. 460&n
Gardner, Benjamin (house carpenter) 39, 178
Garrigues, Benjamin F.
 fees collector/messenger 220, 460
Garrigues, Edward
 fees collector/messenger 38, 103&n, 234

INDEX

Gibson, Thomas 460
Gillaspy, George 461
  medical career in the navy
Girard College 500
Glentworth, James 461
Glentworth, James Jr 461
Grice, Samuel 461
Griffith, Elijah 461–2
  medical career
Haines, John 462
Hallowell, John 462
  education; legal career; public life
Hamilton, James 463
  legal career; public life
Hamilton, William (also see burial ground) 28, 405–6, 408, 427, 433, 463
  landowner, Hamilton estate/village; legal career
Higbee, Joseph 463
Hollingsworth, Paschal 464
Hopkinson, Joseph 464
  family; education (University of Pennsylvania); legal career; political activities; public life; *Hail, Columbia* (1798), composer of
Huddell, Joseph 464–5
Humphreys, Clement 465
Humphreys, Joshua 'father of the American Navy') 465
  naval architect, career as
Humphreys, Samuel 466
Humphreys, Thomas 466
Hunt, Pearson 466
Hunt, Wilson 466
imprisonment 47, 271
James, Thomas Chalkley (physician) 19, 39–40, 41, 110, 211, 213, 215, 317, 340, 368, 466–7
  family; education (University of Pennsylvania); medical career; midwifery, lectures on; editor and essayist; Historical Society of Pennsylvania, founder of
Jones, Bill 13
Jones, Horatio Gates 34–5
Jones, Hugh 7
Jones, Israel 467
Jones, Jonathan 19
Jones, John (fl. 1725) 7
Jones, John
  fees collector/messenger 20, 218
Jones, Richard C. 29–30, 168–70, 468
  testimonial for; yellow fever, treatment of
Jones, Thomas 20n
Jones, William 19, 21, 468
Keble, John 22, 175–6, 183–4, 203, 204
  bequest
Kinsey, Edmund 20n, 468
  public life
Lassalle, Stephen Beasley 468–9
Lazaretto, Delaware County (quarantine station) 38&n, 103&n, 104, 121
Levick, James Jones 12–13
Lewis, Joseph Saunders 43n, 469
Lewis, Mordecai 469–71
  family; business interests (merchant); philanthropy, public life
Lewis, Samuel Neave 471
  business interests (merchant); public life
Linn, Mary 44, 259
Lloyd, Richard (Lower Darby, Delaware) 39
Maddock, Ezekiel C. 471
Maddock, William L. 471

Maris, Richard 18n, 471–2&n
  business interests (merchant);
  portrait of
Meredith, Samuel 19, 32–3, 234,
  237–8, 472–3
  1st President of the Welsh Society;
  United States Treasurer; family;
  education (Dr Allison's Academy);
  business interests (merchant
  and land speculator); military
  and political career; death and
  testimony
Meredith, William 20n, 473
Miles, Samuel 473–4
  business interests (wine merchant);
  legal, military and political career;
  public life
Montgomery, Robert 22n, 177–8
  bequest
Morgan, Benjamin Rawle 19, 475&n
  legal career; public life; portrait of
Morgan, Jacob 19, 475–6
  business interests (sugar refiner);
  military career
Morris, Lewis (Tintern/Barbados/
  New York) 3n
Morgan, Prys 11
Morris, Richard Hill 476
  Philadelphia Stock Exchange,
  President of
Morris, Robert 476–7
  'Financier of the Revolution';
  family; business (merchant) and
  financial interests; political career
  (Declaration of Independence,
  signer of; Articles of Confederation
  and US Constitution, signer of);
  bankruptcy
Morris, Thomas 477&n
  business interests (brewer); public
  life; portrait of
Murdock, Robert 477
Nash, Gary 15–16
Newspapers, advertisements, almanacs
  and reports
  American Daily Advertiser 481
  American Weekly Mercury 9n
  Gazette of the United States &
    Philadelphia Daily Advertiser 18
    &n, 19&n, 24, 449–50, 486n
  London Gazette 10n
  Mirror of Taste and Dramatic
    Censor 501
  National Gazette 484
  Pennsylvania Gazette 8–11
  Poulson's Town and Country
    Almanac 481
  United States Gazette for the
    Country 450, 452
  Western Sky 486
  Y Cylchgrawn Cymraeg (The Welsh
    Magazine) 485
Nichols, William 478
Norris, Joseph P. 478
North, Joseph 478
Ogden, William 1, 18, 19, 24, 25,
  80&n, 221–2, 478
  tavern, Chestnut Street,
  Philadelphia
Otto, Jacob S. 479
  business interests (land agent)
Palmer, John 479
Parke, Thomas 41, 193, 203, 317, 387,
  479&n
  education; medical career; public
  life; honorary membership; portrait
  of
Parry, John J. 480
  business interests (master clock
  maker)

INDEX

Paxton Boys 445
Peace, with Britain (1815) 224
Penn, William 3, 5
Pennsylvania General Assembly 481, 486, 492
Pennsylvania Hospital 40&n, 46n, 50, 185, 284–5, 307, 316, 470, 471, 475, 481
Pennsylvania Infirmary of the Eye and Ear 291
Pennsylvania State Legislature 31, 486, 495
Perot, Sansom 480
Peters, Richard 480–1
 Arnold, Benedict, duel with; financing the Continental Army; military and political career (Speaker of Pennsylvania General Assembly and Senate)
Philadelphia
 general history, incl. demography 14–15
 diversity 15
 cultural activities and societies 15
 ethnic communities 14
 festivities 14
 social composition 14–15
Philadelphia Board of Health (also, see Garrigues, Edward) 38, 103&n, 105, 107
Philadelphia College of Physicians 479
Philadelphia Committee of Safety 31
Philadelphia Society for Ameliorating the Miseries of Public Prisons (Pennsylvania Prison Society) 481
Philadelphia Society for the Encouragement of Domestic Manufacturers 491

philanthropy
 accommodation, provision of 50, 306
 anxieties over relief payments 48–9, 53, 195–6, 309, 312–13, 313–14, 357, 377–8, 391, 394–5, 396, 416
 apprenticeships, placements and problems concerning 39, 140–1, 144, 173, 178
 assisted passage (to/from America and to/from Philadelphia) 41–3, 45, 48, 51
 clothes, provision of 47, 50, 190
 education, provision of 198, 200
 elderly 45
 employment 51, 316, 340, 350, 360, 368
 food, provision of 48
 funerals 45–6, 285, 368
 illness & medical assistance (also, see Pennsylvania Hospital) 37–8, 39–40, 42, 45, 48, 50, 125, 157, 185, 211, 212–13, 284–5, 306, 307–8, 363, 368
 legal fees, payment of 46–7, 362
 letters of gratitude 250
 loans 49, 50n, 53, 88, 130, 322, 358, 363, 383, 385–6, 392–3, 394–5, 401, 407, 411, 416, 418, 419, 422–3, 425, 427, 430
 luggage, retrieval of 50
 women, children and orphans (also, see migrants) 30, 37–8, 42–3, 46–7, 101–2, 140–1, 144, 145, 173, 178, 190, 277, 407
 working conditions and employment rights, securing of 47

yellow fever, assistance for victims
  30, 48, 296
Physick, Dr Philip Syng 50, 363&n
places
  Baltimore, Maryland 38–9, 48, 296
  Beulah, Cambria County,
    Pennsylvania 486
  Birmingham Mills, New Jersey 45,
    342
  Boston 50, 299, 367
  Delaware County, Ohio 295
  Ebensburg, Cambria County,
    Pennsylvania 38, 45, 288, 296
  Lawrenceburg, Indiana 49, 357n
  Mount Carbon, Schuylkill County,
    Pennsylvania 50&n, 362&n, 363
  Muncy, Lycoming County,
    Pennsylvania 162&n
  New York 48&n, 50n, 288, 306,
    309, 312, 360, 363, 367
  Pike Township, Bradford County,
    north-eastern Pennsylvania 45n,
    316&n
  Pittsburgh 43n, 45, 46, 48, 50n,
    247, 281–2, 283, 288, 295, 306,
    312, 351, 358, 363, 407, 418
    visit by members 281–2, 285
  Pottsville, Schuylkill County,
    Pennsylvania 51, 368&n,
    377–8, 381–2, 418
  Steubenville, Ohio 42n, 312&n
Potts, Nathan R. 481
Poulson, Zachariah 17n, 481–2&n
  business interests (printer and
  newspaper; publisher); public life;
  portrait of
Powell, Howell (Brecon / Virginia) 3n
Preston, William 20n, 138, 139, 482
Price, Chandler 482
Price, John M. 482–3

Price, Joseph 483
Price, Richard 17n, 19, 31, 291,
  292–3
  testimony to
Price, Samuel 483
Pugh, Ellis
  Annerch i'r Cymru, author of 6–7
Quakers (see The Religious Society of
  Friends)
Randall, Matthew 483
Read, Collinson 483&n
  legal career and writer
Read, James 484
Read, James Jr 484
Read, John Jr 484
  legal career
Read, William 20n, 484
Relf, Samuel 484&n
  business interests (newspaper
  proprietor and editor); novelist
Religious Society of Friends, The 3–5
  'Free Quakers' 33, 497
Renshaw, William 484–5
  coffee house, proprietor; hotel
  owner (Mansion House Hotel,
  Washington Hall Hotel)
Rhees (Rhys), Morgan John
  (Glamorgan and Beulah) 19, 31–2,
  39&n, 485–6
  education (Wales); political views;
  preaching (Wales and 'Beulah',
  America); publisher; slavery,
  opposition to
Richards, Benjamin W. 32, 486–7, 499
  education (Princeton College);
  family; legal career; political
  activities (incl. Democrat mayor
  of Philadelphia); public life; riot,
  Walnut Street (1798)
Roberts, Edward 487

INDEX

Roberts, John 47, 343, 345–6
  provision for Hannah, his widow
Roberts, Joseph 487
Roberts, Josiah 487
Roberts, Michael 19, 487
  business interests (jeweller & stationer)
Rolph, James 20, 134, 137, 197–8, 487–8
Rubicam, Daniel 240n
  Washington Hotel, Philadelphia, proprietor of
Rush, Benjamin Dr 360, 364, 367, 491
Schlenther, Boyd 7, 13
Sharpless, Jesse 488
  business interests (saddler & merchant)
Shaw, William A. 488
ships (sailed from or docked at)
  Ann (Liverpool) 342
  Bainbridge (Liverpool) 371
  Huskinson (Liverpool) 51, 377
  Julian (Alexandria) 368
  Joseph (New York) 309
  Lavinia (Philadelphia) 38, 101
  Liberty (Wilmington, Delaware) 39, 172
  Liverpool Packet (Liverpool) 295
  Mary (New York) 50, 367
  Mary Ann (Liverpool) 295
  Minerva (Liverpool) 50n, 363
  Moss (London) 295
  Phoenix (Liverpool) 10
  Pilot (Philadelphia) 367
  Sarah Ralston (Liverpool) 319
  Thomas (New Castle, Pennsylvania) 37, 101
  Tuscora (Liverpool) 288
  United States 461
  Washington (Liverpool) 50n, 361

William (Liverpool) 288
Shoemaker, Thomas 390, 488
  testimony to
Simons, Joseph (& wife) 44, 259, 489
  business interests (ironmonger); slavery
  manumission 444
  opposition to (incl. Society for Promoting the Abolition of Slavery) 455, 481
Smith, Daniel 489, 493&n
  business interests (merchant); military career (incl. imprisonment); public life; portrait of
Smith, Jonathan 40
Smith, William 21
Snead, John 22, 172–3
  bequest
Snowden, Joseph 489
  business interests (ship chandler)
Stockton, William 489–90
  business interests (stagecoach proprietor)
Strawbridge, John 210, 490–1
  family; early life and education (Princeton College); business interests (merchant); honorary membership
Strong, Joseph 19, 203, 491
  education (University of Pennsylvania); medical career; inventions
Sykes, Robert Wharton 491
  business interests; legal career
taverns / hotels
  City Hotel, corner of Chestnut and Seventh Streets (Peter Evans) 202n
  Dunwoody's Tavern, Market Street

115&n
Francis's Union Hotel 111&n
Indian King, Market Street (Owen Owen) 9
Mansion House Hotel, Market Street (William Renshaw) 485
Queens Head, King Street (Robert Davis) 9
Sign of the Cross, Market Street 9
Washington Hall Hotel, South Third Street (William Renshaw) 27, 484–5
Washington Hotel, South Sixth Street (Daniel Rubicam) 240n, 248
Thomas, Evan 491
Thomas, Robert 20
Thompson, Edward 492
business interests (shipwright)
Thompson, George 492
business interests ('oak cooper')
Tilghman, Edward 19, 492
family; education (University of Philadelphia); legal and military career; public life
Tilghman, William 493
family; education (University of Philadelphia); legal and political career; public life; slavery, opposition to
Vaux, George 493
legal career
Vaux, Roberts 493–4&n
business interests (merchant); reformer (education and prisons); portrait of
Vincent, William 494
business interests (shoemaker)
Walker, Lewis 494
business interests (ironmonger)

Waln, Jesse 494–5
business interests (merchant, East Indies and China)
Waln, Robert 495
business interests (merchant, East Indies and China); political career; public life
Washington, George 25, 445, 451, 453, 454, 472, 473, 477
Wayne, Isaac 495–6
family; education (Dickinson College); legal and political career; military career
Wells, Gideon H. 496
business interest and bankruptcy
Welsh language 6–7, 13, 37n, 54, 306
Welsh Society of Philadelphia
annual dinner (1 March, St David's Day) 1, 18–19, 92, *passim*
benevolence (also see philanthropy, Orphan Committee) 35–6, *passim*
limits of 256–6, 276–7
conditions of support 366–7
correspondence 43, 309, 312–13, 313–14, 395
early members 29–34
education, provision of 198, 200
expulsion 20&n, 21, 116, 119, 134, 137, 138, 139, 186, 189, 197–8, 221–2, 241–2
finance incl.
appeals 19, 122
assistance to former members and their families 204, 205, 317, 422–3
bequests 21–2, 159–61, 175–6, 177–8, 183–4, 203, 204, 220, 224

INDEX

mismanagement 20–1, 218
debts, 'delinquent' members & fines, 19–21, 96, 106, 108, 116, 129, 244, 263–4, 266–7, 300–2, 326–8, 391–2
investments 23, 51, 177, 183–4, 189, 191, 206, 231, 248, 322, 332, 340, 348, 355, 369, 378, 387, 395, 402, 410, 415–16, 423, 430–1, 437–8
subscriptions (fees and arrears) 19, 86, 87, 119, 125, 154, 211, 215, 217–18, 326–8
governance
   Act of Incorporation 113, 122, 124, 125, 205
   Bye-Laws 17&n, 68, 85, 119, 122, 123–4, 125, 129, 150, 154, 216, 217–18, 328, 334, 358–9
   Charter 17&n
   constitution, drafting of and amending 82, 86, 87, 92, 97, 110
   election of officers 82, *passim*
   First Constitution, 1798 17&n, 57–61
   legality 17
   organisation of 17, 24–9, 248
   Original Association, Copy of 80–1
   Rules and Regulations 90–2
   seal and certificate of membership 83, 85, 88
   Second Constitution, 1802 62–7
   Supplemental Rules and Regulations 17&n, 69

honorary members 100, 109, 113, 210
index of members (1802–3) 71–9
motives 34–6, 313, 332–3
origins 16–18, 80–2
Orphan Committee 30, 39, 140–1, 178
other ethnic societies, relationship with 27, 97, *passim*
patriarchal attitudes 26–7
resignations 21, *passim*
consequences of 299
refusal to join the Society 187
St David's Society, Philadelphia, relationship with 28–9, 189&n, 190, 192–3, 195, 358
women, toast to 26
Wetherill, John Price 497&n
business interests (chemical and white lead manufacturer); 'Free Quakers', leader of; political career; public life; portrait of
Wetherill, Samuel P. 497
business interests (oil and colourman)
Wharton, Fishbourne 497–8
business interests (merchant)
Wharton, Franklin 498
military career
Wharton, Peregrine H. 498
business interests (merchant)
Wharton, Robert 19, 32, 302, 498–9&n
Second President of the Society; business interests (merchant); military activity; political career (mayor of Philadelphia); public life; portrait of
Wheeler, John J. 499
business interests (tailor)

Wheeler, Samuel 500
　business interests (black and white smith)
Wildes, Joseph 500
　business interests (merchant tailor)
Wilkinson, Thomas (Chester County, Pennsylvania) 22, 173
Willett, John Stephenson 18n, 500
Williams, R. (Calcutta) bequest & letter 21–2, 159–61
Williams, William P. 44–5, 295–6, 310, 317
　assistance to the poor; remuneration; Mrs Williams's activities and death
Worrell, Joseph 500–1&n
　business interests (carpenter/master builder); political career; public life; portrait of
Yeatman, Charleton 501
　medical career
Zantzinger, Thomas Barton 17–18&n, 501
　business interests (merchant and publisher)

PREVIOUS PUBLICATIONS BY THE SOUTH WALES RECORD SOCIETY

1. Rice Merrick, *Morganiae Archaiographia* (1578), ed. Brian James, 1983.
2. George Yates, *Map of Glamorgan* (1799), introduction by Gwyn Walters & Brian James, 1984.
3. C. & J. Greenwood, *Map of Monmouthshire* (1830), introduction by Philip Riden, 1985.
4. *The Diaries of John Bird of Cardiff, 1790-1803*, ed. Hilary M. Thomas, 1987.
5. *Llandaff Episcopal Acta, 1140-1287*, ed. David Crouch, 1989.
6. *The Letterbook of Richard Crawshay, 1788-97*, eds C. Evans & G. G. L. Hayes, 1990.
7. *The Diocese of Llandaff in 1763*, ed. John R. Guy, 1991.
8. Sir J. A. Bradney, *A History of Monmouthshire*, vol. 5, ed. Madeleine Gray, 1993.
9. *The Penrice Letters, 1768-95*, ed. Joanna Martin, 1993.
10. *The Glamorgan Hearth Tax Assessment of 1670*, ed. Elizabeth Parkinson, 1994.
11. *The Diary of William Thomas of Michaelston-super-Ely, 1762-1795*, ed. R. T. W. Denning, 1995.
12. *Monmouthshire Wills, 1560-1601*, ed. Judith M. Jones, 1997.
13. *St Davids Episcopal Acta, 1185-1280*, ed. Julia Barrow, 1998.
14. *The Letter Book of John Byrd, 1648-1680*, ed. Stephen K. Roberts, 1999.
15. *The Pennard Manor Court Book, 1673-1701*, eds Michael J. Edmunds & Joanna Martin, 2000.
16. *The Letter-Books of W. Gilbertson & Co. Ltd., Pontardawe, 1890-1929*, ed. P. W. Jackson, 2001.
17. *The Letters of Edward Copleston, Bishop of Llandaff, 1828-1849*, ed. Roger Lee Brown, 2003.
18. *'Women's Rights and Womanly Duties': The Aberdare Women's Liberal Association, 1891-1910*, ed. Ursula Masson, 2005.
19. *Family and Society in Early Stuart Glamorgan: The Household Accounts of Sir Thomas Aubrey of Llantrithyd, c.1565-1641*, ed. Lloyd Bowen, 2006.
20. *In Conversation with Napoleon Bonaparte: J. H. Vivian's Visit to the Island of Elba*, ed. Ralph A. Griffiths, 2008.

21. *Men At Arms: Musters in Monmouthshire, 1539 and 1601-2*, ed. Tony Hopkins, 2009.
22. *The Swansea Wartime Diary of Laurie Latchford, 1940-41*, eds Kate Elliott Jones and Wendy Cope, 2010.
23. *The Origins of an Industrial Region: Robert Morris and the First Swansea Copper Works, c.1727- 1730*, ed. Louise Miskell, 2011.
24. *William Downing Evans: Poetry and Poverty in Nineteenth-Century Newport*, eds. Ian and Wendy Dear, 2011.
25. *The Correspondence of Thomas Henry Thomas, 'Arlunydd Penygarn'*, ed. Christabel Hutchings, 2012.
26. *War Underground: Memoirs of a Bevin Boy in the South Wales Coalfield*, Michael Edmonds; ed. Peter Wakelin, 2013.
27. *The Diaries of Margaret Penderel Jones of Garth 1871 to 1897*, ed. P. W. Jackson, 2014.
28. *Cas Gan Gythraul. Demonology, Witchcraft and Popular Magic in Eighteenth-century Wales*. T.P., ed. Lisa Tallis, 2015.
29. *'I Hope to Have Good Passage...' The Business Letters of Captain Daniel Jenkins, 1902-11*, ed. David Jenkins, 2016.
30. *A Spiritual Botanology: Shewing What of God Appears in the Herbs of the Earth; Together with Some of Their Natural Virtues and Uses:In Blank Verse, and Rhime*, S. Lucilius Verus (Edmund Jones), ed. Adam N. Coward, 2017.
31. *Charley's War: The Diary of Charles Parkinson Heare 2nd Battalion, The Monmouthshire Regiment 1914-1919*, eds. Christabel Hutchings and Richard Frame, 2018.
32. *The Diary of William Southern Clark, 1854: Cardiff Steals a March*, ed. Richard Watson, 2019.
33. *A Gower Gentleman: The Diary of Charles Morgan of Cae Forgan, Llanrhidian,1834–1857*, eds. Rod Cooper and Prys Morgan, 2021.